PEDLAR'S PROGRESS

PILDAR'S PROGRESS

PEDLAR'S PROGRESS

A. Bronson Alcott

PEDLAR'S PROGRESS

THE LIFE OF
𝕭𝖗𝖔𝖓𝖘𝖔𝖓 𝖆𝖑𝖈𝖔𝖙𝖙

By ODELL SHEPARD

BOSTON

LITTLE, BROWN AND COMPANY

1937

Published May 1937
Reprinted May 1937

TO MY MOTHER

"The heart of another is a dark forest."
— Russian Proverb

FOREWORD

THIS book will be written out of the assured conviction that America has always been, is now, and throughout her coming centuries will continue to be, profoundly idealistic. That she has never been exclusively so of course I am aware; but neither, I think, has she ever been quite the crude, coarse, and Mammon-minded country of the conventional interpretation. Founded upon a thought, grounded upon a Book, lineally descended from ancient prophets and modern dreamers, she is at heart still passionately dreamful and prophetic, given to spiritual rebellions, to the never-ending wars of intellectual independence, and to migrations of the mind that ignore horizons. The common mistake about her has been due to the headlong haste in which she has set her young strength to her preliminary task. Not her foreign critics alone but even her sons and daughters have been too much deafened, even deceived, by the uproar of her mere preparations. Too easily and too soon they have concluded that America delights in uproar for its own sake, that she foresees and desires no final goal, that she lives for a purposeless activity alone.

Although this is an error, it may become a truth. Preoccupation with the means of living has for too long postponed our consideration of life's ultimate values. Things unquestionably first in the order of time have already come, for too many of us, to seem first in the order of importance. There is a question how long we can

ix

safely continue to ignore the nobler half of our national memories and nature. So central and inherent an idealism as ours can never be wholly lost, indeed, but it can be, and already it has been, distorted, deceived, and put to sinister uses. Little by little forgetting our birth in the spirit, more and more doubting the dream that has led us thus far on, we face even now the dangers that always confront a people who do not really know themselves. It is significant that we choose our national heroes chiefly from those who have most vigorously set heart and hand to the mastery and gathering of material things, and that we neglect the smaller but no less American number who have somehow kept burning that light of the mind, that holy flame in the heart, with which we began. But during all our three hundred years a still small voice has been whispering to us under the noise of the axes and hammers; and they who have listened to it, striving to comprehend and speak forth its oracles, have been Americans too, quite as representative and typical and heroic as any.

Wishing to illustrate if not to prove this conviction, I have been able to think of no better way than to tell the story of a life that began in the very time and place from which the machine, the factory, industrialism, and "big business" also took their American start. And I have thought that I might well choose for this illustration the life of some son of Connecticut, not only because Connecticut happens to be my own State but because she has acquired, among those who do not know her, a certain reputation which I need not now describe. At least in some degree she owes this reputation to the "pedlars" of "Yankee notions" whom she sent forth, especially into the South, a century ago—a tatterdemalion crew of hard-bitten young men who straggled down every road and bypath of the countryside, pinching pennies, higgling and haggling, flying by night, and leaving behind them, according to popular belief, a trail of wooden nutmegs and of clocks that would not go. Very well, then; it ought to be a fair test of my conviction to consider the life-story of a Connecticut pedlar—that is, of a man who surely, if the current notions of my State and country are correct, ought to turn out a close-fisted, hardheaded, flint-hearted American Gradgrind, with nothing in his mind or soul except what the French traveler Chevalier called, a hundred years since, the American passion for *"le make-money."* And so I come to Bronson Alcott.

Of course I know how the experiment, if it can be called that, will turn out. I know to begin with that I have chosen one of the most vivid examples of the way we have always had in America of braiding fact and dream, matter and mind, this world and the other, into one. And yet there is a real suspense and a steady deepening of curiosity in the effort to find out how a Connecticut Yankee who began his active life as a pedlar of trinkets became an acknowledged leader in the most purely idealistic movement of thought that America has ever known. From peddling to trans-cendentalism, from the rocky hills of western Connecticut to the Concord School of Philosophy, is a distance that few men travel; and the fact that Bronson Alcott did cover that distance, did take his stand upon those opposite poles of experience, suggests a paradox in his career which is teasing to the mind. I shall try to solve this paradox, or at least to trace the main stages by which he passed from the beginning of his career to the end of it, while considering him always as an American. And if when I am through any critic shall say: "But after all, your Bronson Alcott was not a *representative* American, not to say a *typical* Connecticut pedlar," I shall reply: "And how have you grown so sure about what is 'typical' and 'representative'? Is it not possible that you are generalizing too soon? Perhaps the examples are not all in. At any rate, add this one."

And now, after laying these plans, and after the slow piling of impressions and thoughts and conjectures, I come to the fierce effort of imagination which may perhaps convert them all into the likeness of a living man. Facts I have in plenty—indeed, ten times as many as I can use. What with the five or six million words of his Journals, his huge correspondence, and the mass of contemporary comment that he called forth in his eighty-eight years, Bronson Alcott is one of the most fully recorded of all Americans. Yet the question remains: What does this ample record mean? For a biographer has only begun his task when he has set it down, with all possible accuracy and fullness of detail, that his man went here and there, did this and that, thought and said so-and-so. Still we ask: "What kind of man?" When Jehovah himself had molded the bodily frame of the first man out of clay and spittle, he had to stoop and blow into the nostrils of that dead image nothing less than the breath of life.

Just so, now that I take the candle of imagination and go down among the miscellany of dead dull facts about Bronson Alcott's career, striving to see and to show them as they were livingly related by some inward law, I too, though a very minor Jehovah, am engaged in a creative effort, with all its exciting chances of success and failure. In speaking of creative imagination, however, I use the phrase in the clear-cut sense which rules out all trivial and irresponsible play of "fancy" and includes only that severe power of the mind by which we sometimes feel that we pierce through the crust of facts to the quick of their inward meaning. My treatment of Bronson Alcott will be imaginative in this high sense if I can make it so, but by this I do not mean to imply that the raw materials with which I shall deal are in the slightest degree imaginary. Alcott has been for long enough the victim of amiable sentimentalists who, in their zeal for Louisa, have been willing to say whatever pleased their fancy about Louisa's father. Louisa herself—who, although she loved and honored her father, never fully understood him—has been the innocent source of much misinterpretation, through passages written as fiction but taken as gospel truth. In more recent years Alcott has been distorted by the facile methods of what is called the "New Biography," according to which a writer concocts whole scenes, conversations, and even elaborate incidents, to suit his private notion of what should have happened even if it did not. I shall deny myself these splendid liberties. In the pages before me—although of course I shall often be obliged to impute motives and to trace processes of thought of which I am not entirely sure—I shall not consciously make one assertion of external fact for which I am unable to cite authority.

My main authority will be the private Journals of Bronson Alcott himself, in which he noted down for more than half a century nearly every important thing that happened to him and what he thought about it. Indeed, I should not now be adding another book to the literature about him if the chance had not come to me, a year ago, of reading these fifty large volumes of manuscript, his chief life work. I believe that I am the first person who has read them thoughtfully through since Alcott laid them down. Franklin B. Sanborn had access to them when he wrote his Memoir of Alcott over forty years since, but he did not use his opportunities to the full. Having the advantage of a long and intimate personal acquaintance with his subject, Sanborn wrote a good book, but the impatience, not to say the arrogance, of his brilliant and overcrowded mind is as evident in this book as in the rest of his always valuable, never quite dependable work. A man of many keen interests and large activities, he did not take time to master the Journals. When he quoted from them he often altered the text, silently, to suit himself. Moreover, he addressed a public different from that of to-day. I have used his book, therefore, with gratitude and with caution, correcting and extending and deepening his estimates, whenever possible, by recourse to the manuscripts that should have been, but were not, his constant source and guide.

In addition to the thirty thousand pages of Alcott's Journals I have read his voluminous correspondence, his "Autobiographical Collections", the numerous records in print and manuscript of his public conversations, and of course the few rather thin and shallow books that he produced in his old age. I have spent a good many hours in Alcott's private library, studying somewhat minutely his reading habits and his use of books. The *Record of a School* and the *Conversations with Children upon the Gospels*, compiled from notes taken by Elizabeth Palmer Peabody and Margaret Fuller, have supplemented what the Journals have taught me about Alcott's ideals and methods as a teacher. Somewhat less intently, I have studied what was written and said about Alcott by those who knew him best, and particularly by his wife, his daughter Louisa, and his friend Emerson. I have talked with persons who knew him, and with several of his descendants. I have stood on the slight depression in the ground which now marks the spot where he was born, have walked over the hills among which his boyhood was spent, have visited the home of his youth and half a dozen of the houses where he lived in later life, and have gone repeatedly to the perfect little museum at "Fruitlands" in which Miss Clara Endicott Sears has brought together, with patient skill and affectionate knowledge, all that can now represent that experiment in ideal living. While engaged on this study I have resided for months in Concord, a town already dear and familiar to me on account of other men, where Alcott dwelt longest and most happily. The houses and trees, the hills and streams, the roads and lanes and wood-paths of that town, are perhaps almost as much my friends as they were his. At "Dove Cottage," at the house now known as Hawthorne's "Wayside," and at "Orchard House," the three chief places of Alcott's Concord residence, I have lingered and loitered many an hour both within doors and without, trying to find my way back through the years. The local legends about Alcott, as they live on to-day in Concord and Boston and in his native town, have not been ignored in my researches merely because they are so often and so manifestly warped from the truth. Also I have read most of the books and papers that have been written about Alcott in recent years by those who have had to depend chiefly upon printed records. Finally, I have had much profitable talk about him with a number of the young scholars who are now, at last, approaching the study of American thought and literature with the respectful attention it has long deserved.

All this, and a great deal of other investigation of the same sort, is no more than the duty of a conscientious biographer. I set it down here partly because I do not intend to clutter the following pages, intended primarily for the "general reader," with references to authorities. As I have said, my chief and final authority will be Alcott's private Journals, and I can see no good purpose that would be served by frequent citation of volumes and pages in a huge collection of manuscript which is not now, and is not likely to become, accessible to the public. Neither will it be possible for me to quote extensively at present from this manuscript, as I expect before long to do in a volume of "Selections from Bronson Alcott's Journals." And the same statement holds for lesser matters. To choose a trivial instance, I shall not feel it necessary to say, when I speak of the team of tall yellow oxen that Alcott drove on Spindle Hill, that I learned about them from Mr. Fred Andrews of Wolcott, Connecticut, who in his turn was told about them, in his boyhood, by Alcott himself. Rather than a footnote, a little trust on the reader's part seems to be called for. I have not merely fancied that those oxen were yellow and tall. I know they were.

A general statement of the authorities upon which I have chiefly depended in each chapter will be found at the end of the book.

There could have been no such book as this if it had not been for the generosity of Mr. Frederic Wolsey Pratt, Bronson Alcott's great-grandson and the present owner not only of the manuscript Journals but of many other Alcott papers, to all of which he has given me the freest possible access. To him I owe, moreover, the opportunity to study in Alcott's private library, which is now a part of his own. My gratitude for his assistance and for his thoughtful interest in my work is not easy to express. I am deeply grateful, also, to Mrs. Bronson Alcott Pratt, who now lives in the house in which Henry Thoreau died and where Bronson Alcott spent some of his last years; and my thanks are due to Mrs. John Pratt Alcott of Brookline, Massachusetts, for helping me to the use of the important Journals for 1834 and 1835, at a time when I had given them up as lost.

Several other friends and associates have gone with me over some part of the winding and rocky but always pleasant road, or have pointed out my way at the turnings. The whole journey was suggested by my son, Willard Odell Shepard, to whose close and enthusiastic knowledge of Concord history and of the Alcott family I have been constantly indebted. Mr. Bliss Perry was helpful to me, by no means for the first time, at the beginning of my task. Mr. Fred Tower and Mr. and Mrs. Thomas Sanborn of Concord sent me onward. My friend Dr. Dorothy McCuskey, of the Connecticut State Teachers' College, has saved me from several errors by her exact acquaintance with Alcott's work as a teacher. My friend Professor Paul Spencer Wood, of Grinnell College, has read a considerable part of my text. Mr. Allen French, the historian of Concord, and Miss Margaret Lothrop, the present owner of Hawthorne's "Wayside," have shown me in many ways that the intelligent hospitality of their classic town is by no means confined to the past. Mr. and Mrs. Henry Norton of Wolcott, Connecticut, have told me the Alcott traditions of their town. To Miss Clara Endicott Sears of Boston and of Harvard, Massachusetts, I owe much, not only on account of her book, *Bronson Alcott's Fruitlands*, and the admirable museum in which she has commemorated the most famous episode of Alcott's life, but for the loan of valuable manuscripts. To Miss Sarah Bartlett of the Concord Free Public Library and to the library staff of Trinity College I am deeply indebted for many patient courtesies. And my wife has gone with me all the way.

I wish to thank the Houghton Mifflin Company, publishers, of

xvi

Boston, for permission to quote freely from the Journals of Emerson; and I am grateful also to the Trustees of The Concord Free Public Library for allowing me to quote an extended passage from an unpublished manuscript, now in their possession, by Ellery Channing.

The title of my book, it should perhaps be said, is not so much mine as Alcott's, having been used by him as the name of a string of verses in which he tried to narrate his peddling experiences in the South. I have thought it appropriate to the inner spirit as well as to the outward events of the man's entire career, in addition to the fact that it brings to mind that English classic which was the light and guide of all his days. The spelling "pedlar," still preferred in England, is the one that Alcott regularly used.

ODELL SHEPARD

Trinity College,
   Hartford, Connecticut. August 14, 1936

CONTENTS

ILLUSTRATIONS

The five pen-and-ink drawings are by Conrad G. Robillard

PEDLAR'S PROGRESS

ON SPINDLE HILL

*New England's frontier—Country school—Home and family—
An independent rural community—Labor on the land—A hill
of vision—The juvenile library—The cry of the factories—
The way of a boy with a book—A man clothed in rags*

AMOS BRONSON ALCOTT was born at four o'clock in the
morning on the twenty-ninth day of November, 1799, on
Spindle Hill, in the town of Wolcott, Connecticut.

Although the nineteenth century was only one month away,
that high hill town—twenty-five miles north of New Haven and
thirty miles from the State's western line—still bore many marks
of the pioneer settlement. Less than seventy years had passed
since the newborn child's great-grandfather had ridden up from
New Haven with his young wife on the pillion, had bought
twelve hundred acres of wilderness, and had begun his struggle
with oak and pine and stone. Now there were descendants of his
everywhere along the plunging sandy lanes, though many of them
still lived in log cabins shadowed by the lingering forest. They

talked a terse and racy English that would have amused the people of Hartford, less than twenty miles away. They spoke of "kickin' up a bobbery" and of "feelin' dreffle pokerish." To "lope" was the same as to "laze about," a fool was a "nimshi," and the plural of *house* was "housen." When they wished to assert a thing with emphasis they said "I vum," "I snore," or "I swow." They grew their own food among the rocks of the hilltop. They ground their own corn at the gristmill on Mad River. They spun, wove, dyed, and fashioned their own clothing. They made what simple tools they needed for the workshop, hearth, and field. They thought their own few thoughts, and made up their own opinions. Knowing very little, they cared somewhat less about what might be going on beyond those twelve white steeples to be seen from their highest hill.

John Alcock,* the first settler and the patriarch of the family, had given a farm and a dwelling place to each of his many children. For his eldest son, Captain John, a Revolutionary soldier, he had built a house that missed being a log cabin by a narrow margin; and it was in this home of his grandfather that Bronson Alcott was born. Rather large for the time and place, with widely jutting eaves and gables, the house had but one story and probably not more than three rooms, together with a "lean-to" on the northern side. It was built of the local pine and chestnut, and the clapboards were very wide. From its front door one looked southward toward Long Island Sound over a tumble of rounded hills, intricate and mysterious, going from vivid green to a distant blue; yet because the house stood higher than any land between it and the Sound, a level or an upward gaze did not meet these hilltops, but only the hawk that wheeled and soared, the floating cloud, or the empty blue of the sky.

* During the eighteenth century the ordinary spelling of the surname had been first "Alcock" and then "Alcox." The change to "Alcott" was made arbitrarily, about 1820, by the cousins William and Amos, "for the sake of euphony." At the same time Amos Bronson reduced his first Christian name to an initial and began to sign the second one in full.

[4]

To Bronson Alcott, for whom all things and events were symbols, it must have seemed fitting that the house of his birth disappeared long before he himself moved on to the House not Built with Hands. Was it not as though everything that might entangle him with earth must be swept away? At any rate, the heavy hand-hewn beams and wide floor-boards of his birthplace have been crumbling back, now, for almost a hundred years into the earth from which they grew. The older inhabitants of Spindle Hill can remember that there was once a shallow cellar-hole on the spot where the house had stood. To-day there is a garden of flowers.

A few months after he was born, the infant Amos—for by that name his father and mother always called him—was carried down the hill perhaps a mile to the new house his father had been building at Petuker's Ring, a clearing made by an Indian who, while driving deer together within a circle of fire, had perished with his prey. There, in a flimsy house which also went to ruin before he reached old age, Alcott spent the first five years of his life, and there his brother Chatfield was born. When five years old, while his father was in New York State looking for better land and being cheated of his money, the lad lived with a neighbor, Colonel Streat Richards, and attended his first school, in the Babylon District. In 1806 his father returned to his own kindred, took up eighty acres of land lying near the summit of Spindle Hill, and there pieced together two old buildings for a house. At the age of six Bronson Alcott moved into the first home that he could clearly remember in his later years.

Earliest of all his recollections was that of a "quilting"—of the custards his mother had made for the occasion, of the couples dancing in their fine clothes from New Haven, of the amazing length of the ladies' trains, and of the black fiddler, probably a slave, bobbing and sawing over his violin in one corner of the candle-lighted room. For more than eighty years he remembered how he had practised his A B C's, laboriously conned out of Noah Webster's Spelling Book, with chalk, upon his mother's parlor

[5]

floor. The kitchen was large and airy, filling almost half of the house. It had a brick oven in the fireplace where most of the cooking was done, besides an ample buttery. This was the room where the dreamy boy, by no means precocious, first became aware of the world about him. It seemed to him a warm and friendly world, completely sheltered from all danger by his mother's constant presence. His mother worked incessantly from sunup to sundown, and apparently for long hours after he had climbed to bed with his brothers and sisters in the loft. So did his father work all day and, as far as the young Bronson could tell, all night. For grown-up persons there seemed to be nothing but work in life. And yet his mother did not mind it. A boy could tell from the way she smiled at him, from her always patient words, but best of all by the quiet light that shone out of her eyes, that she had some inward joy. Probably everyone had that kind of joy, although not everyone—not even his father—could show it as his mother did. He had that kind of causeless joy himself. He thought it was like the spring his father had showed him once up in the meadow—the little pool of clear cool water in which the grains of golden sand kept dancing, dancing, hour after hour, for no reason that a boy could guess.

Looking back in later life upon his childhood, Bronson Alcott could not remember many boyish games and pastimes. This would be partly because there were so few playmates to be had in that thinly settled corner of the town. His own cousin, William Andrus Alcott, only a year his senior, did indeed live just down the road; but William was already of a serious and timesaving mind, as though he foresaw the one hundred and eight books and pamphlets he would have to write, the thousands of lectures he must give, and all the good he had to do in a rather short life constantly plagued by ill-health. With the grave and earnest William, he remembered, he used to trudge barefooted down the sandy lane to the little gray schoolhouse at the crossroads. How small and gray and bare it had been!—with not a tree to shade

[6]

ALCOTT'S BOYHOOD HOME

SPINDLE HILL
WOLCOTT, CONNECTICUT

After an original pencil sketch by Bronson Alcott

it in summer or to break the winter winds. It had stood so close to the road that the hubs of the farmers' wagons scraped against it in rounding the corner. Not a square yard that might grow another hill of potatoes must be sacrificed, those farmers had decided, to the mere comfort of children. Boys and girls, but especially boys, were the cheapest crop one could raise; and yet they paid well too, if one did not become soft and foolish about them.

The schoolhouse that Alcott attended from six to ten years of age had a single room, twenty-two feet long by twenty broad and seven feet high. It was lighted by five small windows, and was unequally warmed in winter by a large fireplace at the entry end, which often consumed a cord of green wet wood in a week. There was no provision for ventilation, and little care for cleanliness. As the children entered the room after recess, they stopped at the door to drink out of a common cup dipped into a bucket of water —with the quite mysterious result that large numbers of them were frequently absent at the same time, suffering with the same childish disorders. The master's desk stood in the middle of the room, equipped with inkstands, goose quills, leaden plummets for the ruling of paper, a few books, and the proper instruments of chastisement. Narrow benches, without backs, were ranged about three sides of the room for the reception of the larger pupils, and the "infants" sat upon lower benches, also backless, near the instructor's desk. The desks of the pupils, like the benches, were not individual, but merely long planks of wood laid upon trestles.

School held from nine to twelve and from one to four on five days of the week. Punctuality, however, and regularity of attendance, were virtues for which instructors pleaded in vain, not only because of the distance that many children had to walk and the uncertainties of the weather, but also because, at several seasons of the year, the labor of the children was thought necessary for the maintenance of the home and farm. The winter school opened

[7]

in December and lasted sometimes until the end of March. It was taught almost always by men, who were paid from seven to eleven dollars a month, and "boarded round." The summer school, opening in May, was often taught by "females," whose remuneration might be as high as four dollars a month "and found," and seldom was less than sixty-two and one-half cents a week.

The social rating of the schoolmaster had declined rather rapidly in the decade before the Alcott cousins first went trudging down the sandy lane to learning. Once he had been almost a fit companion for the clergyman, that very august person; but that had been in the days when the people of Connecticut had paid him chiefly from their own pockets. Now that he was paid in large part out of a State fund arising from the sale of Western lands, he was rather despised because he cost so little. If he complained of poverty it was pointed out to him that his hours were short and his work was very easy, so that he might supplement his earnings by work of a more lucrative sort; but to this he usually made some weak and evasive reply. There was a general feeling, by no means gone even to-day, that teachers, and especially the "females," ought not to marry, for the alleged reason that their doing so might cause them to neglect their work—but perhaps also because a married teacher might be tempted to ask for a larger income. It was also believed that no teacher ought to be employed in the same school for more than two successive terms.

Under these circumstances it was often difficult to find able-bodied, not to say able-brained, young men and women to do the work of teachers for a hire rather less than they might have made at farm labor or in domestic service. Every town wished, of course, to have its children taught by persons of the most exemplary morals, with precisely the correct opinions upon matters of Church and State; but such was the unwillingness to pay for what was sought, or to treat with ordinary human consideration the teachers who were secured, that in some towns—at least so it was whispered—only jailbirds would apply.

[8]

In their school on Spindle Hill, which was no worse than schools elsewhere in Connecticut and was rather better than those of most other States, the Alcott cousins learned to read and write and spell by processes ingeniously devised to produce the least possible reward for the greatest expenditure of effort. They also learned the catechism by heart and made some acquaintance with the New Testament. Such scant arithmetic as Bronson Alcott was ever to know—or, in fact, to stand in need of—he seems to have acquired outside of school hours. Nathaniel Dwight's *Geography* may have done something to expand his notions of the world beyond his native hills, and Caleb Bingham's *American Preceptor* can certainly have done no harm to his "morals." The main fault of the school was that it did nothing to stimulate intellectual curiosity, to excite and train imagination, or to call forth and guide the process of thought. Everything possible was done by rote, and the teacher's ideal was that his charges should commit to memory all that was told them and all that they read.

Yet there can be no doubt that the young Alcott enjoyed his school, of whose many defects he was then quite unaware. He had a liking for books which, without ever amounting to a real passion for knowledge, made him always an eager and wide-ranging reader. His mother, herself barely able to read and write, never allowed him to forget that in her brother, the Reverend Tillotson Bronson—a graduate of Yale, and Principal of the Cheshire Academy—the family boasted one scholar already, and that it might some day have another. And besides, there was something in the conduct of the schoolroom that the lad found attractive. He liked to watch the master trim and mend the goose quills, rule the foolscap with his leaden plummet, and set copy—"Avoid alluring company"—for the writing exercise. He liked to manufacture his own ink before leaving for school, steeping maple and oak bark in indigo and alum. Although he was by no means brilliant, he did his lessons well and was obedient and attentive. Only once during his school years was he punished,

[9]

and then for another's fault. Might it not be—seeing that the career of a clergyman, that supreme human dignity, was shut away by the unlikelihood of his ever going to college—that he too might some day be a schoolmaster, earning his seven dollars a month, or perhaps as much as eleven, while boarding round? Then he would never have to leave the books he was growing to love, or the quills and paper for the use of which his clever young hands were finding a natural aptitude. In that case, better still, there would always be a company of children about him, and he would never feel lonely again.

When he was ten years old, however, the boy had become so valuable an assistant about the farm and in the shop that he was not allowed to waste any more of his summer time, at any rate, over his books. The iniquities of child labor had not then been realized; and so far were they from becoming the subject of legal enactment that, as a matter of law as well as of immemorial custom, a boy's time and earnings until he was twenty-one belonged entirely to the man who had been at all the trouble of begetting him. No one, at any rate in Wolcott, had ever questioned this folkway. Any objection to it would have been met by a quotation of Biblical authority, and by a request to be told what else boys were good for. The "Century of the Child," although it was opening, was not yet far under way, and the lad who was to do as much as anyone toward the emancipation of childhood was not himself yet free. While still a child himself he began to work for his father— folding the sheep under the great rock on the hillside, guiding the oxen along the furrow, mending the stone walls that surrounded the woodland pastures, husking corn, flailing grain, milking cows, molding candles, bringing water from the well, and doing whatever else might be asked of him between dawn and dark. He managed some attendance upon a few more winter sessions at the district school and he was to have a very little tuition elswhere, but when he was thirteen his regular schooling came to an end.

Alcott was accustomed to say in his old age that the district school gave him little or nothing; but this was the remark of one who had come to think of himself, perhaps with a touch of pride, as a "self-made man." In that crowded, dark, stifling little room at the crossroads, so cold at one end and so hot at the other, where the boy had sat motionless upon a narrow bench for six hours a day, listening to the gabble of lessons and to instruction from gawky youths and maidens who were only a little less ignorant than their charges, a good deal had been done for and by him. He had at least learned to read and write—and for a man of the sort he was going to be what else was needed? There was thinking, to be sure, but even at college he would scarcely have found instruction, or example, in that rare art. Thinking, if he should turn out to be the one man in the million with courage and energy for such an ill-paid task, he would have to teach himself.

But he had learned more than this. He had absorbed Noah Webster's *American Spelling Book,* then in its revised edition, which had already sold two million copies and was still more actively at work in shaping the national speech and character than all the colleges in the land. As young Alcott pored over those crudely printed pages, there fell and lay in the fallow of his mind who can say what seeds of future dreams and doings? Webster's dull iteration of a shallow and shopkeeping morality did not seem dull to him. Somehow he must have winnowed out all that was ignoble, worldly, and self-seeking, and retained chiefly the conviction—which was Noah Webster's too, but on how different a plane!—that moral instruction is a main ingredient in all right education of the young. And then the woodcuts and fables—the fox and the grapes, the dog that kept bad company, the boy who stole apples, the milkmaid who spilled the milk! He was never to escape from the spell of those apologues. Starting with a picture, going on with a brief tale, and then deducing a "Moral," they left an indelible mark upon his mind and were to play some part in guiding his own future practice as a teacher, perhaps in shaping his thought as a transcendentalist and in confirming his lifelong

[11]

dependence upon symbols and emblems. Thus the seeds blew across to him from that other Connecticut farmer's boy who also, forty years before and only fifteen miles away, had so often snatched up a book to read under the oak tree while the oxen rested at the end of a furrow.

Among other things, the Alcott cousins learned at school what a school ought not to be and how children should not be taught. By the ache in their backs and legs, by the suffocation of their lungs, by the heat and the cold, by the noise and ugliness and disarray of the place, a dim dissatisfaction was suggested even to their boyish minds. There is no saying which of the two first began to think about such matters, and to conceive the possibility that school, an all but divine institution, might in some ways be improved. For years they were to think and feel together, pushing each other onward, pulling each other up. They were tied together, as it were, by a rope, so that if one got a firm hold with hand or toe they both moved upward, and if one of them slipped they were both likely to catch a fall. William, less robust, suffered more than Bronson from the physical discomforts and dangers of the school, and it seems more than possible that he contracted in that foul air the tuberculosis which conditioned and shortened his life. Therefore it was fitting that he should have been the one to go to Yale College for the degree in medicine which might assist him in his teaching, and that many of the reforms in the physical properties of the schoolroom, later used by Bronson, should have been suggested by him. It is certain at any rate that, as time went by, the two earnest youths became equally convinced that there was something deeply wrong with primary education in America, and that they must do their best to change it. In the planting of this conviction the little gray schoolhouse at the crossroads must have played some part—as a horrible example.

Yet there is little to show how and why it happened that the virus of reform began to work in these two crude and ignorant lads, shut away among the hills from all the fresh thought of the world. Was it some book that they read? Was it the influence of the Reverend John Keys, the Wolcott minister? Or shall we say that it was the sudden awakening in them both of some common ancestor, say Thomas Alcock of Boston's earliest days or Phillip Alcock of New Haven? One may scrutinize all the existing facts—really rather abundant—about the influences that played upon them, and it still remains a mystery why they two should have turned aside from the comfortable ruts of convention, should have defied that public opinion which is never anywhere more tyrannical than in just such communities as theirs, and should have dared to think for themselves about an institution which had been droning on without appreciable change since New England began. They did not know that education, in all its branches and stages, is always inextricably enmeshed and tangled with the entire social, economical, political, and theological scheme of things, so that one cannot propose the slightest improvement without seeming to threaten the whole structure. They were to find that out. What they did know was that their parents and teachers, all their neighbors, even their minister who knew everything, seemed to regard the school system as perfect. By what right, then, did they begin to ask questions? There is no answer. The problems that a serious biographer wishes most of all to solve are just those that lie most deeply involved in the mystery of life.

There was one thoroughly heretical opinion upon which the two cousins may have agreed when they walked back up the lane after their last day of school. Then and there they may have decided what they afterwards firmly knew and taught, that a formal schooling, even when good, is not the only means of securing an education. Against the American worship of the school, so stupid in itself and so stultifying in its effects upon real intellectual life, one would be glad to think that they set their young faces, even then, like flint. To Bronson in particular there may have come some vague premonition of his future knowledge

[13]

that the school, at its best, is only a substitute for the family and the home, that it is a microcosm of society, a place in which one learns by doing, and, as Thomas Carlyle was to say, "a collection of books."

Well, then, there were books to be had in Wolcott. There were, in fact, about one hundred of them. There was more than enough to be done in the shop and on the farm by which a boy might learn. Moreover, there was the close-knit, interrelated society of the township, somewhat disturbed by local gossip and dissensions, no doubt, and seriously divided by the feeling of the people on the eastern or Farmington side that they were somewhat superior to those of the western or Waterbury half of the hill, yet full of possibilities to a boy of Alcott's strongly social nature. Finally, and best of all, there was the family, the home—in short, one's mother. All these things, taken together, would constitute a school, and it would go hard if one did not get an education out of them.

The family, the home, one's mother—there was the best school of all. It was not that Bronson's mother was particularly well informed. She could not say the table of weights and measures, and when one looked into the little diaries she had been keeping since her girlhood one discovered that she did not always spell her words in quite the ways approved by Noah Webster. Already, though he was but ten, the lad could feel, with a strange mingling of pride and regret, that he could write a better hand than his mother did. Yet what of that? Was not his mother a far wiser, kinder, gentler, and in every way better person than the schoolmistress? And what could that mean, unless that there are more important things in the world than reading, writing, and exact knowledge of the length of the Zambesi River? His mother knew things too, although one never found them set down in books, and even she seldom tried to say them in words. She said them in the way she acted, in the touch of her hand, in the smile of her eyes; and often she seemed to be saying them when sitting quietly beside him, paring apples or mending a hole in his homespun coat.

[14]

There was indeed a strong natural sympathy, which had no need of words, between this little fresh-faced woman and her eldest son, now a well-grown lad of fourteen—sandy-haired, rosy-cheeked, and with eyes of Saxon blue. Her good mind had been one of the many sacrifices made in the interests of her brother Tillotson, who was already a famous man. Often she told her son of how her own mother used to put her daughters to the spinning-wheel and seat herself at the loom for days together, and how then she would saddle her horse, carry her cloth over the twenty-five miles of hill and dale and roaring ford to New Haven, and there sell it for the money to pay her Tilly's college bills. Her father, too, Amos Bronson, had been and still was a man of exceptional parts. A venerable man, of strong features and frank manners, he still maintained something of a patriarchal state on his farm at Plymouth, four miles northwest of Spindle Hill. His young name-sake had seen for himself that the white-haired man, eighty-eight years old, deserved high standing both in the world that now is and in the world to come. Had he not built the turnpike road along the banks of the Naugatuck, thereby saving six fordings of the rapid stream between Jericho and Waterbury? And all the countryside knew how Amos Bronson had long ago turned against the prevailing Calvinism of the district, had joined the Episcopal Church—then a despised form of dissent—had named his eldest son after an archbishop, and had raised all his family in the strange new faith. On Sundays he would saddle two horses, take his wife or a daughter with him on one of them while a daughter or a son and daughter rode the other; and thus he went to church, four miles away, in all seasons and weathers. Arriving there, he rang the bell, read the service, preached the sermon, and led the singing. That was a man to be named after!

Equally well Bronson knew his other grandfather, who lived close at hand in the house with the jutting gables where the lad had been born. Grandfather John Alcock was a far less imposing figure than Grandfather Amos Bronson, and yet it was a convenient thing, especially on Field Days and Training Days when all the boys of the township turned intensely patriotic, to have a grandfather who had seen Washington, had known Israel Putnam, had received his commission from no less a man than Jonathan Trumbull, a distant kinsman, and had served in the War of Independence together with three of his sons. The old soldier went about on crutches now, and his white hair fell to his shoulders, but all the countryside respected him and called him "Captain John."

Bronson's father, Joseph Chatfield Alcox, would scarcely have taken part in the War of Independence, as his father and elder brothers had done, even if he had been born in time. Almost morbidly shy, silent, and retiring, he had a positive genius for minding his own affairs and letting the rest of the world alone. Out of the two hundred householders that Wolcott contained during his mature years, he was one of the few whose names never appeared on the town lists as the holders of any office. A skillful mechanic, he made the plows, yokes, chairs, cradles, and baskets that were used in the neighborhood, and at the same time kept what was considered the most thrifty farm on Spindle Hill. If he had little prominence, no one spoke ill of him. He was frugal, industrious, temperate, honorable in all his dealings, and he reared a family of four sons and four daughters. Although married to a woman in some ways his superior, he was the master of his household. His eldest son felt toward him rather a deep respect than any warmth of affection. Joseph Alcox could not comprehend that son's apparently insatiable thirst for reading. He himself, so he averred, had been a reader once; but he had "got through" with all that, and he long continued to hope that his son would some day do the same.

Of Bronson Alcott's three brothers and four sisters there is less than might be expected to be said. Between him and his brother Chatfield, born in 1801, primarily mechanical in his aptitudes and little inclined toward the "ideal," there was no strong sympathy. His twin sisters, Pamela and Pamila, who were born in 1805, he seldom mentioned, and the same may be said of his sisters Betsy and Phebe, born in 1808 and 1810. Junius Alcott grew to be a sensitive and thoughtful man for whom Bronson, nineteen years older, felt almost a fatherly affection. The youngest brother, Ambrose, born in 1820, Bronson hardly knew.

Such, then, was the immediate family in which Bronson Alcott grew up, and which he did not permanently leave until he was twenty-eight years old. But his family in the larger sense of the word included most of the people on Spindle Hill and more than half, as he calculated in later years, of the thousand inhabitants of Wolcott. His great-grandfather John had been blessed with eleven children, almost all of whom had settled on the Hill and had raised their own large families. Of these eleven Bronson's grandfather, John, had nine sons and daughters, who also lived for the most part in the town where they were born. Thus it will be seen that the Alcock family tree—which, as time went by, came more and more to be called "Alcox"—was like a banyan, covering all the Hill and stretching its creepers and shoots into the adjacent towns. This meant that wherever the young Bronson might turn in, on his wanderings about the Hill, whether at a stately salt-box house like that of James, or at a rude log cabin such as John's, he was likely to find an uncle, or at least an aunt, together with his or her brood of cousins. Eighty years and three generations had crowded Spindle Hill with Alcocks. Another generation of them it could not possibly hold and support, but, during Bronson's boyhood, there they all were, or most of them, forming a re- markably close society.

Not one of them was rich, and none was very poor. If any of them should fall into real need, there was no doubt—although the occasion seems never to have arisen—that he would be supported by the others. Many things they did in common. If one had a house to build, a barn to raise, corn to husk, or an unusually good

[17]

barrel of cider to drink, he let his neighbors—that is, the larger family—know. Each man helped several others get in their hay, and they in turn helped him. When any one of them killed a pig or a calf, the whole neighborhood had fresh meat. When one of them broke his leg or his arm, his crops were somehow gathered. One bull served the whole region. One cradle would have sufficed if the babies had not come quite so thick and fast. One maker of plows and yokes and baskets was all that the community required, or could support. Widows and orphans did not starve or go on the town. In short, here was society spreading out from the family, its only source and justification as Bronson Alcott was later to think and teach. Here was the small beginning of an ideal State.

The farmers of Spindle Hill and of Wolcott were a rugged, sufficiently honest, hard-working, moderately temperate, and not very intelligent lot. Some of the older men had known hard times, in the backwash of the War of Independence, when they had been glad to walk before dawn to the lower fields of Southington, four miles off, labor all day at the harvest, and carry back half a bushel of rye as their day's wages. Since the turn of the century, however, they had been doing better. The expectation that a turnpike road would be built from Torrington to New Haven, with Wolcott as a main station for the changing of horses, had greatly stimulated speculation in land. Indeed, the town records show that during the first thirty years of the century there were no less than two hundred and eighty transfers of real estate in which persons by the name of Alcock, Alcox, or Alcott were involved. The little green at the center, nowadays so drowsy and world-forgotten, had in 1810—even without the help of a turnpike road—a tavern, a general store, a schoolhouse, and a wheelwright's shop, in addition to its dozen houses and two churches.

The rest of the town—using that word in the New England sense, as equivalent to "township"—was still, to be sure, rather wild. Probably not half of the land had ever been thoroughly cleared, and the roads were bad beyond imagination. Add the fact that Wolcott lay eight or nine hundred feet above the sea, and it will be clear that new ideas, which in those days moved along the watercourses, climbed rather slowly up that way. The *New Haven Register* was occasionally obtainable, and the *Connecticut Courant* was brought by post-rider once a week as far as Woodtick, two miles down the Hill. Thither young Bronson was often sent to get the one copy that was slowly read to pieces by those members of the Alcott clan who could read at all. There had been little infiltration of new blood since the coming of the first settler, and nothing indicates that newcomers would have been welcome. In speech and thought, in knowledge and culture, the community was not noticeably different from any that might have been found in one of the older Connecticut towns toward the end of the seventeenth century.

Even for Connecticut, which had long been the most purely English of the colonies and of the States, the population of the little town was remarkably homogeneous. None but English names are to be found on the tax lists of the time or on the older tombstones. Common blood, common racial traditions, common religious faith, and—in the larger outlines—a common political theory, made for a kind of social confidence and ease that has slowly disappeared from the life of New England during the last hundred years. We have scarcely begun to estimate what this loss has meant to us, and how deep a rift it has made between our time and that in which Bronson Alcott grew to manhood; but yet it should be clear, for one thing, that the individual who attacked beliefs and folkways so strongly established as those of Spindle Hill would meet an opposition unknown to the "radicals" of a day in which most orthodoxies have been shattered.

After he had come to know the poems and prefaces of Wordsworth, Alcott liked to compare the rural neighbors of his boyhood with the "statesmen" of the English Lakes, occasionally even speaking of them as though he thought they had actually emigrated in a body from Lancashire or Westmoreland. And no doubt there was some likeness. The farmers of Spindle Hill held their lands in freehold. One does not learn of many mortgaged farms among them. They raised some sheep, though in haphazard ways that would have made a Westmoreland shepherd gasp and stare. They had kept alive many old locutions which, without amounting to a special dialect, gave a distinct tang of oddity to the local speech. Their farming implements and methods were of an older fashion than those to be seen in the valleys below. On a November afternoon, the thud of the flail could be heard for miles around almost any of their barnyards. The first wagon ever seen in the town, a wonder to young and old, appeared there after Alcott was born. It is significant that the Spindle Hill people seldom troubled to lock their doors at night or when they were leaving for the day. What was there for anyone to take, to which he would not be quite welcome; and who was there to come and take anything which he would not return in kind? The whipping post on Wolcott Common was used only once in Alcott's recollection, and then to punish a man from out of town who had stolen a shawl at the tavern. The stocks, which lay out of the weather in a horse shed beside the church, were probably never used at all.

Of drunkenness at Wolcott one hears nothing whatever, although this does not necessarily mean that there was none. Hard cider and fiery applejack were a universal tipple, apparently used by young and old of both sexes on every possible occasion, and Bronson Alcott himself, never a "tee-totaller" and temperate even in his interpretation of the word "temperance," acquired in childhood a love of cider, both sweet and hard, which lasted all his life. Far more deleterious, one would say, than the drinking habits of the people was their excessive consumption of meat, especially of the salted varieties; but this was due in some degree to their lack of fresh vegetables and the almost total lack of refrigeration. The year's supply of meat was laid in all at once when the "creatures" were slaughtered in the autumn.

Calico and cotton were worn on Spindle Hill only on state occasions, because they were very expensive. Homespun woolens for the winter and linen for the summer months were produced and manufactured on the Hill itself, and shaped into garments by the itinerant tailors who came but once a year. In every larger homestead a room was given over to the spinning wheel, and before the woolen mill was set up on Mad River many houses were also equipped with looms. Until he was twenty-one Alcott wore nothing but linen and homespun, and until he was eighteen his clothes were made by his mother.

If one feels a twinge of pity for the lad, it is more than Bronson Alcott himself ever felt in looking back upon his earliest years. He always thought that his boyhood had been most fortunate and happy—fortunate in the romantic country round about, and happy in the kind of work he did, in the sports he had, and, most of all, in the deep contentments of his home. The festivals, celebrations, and junketings that drew the neighbors together on Field Days and Training Days, at harvest homes and huskings, at quiltings, barn raisings, and spelling bees—such were the occasions he remembered longest and with most heartfelt delight. And one can easily see why this was. Profoundly social and yet extremely shy the boy was. Even on these public occasions he always hung back from the girls, and if he came to know them at all it was because they made the advances. He did not know many boys, and after he left school he had few chances to be with many. And yet such gatherings, chiefly of the Alcott clan, swept him out of his otherwise almost unconquerable bashfulness. They helped him to withstand that dull ache of loneliness which has been from the beginning the most terrible foe we have met on the American frontier—more insidious than the Indians, more deadly than wild beasts, and counting more victims by far than slow starvation. After we had crossed the Appalachians we banded together in

[21]

secret societies against this foe; on the plains we shouted and sang and prayed it down, temporarily, in the camp meeting; among the Western mountains, and indeed throughout the land, we have tried to drown it in strong drink; and to-day, in every State of the Union, it drives our women into social and literary clubs and herds up our business and professional men in organizations which strive to make them feel, for an hour or two in the week, that they are really boys together. These devices were not required on Spindle Hill because it was not quite a frontier community and also because the network of family relationship tended in itself to hold loneliness away. Social gatherings which still bore some slight resemblance to those of Merry England, and which were related, like those of England, to the more compact and settled forms of village life, were there sufficient; and these, to the young Alcott, were very dear. But Saturday evenings in the summer months were good times too, for then all the male youth of Wolcott converged toward the mill pond on Mad River for the weekly swim. From the age of eight until he was eighty Bronson Alcott was a powerful swimmer, but the chief reason for his delight in these Saturday evenings was that they brought so many boys together in the glad freedom of nudity and sport. Almost anything that could be done with many others was to him a joy. It fed some hunger at his heart. Companionship, he always knew, was one great good of life.

To a twentieth-century eye the picture made by these details is likely to seem somewhat idyllic, and it seemed so to Alcott himself when the distances of time and space began to give him its total effect. Not solely because it was the home of his childhood and youth, he came to regard Spindle Hill as a little masterpiece, almost a model, in the arrangement of human society. He delighted in the partnership he had seen there between Man and Nature, each contributing toward a result more beautiful than either could have attained alone. Halfway between the city and the wilderness, subtly mingling the past and the present, almost entirely free from the outer world and yet continually sending down into that world its own small surplus of goods and brains and labor, maintaining most jealously every real right of the individual while mingling the individual's thought and work into that of a closely integrated social group—why was it not at least a clear indication of the ideal republic toward which all American institutions ought to strive? The town of Wolcott, with its thousand inhabitants, was in itself a state and a society large enough. Should it grow still larger, not all of those who lived in it would be able to know all the others, so that a kind of social waste would set in. And what was perhaps the most satisfactory thing about this tiny state was the way in which it constantly grew out of and came back to the home.

The bare facts about Wolcott and the Spindle Hill community may not have been quite so idyllic as Alcott's ardent fancy made them out. There was some element of dream and illusion in his recollection of the scenes his infancy knew. Odd and amusing though it may seem that an Irish and a Scottish poet, writing about England, should have deepened the affection of a Yankee for a Connecticut town, the fact is that Alcott came to see Spindle Hill through the glamorous veil, so to speak, of Goldsmith's *Deserted Village* and Thomson's *Seasons*. One would say that Goldsmith's poem might at least have prepared him for inevitable change, but in fact the worst phase of his mistake about Spindle Hill was the illusion of permanence. Ignorant as he always was both of history and of those mechanical and economic forces that were already thrusting his America into constantly accelerating transformations, he naïvely assumed that the little towns of New England would last forever as he had known them, and that their kind would be reproduced throughout the land. In fact, they never got beyond the Appalachians. Even before he had reached middle age the village organization which had come to these shores all the way from ancient India had met its deadly foe, the machine, and had begun to die. Alcott never understood this, and never fully admitted the facts. During his last visits to Spindle Hill, in extreme old age, he would stand peering into empty cellar-holes that marked the homes of his boyhood friends, or would gaze into impenetrable thickets covering land where he had once driven the plow, not knowing precisely how this ruin and desolation had come about. In the course of one lifetime he had seen a human society pass from flourishing youth into senescence and decay. Brought up in a district which still bore many marks of the American frontier, he returned to find it, in general appearance and in emotional effect, one of the oldest places on earth.

If Alcott dreamed, he also labored. Whatever may have been the effect of English poetry upon him, his pastoralism was not of the soft and sentimental kind that has never been put to the proof of toil. In early childhood he began to learn the cost of food and raiment, of warmth and shelter, in terms of bodily strain; and that knowledge, so sobering, making so huge and unbridgeable a distance between those who have it and those who have it not, he never lost. In our effort to solve the perplexing problem of his attitude toward money and self-support it simply will not do, therefore, to assert that he was ignorant of the cost of things. Far better than most of those men upon whose bounty he subsisted, Alcott knew that subsistence is won, ultimately, at the price of human toil. Partly this knowledge it was which made him, as Emerson once said, somewhat reluctant to shake the hand of a millionaire.

Bronson Alcott was thoroughly acquainted with the harsh and angular facts of the farmer's life on a rocky New England hill; for he had himself lived that life, though not continuously, during almost twenty years. It taught him once and for all that Nature's drift is counter to ours, that her vast obscure will is not to be broken, that man is not her master, nor ever can be, and that all the puny successes of which he is so proud have been won by a

[24]

lowly imitation of her great mysterious ways. And there already was a lesson that no school or college could have taught him, then or now. It put into him an almost religious humility, just as he entered that century which was to show itself the most ignorant braggart of all the ages.

Quite clear it was on Spindle Hill, however the fact might be hidden to Emerson beside the old fat meadows of Concord, that Nature is not man's handmaid. It was hard not to think her a foe. The forest, threatening, ever at the door, could never be permanently beaten back. The briars, the hardhack, and the sweet fern came on against scythe and sickle like an army with banners. If there was rain, the weeds triumphed; and if there was drought, the grain died. In almost every field the young plowman encountered boulders that seemed to be anchored in middle earth, big enough to build a house on. He plowed round them. In every pasture and on every hilltop the bare bones of the planet showed through. He did not plow there at all. The smaller rocks were a perennial crop in meadow and pasture and field—springing up year after year, when the frost loosened, from the seed that retreating glaciers had sown long ago. He dug them up and rumbled them out, piled them on stone-boats dragged by straining oxen, and wedged them firmly into the old stone walls; yet every year there were more. And the soil itself, when he did get down to it, was never greatly rewarding. Had it been really a good soil it would not have been ignored for almost a hundred years after the settlement of the Colony, and Spindle Hill, so near the sea, would not still have borne the marks of pioneering.

Spindle Hill was a place where one might learn to love the earth, certainly, but hardly to trust her. It did not suggest a luxurious or an easy way of life. It would drive a man either toward brutality or to asceticism. An ascetic district it was in itself—so plainly beautiful, so pure, so bare. From the great cap of granite on his father's highest hill the young Alcott could see three quarters of the horizon's round, with a hundred hills of intricately

[25]

beautiful contour interfolding and dimming away toward the faintly visible sea. Was he not right when he said, standing on that hill at the age of eighty, that this lofty and outstretched prospect was enough in itself to make a transcendentalist? And then the physical life had been so hard, its rewards had been so little attractive, as constantly to hint that the real worth of living, and indeed the inward truth of all that we see, must lie not in material things but in the mind, perhaps, or in the spirit, or, it may be, in the service of others. How could he have failed to be a dreamer in that place where so little except dreams would grow? Why should not the rocky hills of Connecticut have taught him to despise the things of earth, somewhat as the desert had taught the prophets of old days?

A laborious and yet a happy life was that of the boy on the farm at the base of the granite hill. The people of the region called that hill "New Connecticut," perhaps because it seemed to them a kind of Farthest West. And indeed it was a wild place, splendidly uplifted and airy, with its high woods of oak and chestnut and beech. Old men could tell the lad of catamounts, wolves, and bears that had ranged there, and wildcats were a present possibility. In July, when he wandered up along those gritty paths, looking for a lost sheep or gathering the lustrous blackberries that were larger than his mother's thimble, something spoke to him, out of the silence, a message too deep for words. The flash of a tanager, the plaintive cry of the peewee, the fountainlike cadenzas of the hermit thrush, and, most of all, that mysterious sorrow of the mourning dove, far off, hallowing the afternoon, became a part of him. He did not know the names of these birds, nor was he ever to know them, and he scarcely knew that he heard their songs. Yet every note, woven in with the sound of the wind and the scent of the sweet fern and the haze of the distant hills, had its share in the making of an American. In late October, too, he would be on the ridge of the hill, gathering chestnuts, hickory nuts, hearing the high-up call of the crow and the faint dry tick

[26]

of the golden leaves as they twirled and sidled and struck the ground. The place was very lonely—yet was there not some Presence there? At times it would frighten him, the bodiless Presence that held its breath and made no sound and was nowhere and everywhere at once, within and without him. Then the boy might turn and walk more and more swiftly away, looking over his shoulder, until he began to run. But again, at other times, he would make his way with set purpose to the loneliest sanctuary on the hill, perfectly assured that the Being who dwelt or hovered there meant nothing but good. So the fear and the love of God fused together and were interchanged.

No school or college, no institute of theology, could have taught what the lad learned on the solitary hill. Precisely such things as theology has always hardened into the rigor of death, and such as erudition first doubts and then forgets, were what he learned there. Keeping the innocence of his mind and heart, he moved as naturally into the world of Spirit as the young American Indian does when he too goes up alone to the top of the highest hill and stands there naked, fasting, with nothing but his holy tobacco-pipe for companion, looking into the sky and waiting for the vision that shall transform and guide his life. "New Connecticut" was Bronson Alcott's hill of vision. It was his Sinai. Just at the time when his future friend, Ralph Waldo Emerson, was meeting "God in the bush" at Roxbury, Alcott was doing the same thing on the granite hill above his father's farmhouse. It was as likely a place for such encounters.

The religion of the household was unspoken, undogmatic, not at all an affair of creeds and public profession but one of inward conviction and simple practice. The father, a silent man, and yet with gleams and glimmers far down in him like those of a deep dark pool, was content to let his life show what he believed; and the mother, though her talk ran and rippled cheerily as a brook in the sunshine, phrased most of her religion in her quiet smile. She

[27]

had been born and bred an Episcopalian—a fact which, in itself, suggested no slight independence of mind and character on the part, at any rate, of her father, Amos Bronson. This meant that she did not share those extremely logical, precisely stateable, and somewhat depressing views of the Here and the Hereafter which had been promulgated with huge success, three hundred years before, by a certain sour-faced cleric of Geneva. Calvinism, which was at least the ostensible theology of nearly all her neighbors, somehow left her cold. It seemed to her a kind of thought-trap that snapped and caught people who depended too much upon their brains and too little upon their hearts. There was something wrong, though she could not say just what, about the hardheaded, hardhearted, man-made argument that Parson Israel Woodward used to run through every Sunday over at Wolcott Church, and that Lyman Beecher of Litchfield had enforced from the same pulpit, on one or two terrible occasions, with all the assurance of a man straight from hell with the latest news. Parson Beecher and Parson Woodward both said that because Adam had sinned against God, therefore all of Adam's descendants—and this would include not only herself, but her beloved husband and even her children as well—must suffer torment throughout eternity, unless indeed that same righteously angered God should, as a matter of whim, change His mind about a very few of them. Did this queer and complicated belief seem likely? Parson Woodward and Parson Beecher, having nothing to do except to study out such things, ought to know; and yet, on the other hand, her own father had also given the matter some thought and had reached quite a different opinion. Her father had a way of being right. Besides, there was her brother Tillotson, who had read as many books as either of these learned gentlemen; and he did not agree with them. What was a simple-minded woman to decide?

She had little time to think about it, for when she was not churning butter or baking bread or mending clothes, then she would be spinning yarn in the little room up-stairs, or banging the loom, or else bringing water from the well—besides all of which, more children were always coming. Coming—for what purpose, and to what end? To fill the vacant rooms of hell? To help assuage the inappeasable appetite for vengeance of an infinite God? Oh, perhaps, now that the learned and very logical gentlemen of the cloth had had their sufficient say, it would be well to use a little common sense. Look at young Amos, here by her side, quietly reading his book in the nooning while she knitted, with the sunshine of the south room on his ruddy hair. Amos had never said an unkind thing, or done a mean one; and if God was planning to burn Amos forever, only because He could not get over something that Adam had done a great while ago, why then, why then . . . But she must go and see whether the potatoes had boiled.

Anna Bronson Alcott sometimes went with her husband to the little church on Wolcott Hill to hear what the Reverend Mr. Woodward had to say about the Lord's plans for her and her family. It was a long way to walk in her clumsy shoes, and the last long hill from Misery Brook to the church was often a wearisome climb when she was gravid with child. Sometimes she could go in the cart, but in winter, when the snow had drifted deep in the hollow lane, the two miles seemed like ten. Her husband was unable to afford a "Sabba' Day house" where she and the children might warm themselves before going into the unheated church; but at least she could see that their foot-warmers were filled with coals at the tavern, and also that Joseph, never very strong, was properly fortified with something from jug or barrel before the service began. And then, how odd it would seem to hear the Reverend Mr. Woodward discoursing about the fires of hell as their future destination, while the children's noses were turning blue and the Parson himself stood in his high pulpit with his greatcoat about him and with black mittens on his hands!

Anna Bronson Alcott attended church with her husband because she would not have the women of the neighborhood saying that her Joseph was unable to manage his own household. She was happiest, however, on those summer days when she was able to take young Amos behind her on the horse and ride the five miles down to her own church, St. John's, in Waterbury, where her brother Tillotson had once been rector and where Amos himself had been christened by that famous uncle when an infant. Down Clinton Hill and Spindle Hill they would jog together, with the sunny land opening out before them, down Chestnut Hill and steep Buck's Hill, where the steeples of the small white town came into view, and at last they would reach the green, then half a frog-pond and a reedy fen, where the boy would dismount and pluck sweet flag to chew during service-time. Those were good days. The rides behind his mother were the lad's first sallies into the great world.

Presently Anna's husband, without saying much about it, took to going with them. A strong interest in Episcopalianism was growing in the town, for reasons not wholly unconnected with politics. When Amos was sixteen he and his cousin William began to read prayers and services for the townsfolk in the little schoolhouse at the crossroads. A year later, in October, 1816, both of them, together with Joseph Alcox, were confirmed at St. John's Church.

The education of the boy who had left school at ten was rapidly proceeding. At twelve he began the lifelong habit of keeping a diary, perhaps in imitation of his mother. At fourteen, and for several years thereafter, he was engaged in an extremely formal and dignified correspondence with his cousin William, who lived in the little red cottage just down the lane. "Sir," wrote William, to the barefooted lad with whom he had just been kicking dust beside the fence-rail:—

Sir:—

In commencing the present correspondence our motives, it is believed, are mutually understood; and in its

[30]

continuance the exercise of candor to each other's opinions, it is hoped, will be scrupulously regarded. We write to benefit each other. Let us then be plain and familiar.

That is precisely what they were not. The stilted "schoolmarm English" seen in William's letter, the determination to avoid every free and hill-born expression, vitiated the correspondence, at least as it has been fragmentarily preserved. This was natural enough, and was indeed inevitable. As we have seen, the two lads were engaged in pulling each other up, out of the crudities of their immediate environment; and they found their first toe-hold in a stiff and prim gentility of style which was far less to be desired, of course, than the illiterate simplicities they left behind. They scorned the home-bred Saxon of Spindle Hill and reached out for a tasteless Latinism which they believed— and, one fears, with some warrant—was then the language of "educated" persons in more favored regions. One does not blame them, but only deplores the fact that this necessary stage of progress was so prolonged in the development of Bronson Alcott's style. The sad truth is that he never quite passed through this stage. During his years of daily talk with children and in his later association with the plain speakers of Concord he did indeed learn the worth of that downright Doric from which his pen, though not his tongue, was always flinching away; but all this came too late. The bombast and fustian of his boyish correspondence with William clung to his prose style to the end, like a vice in the blood.

Whence it originally came is not quite clear. We know that the cousins spent three months, in 1814, under the tuition of Pastor John Keys, on Wolcott Hill, giving "special attention to English grammar and composition," so that there is a temptation to find the culprit in that reverend and learned gentleman. But the temptation is to be resisted. One need only turn to the articles which both of the young aspirants to culture were then reading in the *Connecticut Courant* in order to see that the swelling and dropsical diseases of style were just then epidemic. All America, and all of New England in particular, was striving toward the "elegant" and the "genteel." Nearly everyone who drew a pen was laboring to forget the homely words and turns of idiom he had learned in childhood, so that it was soon to be a chief wonder of those who read and listened to Emerson how he, with all his advantages, could so crudely refer to "the meal in the firkin, the milk in the pan." The situation was not unlike that of England some fifty years before, when almost every natural expression was considered by the writers of the time— three fourths of whom were strenuously clambering upwards from the petty bourgeoisie—to be "low." Indeed, if one were seeking a single scapegoat upon whom to heap all the blame for this literary sin, it would not do to ignore Doctor Samuel Johnson.

Of that supreme master of the sesquipedalian style, however, Bronson Alcott probably had not yet heard. A more proximate source of corruption is revealed in one of his undated letters to William:—

Dear Friend:

I have been so busied about many things since your letter came to hand that I have hardly had any time to reply as I wished.

About my summer: I have concluded to remain at home and work on the farm, giving my leisure time to studying Burgh's *Dignity*. I can borrow the book of my aunt. Having read it yourself, you know its value. Does it not illustrate Pope's line in making the reader

"To see all others' faults, and feel his own"?

Wishing you much pleasure and profit in reading Rolin's *Ancient History,*

I am yours truly,
Amos B. Alcox

In directness and ease of expression this is far better than the passage just quoted from William, but one is sorry to say that as more and more leisure was given to the study of James Burgh's *Dignity of Human Nature,* that masterpiece of consummate and ineffable gentility, the prose style of young Amos B. Alcox grew worse and worse. It discovered new bogs and mudholes of magniloquent bathos, through which a sensitive reader wades with pain and a kind of loathing. Why could there not have been one man really educated in the neighborhood—perhaps the Reverend John Keys, or Uncle Tillotson—to make the young aspirant throw James Burgh's *Dignity* out of the window, open his ears, and write the English that he heard? But there was no such man. There was only William. Accordingly, one does not blame Bronson Alcott for what was vicious in his style of writing. One bemoans it.

The cousins formed a "Juvenile Library," of which Bronson was the President and William was Secretary and Treasurer—for even then, apparently, it would not have done to make Bronson the treasurer of anything. So far as the record shows, they two were the sole subscribers and beneficiaries of this institution, to which each of them contributed the few books that he already possessed and perhaps a dollar a year for the purchase of more. Scouring the region round about, they found perhaps a hundred volumes in the kitchens of their kinsfolk, and these they borrowed and read—some of them again and again. Pope's poems were among them, as the letter from Amos B. Alcox has just shown, and so were the poems of James Thomson, from whose glamorous and somewhat sentimental pastoralism one of the two young readers never quite recovered. They found a Milton, a copy of Young's *Night Thoughts,* and Hervey's *Meditations among the Tombs,* together with plenty of Bibles. Also they found a *Robinson Crusoe* and a little dog-eared and grimy *Deserted Village.*

[33]

One is interested to learn what sort of mental pabulum two voracious young minds could find for themselves in a remote New England village one hundred and twenty years ago, and it is worthy of remark that none of the books thus discovered by the Alcott cousins were of American authorship. Young Bronson might have read all those that have been named, however, without much result to himself or to the world; but when, one rainy afternoon over at Wolcott Hill, he came across his cousin Riley Alcox's copy of Bunyan's *Pilgrim's Progress*, then indeed, according to his own later belief, really important things were decided. It was a Dublin edition of 1802 that he had in hand— an octavo bound in legal calf, with about a dozen steel engravings in the manner of Flaxman. Every page of the volume as it exists to-day is browned and polished by diligent thumbing. Aside from its associations the volume is not particularly pleasing, and one would hesitate to pay as much as half a dollar for it at a bookstall; but when its history is considered it shines forth in the precious little library of Bronson Alcott like a planet among stars.

There is no guessing the way of a boy with a book, and no foretelling what a book may do to a boy. At just the time when Bronson Alcott fell, with every mental tooth and nail, upon Bunyan's little homespun classic, the other lads of the Wolcott region were being drawn down from the farms to the few factories in the valleys below. Eli Terry had established a clock factory at "Ireland," on Hancock Brook, close to Spindle Hill, and Silas Hoadley soon had another. They paid better wages than one could make at farmwork or schoolmastering. Why should not Bronson Alcott go with the other lads, as even his own brothers were soon to do? For a time, to be sure, he did, and spent some nine months assembling clocks at Hoadleyville; but he went reluctantly, and returned as soon as he could. The little shop in the barnyard where he and his father worked side by side in winter was factory enough for him.

And then there was Seth Thomas, that redoubtable captain of industry, who had been born and reared, by a delightful co-incidence, on a farm close to Bronson's home. Thomas had once negotiated for the water power, then owned by the Alcocks, below the dam on Mad River where Bronson went swimming. Failing in that, he had gone elsewhere, had cheapened the processes of clockmaking by "standardizing" parts and men, had hired more and more hands, had filled the country—and England as well—with cheap clocks, and was to die very rich before long with a flourishing town named after him. Bronson met Seth Thomas' young men when they came to his father's farm after the "ivy" or mountain laurel which they used in making clock pinions. His own sisters were learning to spin clock cords out of the native flax. Could he not see that a new age was beginning? And why should he turn aside? He had as much Yankee ingenuity as Seth Thomas, and no little skill with mechanism. Even as a child he had learned to handle tools, and he was always to delight in any sort of handicraft or manual labor that came his way.

The question has already been asked, and left unanswered, what it was that first turned Bronson Alcott out of the conventional ruts of his time and place into the hard ways of the educational reformer. Now we have to ask why he turned aside from the bold and splendid mechanical work of his generation—from the bridge-building, railroading, mining, inventing, and manu-facturing of half the things that ran the world—into those paths of ideal thought upon which Plato, Pythagoras, and Jesus often seemed to be his only companions.

What tiny difference in brain cells, what tick of time, what hair's-breadth distinction of circumstance, caused the chasm between Seth Thomas's glorious "success" and Alcott's "failure"? And again there is no final answer. To say that the one was a "representative American" or a "typical Yankee" and that the other was not is merely to mouth words. Both were typical and representative in some degree, though both were partial and in-

[35]

complete. If obliged to choose, one would certainly say that Alcott was the more typical of the two, for the reason that he struck his roots much farther down into New England time. In his preoccupation with things of the mind and spirit he belonged with the men of our Heroic Age, such as Thomas Shepard and Richard Mather and Jonathan Edwards, while the tribe of the clock merchant reached little farther back than Benjamin Franklin.

Bronson Alcott thought he knew what it was that kept him out of the factories. He would have said that it was *Pilgrim's Progress.* He believed that this book lay so close to the watershed of his life as to turn his thoughts permanently aside from machinery, from money-making, and from all the clatter and din of the age coming on, toward the ancient and infinite seas of Spirit. Of course he may have been wrong. A cautious biographer ought to hesitate before so simple an explanation. But that is what he himself believed.

It is certain that young Alcott read Bunyan's book over and over, memorizing large parts of it and acting it out in some rude dramatic form of his own devising. The book entered into him, shaping and coloring his thoughts. It affected, for a time, even his choice of words in daily speech. Why it did not also affect, and greatly improve, the style of his written prose is an easy question. It lay too close to his life. *Pilgrim's Progress* could not be "literature," he felt, because it was so obviously real. The language of it could not teach him anything he needed to know, he was persuaded, because it was so like the plain speech he had always heard. But the book could teach him everything except how to write.

Little by little the great allegory fixed upon the youth's mind a habit, perhaps already begun under the influence of the Fables in Noah Webster's Speller, of seeing all things double—here the fact and there its significance; here the event and there its universal meaning; here the concrete temporal instance and there the everlasting law. After such teaching he needed only a Cole

[36]

ridge or a Plato to show him that reality lies always in the law and never in the instance, and he would be a complete "Idealist." Add to this what he already knew, or surmised, about the Presence on New Connecticut Hill, and he would be a transcendentalist fully equipped.

There was really no reason, then, why he should descend into those western valleys along the Naugatuck, where young America was beginning to lift up its raucous voice. He had heard the first infant cry of the machine, which was to swell in his lifetime into so huge a roar, and he vaguely knew that it was calling for him—for his heart's blood, his love and devotion. But he had also heard a quite different voice. It had come from "a man clothed with rags, standing in a certain place, with his face from his own house . . . and he wept and trembled; and, not being able longer to contain, he brake out with a lamentable cry saying, 'What shall I do to be saved?' "

It is true that *Pilgrim's Progress* did not induce in Alcott, even at first, anything like the Christian piety which Bunyan had hoped it might increase; and yet the first reading of the book was a religious experience, in some ways amounting to a "conversion." This one may say in full recognition of the fact that, according to the spirit if not the letter of Alcott's own declaration, it led on to his denial of the divinity of Jesus and to the sober statements of such liberal men as Dr. Channing and George Ripley that he seemed hardly distinguishable from an atheist. How, then, can the book be said to have had a "religious" effect? It convinced the young man, once and for all, that "here we have no continuing city." It made all the remaining course of his life one long pilgrimage, like that of Christian, "from this world to that which is to come."

A GENTLEMAN OF THE ROAD

{ 1818–1822 }

What shall the lad do?—The American Autolycus—A maple-
wood fiddle—An innocent abroad—The Old Dominion—A sham-
bling Odyssey—Fever—The gorgeous coat—Quakers—Repentance

IF YOUNG AMOS was not going down into the factories,
what should he do for a living?

When the lad was about seventeen he and his parents began to
discuss this problem as they sat together, in the winter evenings,
by the huge kitchen hearth. They talked it over without haste or
anxiety while the father smoked his pipe, the mother went on
with one of her thousand tasks, and Amos held his place with
one finger in the book he was reading. There was no need of
haste. Amos himself was not to come to a final decision about
the matter, if indeed he ever did, for the next forty years. He
was never much interested in the problem. It bored him. He
could see that to other lads it was the one thing worth thinking
about, but he found it hard to think about at all.

Neither were his parents anxious. The whole country was crying out for young men, and anyone with eyes in his head would be glad to employ a young man like their Amos—so well-grown and strong and good-looking, so clever with his hands and in the use of all common tools, so fond of hard work, so completely honest and good.

Of course a young man could always go out West, as a few youths of the clan had already done; but Anna and Joseph Alcox did not like that plan for their eldest boy. It would mean a separation almost as final as death.

How about farming, then? Why should not the lad go on as he was going now, inherit the farm some day, marry a neighbor's daughter, and live as all the men of the family had lived for as far back as any one knew? Well, there were a number of things to be said about that. In the first place, although no one ever starved at farming, it seemed almost impossible to get ahead, at least on Spindle Hill. There was never any money there—and money was going to be needed if they were ever to put up the new house. And then, too, the son was not particularly fond of farming. He was good at it, because he was so strong, but one could see that he was always hankering after something else. He liked the winter work in the shop. He liked spring plowing, cradling, and getting in the hay. He was a great hand at the flail. In fact, he seemed to be fond of almost anything that had to do with plants. It was the creatures that he did not like—one could hardly tell why. Father Joseph smiled to himself when he thought of the day he had sent the lad up with the two tall yellow oxen, to plow the little meadow near the top of New Connecticut. He would have said, if it had been anyone else, that Amos was really vexed when he came down from that day's plowing. Well, it *was* somewhat rocky up there, and those yellow oxen were two tough brutes to handle. They needed a man—a man who knew about creatures. It was a queer thing: either a man did or he didn't—and the creatures always knew which kind a man was. Amos

[39]

was not the kind that did. One might almost say that creatures disgusted him. He never cared for dogs, even; and as for hogs! Why, time and again the boy would leave his salt pork untouched on his plate, after a hard day's work. And then in the middle of the winter you could hear him hankering after fresh vegetables when he knew that for nine months of the year there wasn't any such thing. And trying to live on apples! It was a wonder how he had ever got his growth, and all that muscle. But no; if a man was going to be a farmer he had better not begin by turning up his nose at good salt pork.

The mother had no dearer dream than that her son might be a minister like her brother Tillotson, full of old languages and mathematics and able to write poetry. It would mean going to Yale, of course, and that, in turn, would mean money; yet her own mother had woven Tillotson himself through Yale, and she too could weave. The question was whether the boy really wanted it—for what was the use unless he did? He had been down to New Haven with his father when he was thirteen, and had come back all agog at the shops and the streets full of houses and the stately college buildings, three or four of them, under the elms by the green. But what did that mean? When you pressed the question home to Amos it was hard to tell whether he really wanted to go to Yale College. Was it because he was shy, because he thought he would not like the routine of the work there, or because he felt that his father could not spare him? There was something in each of these explanations; but, in addition, one might almost think the boy was holding back because he thought he had something in him that a college might spoil or take away. He liked to teach others, but to learn from anyone—ah, that was a different matter.

Brother Tillotson had taken Amos to live with him at Cheshire thinking perhaps that if the boy showed promise a way might be made for him to go through the Cheshire Academy and so on to the pulpit. Amos had run on errands for his uncle and had gone

[40]

to the district school. His uncle's library, containing perhaps as many as a thousand books, had deeply impressed him. He would have liked to sit there forever, reading those books. Yet he had not been happy at Cheshire. He was very bashful; and he thought —no doubt wrongly—that the young gentlemen of the Academy had laughed at his homespun clothes, at his language, or at his lack of their kind of school-learning. At any rate, he had been so homesick that, after two months of the experiment, they had allowed him to come back home. It had been an unpleasant experience. Amos himself did not like to talk about it, and for her it had been a deep disappointment which seemed to close a vista.

There was schoolmastering, of course. Not that it was to be compared with the life of a minister, but it would keep Amos at the books he liked so well and would give him more of that "leisure" about which he had so much to say. (What could he mean by "leisure"? Amos was not a lazy boy.) Already he had passed the tests for his teacher's certificate, but for some reason the School Committee had not given him the school at Woodick that he had asked for. Perhaps they thought he was not old enough. He was seventeen.

And, again, there was peddling. Amos had done a little of it when he was only fifteen, journeying on foot with his cousin Thomas as far as western Massachusetts and trying to sell small articles from house to house on the way. He had in fact made two of these trips in the spring of that year, extending his knowledge of geography and of mankind not a little. During one of them he had visited Newgate Prison, in the northern part of Connecticut, and had seen the pale, gaunt men—two of them father and son from his own town—brought up from the frightful darkness of the pit where they slept. He had been faint for weeks at the thought of them. Also he had gone into eastern New York in October of the same year, peddling Flavel's book on *Keeping the Heart*. He had made little money, but he liked

peddling. He liked it because it took him to new places and people
It satisfied the instincts of the wanderer in him, which were al
most as strong as his need of home and of a settled society.

Western Connecticut, where the soil was thin and the water:
were swift, was beginning to pour her surplus of young men into
the trails and tote-roads, turnpikes and highways of America
They went South and West and even "way down East," carry
ing in handbags, valises, carts, and wagons everything portabl
that they thought might sell. They carried news from the sea
board towns into faraway farmsteads and huddles of huts whither
without their help, it would never have come. They carried las
year's fashions, public opinion of a decade gone by, and th
prejudices that never die out, together with assorted heartbrea
for many an uplandish maiden. One fears that they were not al
ways well-bred or perfectly well-behaved. They could not shav
often. Their baths were mostly those that they took perforc
while fording unbridged streams. Country dogs regarded then
with strong and well-founded dislike. When they slept at inn
and taverns, as they were sometimes allowed to do, the rate wa
usually fourpence a night, with two pence added for supper o
breakfast; and it was occasionally stipulated—or so we are told—
that not more than five pedlars were to sleep in a bed and tha
all boots were to be removed before retiring. More frequentl
they slept in barns.

A virile lot, bold, carefree, and adventurous, the Yankee pec
lars of a hundred and more years ago made up one of the mos
picturesque classes of men that America has ever produce
They stood halfway between the merchant and the gipsy, with
faint touch added of the mountebank. One might term them th
"commercial gentlemen" of those days if one remembered th:
they carried the goods they sold, that they seldom returned c
their own tracks, and that they did not even try to secure wh:
is nowadays called "the confidence of their buyers."

[42]

To say that the Yankee pedlar was a consummate liar was considered, in Bronson Alcott's youth-time, an assertion of the obvious. To have called him "dishonest" would have been thought a violent understatement. In estimating these opinions, however, we should consider that pedlars had been going up and down the land for more than a century, spreading a reputation about themselves which was not in all instances entirely deserved. It was the kind of reputation that a wandering people or class, or even individual, will always acquire among those who stay at home and peer suspiciously through the narrow crack of the door. There was something in it of *caveat emptor,* "let the purchaser be cautious," but there was rather more of the homebody's fear of the homeless, foot-loose man. Moreover, people had come to delight in the pedlar's real or alleged iniquities. He was an institution, a treasure, something to be proud of, like the town fool of New England, the champion liar of the Middle West, or the cowboy who wins a prize belt for profane vituperation. If a pedlar from Connecticut was only moderately dishonest and had "taken them in" rather less than they had expected, people liked to help him out by asserting that the desiccated and wormy nutmegs he had sold them were made of wood. Thus he became the hero of a legend, and eventually filled an honorable place in the "tall tales" with which the popular imagination was seething from the Atlantic to the Mississippi. He enjoyed these tales as much as anyone, and used them in his business.

In considering the Connecticut pedlar's reputation, furthermore, one needs to see it in historical perspective. Barter, trade, commerce, business, merchandising, have never been a whit more "honest" than the conditions about them have compelled them, or made it profitable for them, to be. They have given up seeking a profit of a thousand per cent. only when, by taking only half as much, they could hope, in the long run, to make more money; and this would be only when they expected to deal with the same customers year after year. There is, in fact, one scale of com-

[43]

mercial "honesty" for the established and stationary business
serving a settled community, and quite another for the merchant
who needs to think only of the single transaction. Benjamin
Franklin, when he said that "honesty is the best policy," spoke like
the city-bred shopkeeper that he essentially was. It was not that
he and other members of his comparatively respectable class were
really more honest than pedlars, but only that they had found it
profitable to seem so.

And so Bronson Alcott, seventeen years old, studious and
dreamy and invincibly innocent, was thinking that he might lay
aside Burgh's *Dignity of Human Nature* for a while and go South
as a pedlar. The force of example, though he was never much
led thereby, strongly suggested this course. The new factories
on the Naugatuck were turning out ever more and more goods
which must be sold ever farther and farther away. The War of
1812 had established even in the South a definite preference for
American manufactures. The hills of New England were crowded
with young men who could no longer find enough land to work
even if they had the patience to work it. In western Connecticut
where the hills left the least arable land and also sent down the
best mill-water, the development of a race of pedlars was as in
evitable as the springing up of blueberries where fire has burned
the woods. From Meriden, it was said, thirty men went South and
West each year with their packs or wagonloads of tinware, plated
silver, and "Yankee notions." From little Wolcott itself Lyman
Higgins, Sam Horton, and two of the Hotchkiss brothers had gone
forth as early as 1810, and more of the local youth were taking
to the roads every year. Usually they traveled in Virginia and
the Carolinas, sometimes buying their outfit at Berlin, Connecti
cut, and at others hiring themselves out to a firm in Southington
just down the hill from Wolcott.

Amos pled for permission to go, but for a long time in vain
Some concession was made to the wanderlust by allowing him to

[44]

spend a few months with his grandfather, Amos Bronson, and to help the old man get in his autumnal crops. He enjoyed that visit greatly, and was to keep throughout his life the recollection of the strong and gentle octogenarian who lived with a simple dignity unusual for those parts in his comfortable house at Plymouth, beside the Naugatuck. Returning home again, Amos spent the winter at his now familiar occupations—making baskets and plows in the workshop beside his father, carrying on his stately correspondence with William, reading the services on Sundays at the schoolhouses of the Spindle Hill and Babylon districts, and farming. But he was beginning to feel awkwardly large for the nest. His wings were aching for flight. He had borrowed and read all the books, the almanacs, even the flying stationers's leaves that were to be discovered for miles around. Surely there must be more books somewhere. He had heard of many more than he had been able to find. But how get at them? In default of books by other minds he made books with his own, toiling at his diaries and fastening upon himself a habit that was to last until the pen should fall from his palsied hand. He made himself an excellent penman, perfecting the first and best of the half-dozen quite distinct chirographies to be seen in his manuscripts. Probably it was at this time that he taught himself to draw, and also began those decorations of the barn floor, made with a jackknife, which were the admiration of Spindle Hill boys for the next half-century. The two chief figures, as he explained it to them, were intended to represent the same man before and after partaking of a dinner of clams.

These are trivial details, yet worthy of mention because they show a strongly æsthetic nature groping, with no guidance or encouragement, toward some kind of expression, it knew not what. At this time in his life Bronson Alcott had probably not seen one good picture or statue. He hardly knew that such things existed; and yet he was reaching toward them in the dark. It may well be that in his lifelong effort to make himself a good writer he was working against some inward grain, and that his real gift lay rather in the arts of form. In that case, he would be one more victim of the great initial misfortune from which America has always suffered—the enormous headstart that was given here to the arts of speech and writing over all the others.

"Whatever the eye can do," Alcott once said to Emerson, "I am good for," and it may be added that he had a remarkably steady and skillful hand to carry out the orders of the eye. Certainly he never worked in a more continuous, creative rapture than he did when building the summerhouse in Emerson's garden after a design entirely his own. But style in writing is largely an affair of the ear.

Of good music, too, Alcott knew in his youth exactly nothing; but even toward this he could fumble and grope. He had felled a large old maple tree in the bilberry swamp on the edge of the farm—a place which his boyish fancy had once invested with a peculiar wizardry. From the wood of this tree he carved himself a violin. Varnish and strings were bought in New Haven and the bow was strung from the tail of the family horse. The young artist was not proud of the music he drew from his homemade instrument, but he says, significantly: "My eyes were delighted with its beauty."

And all the while the plan for peddling "at the South" was by no means forgotten. There came a Hessian tailor to Spindle Hill and Bronson, now eighteen and a man grown, decided that the time had come for him to have a suit of clothes made not by his mother but by a man. He provided the material—which was still, to be sure, only homespun from his mother's loom—and had himself duly measured. In a few days he stood forth arrayed in the latest New York fashion, at least so far as the cut of his coat was concerned, and his precious violin had been carried off by the Hessian tailor as payment for professional services.

Then it became apparent to all that Bronson must see the world without delay—or rather, perhaps, that the world must see him. On the thirteenth of October, 1818, he sailed from New Haven for Norfolk, Virginia, on the sloop *Three Sisters*.

There were fifteen pedlars and tinmen on board, mostly from his own region; but these soon dispersed into the surrounding country after reaching Norfolk, leaving Amos in lodgings at the "tinnery" until he could spy out the land and discover in what way his talents might best be employed. One would not care to say that he had sailed under false colors, but he had certainly not been very explicit with regard to his hopes and expectations. Peddling was a thing that he might do if he could find nothing more dignified, but he hoped for teaching. He shared an opinion then held by most of New England that the South stood in need, chiefly, of "education." Equipped, therefore, with his four or five years of training in the Spindle Hill school and with the certificates of the Wolcott School Committee, he set forth into Virginia to offer his services. But here he met a rebuff. After a few days' jaunt into the Norfolk hinterland, "exploring," as he says, "the wishes and views of the planters," it became evident that these views and wishes did not at all correspond with his own, and that he was "as ill-qualified to serve the common people as he was their more courtly and aristocratic neighbors." Like Mr. Micawber in this respect as in a few others, Alcott was likely to be most magnificent in his language when he had to record or to gloss over an incident somewhat wounding to his pride. His present remark would appear to mean, then, that the "common people"—a phrase not often heard at that time in Connecticut—did not wish to be taught, and that the "aristocracy" had already been instructed at least as well as he.

Both of these observations were probably surprising to the youth from the New England hills. However, he was out to see the world and to meet its "views" as well as he could without lowering the never-sullied banner within him. The Christmas holidays were now at hand, and the "countrymen," as the farmer's son had already begun to call them, were flocking into town for their holiday shopping. These people, of course, were the pedlar's legitimate prey. With one of his few remaining dollars the young man purchased a number of almanacs for the new year and hawked them about the town, buying them at threepence each and contenting himself with a profit of only three hundred per cent. He found so ready a market that by the end of the first day he had cleared two dollars—a mighty sum. For two weeks he continued to do as well, until he was not only able to defray his somewhat embarrassing bill for board and lodging at the "tinnery" but even had something left over for more audacious speculations.

There was in Norfolk at this time a certain dealer in "fancy goods," J. J. Allen by name, who preyed upon pedlars as they meant to do upon the general public. He was a Yankee himself, as it happened, and extraordinarily "accommodating." From him young Alcott ordered, regardless of expense, two handsomely japanned tin trunks such as pedlars carried, fitted with strong and easy handles and an intricate arrangement of interior fastenings for holding the stock in place. The stock itself, to the value of some three hundred dollars, was sold—or rather lent—to him by the same high-minded benefactor, and was neatly packed into the two portable bazaars.

Here, according to the pedlar's own inventory, were: "combs of tortoise-shell of the latest fashion, jewelry & amulets & garnets & pearls, reticule-clasps & rouge-papers, essences & oils & fine soaps & pomatums, silver thimbles & gold & silver spectacles with shagreen cases for all ages, sewing silks & cottons & threads & buttons & needles with silver & gold eyes (Hemming's best), pencil cases, pen knives, scissors of Rogers' make, with steel purses, playing cards, & wafers. And, for the gentlemen, the genuine magnum bonum rasors & straps. Also picture-bricks and puzzles for the children. Then we have fans & fiddle-strings, etc. etc."

This delightful list of items probably runs fairly close to that

[48]

of the ordinary pedlar's pack, but yet it does seem to indicate a remarkable preponderance of articles for the fair sex and for the darling young. Indeed, the pedlar himself remarked that "the ladies and the children were especially cared for." It would always be his way to care especially for them. Men were coarse creatures who shaved, or ought to do so; and a sufficient provision for them would be "rasors & straps." But whisky flasks, cigar cases, chewing tobacco, and the other paraphernalia of masculinity seem to have been entirely forgotten.

According to Alcott's own later belief, no customer ever paid more fabulous prices for a pedlar's outfit than he did to his accommodating friend from New England. Still a perfect novice, and destined always to remain a pure idealist in matters of purchase and sale, he seems to have agreed to any price that was asked of him, being chiefly anxious not to wound the feelings of this new friend who was being so helpfully kind. And what must have been the bewilderment of that Yankee dealer in "fancy goods" as he placed more and more fantastic valuations upon his wares and had them all instantly accepted! "Is this really a Connecticut pedlar," he may have asked himself, "or is he not rather a wandering philanthropist?" But the full rich humor of the situation, and its tinge of pathos as well, must have escaped him. He could not know that this tall young man, apparently preparing to go forth and fleece the innocent countryside, was himself one of the most innocent souls that have ever withstood the slow stain of the world. He could not possibly guess how slight and negligible, among the young man's motives, was the mere desire for gain. One could scarcely have made him believe what was really the fact, that his customer was mainly driven by a desire to see the world, to meet many people, to enlarge his horizons. It would have been a waste of breath to tell him that the raw youth was himself so dazzled by the beauty of these gewgaws and of the two tin trunks as to care not at all what he promised to pay for them. The pedlar was chiefly thinking of how he would soon amaze the ladies and children in a thousand country parlors, as he opened these lustrous crypts and let their "amulets & garnets & pearls" blaze forth. Would not some reflection of that luster fall upon the pedlar himself, young though he was, and a greenhorn, and clothed in country homespun? He was beginning a long public career in which the hope of doing some good to the world, a simple love of beauty, and the longing for a light reflected upon him from happy faces, were to be the main motives from first to last. A pedlar he certainly was, and would always remain; but he was not therefore mercenary.

The Yankee dealer in "fancy goods" may have laughed a little to himself after Mr. Amos B. Alcox of Connecticut left his shop, but we can hardly suppose that he laughed deeply and tenderly, as he should have done, or with any suggestion of tears.

Soon after the holiday season the newly equipped pedlar took the Hampton packet boat and went forth among the plantations on the River James. From thence he crossed country to Yorktown and visited the plantations on Chesapeake Bay as far as Hampton, returning from there to Norfolk. And this his first expedition was entirely successful. It succeeded, if one may put first the matter which he always thought of last or not at all, even in making money. In spite of his incurable tendency to give his trinkets away instead of selling them, Alcott made perhaps a dollar a day during this hundred-mile walk with a heavy tin trunk in either hand. But far more important than this were the intellectual gains. For the first time in his life he talked on terms of something like equality with cultivated men and women. Furthermore he was able to read, or at least to look into, several of the books—Cowper's *Life and Letters*, Lavater's *Physiognomy*, and John Locke *On the Human Understanding* among them—which he had known must exist somewhere but which he had never been able to lay his hands upon. A few Sunday afternoons in the libraries of certain nameless country gentlemen of Virginia probably did more to determine the

permanent slant of his mind than all the weary hours he had spent
in the little schoolhouse on Spindle Hill.

For the social success of Alcott's first jaunt into the world was
the most gratifying and remarkable thing about it. Toward
Yankees in general and Connecticut pedlars in particular the
Virginians of those days felt no strong yearnings of affection,
and this young pedlar fell exactly within the category which was
soon to be described by Fitz-Green Halleck in his poem on
"Connecticut" as:—

> . . . a few apostates who are meddling
> With merchandise, pounds, shillings, pence, and peddling,
> Or wandering through the southern counties, teaching
> The A B C from Webster's spelling-book;
> Gallant and godly, making love and preaching,
> And gaining by what they call "hook and crook"
> And what the moralists call over-reaching,
> A decent living. The Virginians look
> Upon them with as favorable eyes
> As Gabriel on the devil in Paradise.

And yet the Virginians liked Mr. Amos B. Alcox—perhaps
partly because he liked them.

The social success began with the planters' dogs, which were
supposed to have been carefully trained to bite Connecticut
pedlars. They did not bite Mr. Amos B. Alcox, possibly because
he had already acquired that piece of rural wisdom—applicable in
so many difficulties of life besides the canine—which Henry
Thoreau was to phrase thus: "If a dog runs at you, whistle to
him." Or possibly, as Alcott suggested in his old age, those fierce
and formidable beasts recognized in him not so much a pedlar as
the spirit of Pythagoras come back to earth. At any rate, he addressed himself to the gentleman whom he believed to be imprisoned in each of those shaggy breasts, and the deepest-mouthed
Cerberus of them all would suddenly relent into tail-wagging as
soon as he came within sight of the pedlar's benignant smile. The

success included also the slaves, in whose cabins the young pedlar often slept. (One recalls at this point that Emerson, forty years later, was to find his friend Alcott deficient in the sense of smell; but one is also reminded that the time would come for this young man to return the hospitalities of his dusky hosts by sheltering more than one refugee slave at his own home in Concord.)

With masters and mistresses, and most emphatically with their children, the pedlar's success was complete. In speaking of him the Southern gentleman modified the usual formula "Damn Yank" by omitting the adjective—a distinction not without a difference, but one that required a feeling for nice discriminations. Every presupposition was strongly against the stranger. He came from New England, even from Connecticut; he was a pedlar, a landless wanderer, a fly-by-night; he talked eagerly, in a cadence and pitch and vocabulary that seemed almost a foreign tongue; he had "idees," which, however, he was more likely to call "idears"; he walked on his own feet instead of riding a horse like a gentleman, and he carried his own luggage instead of handing it to a "nigger." These were damaging facts, but he somehow managed to smile them all down. By his bashful modesty and shy friendliness he warmed the hearts of those Southern gentry even while he puzzled their brains. They saw that there was something irregular about him, bursting through the familiar categories. Though a Yankee, he was a human being. In short, he was an exception. They treated him as such.

Whatever the pedlar's previous notions about the Old Dominion may have been, he soon came to regard it with strong enthusiasm. Day after day, as he sat by the roadside on one of his tin trunks and wrote down reflections in his diary, his remarks about Virginians became more favorable and those about Yankeeland more caustic. Though entirely new to him, the social refinement and the courtesy which he found in the great houses beside the York and the James were recognized at once as things of his own kind.

[52]

There it was that he began to acquire what an English acquaintance of later years was to call "the manners of a very great peer." There the raw country youth began those lessons in demeanor which were to make him, in the words of Emerson, "very noble in his carriage to all men, of a serene and lofty deportment in the street and in the house, of simple but graceful and majestic manners." Through the mask of extreme diffidence and from beneath the disguise of a traveling salesman, he was observing every motion and gesture, hearing every nuance of tone, catching and remembering every hint of true gentleness and decorum. It was nothing less than a school of manners that he was attending, this awkward youth from the New England hills where crude blunt candor was thought the chief social virtue and where honesty consisted most of all in "speaking one's mind." The contrast between what he saw and what he had previously known could scarcely have been more startling if he had gone to China.

All such experiences are based upon comparison, and in this instance everything that was fair and dignified and of good report in the life of the Old Dominion was thrown up sharply against the bleak two-handed struggle for existence on Spindle Hill. What he took for an unqualified opulence and elegance and lordly ease in the plantation life made the young man feel that he was moving through an ideal country of romance. He was not, and he was never to become, an admirer of ordinary riches, but when wealth had been purified by long inheritance and culture, as he thought it had been in Virginia, it seemed a different thing. In the houses of the planters he saw, for the first time, an architectural magnificence which was somehow in keeping with their manners. Their parks and grounds, their hunting and games and festivals, their gallantries, their balls and dances, their many songs, amazed him. He saw that these people were making a game, a delight, almost one might say a lovely art, and not a dire necessity, out of living. Instantly the Connecticut pedlar realized that they were right in so doing—and at that moment every rag or tag of a merely negative Puritanism which may still have been clinging to him fell away, forever.

The life of the plantation did not remain to him a mere spectacle. Without the slightest intrusion, he became a participator. He entered the family life, and spent much time with wives and children. He was a privileged guest, remaining as long as he liked, and was sent from house to house with a hint to the next planter that there was something more here than met the eye. It might take a brazen face, he said, to get into one of these great houses, but it always took a gentleman to get out of one. When it came to thanks and farewell, the reticence of the tongue-fast North betrayed him and left him stammering.

At taverns he seldom stayed. He had a shrinking dislike of barrooms and of all the "huddle and impudence" of public places. Often he slept in the slave quarters rather than the tavern. Court days and muster days, bringing the people together from far and near, confused him. He did not like a crowd. Why trouble with places in which only men would congregate? What did men matter? What did men know? He came from a home; and he made his way by the shortest possible route to homes, to mothers and children.

Alcott went through Virginia just as he would have gone through life if the world could have let him, seeing only what was fair, gracious, and stately. That the beautiful tapestry had a seamy side, he did not guess. So far as he knew the silver lining that he saw was all there was of the cloud. No one undertook to tell him about the darker aspects of slavery. He stayed away from overseers, and saw no flogging, no slave-auctions. The maimings and disfigurements that he could not fail to see he tried, with some success, to forget. The fact that few of the slaves he saw were really very black, and that some were hardly distinguishable from whites, suggested nothing to his clean young mind. What he remembered was the genial and friendly relations between master and slave, and, still more, the strong fidelity of affection that

[54]

often existed between slave-girl and mistress. He did indeed believe, and continue to believe, that slavery was a serious blot upon this fine civilization of the South; but in that he did no more than agree with many of the kindly gentlemen and ladies who entertained him. He hoped and believed, as many of them did, that it would gradually pass away. He heard planters denounce the whole system as a curse to all concerned, and he came to think that the owners of slaves were the greatest sufferers.

Such was his preparation for the day when he and four or five other men of Boston were to establish the first Anti-Slavery Society in Massachusetts.

Thus three months went by. The pedlar worked out from Norfolk into Portsmouth, Smithfield, Jamestown, Williamsburg, Gloucester, and Mathew's Court House. In April he found that he had cleared a little over one hundred dollars. Late in that month he sailed for New York, where he bought himself "a plain suit of clothes" as his own reward for the winter's work. A few days later he was at home to find that a brother, Junius, had been born in his absence. He turned over to his father the sum of eighty dollars, and on the twelfth of June his father raised the frame of a new house, which is still standing, on the site of the old one.

It was a little hard to say farewell to the old house, where Amos had lived since he was six. By far too small it was now, with a family of nine to be accommodated, and perhaps it had never been very comfortable or roomy. One story and a half in height, with three rooms and a lean-to on the ground floor, it had never been painted and had come to look rather dingy. The loft in which most of the children had slept was a mere storeroom, unpartitioned and unfinished, and the cellar, entered through a trap door in the kitchen, was only a dark hole in the ground. Yet this had been Amos's boyhood home, and it had been dear.

The new house, ample in size and handsome in lines, was a different affair altogether. The kitchen, running almost the whole length of the house, would give plenty of room for the varied work —cooking, washing, spinning, and dyeing—that would go on there. The "South Room" had a double window where his mother might sit on winter afternoons. There was not a larger chimney on Spindle Hill than the one it boasted, and the kitchen fireplace —not counting the brick oven—was six feet wide. The young man was not to see so much of this house as he had of the old one, but he would always be proud that he had done some of the carpentry upon it and that eighty dollars of his first earnings had helped to pay for its construction.

The building of this new house left the father of the family some two hundred dollars in debt, and it was with this fact in mind that his eldest son wrote to him:—

> Two hundred dollars, owed by a farmer who has no other means of accumulating that sum than by the cultivation of a farm of 80 acres, & when the times are extremely dull & the cultivation to be chiefly done by the owner, who is over 45 years of age & considerably debilitated, is a great sum. If that parent has two sons, who can earn him but very little during the winter season at home, & can, by running a little risk, by going five or six hundred miles from home, earn him in 8 or 9 months, with prosperity on their side, that $200, it would be considered by most as managing business the best way.

The logic of these remarks having been accepted, young Alcott set out for Norfolk a second time, taking with him his brother Chatfield, in November, 1819. The younger brother returned in May with sixty-five dollars, and Amos at the end of July with one hundred, all of which he gave to his father. While on the way home he nearly lost his life in the James River, having been seized and pulled down by a drowning fellow-pedlar.

By this time the peddling fever was nearly at its height in western Connecticut. From little Wolcott alone ten or fifteen young men were going forth each year, and a number of them, like "Amos B. Alcox," had already gone more than once. Even cousin William, that extremely sober young man with the studious countenance, was becoming infected, thinking that it was time for him too to see something of the world, and especially of those wonders at the South of which he had recently been hearing. Peddling, to be sure, did not attract him; but he had been told that schoolteaching was more profitable in South Carolina than in Connecticut, and he resolved to try his fortune. On the fourth of October, 1820, the two cousins set out from New Haven bound for Charleston, together with almost a hundred other Connecticut men and boys who expected to be employed upon a canal "project" at Columbia.

William Alcott's account of his first journey, and Bronson's third, away from home is a document which, though not well written, brings the America of those days before a twentieth-century reader with startling vividness. It is a shapeless and shambling prose Odyssey, telling a meaningless tale of how two young men went very vigorously no-whither with no settled plan, how they rambled about at sea and in swamps and in forests, escaping death repeatedly through sheer luck, going through toils and privations and exposures that always stopped a little short of killing them, making their way among whores and rascals and ruffians by the force of pure innocence, and returning home, after a prolonged search for their fortunes, far poorer than when they set forth. Their adventures were prosaic. Their heroism consisted for the most part in the cheerful facing of physical misery. There was no epic grandeur in what they went through; and yet there was a kind of beauty, a sort of symbolic foreshadowing, in the whole series of events. One sees that there was something invincible about the cousins from Spindle Hill, and that after such a trial they would be able to live through almost anything.

The schooner *Enterprise*, though aged and battered and a dull sailer, would have served them well enough on the outward voyage if she had not been overloaded with freight, if she had not met a steady alternation of dead calms and of hurricanes, and if either the captain or the mate, or else some member of the crew, had known a little seamanship. Under the circumstances, however, she took sixteen days between New Haven and Charleston, during which the passengers—most of them continually sick—rattled about on the bare boards of the hold in the nighttime and tried to work the ship in the day. The water was foul. The bully beef had been bad when it was taken on board. When they finally made a landfall the captain did not know what it was. They were blown as far as the Gulf Stream, and then almost down to Bermuda, at the mercy of wind and wave. And yet at last, without the slightest justification, they did make Charleston Harbor and even picked up a pilot—a pilot of whom William spoke most ungratefully, "daring to indulge the hope that he was not a fair sample of his countrymen, for he was a profane swearer, and in many respects a very vulgar man."

After withstanding numerous "temptations to vice" in Charleston—using certain maxims from Webster's Speller and the old writing-master's motto, "Avoid Alluring Company," for the purpose—the cousins started to walk the one hundred and twenty miles to Columbia in company with certain other vulgar persons and profane swearers. These companions were a group of Dutch wagoners who had come down to tidewater with inland produce and were now returning with rum. They carted the young men's trunks, but everyone walked—walked twenty miles a day on wood-paths and tote-roads that were either flowing with water or deep in mud. At night the Dutchmen slept under—not in—their featherbeds, but the cousins from Connecticut, being unprovided with a blanket, piled pine needles over themselves and lay on the bare hoarfrosty ground. A great hole was burned in the tail of William's coat on the first night, after which he lay a little farther from the fire. The Dutchmen drank rum and the cousins drank the water of the stagnant creeks. William, who had been seasick for two weeks before the walk began, did not recover so rapidly as he expected; but Bronson stepped and waded and climbed and jumped his twenty miles a day with his accustomed serenity.

Columbia, even when they reached it, was no place in which to tarry, for there too the water was bad and such schools as there were had already their quota of masters. Out again they walked, therefore, going westward through the sand hills, sleeping one night actually in a bed and breakfasting on sour milk and corn bread at the log cabin of a hospitable Dr. Smith, who was most curious about the North. The houses were few and poor—and as for villages grouped about a steeple in the right New England way, there were apparently none. When one did discover a church it would be in the woods, perhaps made of rough logs, without a floor or any discoverable pulpit. The preacher would be almost as ignorant as his audience, and he would deliver his extemporaneous sermon in a whining singsong very strange to Northern and un-Methodistical ears. The schoolhouses were even more amusing than the churches. They too were built of logs and were without floors, but differed from churches in having large fireplaces—which always smoked. William and Bronson leaned for a while at one schoolhouse window and heard a class of youngsters laboriously spelling "Gizzard," using the old name for the letter "z": "G-i-iz-zard,—giz! izzard-a-r-d,—zard; Gizzard."

With a characteristic contempt for times and seasons, the cousins had reached South Carolina in the middle of the school term, when it was impossible to secure a teaching position. They had thought, to be sure, that if this should happen they might at any rate secure jobs as common laborers on the Columbia canal; but no sooner had the prospects of teaching faded than the contractors for the canal project also failed.

Thus the two prodigal sons came to themselves at the town of Newberry, South Carolina, far from anywhere, with thirty dollars in their pockets. In default of anything better to do, they decided to walk to Norfolk, Virginia, which was about six hundred miles away.

The distance itself, as they soon found, was not so important as the fact that over a great part of their route they were obliged to walk in loose sand. There were hundreds of rivers, creeks, brooks, swamps, and bogs to be crossed on their way, but only one bridge in all of those six hundred miles. They waded or swam the streams and jumped from tussock to rotting log in the swamps. Human habitations were often many miles apart. They ate deer's meat, bear's meat, crackling bread, and johnnycake when they could get them, and went hungry when they could not. As they had already done on the road from Charleston to Columbia, they drank, for the most part, stagnant water—William cautiously, but Bronson without regard to consequences. In eighteen days they were in Norfolk.

Bronson already knew this town. He knew an old man there, formerly a Yankee pedlar but now living in reduced circumstances, who kept a grocery store and took in lodgers. To this man's house in one of the lowest and dirtiest streets of town he led the squeamish William, who was fairly sure that no man who had followed the trade of tinware peddling for many years could be really respectable. Probably this man was not so; but his rates were low and his heart was kind, so that the cousins finally hired a narrow little room with one window at the top of his house.

Returning on the fourteenth of February from a jaunt into the country, William found Bronson lying on the bed in that stifling room, evidently very ill. The doctor called it "typhus fever," meaning what is now understood by typhoid. Four months of bad food and worse water had produced their natural result.

For the next five weeks William sat in the narrow room at the top of the decayed tin-pedlar's house, nursing Bronson. He had not yet listened to the single course of medical lectures at Yale College which was soon to enable him to write himself "Doctor," but he already had some skill in nursing the sick, together with no

[60]

slight affection for the playmate of his boyhood and the earnest correspondent of his youth who lay before him, desperately ill. What pulled him through, however, was a simple and unquestioning sense of duty, strongly reinforced by a number of maxims from Noah Webster's Speller.

Even if there had been room for a nurse, William could not have afforded such a luxury; and if there had been anything in the way of a hospital he would have thought its rates prohibitory. The few men from the North to whom he told his plight—and apparently he never thought of asking help from a Southerner—were either indifferent or afraid of infection. There was nothing for it, therefore, but to sit quietly by the sickbed day and night, administering medicine almost every hour. His patient was much of the time delirious, abusive, even violent; and, with a physical strength much greater than William's, he occasionally became dangerous. William records that, in the insanity of fever, Bronson once struck him on the head with such force as almost to fell him to the floor; but to this the only possible reply was to pick himself up and administer another spoonful of medicine. He also tells us that he became positively despondent and lost his appetite for several days when he learned by letter from Spindle Hill, just at the climax of Bronson's illness, that his own mother's life was despaired of and that his brother and sister had recently died in a local epidemic. But now and then he could sleep a little, and now and then he could go to the narrow window for a breath of air that was not foul. Toward the middle of March he saw that Bronson would probably live.

In the career of William Andrus Alcott—quite as serviceable a career in its different way as that of his cousin, and in some respects even more heroic—that five weeks' vigil in the upper room at Norfolk may have been the turning-point. Serious before, he now became profoundly so. Indeed he laid in such a surplus of seriousness that he would soon be able to spare a little for Bronson himself when that young man, quite well again and unmindful of his narrow escape, should most need it. His sense of utter helplessness, as he watched his companion sink down toward death and then so slowly come back again, may have been the source of his determination to learn what he could about medicine, out of which determination there grew certain beneficent reforms in the physical arrangements, at least, of the New England schoolroom. These reforms, adopted by Bronson Alcott, led on in his richer and more aggressive mind to certain quite different and independent educational advances; and from radical theories in education to an idealistic philosophy the path, though intricate and long, was to be found.

Our lives are woven in strange and incomprehensible patterns. Was there any causal relation between the stagnancy of the streams in Carolina, on the one hand, and the Concord School of Philosophy on the other?

When Bronson's recovery from his fever was complete William felt that he had seen enough of the world for the time being, and he returned to Spindle Hill alone in May. Bronson, however, had a doctor's bill to pay, and so he went peddling with another cousin, Thomas Alcox, through Alexandria, Washington, Baltimore, and Philadelphia, until he reached New York. And whether it was the rebound from his long illness, the change from the serious William to the blithe Thomas, or for some other reason, he seems to have had a gay and joyous time on this trip. There is even a possibility that his constantly roving life, in frequent association with a class of men by no means exemplary in conduct, may have begun at last to have some effect upon him.

At almost exactly this time it was that President Timothy Dwight of Yale College—"Pope Dwight" his political and clerical enemies called him, for he was an imposing but rather stuffy person, and the champion of all conservatives—was writing certain highly derogatory remarks about pedlars.

"Many of the young men employed in this business," said he

"part at an early period with both modesty and principle. Their sobriety is exchanged for cunning, their honesty for imposition, and their decent behavior for coarse impudence. Mere wanderers, accustomed to no order, control, or worship, and directed solely to the acquisition of petty gains, they soon fasten upon this object and forget every other of superior nature. The only source of their pleasure or their reputation is gain; and that, however small or however acquired, secures both. No course of life tends more rapidly or more effectually to eradicate every moral feeling."

One may smile at the Reverend Doctor's smug and prudish condemnation of a whole class of men in which he probably did not know a single individual, and yet there was a modicum of truth in his grossly exaggerated strictures. Those who know anything about the career of Bronson Alcott will not need to be told that he, at any rate, did not succumb to the pedlar's alleged passion for gain. It should be almost equally clear that, whatever may have been the influences about him during the years of his early wanderings, his mind and spirit took no stain from them. But on the other hand he was always a social person, eager for companionship. His recent observations of Virginian life had shown him that gaiety need not be sinful, and they had awakened in him a longing for an "elegance" such as he had never before aspired to, or even known.

Beginning, then, with this peddling journey from Norfolk to New York, Bronson treated himself to a short period—and it was almost pathetically short—of elegance and gaiety. Lest this statement should be too liberally interpreted, however, one must hasten to say what was the head and forefront of his offending. It was this: when he reached New York he bought himself a costly coat, the best that he could find on Broadway, together with a ruffled shirt, drab trousers, a handsomely figured vest, and—perhaps, although one cannot be quite sure—a watch. In these splendid habiliments, the like of which had probably never before been seen on Spindle Hill, he returned to his home in July, to the great

[63]

surprise, as he says, of his townsfolk, and to the deep chagrin of his father and his cousin William.

The father's chagrin was probably increased by the fact that Bronson had spent for these fine feathers the money that should have gone toward defraying certain debts. Indeed, Joseph Alcox had to sign his son's note, at about this time, for two hundred and seventy dollars owing to a Norfolk merchant for pedlar's goods. The situation was alarming in the extreme, for frugality was considered on Spindle Hill the chief of all the virtues, certainly the first to be sought and one of the last to be lost. There was nothing in the experience of Joseph or of Anna Alcox that could help them to understand what had happened; and the conduct of the young man during his summer at home—no longer working in the field or shop, neglecting books and diary, spending his days and nights in idle gallantries with the girls of the neighborhood—did not allay their anxiety.

It is not hard, however, for one who has in mind the total picture of Bronson Alcott's life and character, to see what was occurring and to excuse the young man entirely. He could not immediately pass from what had been to him the brilliant and beautiful spectacle of Virginian life, so gracious and leisurely, to the toilsome obscurities of Spindle Hill. Always quick to discern the goodness in every social scene, always slow to discover defects, he was convinced for a time that the Virginian way of life was in every way superior to what he had known at home.

What better thing could he do for his humble village than to take back there some of that "elegance" with which he had fallen in love? His broadcloth coat and ruffled shirt were hardly more than symbols of things far more important. It was not so much that he was vain as that he was beginning his lifework as a missionary of what would some day be called "culture." He was trying to import as much as he could of the Old Dominion's sweetness and light into the Land of Steady Habits.

But why was it necessary to choose for the opening of this

[64]

mission a time when he was already, on account of his recent illness, in serious financial difficulties? Why was it necessary to drive
his father still more deeply into debt? Did he expect his mission
to be more persuasive because he began it by flouting the economic
and even the ethical standards of the very persons he hoped to
enlighten? These questions raise one of the most puzzling problems
that his life presents—a problem the study of which, in its larger
aspects, must be postponed. At present it need only be said that
Alcott does not seem to have shown his curious stupidity, innocence, or idealism—call it what one will—about money until he
made his superficial acquaintance with the ladies and gentlemen
of Virginia.

Is it possible that the spectacle of their unlaborious lives, apparently so unconcerned with vulgar questions of livelihood, may
have caused some permanent lesion, so to speak, in the mind of
the young man from a district in which those questions had always
been kept well to the fore? May it be that Bronson Alcott, who
after his Virginian journeys was hardly ever again to pay his own
way in this world's coin, was trying to live in New England as he
had seen gentlemen living by the James and the Rappahannock?
Was he, the future Abolitionist, imitating as closely as possible a
kind of life that had thus far been possible in America only when
supported by the labor of slaves?

The young man's new-found "elegance"—it is his own word—
was not confined to ruffles and broadcloth, or to evening calls upon
the astonished maidens of Spindle Hill. It extended, he tells us,
even to the style of his writing, although it is hard to imagine any
more sedulously candied and dephlogisticated discourse than that
which he had already been manufacturing for years in his correspondence with his cousin. That correspondence languished for
a time. Perhaps William found it difficult to address, in terms
suitable for the salutation of a Roman Senator, a young man who
had so short a time before knocked him violently on the head. A

[65]

more probable cause of the silence, however, was the fact that, in the eyes of William, Bronson was now in deep disgrace.

The cousins did reach an agreement upon one matter closely related to Amos's passion for "elegance." How long the jibes of their obscene playmates and fellows had been making them ashamed of their family name there is no telling. They knew that "Alcock" had been silently changed to "Alcox" about 1780, in the days of their grandfather John, but they also knew that the change had been no great improvement: it did not prevent coarse-minded and ribald persons from wearisome repetition of a perfectly intolerable pun. To one or the other of them it occurred that these humiliations might be avoided by a slight change in the spelling of their name which would enforce a change in pronunciation. Such changes were easy and frequent at the time, as even a brief study of New England gravestones will show. There is, for example, a forgotten graveyard in eastern Connecticut which began as the private burying ground of the Higginbothams. That graveyard shows quite clearly, however, that at about the middle of the eighteenth century the name "Higginbotham"—perhaps because it came to seem too long—was split in two, one part of the family being known thereafter as "Higgins" and the other part as "Botham." Quite easily, therefore, and without any recourse to law, the cousins altered their name in the direction of elegance, and Amos B. Alcox became, thenceforth, A. Bronson Alcott.[1]

Once he had begun to slip, the young man whom we may now call regularly by his more familiar name found his descent into the Avernus of debt very facile indeed. In October, 1821, he borrowed more money from his father, who also gave him a horse; he bought a pedlar's wagon at Berlin, Connecticut, purchased a load of goods on credit at Meriden, and started on the long ride

---

[1] The alteration was much older than either of the cousins knew at the time. There were in Hartford in 1640 both a Thomas Alcock and a Thomas Alcott—the latter's assignment of land lying in the north part of the town within one lot of that assigned to John Brownson—*i.e.* "Bronson."

to Virginia with his brother Chatfield and his cousin Thomas—two very unstable companions. The end of November found the trio at Alexandria, where Bronson was once more in the neighborhood of those Southern "aristocrats" whom he had been emulating from afar. We catch a glimpse of him riding horseback, somewhat later, at Norfolk, on a "silver speculation." He was finding that "the costly coat scorned peddling, and sank money fast."

By the end of March Alcott was in Richmond. One would like to know whether, in his peddling there, he ever went up to the door of Mr. John Allan, the wealthy tobacco-factor, and whether a dark-eyed lad of twelve with a beetling brow came to the door and glanced contemptuously at the plated silverware from Meriden, treating the pedlar with that disdain which he was usually to show toward persons from the district of his own birth. Did Edgar Allan Poe help A. Bronson Alcott to see that "peddling would never do"? At any rate, that is what Alcott decided before he had been long in Richmond. On the seventh of April a bill of sale upon his horse, wagon, and stock was taken on account by his principal creditor—that same Yankee dealer in "fancy goods" who had been so "accommodating" to him in Norfolk at the outset of his peddling career. Shortly thereafter he was teaching penmanship at Warrenton, North Carolina, to a class of fifteen pupils whom he charged three dollars a head for a course of fifteen lessons.

Alcott's fourth expedition, which he had hoped might retrieve the errors and misfortunes of the third, was a complete failure; and he felt for a time perhaps a little downhearted. His admiration for the Southern gentry remained as strong as ever, but he began to suspect that there was something incongruous in his effort to imitate a slaveholding planter on the income of a Yankee pedlar who had somehow acquired, rather early in life, the habit of failing at everything he undertook. The South itself was losing some of the charm it had once had in his eyes. He was beginning to feel the disillusionment so vividly expressed at about this time in the diary of his brother Chatfield:—

[67]

O this being to the South is bad business. It is the lonesumest place & unhelthy place & once more I reppet it I never intend come to Virginia again if ever I get home again I will stay away from here & bid good buy but neaver have I sorrow that I came here. It has been the worst travelling the weak past that ever I saw.

In June, after the close of his little school in penmanship, Bronson Alcott walked from Warrenton to Spindle Hill, approximately five hundred miles. While he was on the way his shoes gave out, so that he arrived in New York City barefooted. He slept in tobacco barns, and wherever else he could sleep most cheaply. Early in July he reached home, with exactly sixpence in his pocket but "many penitences at heart." By this time he owed his father—whom it had been his primary purpose, in all his peddling, to help—about six hundred dollars. It would seem, in fact, that Joseph was obliged to sell some part of his farm in order to defray, or postpone, the debts of his improvident son. Short of downright criminality, a deeper disgrace than this was hardly conceivable by the frugal and debt-fearing people of Spindle Hill. In Cambridge, one hundred miles away, a youth by the name of Ralph Waldo Emerson was about to be graduated from Harvard College.

Bronson did what immediate penance he could by working hard, during the summer, on his father's farm. In October he had a letter of expostulation from William, most earnestly pointing out the errors of his recent course and whither it would lead. Faithful were the wounds of that good friend. And although William's letter, which has not been preserved, probably did not rise above the conventional and parochial moralities of the time and place it was just such utterances of the common sense that Bronson needed at that time, and always, to hear. It touched him to the quick. He resolved to punish himself by going South once more—this time really to make money which would relieve his prematurely aging father of an unjust and intolerable load of care

Late in October he set forth in a wagon with his cousin Thomas, who owned the whole outfit, on his fifth and last business expedition. From the business point of view it turned out worst of all.

Yet here, in this final peddling trip, we see the first clear instance of a law that ran throughout Alcott's life: when his outlook on material things was darkest, just then it was that his intellectual and spiritual vision grew keen. It was only in the night or in the deep dark pit that he could see the stars. It was when the tide ebbed lowest for him on the shores of this world, leaving him poor and outcast and despised, that it washed up into the creeks and bays on the opposite coasts of infinity.

The people of Chowan and Perquimans Counties, on Albermarle Sound in North Carolina, were of another sort entirely from the Tabbs and Taliaferros, the Nelsons and the Dabneys, whom the pedlar had seen, admired, and imitated in the great houses of Virginia. Comparatively few of them kept slaves. Though not poor, they lived plainly. Though courteous, their speech was frank and forthright. They were hospitable, but more to the mind and heart than to the body. The young man went among them as he had among the "aristocrats" of Virginia, and as he was to do among the settlers of Indiana, Wisconsin, Iowa—talking with everyone, making friends, "sharing views"; but the views he took in exchange were remarkably different from those he had found in Virginia, or on Spindle Hill. Here too he read the books that were lent him; but these were of a strange new kind. Instead of Locke, Thomson, Pope, he found here William Penn's *No Cross, No Crown*, Robert Barclay's *Apology*, William Law's *Serious Call*, Thomas Clarkson's *Portrait of Quakerism*, and, most important of all, the *Journal* of George Fox and that of John Woolman. For these people were Friends, or Quakers. He read their books with absorbed attention. He talked with them long and earnestly about things of the spirit that Spindle Hill had never heard of, things that the elegant ladies and gentlemen of Virginia would have disdained as mere enthusiasm, things that all New

England had once expressed its feelings about rather vigorously with the hangman's whip administered at the cart's tail.

It was not a detailed theology that Alcott took from the Quakers but the innermost quintessence of their teaching, which was perfectly in keeping with his own vague awareness of a Presence on the summit of New Connecticut Hill. They told him, they taught him, or at least they reinforced in him, a basic belief which he was never to forget or for one moment to doubt: that the sole and unsupported spirit of a man may come into an immediate relation with its Maker. They said, and he agreed, that all true religious experience is inward, personal, essentially and exclusively spiritual. They held, and he also held from that time on, that God speaks directly to the soul of a man, telling that soul what to be and do and say. For them, and thenceforth for Bronson Alcott, creed, ritual, priesthood, and tradition were of no worth in comparison with the "inner light"; and when these things tended— as, for the most part, they thought such things do always tend— to dim or hide that inner light, they must be brushed aside.

Under this tuition Bronson Alcott did not become a Quaker, any more than he had become a Puritan under that of John Bunyan. The external characteristics of the sect left no mark upon his speech, his dress, or his general way of life. With the power of piercing to inner essences which he was to show on many other occasions, he singled out as the central teaching of the Friends their doctrine of the "inner light," their belief that the individual soul may be so illumined by the divine spirit as to speak its word to men. This belief and doctrine he made his own—or perhaps one might better say that it made him. It helped him, or forced him to take his first long step toward transcendentalism.

Under the influence of the Quakers, as Alcott said in late years, "the moral sentiment superseded peddling clearly and finally." The change may have been hastened by a recurrence of the fever of the preceding year which kept him in bed for several weeks in May. He returned to Spindle Hill in July, 1823, sallow

nd spiritless, still owing his father six hundred dollars. His brief
period of "elegance" and of gaiety was over. Even his reading
was changed. Cowper's poems, Hervey's *Meditations among the
Tombs,* and the New Testament were now his mental fare. In
November he applied for the position of teacher in the Fall
Mountain District of the town of Bristol, three miles from home,
nd was examined and approved. From that time forth he was to
peddle only immaterial wares.

There is danger in the sudden uprooting of a provincial mind.
Swift ruin or a slow decay often follows a withdrawal from those
restrictions of local custom and opinion which in many lives take
the place of an inward morality. Mere stubbornness without intelligence hardens into bigotry when confronted by the new and
strange, and intelligence without inward strength may soften and
rot away. The test is a severe one. During the history of America,
which has been one long continuous pulling-up of roots, hundreds
of millions have had to take this test, and many of them have
failed. If we ask why the American mind is so often shallow and
flat, why it is less earnest than excitable and why it seldom maintains any inner quiet and poise, we must not forget that most
American lives have been transplanted, some of them again and
again, and that many of us are now trying to live with our roots,
so to speak, in the air. To a few minds, however, this escape from
provincial boundaries brings neither bigotry nor corruption, but
freedom. Bronson Alcott was one of these.

Spindle Hill, a thousand feet high, with only one traveled road,
steep and rocky, rambling up from the outer world, was a good
place for the innocence of a boy to shelter in, but thoughts stood
still there, if they ever climbed so high. It was a good center for
the stationary leg of one's compasses, but the other leg was somewhat confined within it. Bronson Alcott was never to lose his
boyish innocence, though he saw a good deal of this wicked
world. The standing leg of his compasses never wavered from the

tiny spot on the map marked "Spindle Hill"; but the other drew larger and larger circles until it rose from the map of earth altogether and swept out toward the stars.

Alcott often said that his five peddling journeys into the South taught him more than he could have learned at any college. It is a moderate statement. They made a wanderer of him without weakening in the least his love of home. They changed a shy and awkward rustic into a man remarkable for the dignity, grace, and ease of his social bearing. By the time he settled down to teaching he had met thousands of strangers under difficult circumstances. In a time when very few Americans traveled in their own country, and when the ignorant provincialism of the New England mind was at its worst, he saw thousands of miles of America in the close and intimate way of the pedestrian. When his peddling days were over he knew both the Old North and the Old South, had his base-line mapped and measured, and was ready for his future triangulation of the New West, the America that was to be. Colleges did not and do not teach such things. Yale or Harvard would have pointed the young man's thought eastward and toward the past. His wanderings up and down his base-line, from Connecticut to the Carolinas, gave his thoughts a westward bent and a reach into the future. For that strong contrast between North and South, that tension and polarity, must be resolved somehow, he saw, and soon. The Southern plantation and Spindle Hill must come together and marry and have many children.

Thus he discovered America.

Who else, among those with whom his thought-life would be spent, ever knew or guessed at America in his fashion? Walt Whitman knew something of the Southern States, and so was able to work out a dim and grandiose dream of the West that was coming; but his Brooklyn, his Northern point of observation, gave him no such contrast with the South as Alcott found at Spindle Hill. Brooklyn or "Manhattan" was as much a sprawling improvisation

[72]

as anything on the lower Mississippi. But Spindle Hill, for better and worse, stood sharp and clear against the Northern sky. From the start, that community was old—was based upon old traditions, old thoughts and moods and ways of living, that must soon die into the future. So was that leisurely patriarchal life that Alcott found on the banks of the Rappahannock and James an old thing, almost visibly crumbling away. He knew that it was dying, but also he saw that it was beautiful. What other Yankee of his time saw that? Whittier, Parker, Thoreau, Ripley, never had the chance. Garrison had a brief glimpse of the Old South, but used it chiefly to gather materials for future indignations. Hawthorne, Melville, Longfellow, Lowell, Prescott, Jones Very, the Channings, the Peabodys, like the rest of New England, were simply not interested.

There was one person among Alcott's future associates whose knowledge of the South, though by no means so extensive, was comparable with Alcott's own. That person was Ralph Waldo Emerson. When he was twenty-three Emerson spent a winter and spring at Charleston and at St. Augustine, nursing his health, seeing few people, thinking few thoughts. Yet even this enabled him to say to Margaret Fuller, many years later, that his Southern travels had helped him "to cast out the passion for Europe by the passion for America."

Alcott, of course, never had any passion for Europe, unless it was for the ancient Greece of Plato and Pythagoras; but he might easily have succumbed to that puling homesickness for England which has warped the lives of so many New Englanders if the dream of America had not come over him like a cloud of glory in his youth. As it was, he thought even Emerson an incomplete American—perhaps because Emerson had not remained in the South long enough. Emerson spent about five months there, and Alcott, first and last, three years and a half.

Upon both men, however, Southern life made the same kind of impression. When Emerson was writing *Society and Solitude* and

needed an example of "good society," he did not turn to the
drawing-rooms of Boston or even to the salons of Europe and
England, which by that time he had seen. He remembered, rather,
some of the Southern youths whom he had admired from a cool
distance at Harvard, and especially that Southern planter, Achille
Murat, with whom he had struck up an odd friendship at Talla-
hassee. Manners, courtesy, social decorum, an easy and graceful
savoir faire, meant more to Emerson all his days than it did to the
blunt Yankees about him—and it does not seem likely that he got
his preference from his observations of his Aunt Mary, of Father
Taylor, or of Edmund Hosmer. Certainly he found no such taste
for the art of social intercourse in his young friend Henry Thoreau. But he did find it in his older and his closer friend, Bronson
Alcott. And for good reason. During most of the time that Emerson had been living in the little brick buildings at Harvard—so
cold, so grimly chaste, so bare—Bronson Alcott, three years
older, had been wandering up and down among the Virginian
plantations, liking everything he saw, liking the very dogs that
threatened to tear him to pieces until they saw his smile and suddenly changed their minds. He had gathered no Latin and less
Greek in his peripatetic college. Least of all had he gathered
money. But he had brought into the barns of memory his "harvest
of a quiet eye." He had seen enough of his own land so that he
would always love all of it. He had attended one of the world's
best schools of manners. Whatever else he might fail in from that
time forth, Bronson Alcott would always be a gentleman.

COUNTRY SCHOOL-
MASTER

 1823-1828

Fierce concentration—A holy calling—"Young vipers" or
"Mighty philosophers"?—An American Pestalozzi—Connecticut
schools—Jesus of Nazareth—The Church of Mammon—A dan-
gerous heretic—A long farewell—The intellectual frontier

THE EXTERNAL history of Bronson Alcott's teaching in
Connecticut is soon related. During the winter term of 1823–
1824 he taught the Fall Mountain District School at Bristol.
A recurrence of ague and fever made it impossible for him to
teach in the summer term, but he cured himself by bathing in a
running stream and in the autumn was able to follow Cousin
William as the master of Bristol's West Street School. He passed
the spring and summer of 1825 with his Uncle Tillotson at
Cheshire, reading widely in philosophical literature and helping
to edit the *Churchman's Magazine*. He then taught during four
successive terms, a most unusual period, as master of the Centre

[75]

District School in Cheshire. The winter of 1827–1828 found him back at the West Street School in Bristol for a single term, after which he went to Boston and never again taught in his native State.

One thing to be observed in this brief history is that Alcott's Connecticut schools were all close to his home, Cheshire being only six miles from Spindle Hill and Bristol hardly four. Another consideration, the importance of which cannot be exactly estimated, is that during this whole preliminary period of his teaching career he was near his cousin William, who was already known as "a smart teacher." His own salary, when he taught in the Fall Mountain District, was ten dollars a month and board, increased to fifteen dollars at West Street. In Cheshire he was paid one hundred and thirty-five dollars for a term of about four months—a salary which would have meant something like opulence to him if he had not expended more than half of it upon alterations in the schoolroom and books for his children. While at his last school in Bristol he received the comparatively large salary of twenty-three dollars a month, but "found" himself.

Bronson Alcott had no teaching license from the State of Connecticut when he began to teach, such matters being managed by the School Committee of the town concerned. Before he was engaged at the Fall Mountain District he underwent an examination, which was no doubt rather perfunctory because he had a certificate of his fitness for teaching from his Uncle Tillotson, an unimpeachable authority. His knowledge of the elementary branches was entirely adequate, but in the general theory of teaching he had no instruction whatever. His schools were common or "District Schools," attended by children from the age of three or four to ten or twelve. Ordinarily he would divide the school into two classes, a higher and a lower, conducting both himself. The numbers of his pupils ranged from about fifteen to more than eighty. As a consequence, his classrooms were often crowded, and his efforts to secure comfort and beauty were seldom successful

[76]

Observing that Alcott was comparatively well paid, that he had a remarkably long term at Cheshire, and that he was asked to return to a district in which he had once taught, one might infer that his teaching in Connecticut was highly successful. The inference would not be true, if by "successful" one should mean that he gave "satisfaction." His success lay in his own growth, in a steady deepening and extension of his thought, in his rapidly strengthening grasp of the motives and means of education. But this growth itself meant that the gap was constantly widening between him and the conventional minds about him. To those for whom the word "success" means chiefly a worldly advancement, pleasing everyone, scrambling up an economic, a social, or professional ladder, it can only be said, then, that he failed—splendidly.

Bronson Alcott's schools, and particularly the one at Cheshire, attracted wide attention; but much of it was hostile and even belligerent. In districts where no one had ever given teaching a second thought, where everyone tacitly assumed that the schoolmaster's task was simply to beat the three R's well into the children and to keep his hands off of everything except the ferule and the birch rod, this young man made trouble. His pupils came home with the most amazing and alarming tales of what their teacher had said. He seemed to believe that children, even the youngest, had minds of their own, and should be encouraged to use them. He had even been known to talk about their souls and to meddle with their morals—the parents' exclusive prerogative. He let the children dance in school—or something like it. He tried to make them comfortable. He put backs to the benches. He changed the long tables into individual desks with separate seats. He had newfangled notions about lighting and heating the schoolroom. He set up a blackboard made of slate brought from Wales, to write on, and he thought the children should have little slates of their own upon which they might draw and scribble for their own pleasure. All this seemed vaguely dangerous to a good many, chiefly because it was so different from what they had known in their own schooldays.

If the young teacher had asked the parents to pay for any of these notions they would have refused with emphasis; and the fact that he was fool enough to pay for most of them himself was not reassuring, for it could only show that there was "a screw loose somewhere." So did his almost total abandonment of the birch rod. The children were not afraid of him. Some of them had been known to say that they really liked Mr. Alcott. He made up little games for them, in which he sometimes joined himself. Now and then he asked a number of his pupils to visit him in the evening. Surely this sort of thing would break down all discipline and familiarity would soon breed contempt.

There were a few persons in each of the districts that Alcott served, of course, who were intelligently interested in his purpose and method. Before he had quite found his way, he often talked over his problems with his two friends Bull and Mathews, Bristol schoolmasters, with Dr. Byington and Dr. Pardee, his Bristol friends, or else with Uncle Tillotson. At the home of Cousin William, who was more responsible than any other person for Bronson's ever teaching at all, he had, one may be sure, many an earnest conference, from which he drew comfort, encouragement, and at last an unshakable conviction that he was right. From William he probably derived most of his novel ideas about the furniture of the schoolroom. William it must have been who breathed into the young man—so recently a waverer, a wanderer and a spendthrift purchaser of expensive attire—the absolute devotion which he now gave to the task in hand. William had no intention that those five sleepless and airless weeks he had spent in the sickroom at Norfolk should be wasted. Having brought his cousin back from the half-open door of death, he would make it worth while to have brought him.

As one reads the first volume of Bronson Alcott's Journal begun at Cheshire on July the third, 1826, it does indeed seem that

[78]

a double portion of William's spirit has entered into the writer. The loose and drifting habit of mind which might so easily have been fixed upon him by his years of rather aimless knocking about in Southern regions is just what one does not find in this volume. Instead, one finds a fierce concentration of thought, sustained and driven by moral earnestness. The young man is bringing his total force to bear upon one task, and he is to hold it there, steadily, in sharp focus, year in and year out. He is twirling the fire-stick of thought into the dead dry wood of educational theory and practice; and one can see that in spite of his ignorance and awkwardness he will soon, by sheer persistence, bore down to the living flame. Nearly every sentence of the early journals pertains to teaching. All that he reads, hears, thinks, must converge upon teaching. It is a monomania, an obsession.—And for so abrupt and complete a change, both in the method of thought and in its object, there seems to be no explanation other than William.

Alcott is not unduly modest in the claims he makes for his new-found profession. The teacher, he repeatedly asserts, is a far more important man in the community than the preacher can ever hope to be, for the reason that he works as it were from the ground up, and while there is yet time. He is practical, shaping the molds of conduct, whereas the preacher is ordinarily a bookish theorist. The task of the teacher is holier than that of the minister because it deals with souls new-come, unstained, and still "trailing clouds of glory." It is also a much more delightful task, not only because it holds one in the companionship of innocent minds and hearts but because it deals with simple and direct affections rather than with tedious thought. Upon the whole, then, a teacher's task is the greatest task to which any man can devote his life.

The underlying, subconscious motive of this comparison between the minister's and the schoolmaster's work is not hard to

[79]

discern. Something more than egoism is concerned. A struggle for spiritual breath, for intellectual life, is going on. In the many passages of these early Journals in which Alcott declares himself the minister's superior, asserts that he is engaged upon a more delightful, a more practical and effective, and indeed a holier task than the preacher's own, he is throwing off an intellectual and spiritual tyranny which had ruled and thwarted and tormented the New England mind for two hundred years. A lay mind is coming of age. A mind naturally and intuitively religious is asking whether there is in fact any justification for supposing that spiritual things are exclusively the clergy's own. Or rather, such a mind is answering that question, once and for all. It is a mind that has been overpoweringly aware of a silent Presence on the crest of New Connecticut Hill, where there is neither church nor priest. It has been shaped and deepened by long readings and talks among the Friends, who hire no man to tell them what God says. It is an American mind issuing its own declaration of spiritual independence of the pulpit, which had long been far more tyrannical than any throne. Protestantism is approaching its final term.

Not only does the young schoolmaster relegate the clergy to its subordinate place; he tells all statesmen, reformers, politicians and social workers just where in the lower ranks they too belong. At any rate he tells his Journal. Such persons, he says, have been at work in the world, together with plenty of preachers, for a long while, and yet one sees that "Mammon reigns; oppression and war and misery still grow in rank luxuriance; Virtue sleep confined; Benevolence is doomed a beggar—unclothed, unshod without a friend, without a home." And the reason for this Children have not been properly taught.

The love of children, intense but unsentimental, sprang up in the young man's heart. He saw that they needed discipline and were far from perfect, but he also knew that they needed love; and

[80]

even if there had been no need he would have been unable to withhold that. He saw that they were beautiful, and would have loved them for that alone. He thought he saw, too, that they were strangely wise. Without the least effort or the slightest self-consciousness they babbled a wisdom that would confute the sages. And whence could this beauty and wisdom come? Wordsworth's *Ode on the Intimations of Immortality*, already working like yeast among all his thoughts, suggested an answer:—

> Our birth is but a sleep and a forgetting:
> The soul that rises with us, our life's star,
> Hath had elsewhere its setting,
> And cometh from afar.
> Not in entire forgetfulness,
> And not in utter nakedness,
> But trailing clouds of glory, do we come
> From God, who is our home. . . .

And then there was that young man of Nazareth in whom Bronson Alcott was growing more interested every day, regarding him as a perfect model for schoolmasters. He too, though never a father, had felt this same deep love of children, and had been amazed at their wisdom and beauty. How had he explained the way a child's face might sometimes make one laugh with sudden joy, even while the tears stood in one's eyes? What did he think was the source of a child's deep unlearned wisdom? He had said precisely what Wordsworth said, but in only seven words: "Of such is the Kingdom of Heaven."

The Reverend Jonathan Edwards had taken a different view of the matter when he declared that children are "young vipers, and are infinitely more hateful than vipers" in the sight of God. That remark had been made years ago; it probably had not expressed the opinion of the community even when it was made, and the rigors of Calvinism had been considerably modified during the interim; yet it was nearer to the ordinary belief of western Connecticut, even in 1828, than was the feeling of Bron-

[81]

son Alcott that children were angelic visitants, innocent exiles of heaven, "mighty philosophers" and "eyes among the blind." In spite of the encroachments of Arminianism and notwithstanding the serious blow that had recently been delivered against the Congregational theocracy, there lingered still a fairly common conviction that the soul of man is everywhere and always "deceitful and desperately wicked" until it has been redeemed by God's mysterious Act of Grace. For those many persons who thought thus, it was simply impious to assert that children are "innocent." Bristol and Cheshire contained many a tax-paying citizen in the eighteen-twenties who thought he could prove, by the most logical deductions from God's unerring Word, that children were limbs of Satan, wholly depraved and indubitably damned—except always for the Act of God's Grace, which it would be wise not to count upon. The young teacher's educational heresies might have been condoned by these logicians, for it mattered comparatively little what he did or did not do to his pupils' minds; but what he was doing to their immortal souls was important. Of course a logic even more severe might have pointed out that if the children were damned already it would matter little what Alcott did to their souls; but that would have required some thinking, and would have deprived them of the joys of persecution.

Bronson Alcott was not yet a theologian, if he was ever to be one, nor was his thinking always strictly logical. He had not derived from Arminius, Rousseau, Wordsworth, Pestalozzi, or any other literary source, his conviction that childhood is essentially innocent. He did not ask what the Reverend Jonathan Edwards or any other Calvinistic pundit had thought and taught about the essential nature of children. He simply looked at the children he had daily before him; he watched them more and more intently; he wondered at their simple graces and pondered what seemed to be the artless wisdom of their words. From surprise he went on to respect, and finally to a kind of reverence.

[82]

They taught him far more than he taught them. The question arose: Did they really need to be taught? Was it not enough to remind them? And then the further question: If one listened very intently would it not be possible to catch some echo, from their tones and words, of an eternal music, a supernal wisdom—just as from the lights of their eyes and in their smiles of inspired recollection one seemed to catch faint glimpses of an everlasting beauty?

And so the young schoolmaster—hired to teach the table of weights and measures, the multiplication table, and such other items as mill hands and farmers need to know—began, instead of telling his pupils much of anything, to ask them questions about their souls.

It was rather absurd. People began to think that it might also be dangerous.

Precisely what influence it was that lifted Bronson Alcott out of the conventional ruts of Calvinistic teaching and educational practice, there is no definite telling. He had no sudden conversion of mind and heart like that of Saul on the road to Damascus, like Rousseau's on the way to Vincennes, or even like the one that came to young Channing as he paced up and down under a clump of willows by the Charles in Cambridge. One can only say that his theory of the essential innocence of childhood, though not the pedagogical deductions from it, was already complete when he began the first volume of his Journals in July, 1826. In that very month, to be sure, he was reading Adam Smith's *Theory of Moral Sentiments,* finding its strong emphasis upon benevolence much to his liking. Robert Owen's *New View of Society* was strengthing his conviction that right teaching of the young is the surest way of reforming the world. The first volume of William Russell's *American Journal of Education,* just then beginning, taught him much and suggested much more.

[83]

And all the while there were those few lines of Wordsworth's great Ode, glowing in his mind and lighting up his thoughts.

But where, in all this, was the influence of the great Swiss teacher Pestalozzi, whose beneficent life was just coming to a close? Bronson Alcott was to be called "The Pestalozzi of America" in later years, and with some reason, yet it has often been said that he scarcely knew the educational theory and method of the man whom he so much resembled. The fact is that he knew them very well, from a number of sufficient sources, and at an early period of his teaching career. Two little books by two men who had been closely associated with Pestalozzi were read by him almost as soon as he began to teach: Joseph Neef's *Sketch of a Plan and Method in Education,* published at Philadelphia in 1808, and Hermann Krusi's *Coup-D'Oeil on the General Means of Education,* printed at Yverdon in 1818. William Alcott, furthermore, was a friend and associate of the Reverend William C. Woodbridge of Hartford, who had spent some time at Hofwyl, Switzerland, in the school founded by Fellenberg, one of Pestalozzi's assistants. Dr. J. M. Keagy, a Swiss physician who was conducting a Pestalozzian school at Harrisburg wrote Alcott about the principles and methods of his master in April, 1826. Eight months later there came a long epistle on the same topic from William Maclure, the wealthy philanthropist, geologist, and President of the Philadelphia Academy of Natural Science who was at that time managing a Pestalozzian school at New Harmony, Indiana. In July, 1826, Alcott read a little book called *Hints to Parents . . . in the Spirit of Pestalozzi's Method,* from which alone it would have been easy for him to secure a clear knowledge of the system. Upon the whole, therefore, he was not making a vague and boastful reference to matters of which he was really ignorant when he entitled the first volume of his Journals "The Cheshire Pestalozzian School."

But this was not all. At Philadelphia, in May 1828, Alcott got from the famous bookseller Matthew Carey a Pestalozzian pam phlet called *Exposition of the Principles of Conducting Infant Education,* written by one J. P. Greaves—a man, then unknown to him, who was to have a deep effect upon his later life and thought. Early in 1829 Alcott compiled for William Russell's *Journal* an article on "Pestalozzi's Principles and Methods of Education." Two years later he was reading with close attention an admirable book by Dr. E. Biber entitled *Henry Pestalozzi,* then just published in London.

And so one might continue at tedious length; but these citations are enough to show that Bronson Alcott was far from ignorant of the theories and practices evolved by the foremost educational genius of his time. During the second and third decades of the nineteenth century, Pestalozzi's teaching was inescapable anywhere in Europe, England, or America. Bronson Alcott did not escape it even in the Connecticut hills. Before he had been many months in Cheshire he certainly knew the chief Pestalozzian principles, which taught that education ought to be: moral and religious; organic, harmonious, and complete; not mechanical but designed to penetrate and regulate the entire being; free, natural, and individual; based upon intuition rather than upon memory and the lower reason; gradual and progressive and linked, like a chain; social and domestic, and closely related to life. All this sounds very like Alcott. It actually is Pestalozzi.

And yet it would not be wise to conclude that Alcott's theory and practice of teaching, even in his apprentice years, were dependent upon the Pestalozzian example. He had not a dependent mind. Always remarkably quick to seize the essential idea of a man, a book, an institution, he was equally quick in converting it into the substance of his own thought, in making it over into himself. This faculty makes him a difficult problem for a student more concerned to discover where a man's ideas come from than what he does with them and what they are good for. So difficult it is to find out precisely where Alcott learned this and that element of his thought and practice that even the most pa-

[85]

tient "source-hunter" may well be tempted to suspect that he sometimes made them up himself.

That suspicion would be well founded. During the very months in which his theory of teaching was most rapidly growing, Alcott was declaring his independence of all books, reminding himself that they must always be held subservient to his main purpose of working out his own thought and destiny. "Adherence to them," he says, "has been the cause, and still continues, of perpetuating error among men, and that to an alarming extent. . . . They often impose the most irrational and absurd conclusions on the fearful understanding. It dare not doubt. Fear keeps it ignorant. Authority lifts her head and commands instant belief."

These are not the words of a young man for the source of whose opinions we need look into the books of other men. He is beginning to think for himself. As though to complete his anticipation of Emerson's essay on *Self-Reliance,* he goes on in the passage just quoted to ask how one may escape from the tyranny of conventional public opinion. To this he replies that free men must "rebel, think for themselves; let others grumble. Dare to be singular; let others direct. Follow reason; let others dwell in the Land of Enchantments. Be men; let others prattle. Practice; let others profess. Do good; let others define goodness. Act; let others sleep. Whatever thy hand findeth to do, that do with all thy might; and let a gainsaying, calumniating world speculate on your proceedings."

The conditions in the schools of Connecticut against which Alcott was beginning to pit his young strength have already been briefly indicated in the description of the school on Spindle Hill These conditions would vary, of course, from one town to another, and even from one school to another within the single town because as yet there was no general supervision exercised by the State. No doubt there were many intelligent teachers at work here

[86]

and there; but most of the instruction was still given in the deductive way, beginning with "generals" and gradually descending to "particulars." Usually this would be proceeding from the unknown to the known, in the inverse order of interest. The method had apparently been designed in complete ignorance of the learning process—unless, indeed, it had been invented by some enemy of the human species with the deliberate intention of making schoolwork as dull and profitless as possible. Children began the study of geography, for example, by memorizing a few general statements, quite beyond their comprehension, about the astronomical universe and the solar system. When they finally arrived at the earth they would be required to memorize statements about its girth and diameter and weight, after which they would proceed to more rote-work concerning poles, meridians, and zones —all conducted without a terrestrial globe and frequently without even a map. Grammar too was an affair of definitions and abstract principles, always learned by heart but seldom applied. In arithmetic, when it was taught at all, definitions and rules were memorized and copied into notebooks; and there the matter frequently ended. Reading was taught by the time-dishonored method, which has been generally abandoned only in recent years, of spending weary months in getting children to recognize the letters of the alphabet and to render their several phonetic values. There was, to be sure, as there had always been in New England, a strong feeling that the school should teach "morality"—a word which had a far wider connotation during Alcott's youth than it has to-day, but which had already been pitifully diminished so as to cover chiefly the prudential virtues. But even this morality was "taught" largely by the setting of crude maxims, abstract and general, which were to be committed to memory and parroted upon demand.

In few district schools of Alcott's time, apparently, was there any effort to secure real comprehension of what was learned. Memorizing was everywhere grossly overemphasized, in part be-

[87]

cause it served the purposes of those public exhibitions upon which the teacher's reputation too much depended. The impression was given, because the teacher often had it himself, that an educated person was simply one who had a large body of facts lying separately and quite unassimilated in his brain. That such a person should be able to think, imagine, feel, and act in terms of the facts he had acquired, or that his knowledge should permeate his whole character and personality, making him a wiser, gentler, and happier being, was a conception that seldom entered the heads of the "jailbirds" toiling at eleven dollars a month, or of the "females" whose wages were seldom allowed to fall below sixty-two-and-a-half cents a week. The processes of education were not supposed to be pleasant, but definitely painful, as befitted the training of "young vipers" and "limbs of Satan." The parents had found them so, and did not wish their children to be defrauded. Because all children were thought to be naturally bad and all learning was considered in itself distasteful, physical chastisement, administered severely and at frequent intervals, was almost universally regarded as an indispensable part of the system.

But Bronson Alcott, and perhaps his cousin William before him, disapproved fundamentally, and as a matter of settled principle, of all of these tendencies and practices. Either on account of something he had read or, more probably, because he had studied the processes of his own learning and thinking, he understood that interest proceeds not from the unknown to the known, from the abstract to the concrete, from the far to the near, but in the opposite order. Therefore he resolved to teach not by the "deductive" but by the "inductive" method, starting always with that which the child already knew and with interests already developed, and proceeding systematically outward from that point, with constant care to link every novel fact or conception to what was familiar. Thus, in the teaching of geography he began not with the stellar universe but with the schoolyard, and had

[88]

his pupils make a map of it. After this had been accomplished they might go on to draw maps of the adjacent district, with its farms and woods, brooks, roads, and houses, until eventually they had a fairly accurate knowledge of the entire township. Thus he made geography "begin at home," and rendered it concrete, real—in a word, poetic. Arithmetic he began not with a set of meaningless rules but with the adding and subtracting of tangible objects. Grammar was an induction from the child's own discovery that words fall easily into certain classes denoting the names of things, acts, qualities, relations, and the like. Reading, too, was begun not with a study of separate letters but with a relating of printed words and pictures.

For the rest, Alcott strove to appeal to the child's several "faculties" as they arose, beginning with the "affections," and going on to imagination, association, attention, taste, memory, judgment, reflection, and reason. All good educational processes, he believed, should be "spontaneous, social, and rational." The purpose of education, he held, was "to form mind, heart, character; to make its subjects wise and happy; and to make them so by a simple, natural, and rational process." To this end he thought there was no need of coercion. More and more, as the months passed, he "spared the rod," and found that his children were by no means "spoiled." Occasionally he absented himself from the school for a day or two, and found on his return that the children had taken care of themselves, had taught themselves, and that all had gone on much as usual. He set them to writing diaries, in which they tried to enumerate the "ideas" that came to them day by day. He joined in their games. He let pass no opportunity to gain their confidence and affection. An intelligent visitor of one of his early schools remarked that the teacher seemed "to invite rather then compel attention, to awaken thought rather than load the memory, and in one word to develop the whole mind and heart rather than a few of the properties of either." Alcott himself summed up his theory in saying that

[89]

"infant education is founded on the great principle that every infant is already in possession of the faculties and apparatus required for his instruction, and that by the law of his constitution he uses these to a great extent himself; that the office of instruction is chiefly to facilitate this process, and to accompany the child in his progress rather than to drive or even to lead him."

Bronson Alcott went about his schoolmastering with the conviction that it was the most important and responsible task on earth. What others might think of it troubled him not at all. If the task had little social respect, he dignified it from within. To instruct a few ragged children in an obscure village, working at starvation wages, surrounded by ignorance and taunted by bigotry, fulfilled his notion of the good, the noble, the holy life. Let others win fame, gather wealth, command armies, rule realms, and preach to the old and dying. All of that took hold upon death; it all looked backward; but he looked to the great time coming, the western time, the American, which these young lives he was shaping would certainly help to make. He stood beside the mountain springs, where the tiny tricklets first gushed forth out of mystery, and paused, as though reluctant, before they set out on their never-ending way. By a single motion of his finger, by a breath almost, he could turn those infant rills to left or right, toward destruction or toward the life eternal. The issues of his thoughts and words and deeds would be everlasting. Let fools despise him if they must. What did that matter? Let wise men aid him. And ah, let all good men everywhere pray for him, that he might be true to his great trust!

Unsympathetic persons were to wonder, in the years coming on, whether Bronson Alcott had not, perhaps, slightly too exalted a notion of himself. Why, no! How was that possible? He had done the work of a schoolmaster, than which, as he would have said, there is none nobler. He *did* say it, addressing himself in a most magnificent language, as though talking to a king:—

"If there be any employment which, among the inhabitants of

[90]

our earth, claims a precedence, that of instructing the young in the duties and pursuits of time and eternity seems to hold itself conspicuously to notice. And this deservedly. No other employment in which men can be engaged is more intimately connected with the welfare of human beings. . . . It is the employment of God."

But with the sense of opportunity there came an equal sense of obligation, and the young man was tormented by doubts of his own worthiness for this high calling. Indeed, one might almost ask whether it had been worth his while to climb up out of the Puritan's terrible anxiety about "salvation" only to fall at once into an equal anxiety about his fitness to teach children. Well, yes, it had been; for now, at any rate, the reference and object of the struggle was outside himself. Yet the tone of his meditations is often curiously like what one would expect to find in some spiritual diary written in the days of the Great Awakening, a hundred years before.

"What moral attainments are there," he asks himself, "of which our Instructor is *not* in want? Of what injury may the want of a single one prove to the individuals under his care, to the community in which he dwells, to the world of intelligent minds! How does it become him to husband well his passing moments in the study of Morality, and to illustrate it in practical clearness before his imitating charges—to take care that his feet depart not from the path of wisdom, that his lips speak no guile! . . . Let him see that his practice be an unwavering comment upon his principles, that the correspondence be visible and connected to the apprehension of his disciples."

It is clear that the young schoolmaster went about his work in a mood of religious self-dedication. He was not pious. He was far from orthodox by any test then known. Already he had the gravest doubts concerning the basic assertions of Christianity. As Jesus of Nazareth became more and more his master, his model of all conduct, his ideal of all good teaching, precisely to that degree Jesus descended from his alleged divinity and took his equal place on the earth, a man among men. Alcott was already confiding to his Journal such audacities as these:—

> Those who . . . idolize the person of Jesus Christ, asserting him to be God, exhibit the disposition of men in ancient times to deify such of their fellow-men as performed great and magnanimous actions . . . I cannot persuade myself to admit such things. I hold that the Christian religion is the best yet promulgated, but do not thence infer that it is not susceptible of improvement; nor do I wish to confound its doctrines with its founder, and to worship one of my fellowbeings.

Yet Bronson Alcott was religious through and through, in the sense that his whole proud nature continually adored the Spirit he saw pervading all things, but saw most clearly in children. Unmistakably, he regarded himself as that Spirit's priest, dedicated, holy, uttering God. There had been no laying-on of human hands, no mediation of human ritual, but only that eloquent Silence of New Connecticut Hill, which had seemed to say: "Go thou, and preach this Gospel!" He had written his own ordination sermon in the first pages of his first Journal, reminding himself what he had to do:—

> To teach with reference to Eternity, to teach as an agent of the Great Instructor, to teach as the former of character and the promoter of the collective happiness of Man.

So it runs on, to fifty-eight items of self-adjuration, this credo of a young teacher whose training had been chiefly in the peddling of "Yankee notions." It takes the place, for him, of a young clergyman's confession of faith. Also it takes the place, in Alcott's career as a schoolmaster, of the two or three years that must nowadays be spent at Normal School, by persons who

[92]

wish to teach, in the study of pedagogic method and the psychology of the learning process. Bronson Alcott knew more about these matters than one might at first suppose, but he had to get his knowledge from his own observation as he went along. He got it rapidly, making in the first two years a greater advance in teaching-method than all the schoolmasters in America had made in as many centuries. But this is not so remarkable, or at any rate so interesting and significant, as the high motives that he gives himself for his work, or as the mood—firm without belligerency and courageous without impudence—in which he advances upon the old entrenchments of prejudice.

One is to consider that Alcott had had no special training for his task. His own schooling had ended when he was thirteen. He had read only the hundred books he had been able to find in his native town and such others as he came across among the plantations of Virginia. He did not know, at first, how the district schools of other towns in his own region were being conducted. At first, he did not even inquire. The total effect of the "General Maxims" which he sets down for the guidance of his teaching is, simply, that he is listening inward, hearkening upward, for the voice not of human experience but of divine wisdom. He intends to teach by "inner light."

That would have been his unabashed apology for any suggestion of arrogance which an unsympathetic reader might have found in his "Maxims." He told himself to "teach with independence," to "teach unawed by the clamors of ignorance," and to "teach nothing merely from subservience to custom." Was there not just a hint of the "toplofty" in those sentences, coming as they did from a young man who had never been to college, who had recently hobbled into New York with no shoes on his feet, and who owed his father six hundred dollars? Certainly not, he would have answered. Of course if those sentences really meant that he was going to depend upon Bronson Alcott alone, as against the accumulated knowledge and experience of the rest of the world, then indeed they would be absurd; but a dependence upon divine wisdom as against man's knowledge was a different thing. There was nothing absurd about that, and nothing arrogant. So much he had learned, once for all, from the Quakers of North Carolina.

The lives of most men who really live at all are divisible into periods. They seem to pass out of one mood, one set of interests and ideas, into another. Goethe's life is a clear and familiar example, and the intellectual experience of Shakespeare as it has been conjecturally reconstructed is another. In speaking of Beethoven, of Plato, or even of Napoleon, we feel it necessary to distinguish the particular phases to which we refer in each of their careers. But then there is another kind of life which, although moving as we all must through a constantly changing scenery, remains always visibly one and the same. Bronson Alcott's life is of this less common kind. Take it up where one will, one finds in each aspect or episode of his mature experience all the ingredients to be found in any other. It is true that his life had a wide range, and that he was "adaptable" to an extraordinary degree. Superficially, like the chameleon, he took on the color of his surroundings, but inwardly he remained for sixty years the same man—serene, poised within himself yet strongly social, idealistic in every sense, and profoundly though heretically religious. And his teaching career is no exception. The obscure schoolmaster of twenty-five who was smiled at, sneered at, preached against, and thwarted as much as possible in two Connecticut villages was the same person, unmistakably, who was to sit, full of years and fame, as the Dean of the Concord School of Philosophy. Fifty years of life's up-and-down had only confirmed in the old man's mind what the young man already knew. For that young man was an idealist without having read a word of Plato. He was a transcendentalist without having heard the name of Emerson. Already, he had hitched his country wagon to a star.

[94]

The most important of all the "General Maxims" by which Alcott hoped to guide his work as a schoolmaster was this: "To teach in imitation of the Saviour." The phrase is so deceptively familiar that one is tempted to let it slip into one of the well-worn grooves of thought, and regard it as a mere pious aspiration. It was no such thing. Bronson Alcott disliked a shallow, unctuous, and mouthing piety at least as much as the most confirmed skeptic can do—partly because he was himself, by this time, a thorough skeptic with regard to "the Saviour." He was already, without having heard of Channing, a Unitarian. That word "Saviour," itself would soon disappear from his vocabulary, giving place to "Jesus," the simple name of a fellow man. But yet the maxim, as Alcott meant and understood it, was charged with sincerity. As Alcott tried to draw Jesus down to him, out of the godhead, out of the empty skies and emptier theologies, strove to rescue him from the priests and to bring him back from the myth-makers, his devotion to this supreme figure grew and grew. One might say that he was compensated for his loss of a person from the Holy Trinity by finding a companion, a colleague. Jesus of Nazareth was to him simply the most accomplished teacher that had ever lived—the most expert in method, the noblest in motive, and the most obviously inspired. As another earnest young pedagogue might study *The Great Didactic* of Comenius he studied the Gospels, admiring every stroke of the master's technique, the subtlety of his psychological perception, the depth of his knowledge of human nature, the height of his aim. Jesus had taught in the spirit of love. So he would do. Jesus had realized that every mind must teach itself. So he realized. Jesus had seen that unless a human soul can keep or recover the innocent wisdom of childhood, there is no hope for that soul. How true!

Thus it was that Bronson Alcott found a master. One cannot make the statement too simply, nor can it be taken any more literally, more directly, perhaps one should say more naïvely, than he took it and showed it forth in his daily life. He was to find other masters. Pythagoras, Socrates, Plato, Boehme, Berkeley, and Coleridge were to add their wisdom to what the young Hebrew mystic had taught him. He came to see, or to think, that there were many ranges of thought and experience which Jesus never entered. What had he known, at first hand, about the love of man for woman, about physical paternity, or about the broader ranges of masculine humor? And where, after all could you find Jesus tried, as other men are, in the toil and anguish of thought? Jesus reached right conclusions, but you could not follow him step by step as you could Socrates. Always he seemed to stand waiting at the goal of thought, instead of sharing the dust and heat of the way. Was that, after all, the best teaching—or might Socrates, so much more patient, moving with you step-by-step, be a better guide?

In later years such questions would arise; but even then Alcott would say that, whichever way was better, his own way was that of Jesus. Always it was Jesus who taught him how, what and why to teach.

Alcott's first two terms of teaching, at Bristol, were tentative and experimental, attracting little attention from the townspeople At Cheshire, however, whither he went in the autumn of 1825, h seems to have felt that his apprenticeship was over. Within hi first year of service there he managed to get the schoolroom thoroughly renovated and "fitted out" with blackboard, slate: and separate desks, all at his own expense. He also purchase with his own money a school library of one hundred and sixty five volumes, to be lent not only to the pupils but to their parent as well. Against the opposition of those who felt that the Stat should defray the entire cost of education, he secured new tex books in place of those that had been doing service for man years, although for many of these too he had to pay. By the b ginning of 1827 he had established evening classes and regula

[96]

social gatherings of parents and children at the schoolhouse, and was giving one evening of every week to the entertainment of his pupils at his boarding place. The school was rapidly gathering a reputation. Visitors came from far and near. They were much interested in the gymnastic exercises that Alcott had invented to break the monotony of school hours, and some of them listened without complete incredulity to his amazing opinion that the body too stands in need of education and that the complete training of a human being involves all three aspects of that indivisible trinity, Body, Mind, and Soul. They were astonished to find that the children and teacher alike were unmistakably happy. One result of these visits was the appearance, in May, of an unsigned article in the *Boston Recorder and Telegraph* which asserted that, although the Connecticut schools in general left much to be desired, there was one "of a superior and improved kind, viz., Mr. A. B. Alcott's school in Cheshire." The writer was satisfied that this was "the best common school in the State, perhaps in the United States."

When he read that laudatory paragraph, Alcott hoped devoutly that it was not true; and yet he feared that it might be. His cousin William had recently been all up and down the State visiting schools, and had found most distressing conditions. Both the cousins realized by this time that the school which they two had attended on Spindle Hill was decidedly better than most. They knew that the "little red schoolhouses" of New England, so fondly misrepresented in later song and story, were for the most part less comfortable, less sanitary, and less decent than the prisons even of their day. In Connecticut they were, on the average, twenty feet long, eight feet wide, and seven feet high. Hardly any of them had any ventilation whatever, and yet they held thirty or more children each for six or seven hours a day. Less than half of the fifteen hundred schoolhouses in the State, most of which were situated on the public highways, were equipped with "places of retirement for either sex." The long and narrow

benches, often so high that the smaller children could not touch
the floor with their feet, were apparently devised for the torture
of young bodies. The heating was such as to provide a maximum
of discomfort and to leave a minimum of breathable air. As a
whole, the ordinary schoolhouse was an empty shell, thrown to
gether as cheaply as possible. Therein some thirty or forty
children were herded together, under the management of a male or
female ignoramus paid somewhat less than a common laborer
and passed about their diseases. Such were the educational ad
vantages of the more fortunate of Connecticut's future citizens
for only about five in seven of the children in the State ever
went to school at all. And in the other States of New England
excepting Massachusetts, the conditions differed from those o
Connecticut chiefly in being somewhat worse.

It grew increasingly clear to Bronson Alcott that his heretica
views about education pained the good people of Cheshire mos
keenly of all in the pocket-nerve. He himself, as it happened
never had any pains whatever in that region, so that he spen
nearly half of what he earned during his two years in the tow
upon new textbooks, the school library, and repairs for the school
house. Little wonder, therefore, that when he returned to Spindl
Hill his six-hundred-dollar debt to his father had not been re
duced.

This extravagant spending of his own money did nothing t
ingratiate him with a community in which all common sense an
a great part of morality had been brought down to the level c
"New England thrift." Furthermore, these new schoolbooks, ne
desks, new slates and blackboards, the new library, and, worst c
all, the startling novelty that the children were enjoying then
selves and liking their teacher, amounted to an intolerable deal
innovation. Like the redoubtable Jedediah Morse, the parents
Cheshire began to brace themselves "against the insidious e

croachment of *innovation*—that evil and beguiling spirit which is now stalking to and fro in the earth, seeking whom it may devour." Born and brought up in a highly conservative district of what was rapidly becoming one of the most conservative countries on earth, they shrank back from all this reckless novelty. It made them wonder, as people of their good and stupid kind have wondered through all the human ages, "what the world was coming to." They felt that there was altogether too much new-fangled cheerfulness in the schoolhouse of the Centre District, together with a lamentable deficiency of good old-fashioned birch rod. Remembering so vividly the ache in their own young bones which had followed upon hours of immobile perching on backless benches, they could not be expected to like this "hop-skipping" to music, actually in the schoolroom itself. It seemed frivolous. And as for the fraternization between master and pupils, who had always been understood to belong to hostile camps—well, it was weak, it was sentimental, it was crack-brained. Worst of all, it was new.

Thus it happened that just when the Cheshire School of the Centre District first attracted a favorable attention in the outside world, it began to be severely criticised, also for the first time and for the same reason, in Cheshire itself. One week after the laudatory paragraph about it appeared in Boston, Alcott recorded in his Journal that an "opposition school"—it was headed by the Reverend Mr. Cornwall, formerly assistant to Tillotson Bronson —had been established. In June, while he was preparing for William Russell's new *American Journal of Education* an outline of his work at Cheshire, he was obliged to admit to himself that "school languishes now." Seven days later he locked the Cheshire schoolhouse door for the last time and walked back to Spindle Hill, thereby grieving his pupils and disappointing a few friends, but causing a huge relief to many anxious parents. Once more, as in his peddling expeditions, he had made a successful failure.

[99]

Early and late in his career, Bronson Alcott was extremely sensitive to public opinion. He could face it down; he could even go forward in firm opposition to it when that seemed the course of duty; but he suffered more, in such opposition, than most men do who understand the not very formidable ingredient of which public opinion is usually composed. And one should remember that the disapproval of a small homogeneous village such as Cheshire then was, is more daunting by far than that of a huge, diverse, impersonal city. Even half a dozen persons with whom one has been on familiar terms but who now pass one on the walk with no sign of recognition, can become a serious trial to a sensitive man who has to meet them every day, even though he has no sense of personal guilt. Bronson Alcott had been known in Cheshire since his boyhood—ever since that time in fact, when he had shrunk away from the more glossily polished young candidates for the Episcopalian ministry, and had perhaps lost his chance thereby of a higher education. He had been the lodger, the secretary, the nephew of the most prominent man in the village—and that man, Uncle Tillotson, was now dead. Was it any wonder that he decided to take his new ideas elsewhere?

Yet Alcott did not leave Cheshire with feelings of resentment for such feelings were not in his nature. Rather, he went back to Spindle Hill with a sense of mild bewilderment. His motive had been so high and pure; he had thought and wrought for others only; he had given to his holy task every atom of strength that there was in him; and certainly, even in his humblest mood he could not think himself quite without the gifts of the teacher. Where, then, had been the fault? What sort of world was it in which these qualifications were held to have no value? The young man did not yet know.

Concerning the fault of the particular community that he had been trying to serve, Alcott could make a shrewd guess. Once more at home in his father's house, he wrote these words in his Journal:—

[100]

Among the inhabitants of New England the parsimonious and calculating spirit of their forefathers is yet exhibited. . . . Mammon is associated with all our public and private concerns. To him our homage is paid, and he who refuses to worship him is doomed and outcast as a simpleton, a fool.

And in those words, hackneyed and platitudinous as they may seem to us, there is proof of a definite advance; for a young man has made real progress in the battle of life when once he has clearly seen his foe and recognized that foe's nature, so that from that time forth he will know "what weapons to select, what armour to indue."

At about the time when young Alcott was beginning to see the whites of Mammon's eyes, he read the following sage pronouncement made by a Professor at Yale College, that consistently orthodox bailiwick of the Reverend Timothy Dwight:—

We find no advantage in pursuing a different course of instruction from what has hitherto been practised. That has stood the test of experience. It were surely an outrage to alter it. The world talks about improvement in instruction . . . and about a thousand nevertested notions. They are good for nothing. I would not give a straw for all of them. . . . The money appropriated to common schools ought to be applied to better purposes — to the support of colleges. What good can be done in common schools? Our dependence must rest upon colleges chiefly. Cannot some means be devised to get a part, or the whole, of the School Funds applied to the use of Colleges, and save it . . . instead of its being thrown away?

Oh, Mammon! Mammon everywhere! Instead of merely seeing the whites of his eyes Alcott began to feel the enemy's poisonous breath. The unnamed professor's magnanimous disregard of the

[101]

fact that he might himself be a beneficiary of the suggested conversion of School Funds did not placate the teacher of common schools when he read the passage. "Such sentiments," says he, "do, in spite of myself, raise indignant feeling. I cannot, perhaps ought not to, feel otherwise." Furthermore, he is feeling a little lonely as he sees his dearest interests assailed both from above and below, at Yale as well as at Cheshire, by the learned as much as by the ignorant. Almost inevitably, there grows up in him that tendency to undue self-assertion with which a sensitive and a strongly convinced mind first confronts the opposition of the world. He decides, if only in self-defense, that any man who takes reason for his guide "must calculate on contention with the irrational part of mankind. He must expect opposition and calumny The greater part of mankind do not reason. They take their opinions implicitly from others." And so it is not long before he reaches the conclusion that "the number of those who advocate any particular doctrine is no test of its truth; but, on the contrary, is an indication of its incorrectness." Yet he has to live in America, which at least purports to be a democracy and pretends to hear in the voice of every majority nothing less than the voice of God.

The young man, one sees, is being thrown back upon his innermost defenses. Mammon, who sometimes takes on almost the huge looming bulk of Giant Despair, is crowding him hard Social though his nature is, he ranges rapidly through all the earlier phases of moral solitude, soon reaching the conviction that if he is misunderstood, scorned, maltreated, he must find in that very fact the evidence of his high powers and lofty mission—"for so persecuted they the prophets." In his loneliness in his sad contemplation of ruined hopes, he begins to suffer mild illusions of grandeur, begins to develop what may be called "Messianic complex." Must it not be, he argues, that he is messenger of the Divine Will? Partly he has the evidence of the way his thoughts spring up in him without his effort, as though they were given him from on high; and, for the rest, here is this outcry in which all men seem to revile him and say all manner of evil against him, falsely.

There is an error in his logic, to be sure, for not even an absolute unanimity of popular condemnation gives sure proof of the greatness of any man. But we may leave the judgment against him to those very few, if any there be, who have never set foot upon the same strange road of thought.

How strange it was and how far it led him is shown in a curious passage from the Journal of the time:—

Those who . . . attempt in education anything different from old established modes are by many considered as public innovators on the peace and order of society . . . They are regarded by some as dangerous, and by others as ignorant and imbecile. . . . By their friends in particular are they regarded with feelings of distant coldness, as those who by their arrogance and presumption are obstinate in bringing shame upon their own heads. Like the friends of the Great Reformer, they lay hold on a person of this character saying: *"Certainly he is beside himself.* He presumes to dictate to the intelligence and wisdom of men in high office, to men possessed of every means of obtaining accurate knowledge of the subjects in investigation, to men of liberal views and expanded minds, through whose intelligence and efforts our present fair and comparatively perfect fabrick of publick instruction and government has been raised . . . He sets all this wisdom and skill at defiance, attempts to demolish the whole structure, plunge mankind into anarchy and confusion, and bring chaos again. At one blow he is striking at the very root of wisdom. He is levelling the foundations of virtue and happiness, and doing his best to establish the reign of vice, infidelity, and misery. He hath Beelzebub, and by the Prince of the devils casteth

[103]

he out devils. Though to appearance his theory of reformation may be fair and comely, as it opposes the wisdom of wise and good men who have hitherto lived and adorned the doctrines which they professed it must in essence be deformed and poisonous. How knoweth this man more than others? *How knoweth he letters, having never learned?* Who is he? What is his parentage? *Learn and look, for out of Galilee cometh no Prophet.* Hath he ever been the inmate of a University? Hath he ever taught in our privileged seminaries or churches? *Where then hath he these things?"*

The answer is ready: He has studied the Scriptures. He has separated their spirit from the shackles of form, of mode, and ceremony by which they have been so long restrained. He has studied man, human nature. He has traced effects to their causes. He has studied man as he is from the hand of his Creator, and not as he is made by the errors of the world. He has drunk at the fountain, and not at the distant streams. He has listened to the instructions of *Him who spake as never man spake,* who saw as man never saw before, who did as man never before did.—And, making due allowances for the imperfections of human nature, *he is going to do likewise!*

The opportunity to "do likewise" opened up rather strangely. Fifty miles to the eastward, in Israel Putnam's village of Brooklyn, the Reverend Samuel Joseph May—Boston born, a Harvard graduate, and Connecticut's first Unitarian minister—was rattling the dead bones of Connecticut education to some purpose. He had called a convention of School Committees, at which he described the conditions in the schools in Brooklyn itself and then asked whether, by any chance, they might be almost as bad in some other town. Good results followed—among them a letter from Dr. William A. Alcott, then teaching at Wolcott Hill. Without any mention, apparently, of his own work, William spoke in such glowing terms of the school his cousin had kept at Cheshire that May wrote at once to Bronson Alcott, begging him to send a detailed statement of his principles and methods. There was nothing in the world that Bronson Alcott more delighted to do.

"In due time," says May in his sketch of his own life, "there came to me a full account of the school at Cheshire, which revealed such a depth of insight into the nature of man, such a true sympathy with children, such profound appreciation of the work of education, and withal so philosophically arranged and exquisitely written, that I at once felt assured the man must be a genius, and that I must know him more intimately. So I wrote, inviting him urgently to visit me." On the eighth of August, 1827, Alcott arrived in the beautiful drowsy village of Brooklyn. He spent a week there, living in the parsonage, and talking not about the schools of Connecticut alone but about the new "Infant Schools" of Robert Owen's invention that were spreading from England. He found in the young Pastor a mind gloriously seething with heresies, radicalisms, enthusiasms, disgusts, plots for reform, and plans for good works. "The Lord's chore-boy," as Alcott would one day dub him, was already darting here and there on his Master's business. His eager, aggressive, extraverted nature was of just the sort to kindle in the quiet and inwardly brooding Bronson Alcott a slow long-smoldering fire. Samuel J. May, moreover, seemed hardly to know the name either of fear or of discouragement. He was dedicating his life to the prompt and brisk assassination of numerous hoary abuses, and one could already see that he would go in to kill with a perfectly good-humored smile on his face, oddly mixed with a look of studious abstraction.

It was a good week there, under the gracefully balancing Brooklyn elms, for those two somewhat lonely idealists. They recognized each other at the first glance, and each heart said to self: "Here is another American of my own uncommon but

[105]

quite necessary kind!" Two dreamers they were, in Connecticut, and the year was 1827. Two runners they were with the sacred fire which had never quite died out during the centuries of our struggle with the wilderness. How could their hearts not cry out with a hail, each to the other?

This is what the Parson wrote concerning Alcott many years after, when he had encountered thousands of men in the course of a stormy and eventful career:—

> I have never, but in one instance, been so immediately taken possession of by any man I have ever met in life. He seemed to me a born sage and saint. He was radical in all matters of reform; went to the root of all things, especially the subjects of education, mental and moral culture. If his biography shall ever be written by one who can appreciate him, and especially if his voluminous writings shall be properly published, it will be known how unique he was in wisdom and purity.

There was another person in the house at Brooklyn who wa just as immediately taken captive by the tall and handsom visitor. Abigail May, the minister's sister, was a year younge than Bronson Alcott—that is, she was at this time twenty-seven and well past the age at which women then usually married. He form and her rather large and heavy features suggested strength persistence, endurance, rather than sprightly grace and charm She was womanly, but one would scarcely have called her whol "feminine." There was something refreshingly straightforwar and frank about her. One knew what she thought and what sh felt with little delay. If her speech and manner sometimes seeme a little blunt and abrupt to the always courteous Bronson that could easily be set down to her honesty. Most beautiful honest she was; and she was thoroughly good, too, in her positiv downright, self-reliant way. To be sure, one would not think calling her "good" with the suggestion that she had no fault

Oh, far from that! It was rather that she was "good for something."

Miss Abigail May was the first woman with any pretensions to culture and breeding that Bronson Alcott had ever intimately known. She was a daughter of one of the most highly respected families in Boston. Although her educational advantages had not been many or great, she had read a good deal and was delightfully eager to secure the visitor's suggestions for further reading. He was not reluctant to give them. Also he agreed with her that the position of woman was everywhere much lower than it ought to be—it was hard to say just why. He found that he rather liked to discuss the woman problem with Miss May. It was not that he had ever given it much thought before, the problems of young men and of children having hitherto occupied most of his attention; but now that he did come to think about it he discovered that he had a surprising number of opinions. She felt that those opinions did him honor, and said so. During the week in Brooklyn he had a good deal of talk with Miss May—or she had, at any rate, with him. Never before had he talked so much with any woman except his mother. He discovered that she too was lonely, perhaps on account of her mother's recent death. Eight of her eleven brothers and sisters were also dead. He gathered that she was not entirely happy in her home in Boston—although she adored her father, Colonel Joseph May, who was one of the old town's first citizens. He, Bronson Alcott, had never yet been in Boston, the Capital of New England. He would like to go there, especially in view of what Miss May told him about the opportunities the city offered for young teachers. Perhaps sometime. . . . But in the meanwhile the new association was all very pleasant, as well as a little perplexing. Miss May's farewell, when he came to leave, made him think of something in one of Shenstone's poems:—

> So sweetly she bade me adieu,
> I thought she bade me return.

[107]

Later in the summer, while he was reading Locke and Dodd-ridge and Foster's Essays at Spindle Hill, she wrote him a pleasant letter in which she rather strongly urged the advantages, for a man of his tastes and abilities, of Boston.

In November, 1827, Alcott began the five-month term in the West Street District School of Bristol, Connecticut, at the com-paratively high salary of twenty-three dollars a month. The school-house had been arranged at the town's expense in accordance with his specifications, and for the first few weeks all went well. In that flourishing mill-town of two thousand inhabitants he found several intelligent persons with whom he could discuss theology, morals, and even education. Cousin William was only a three-mile walk away. Bronson read Paley's Works. His paper on the Cheshire School appeared in William Russell's *Journal,* the first extended piece of his writing that ever appeared in print. Miss May continued to write to him about the proposed Infant School in Boston, and also about other matters. He began to refer to her letters as "communications of an interesting nature." The taste-less phrase signified that he was finding it decidedly pleasant to hear from Miss May.

Before his second month at Bristol was far advanced, however, Alcott was again in difficulties with Mammon, with bigotry, with parents, or whatever other enemy it was that seemed determined to defeat his noblest aspirations. Using the editorial "we" then habitual to him and slipping into the magniloquence, so prophetic of Mr. Micawber, which was often to prognosticate disaster in his later life, he confided to his Journal:—

> Our plans having been misunderstood and prejudice
> having been busy in attempts to injure us, the minds of
> some are at this time in doubt respecting the success
> and correctness of our plans. Our theological sentiments
> have been so construed as to increase prejudice against
> us. Time, we think, will set all to right.

[108]

But Time had other intentions. One month later Alcott was writing:—

> Prejudices strong and inveterate assail us on all sides. There are only two or three individuals with whom we can freely converse.

And a month later still he wrote:—

> Our opinions are subjects of discussion among those who are bound to the faith of antiquity, determined to support it at all events. The clergyman here, in a recent discourse, alluded to our opinions, attempted to controvert them and establish what he called "the truth." We are unable to bring these men to discuss the points in question. They seem unwilling or afraid to bring them forward except among their own party.

This was no mere squabble over the question whether school children should have backs to their benches and whether to thrash or not to thrash. This was the *odium theologicum,* that peculiarly poisonous hatred which has been known to arise at other times and places within the religion of brotherly love. The town of Bristol was made up at this time, according to Alcott's own report, of "a plain and simple people," but they were "mostly Baptists and Presbyterians, and very determined in their ways—the Baptists particularly." This would mean that he was surrounded by Calvinists of the hard-shelled variety, convinced of the total depravity of human nature and strongly inclined toward the "young viper" school of thought with regard to children. Bitterly and ignorantly logical, thinking with the head alone and therefore thinking badly, devoutly believing that the Spirit of the Universe was an ignorant logician like themselves, they did not provide a favoring climate of opinion for the schoolmaster whose whole theology could be summed up in "God is Love." He asked them to meet him at the schoolhouse on an evening in February for a frank discussion of the trouble between them, but his explanations only made things worse. He talked about the necessity that parents and teachers alike should be what he called "Christians," and he had much to say about "Jesus." Ah, how they hated to hear him use those words! And how it perplexed them! Was it not blasphemous to suggest that Christ had been a sort of school-master? Was it not positively terrifying to hear him speak of Christianity as though it were no more than a way of living? They liked him none the better because it was so hard to find an answer. If he would only stand up and fight them with sound and manly argumentation, instead of being so gentle with them, so courteous and kind! It was uncomfortable, unfortunate, that the young heretic should know his New Testament so well; because of course one did have to admit that the New Testament was a portion of God's Word. And he had a bewildering way of going to the heart of things. He stripped the Holy Bible down to the New Testament, reduced that to the Gospels, and then said that the essence of the Gospels was "God is love"! Oh, it was intolerable that one's own offspring should be taught by a man like that. No wonder he tried to make them comfortable at school, tried to make the schoolroom, as he said, "beautiful," and would not even thrash the children!

One thing Alcott learned at Bristol which Cheshire had not taught him. At the end of a series of "Inductions" based on his experience there he wrote:—

> In introducing improvements, great care is required to graduate their introduction to the state of common opinion.

This was a bit of wisdom which he had taken thirty years to learn. He was to forget it all too soon.

Toward the end of March, in 1828, the teacher whom Bristol had branded as a dangerous heretic delivered up the key of his

[110]

school and began to shake the dust of Connecticut from his shoes. That Land of Steady Habits had borne and reared him, but it could not hold him or feed his further growth. Its homespun culture, its tradition of local independence, and most of all those granite hills to westward where heaven and earth were married, had left a deep mark on him. To the end of his days he would be unmistakably a son of Connecticut, proud to be known as such, with always a hint of the hill-born rustic beneath his "manners of a very great peer." His love of those hills would bring him back to them many a time as he grew old. And yet it was the earlier, the humbler, the agrestic Connecticut that he loved, where men had worked with tools on a few rough acres, and not this clattering factory for making tinware, plated silver, pistols, and cheap brass clocks. Much of the past was in him, and more of the future, but he seemed to skip this present Connecticut, growing fat and prosperous and respectable, where the old adulterous alliance of Congregational Orthodoxy and Federal Politics and "Business" still held grimly on, ten years after its apparent defeat at the Hartford Convention. Where, in such a Connecticut, could he hope to find a home? At New Haven, where the dead hand of Timothy Dwight even yet lay heavy? At Hartford, self-contented, inbred, home of the *Connecticut Courant?*

Men had been leaving Connecticut for thirty years and for many different reasons. Connecticut had become a quiver of men, and her arrows were filling the land. He would leave her for a new reason. He would seek the intellectual frontier. He would go to Boston.

CITY SCHOOLMASTER

 1828-1839

The capital of New England—In quest of minds—Courtship and marriage—A windfall—Germantown and Philadelphia—Daughters—William Russell—Plato at last—The Temple School —A place in the sun—Gathering storm—Emerson—Shipwreck

APRIL 20: Leave Wolcott for Boston, by way of Hartford and Brooklyn. Pass two days at Mr. May's. *24th.:* Arrive at Boston and stop at the Marlboro' Hotel. Call on Wm. Russell, Dr. Coffin, Rev. Mr. Gannett, and others. *27th.:* First hear Dr. Channing on the "Dignity of the Intellect." *30th.:* Invited to take charge of the Infant School.

Such is the laconic record made by Alcott himself, many years later, of his passing from the provincial to the metropolitan scene. It is a highly selective record, leaving out nearly all the busy, voiceful world and getting in precisely those few things that mattered to the traveler: Mr. May's parsonage—with Miss May, as it happened, still lingering there; the editor of the

American Journal of Education; two ordinary clergymen; a clergyman-extraordinary; and the new opening for the teacher.

And the account of those ten momentous days as it stands in the contemporary Journal is no less grimly focused upon matters intellectual, educational, and edifying. Like a horse wearing blinkers, Alcott saw only the road before him, and less the road than its goal. Of the journey by stagecoach across Connecticut—the sandy lanes, the churning wheels, the pines of Manchester, the inn at Windham, the slow laborious climb out of the Willimantic Valley, and the long race down from Pomfret into Rhode Island—there is not a word. To his first sight of beautiful Boston, the lodestone of his thoughts for the following sixty years, he could not vouchsafe a single line. He had taken journeys before, this reformed pedlar. He had already seen cities—Charleston, Washington, Baltimore, New York—and had not been much impressed. The sixty thousand inhabitants of Boston did not astonish him by their mere number any more than the nine thousand of the Hartford he had just left behind, or the one thousand of his own Wolcott; for he was one of those rare Americans who ask not "How many? How much?" but always "How good?" What he wanted to know about Boston was, were there any "Minds" there? Before he had unstrapped his luggage at the Marlborough Hotel, one may be fairly sure, he set out on his never-ending search for "Minds."

Undoubtedly he had come to the right place, and in the nick of time. His action was as unerring as that of a plant that reaches toward the light. No young Boeotian going up to Athens in the age of Pericles was headed more certainly in the right direction. For little compact Boston—standing there on her three still discernible hills, nearly surrounded by tidewater and washed all over by the wandering airs of the sea—was indeed just then, at least for America, the Capital of "the Monarch Thought's dominions." There was probably not a city on earth that would then have assayed so large a quantity of "Mind" to the thousand of population. And even English visitors, swarming across the Atlantic just before the Great Reform Bill and looking for proof of their conviction that democracy could not possibly work, were constrained to admit, in spite of their reluctance to say anything that might sound polite, that Boston was beautiful. They liked her tangle of streets, roads, lanes, and alleys, so like old York or old Bristol. If only she had been able to boast a few bits of Roman wall they would have taken her to their hearts entirely. Some even went so far as to allow her intelligence. They could hardly help it, seeing that Boston was in some ways more English than anything they had left behind. Her proportion of "foreigners" was less than London's own. If England was "insular," Boston was at least peninsular, and made up for the slight geographical difference by looking down not only upon all other countries but also upon her own. Boston was an English city that had come to a stand, as it were, in the middle of the eighteenth century, choosing that as the best of all possible times—except, of course, that she had none of the poverty, vice, or crime that tormented the bad Old World. Or, if she did have such things, then she hid them decorously away—and that would be English too.

Quite seriously speaking, if one were given free choice of a time and place to live in, it is not certain that one could find anything better among all the lands and ages than the Boston of a hundred years ago. She was neither too old nor too young, and neither too large nor too small. The green and blowing country was near at hand, yet the sea lay at her door. Man and nature meshed together, like the folding of one's two hands. The Common was still a cow pasture, and the Frog Pond was what it was called. The streets were paved with cobblestones, and such sidewalks as there were with brick. English travelers found the houses remarkably comfortable and commodious. Not a few were also beautiful. For Boston, in spite of the staggering blows at her commerce in the Embargo of 1807 and the War of 1812, was still a

[114]

wealthy town, though not given to ostentation. She had long sat
at the gate of New England—which, so far as she was yet aware,
was practically equivalent to America—and had gathered tribute
from all comers and goers. Not long since she had been a mari-
time city, sending her ships into the seven seas; but her feeling
had always been that her merchants and captains should bring
home the best of what they found in foreign parts and keep it in
Boston. Instead of ships she was building chiefly factories now.
In politics she was still strongly Federalist at heart if no longer
so in name—a fact for which Bronson Alcott, a natural Democrat
but profoundly ignorant of political matters, could never sufficiently allow. Like ancient Athens and Elizabethan London,
though not to the same degree, she was a talking town. Whatever
occurred in the outer world she was likely to hear of at once, and
to make up her mind about. She had her "first families," who
believed that they had won their privileges by honorable service
and meant to keep them. She had many merchants, who were
likely to be cultivated men at least tolerant of ideas, and she was
acquiring "captains of industry," but she had not yet attained to
"businessmen" in the full rich sense of that term. Such servants
as there were in Boston were recruited for the most part from the
families of New England farmers, as the laborers in the mills at
Lowell were soon to be. There was also a shopkeeping class, almost as distinct from others as the corresponding class in England, and already there were many Irish. Class lines were sharply
drawn, considering that Boston was after all connected with
America, yet the several social strata so clearly recognized their
common origin and mutual dependence that an ugly snobbishness
did not often result.

The real glory of Boston, however, lay in none of these things.
Little by little she had produced or had attracted to her from
many places and social ranks and callings, a body of persons without whose help the fame of that city of a hundred years ago would
now be "one with Nineveh and Tyre." It was of this group that

[115]

Harriet Martineau spoke: "I certainly am not aware of so large a number of peculiarly interesting and valuable persons, living in any near neighbourhood, anywhere else but in London." These were the "Minds" that Bronson Alcott sallied forth to seek.

The minds most immediately accessible to a stranger from Connecticut would be those of the clergy, to whom one needed no introduction. During his first months in the city Alcott seems to have attended church at least once on every Sunday, and he must have spent a large part of the time remaining to him after service in commenting upon what he had heard. He had not done this in Connecticut. Now, in Boston, he was famishing for sermons.

Looking back upon him and his times from the lofty vantage ground of the twentieth century, one may smile at this strange hunger, and infer that if he could turn to such provender his own mental life must have been poor indeed. But it is always wise, as it is also fair, to test a man by the standards of his own day, and not by those of another. The fact seems to be that Alcott heard all the sermons that he could during his early months in Boston not because there was nothing going on in his own head but for the opposite reason. His mind, when he came to the city, was seething with questions, doubts, surmises, and strange new affirmations —all related in one way or another to the religious problem. Almost unaided, until he met Samuel J. May, he had thought his way out of Calvinism, out of Trinitarianism, out of Episcopalianism, and had made much headway toward the Unitarian point of view, or beyond it. Now, what did these profound and brilliant men, in what he took to be the very source of American Unitarian thought, have to say? It was a sensible question. Besides, as a teacher of children he was a preacher himself, not less than these famous men to whom he was listening. In a way, though far less prominent in the public eye, he would soon be above them, working to better advantage and in a more important sphere. It was

[116]

well that he, the newcomer, should learn what his colleagues were thinking. One may add that from his childhood he had thought of the preacher, with good reason, as by far the most important man in the community. "In those days," said the Reverend Lyman Beecher of his own Connecticut youth, "the ministers were all politicians. On election day they had a festival. . . . And when they got together they would talk over who should be governor and who lieutenant-governor, and their counsels would prevail." There was a long tradition behind Alcott's respect for the clergy. In the Connecticut villages of his boyhood the preachers were likely to be the only educated men; and they were usually men of indubitable power, quite worthy of the social respect that was paid them.

But the clergy of Boston! To Alcott, at least, it was a brilliant galaxy that burst upon his hopeful eyes. And they were really a brilliant lot of men by almost any standard of judgment, those twenty or more Unitarian ministers who were serving the city when Alcott arrived there. He seldom mentioned the Trinitarians, such as Lyman Beecher of Bowdoin Street; and that was odd, because many of them were Connecticut men, like Beecher himself, and graduates of Yale, whereas the Unitarian clergy stemmed from Harvard. Among the Unitarians, however, there was Nathaniel Frothingham at First Church, Ralph W. Emerson at Second, Francis Greenwood at King's Chapel, John Palfrey at Brattle Square, Francis Parkman at the New North, Alexander Young at New South, John Pierpont at Hollis Street, Charles Lowell at West Church, Joseph Tuckerman at Bulfinch Street, Samuel Barrett at the Twelfth Congregational, George Ripley at the Thirteenth Congregational, Mellish Motte at the South Congregational, Lemuel Capen at Hawes Place, and finally, leading them all, Ezra Gannett and Dr. William Ellery Channing at Federal Street. Alcott heard most of them, but he returned again and again to hear Channing. He heard Channing, as we have seen, on his first Sunday in Boston—going straightway, as though by in-

[117]

stinct, to the man who could most quickly set him on the lonely path to his future troubles and triumphs.

The ministers of Boston had to be brilliant in order to survive. Two hundred years of absorbed critical attention to sermons had trained the homiletic taste of the city to some purpose. No longer, if they ever had, would Boston congregations endure dullness merely because it was orthodox, and they were seldom called upon to do so. Their preachers had mastered the arts of public discourse in a time when those arts were still honored and splendidly flourishing. They made one think of the Golden Age of the English Pulpit, or of that time in Paris when Bossuet and Massillon had held a frivolous and glittering court spellbound. Ministers and merchants still ruled Boston, as they had for a hundred years. Bronson Alcott did not like the alliance of the two groups, but he would not condemn without trial. The ministers were still the chief readers and thinkers of New England, still the most prevailing talkers and aristocrats of Mind, but in these new days they held their prestige by dint of their own intrinsic power. The sounding-board was no longer mistaken for a halo. The church had rivals to-day: theaters, music halls, newspapers, magazines, an ever-increasing flood of secular books—and now this new thing, so like the sermon that a man could pass from one to the other without feeling the jar and yet so different in effect, the public "lecture." Could the preachers keep the pace of the times? If they could and did do so, then they would certainly be first-rate men.

The stranger from Connecticut, as he went from church to church, did not ask the preachers to entertain him. He chiefly wanted to know whether they were going to set Christianity to work in Boston. For he was severely practical, contemporary, and American in his demands upon the clergy, as he was to become also in his thought about scholars. It mattered little to him how much of the past a scholar or a preacher had impounded in the reservoirs of his brain, but it mattered immensely how much

[118]

thought-power that brain could actually deliver at the mill wheels of the present work-a-day world.

The mere antiquities of the Christian religion, the theory of it, the logic and the lore, concerned him hardly at all. Could it be made a way of life? Could the sayings and doings of a Galilean peasant be made to groove and grip into the cogs of this modern American metropolis? A clerical antiquarianism, maundering over the past, haunting an empty tomb, and canting in the specialized jargon of the pulpiteer, he abhorred. His dislike of it often led him to condemn sermons as "too Biblical" or as "talking too much about Jesus." Any man who brought Jesus nearer and made Him dearer, Alcott admired; but any man who tried to keep Jesus far off there, shut safely away in the past, was to him merely a pedantic archaeologist who gave the people the stone of information, frequently false, when they were starving for the bread of life.

Bronson Alcott had no hesitation in speaking his mind, at least to himself, about the preachers of Boston. For he was an expert. Good preaching differed in no essential respect, he believed, from good teaching. In motive and method and effect it was the same thing. In method particularly; for it too must begin with something near and concrete and known—not with the universe but with the kitchen and shop, and not with "bravery" but with a brave deed. Upon that specific thing or deed it must generalize, of course, carrying the symbols of this always emblematic world as far as possible into the abstract realms of ultimate reality, and then it must return again to the shadowy but actual realm of here and now. Good teaching always showed this movement of thought—from the known to the unknown and back, enriched, into the known. Good preaching must show it too.

Little by little, as the months in Boston grew into years, Alcott gave up his hope of the preachers. It was one of the more serious losses of his life, but he came to feel that they did not deeply mean what they said. Hardly one of them, hardly even the profound and lofty Channing, kept his full respect. And the ultimate reason for this was that, in his belief, they did not accept and follow either the teaching or the example of the Master. Simply they were not Christian. Swathed in precedent and tradition stifled by institutionalism, sticking to the letter that killeth and not even understanding that letter, erudite to the point of stu pidity, they represented the very things, he came to think, toward which the patient Man of Galilee had shown least patience. Did they lead the radical thinking of the land, as Jesus would have done, or did they side with the rich, the entrenched, the "respect able"? When the hue and cry of the mob was up against one of their brothers who had only said "Suffer the little children to come unto me," did they fence his lonely weakness with their serried strength, or did they stand aside, choosing precisely his darkest hour to tell him that he was to them a pariah, an outcast Jesus had said certain quite definite things about rich men and the slow corrosion of gold within the soul. What did they say Jesus had lived and had died a poor man. And they?

So that finally Bronson Alcott stayed away from church and did his own preaching.

But now the current of Alcott's outward life began to move at a speed more nearly corresponding to that of the current within him. Having secured, with the help of Samuel May, an invitation to open an Infant School in Boston, he set forth to inspect such schools of the sort as had already been opened in America. On the fifteenth of May he was in New York visiting the Green Street Infant School, which was under the superintendence of Mrs. Bethune, and two days later he was studying a similar in stitution at Chester Street in Philadelphia. He found both of them "tame, formal, unideal, and sectarian." With just enough of Pes talozzi's and Oberlin's original ideas to attract his attention, they had by far too much of English regimentation to command his respect. The source was pure, but one tasted the lead pipe. Thou professional English philanthropists—Owen, Wilderspin, Wilson, Wilberforce, Brougham, and the Marquess of Lansdowne—had taken as much as they could understand of the Swiss and German ideas, but they had missed the spirit of love, the reverence for childhood, the ideal of the home. They had supposed that running a school was very like a matter they really did understand—drilling raw recruits for an army. They had thought that of course Pestalozzi's real purpose, no matter what he had said, was exactly like theirs: to keep the poor from wrecking the capitalistic realm. Cheapness and military organization was their notion of teaching, and so they had hardened and coarsened a beautiful thing almost beyond recognition.

Bronson Alcott returned from his journey knowing even more fully than when he left the school on Spindle Hill what a school ought not to be. The chief gain of the journey had been his meetings with Dorothea Lynde Dix, philanthropist, with Matthew Carey, the Irish bookseller and author, and with Dr. William Furness, who was to be his friend, and Emerson's, for the following fifty years.

Back in Boston once more, Alcott took "boardings" at Mrs. Newall's, 12 Franklin Street. Everyone, it seemed, was "taking boardings." Rather a new thing in Boston life, the custom was contributing not a little to the currency of thought and opinion. The art of conversation, long cultivated there, was being carried forward at a hundred commensal breakfast-tables until it should be ready for the pen of Dr. Holmes. And even in 1828 this art was a delight to Alcott, eager as he always was for talk, charmed as he could never help being by any innocent human association. To Mrs. Newall's there soon came Josiah Holbrook of Connecticut, a friend of Samuel May's, now hard at work in founding the American Lyceum. Instantly fired by the idea of a broadcast adult education, Alcott helped Holbrook to write a prospectus outlining a scheme of public lectures destined to have profound effects upon American culture. There, too, came William Ladd—

[121]

a large, coarse-looking man, formerly a sailor and later a farmer in Maine but now a flaming prophet of pacifism,—destined to become, as the faraway prophet of the Hague Tribunal and the League of Nations, one of the more influential men of his time. Now and then one could see at the breakfast table the keen ascetic face of William Russell, Scottish editor of that *American Journal of Education* which Alcott had been reading from its first number. America did not hold many men so clear-headed and yet so idealistic, so sure-footedly logical and at the same time so spiritually minded, so thoroughly good for Alcott. His head was stored with the learning of his Scottish University, all neatly laid forth on shelves ready to hand; and yet he had nothing to sell. Russell was a teacher. All that he asked of life was the chance to give his life away.

Bronson Alcott, as social in his disposition as he was bashful in manner, began to stir about in Boston and to call on many people. Dr. Tuckerman, Colonel May, Dr. John Coffin, and even the Cabot family found themselves talking with a tall blond stranger in rusty black of whose family they had never heard. Was he a "climber"? But something checked that crude surmise. In his opinion, at any rate, he was conferring a favor. A man who was about to instruct the "infants" of Boston had no need to hesitate, he felt, before the most brilliant door-knocker that the city contained. When he got round to it, he might call on Dr. Channing himself!

But that would have to be postponed, for he had not been back two weeks from his trip to New York and Philadelphia before Miss Abigail May arrived in town.

Miss May applied for the position as Alcott's assistant in the Infant School which he opened at Salem Street on the twenty-third of June. He strongly felt that some "female assistance" was necessary to the success of his plans, but dissuaded her from urging the application because he hoped that she might be with him in another and better school of which he was already thinking.

[122]

ng. It was not Miss May, therefore, but a Mrs. Brush who
helped him in "taming, awakening, and instructing" the group of
seventeen children, mostly foreigners, with whom he began his
Boston teaching.

These children were much younger, on the average, than those
he had taught at the district schools in Connecticut. For that
reason Alcott felt that his work with them was more important
and interesting. They were nearer to the Divine Original, and
their "clouds of glory" had been less dissipated in the mists and
murk of this world. Therefore all that had seemed so strange in
his methods to the people of Cheshire and Bristol was accentuated
at Salem Street. Alcott departed as far as possible from the English mechanism of the "Lancastrian" or "monitorial" system as
he had seen it at work in Philadelphia and New York. He taught
his children as individuals, recognizing in each of them a separate
soul with which it was his privilege—that is, if he could be patient
and kind and skillful enough—to come into an affectionate parental relation. He addressed the child's affections first of all, then
the conscience, and finally the spiritual nature. He dealt not at all
with abstractions but with the actual scenes, persons, and events
of his pupils' everyday lives. Such a child had done so-and-so.
Had he done well or ill, and why? Stories illustrating principles
of conduct assumed more and more importance in his teaching.
Were the crude woodcuts and fables and appended "Morals" in
Noah Webster's Speller still at work in his thought? He went on
from there. He ransacked the stories that Maria Edgeworth had
written for children, wishing that they were better and that there
were more of them. It was amazing, how little had been done in
this most beneficent kind of writing. He longed and yearned for
better children's books. Would that he might write them—or, if
not he, then someone whom he might teach! The longing sank
to the core of his heart, and lay there, waiting its time.

The Salem Street School flourished. Some of the ladies who had
contributed to its support were disappointed that the teacher did

[123]

not make his charges memorize more verses from the Bible so as to provide a more impressive "exhibition," but he insisted that his teaching was not done for show. His patrons were more intelligent than the hill folk of Connecticut, or at least they knew more about what was going on in the world.

During July there came a stream of visitors, many gentlemen and more ladies, curious and benevolent and believing, to visit the school and appraise its novelties. William Russell came, and was uplifted. "You may think me extravagant," he wrote, "when I say that I left the schoolroom with a clearer conception than I ever had before of the innate excellence of the human soul, and with a deeper reverence for it as the production of infinite wisdom and love." Ah, there was a man who understood! Colonel May came, and gave the school his stately, courteous, and highly influential blessing. The Reverend May came, and wrote an account of what he saw for the *Christian Register*. Miss May came and confirmed the favorable impression she had gained when she first saw the teacher—that he had "a true sympathy with children."

Bronson Alcott expanded with this first unquestionable success that he had ever known. Worldly success, to be sure, was never very good for him, but still, after so many years of continuous failure, he could endure a little. He called on more and more people, laying his plans and confirming his social support for a new, more ambitious venture. He began teaching a class in the Berry Street Sunday School, partly because it gave him more opportunity than he had at the Infant School to talk about Jesus, but also because he found there a chance to affect the teaching methods and the basic religious opinions of adults. Sunday School teaching he found to be "permeated with the leaven of the old philosophy." It offered, therefore, a strategic point of attack, and Alcott gave to his attack upon it much of his most earnest, most radical thinking. Indeed, Boston's slowly growing realization that it had in Bronson Alcott a dangerous

[124]

person, sapping the very foundations of all orthodoxy if not of all morality and religion, seems to have spread at first from his work in the Sunday School rather than from his daily work with children.

If it had been known what books the tall handsome teacher was reading just then, at his boardings in Franklin Street, would the Sunday School children he taught have been sent off from home quite so trustingly? He was reading, for the second or third time, that radical book which he had bought at New Haven two years before—*A New View of Society*, by Robert Owen, the famous British reformer. Boston parents of 1828 would have been well aware that Robert Owen—although it was understood that he was a rich man and had done a certain amount of good in spite of his opinions—was not the sort of person for a Sunday School teacher to be reading, unless with the purpose of refuting him. But Bronson Alcott was reading something worse, even more closely related to that French Revolution in which Boston had been so deeply disappointed. This was William Godwin's *Political Justice*. And there was still a third book, more disruptive and unsettling and radical than either of these, which he was reading now for perhaps the twentieth time, but reading as though he had never seen it before, as though no one had ever before seen it. The words, as he read, flashed up in his brain. They seemed to be spoken inside him. They were not so much human words as divine. They did not tell an ancient story but expressed present fact. They crushed all the past into now. He believed them, utterly, as to their inward significance, although much of their outward assertion seemed to him no more credible or important than an old wives' tale. This most dangerous of the three radical books he was reading was the New Testament.

In September Bronson Alcott was made Superintendent of the Chauncy Place Sunday School, and began weekly discussions of religion and of education with the teachers thus brought under his control. He had been in Boston four months and had heard many sermons, so that he spoke as an experienced mind when he said "Unitarianism looks now a little pale and puny. Does it lack love, knowledge, and faith?" What Unitarianism really lacked was the tang of heresy. It had grown prosperous, powerful, fashionable. Harvard College, even including the Hollis Professorship of Divinity, was solidly Unitarian. So was the Boston Bench and Bar. So was State Street. So was Beacon Street. The atmosphere of Unitarianism was so stifling with respectability that the Reverend George Ripley would one day have to read himself out of it. To Bronson Alcott, coming from a State in which the profession of Unitarian belief had been until recent years a felony, all this was rather disappointing. Still, he could rouse himself to a moderate expression of approval when he heard a certain young R. W. Emerson speak at Chauncy Place late in September. The speaker dealt with "The Universality of the Notion of Deity," and Alcott's laconic comment in his Journal had the exact New England ring: "A very respectable effort."

And yet, try as the preachers might, they could not please Alcott. Within a week after he had heard the "effort" of Reverend Mr. Emerson he was saying:—

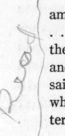

> The intellect of preachers seems still wandering among the mysteries of a dark and antiquated theology. . . . They lead us through a bewildering labyrinth of theory, of book-work, far away from the ever-present and all-pervading Deity. They lead us to what man has said and thought and recorded in books, rather than to what He who made man has recorded in living character.

And on the same day he says that Christianity is to him "a system of education. Its author is a 'Redeemer' in the same sense that an instructor is the redeemer of his pupils, by exerting an influence upon their minds and hearts." But these views, he fears, "are of a character too liberal and charitable for the ge eral mass of thinkers" about him. "They are not decidedly Unitarian; they do not embrace all the minute particulars of that class of opinions; they are not so decidedly Christian. In other words, they do not attach that particular divinity to the person of Christ and the system which he gave us that this denomination does." At present, Alcott is disposed, he says, "to consider the author of the Christian system as a great and good and original man, and the system itself as one of superior merit."

Women, as usual, were winning more of Bronson Alcott's approbation than men, even when preachers, could ever hope for. The reasons lay deep, and were perhaps congenital. Almost certainly they were related to his sharply contrasted feelings toward his own mother and father. Something may have been added by the conscious effort he made in all his teaching to imitate the methods of an ideal mother, as Pestalozzi also had done. At any rate, Bronson Alcott was a gyneolater. His worship of women was one of his most decided American traits. As though he himself were not always as pure as the driven snow in thought and word and deed, he went up and down the world for more than eighty years without ever losing the conviction that women had somehow monopolized "purity." He used the word "pure" by far too often, and never analyzed what he meant by it—perhaps because he thought it would be an impure thing to do. "Pure"? That was what women were, always, and by nature —or at any rate would be if men would let them alone. It was what men might aspire to be, rather hopelessly and from far, far away.

To find a woman who was something more was at first an unpleasant surprise. Alcott called upon Elizabeth Palmer Peabody, then assisting William Russell at Roxbury in a school for young ladies, after he had been in Boston some three months. He did not like her. What he took to be the extreme "negligence" of her manners seemed to him studied and artificial. "She may perhaps

[127]

aim," he said, "at being 'original,' and fail in her attempt by be
coming offensively assertive. On the whole there is, we think
too much of the man and too little of the woman in her familiarit
and freedom, her affected indifference of manner. Yet after al'
she is interesting."

Miss Peabody's offensive assertion probably amounted to n
more than having ideas of her own, and some months later Alco
repeated his visit with better results.

> I was much pleased [he wrote in his Journal] with
> the thoughts expressed in the course of this interview.
> Miss Peabody is certainly a very sensible lady. She has
> a mind of a superior order. In its range of thought, in
> the philosophical discrimination of its character, I
> have seldom if ever found a female mind to equal it.
> Her notions of character, the nicety of analysis, her
> accurate knowledge of the human mind, are remarka-
> bly original and just. Her views of morals are very
> liberal and elevated. I was better pleased with her as a
> whole than I had expected to be, and shall repeat my
> visits, at her request.

So began a friendship which lasted, with a brief interruptio
for more than fifty years. When she first met Alcott, Elizabet
Palmer Peabody was one of the ablest and most thoughtf
teachers in America, and she had, moreover, one of the mo:
alert and well-stored minds in Boston. So far as what is ordinari
called knowledge is concerned she knew far more than Alcott di
Certainly, too, she knew more about his teaching, from firstham
observation, than any other person has ever known. Therefore
is a matter of some significance that she should have bowed
Bronson Alcott as her superior, should have been glad to serv
as his assistant and to take elaborate notes upon his teachi
method. "From the first time I ever saw you with a child," s
once said to Alcott in a private letter, "I have felt and declar

[128]

that you had more genius for education than I ever saw, or expected to see. I am vain enough to say that you are the only one I ever saw who, I soberly thought, surpassed myself in the general conception of this divinest of arts."

These are kind words, whatever one may think of their wisdom; and one hopes that Alcott recalled them at a later time when Miss Peabody showed herself to be something less than a heroine. She was not stoutly courageous. If there was "too much of the man" in her mind, there was quite enough of the woman in her tremulous, timorous heart. She had little of the fierce fidelity of Margaret Fuller; but at any rate she never lost the respect for Bronson Alcott that had grown in her at these first interviews. Half a century later, when she was everywhere spoken of with affectionate pride as "the Grandmother of Boston," E. P. Peabody would sit all day long in her special chair at the Concord School of Philosophy listening to the learned men that Mr. Alcott had brought together—and nod, and seem to sleep, and then, when the lecture was over, show that she had understood it better than anyone.

Bronson Alcott was succeeding well enough with Miss Peabody, but he was succeeding wonderfully and beyond all expectation with Miss Abigail May. He had asked her, as we have seen, not to press her application for an assistant's position at Salem Street because he hoped that she might be with him at a larger and better school. His reason for this hope, so far as he states it, was the purely professional one that he knew of "no young lady equally intelligent on the subject of infant education, and no one feeling a deeper interest in the welfare of the young." When the plans for the new school matured, however, she thought best to write to her brother for advice. The Reverend May replied, judiciously, that he could see "no other objection than the remarks and opinions of the world." A man, he said, might bid defiance to these; a woman cannot without the greatest danger. The circumstances of our acquaintance with Mr. Alcott, and his having gone to Boston at my suggestion and with my recommendation, would lead a censorious world to ascribe selfish views both to myself and you, if you were now to unite with him in his school. For this reason, and for this alone, I decidedly advise you to relinquish the plan altogether."

She did relinquish the plan, and retired to Brookline—which was not, after all, a very long walk from Boston; but another plan, or hope, of hers was not so easily abandoned. At the end of his letter her brother had said, rather prophetically: "Don't distress yourself about his poverty. His mind and heart are so much occupied with other things that poverty and riches do not seem to concern him." No; Mr. Alcott's poverty did not distress her— except that she would like to share it. As the August days came and went, and he often found his way through the fields and over the hills to Brookline, she began to think that this high privilege might be hers.

Reading the letters and journal entries written at the time by these two frank and simple souls, one has no difficulty in discovering which of the two it was that led and which that followed happily after. In his boyhood, as we have seen, Bronson had had little to do with girls, and that little only when they sought him out. At the time of life when other country youths went courting he had been able to go through some of the preliminary motions of that process only when protected by the ruinously splendid coat from Broadway; so that now, at twenty-nine, he had no practice, no confidence, and it is not even certain that he quite knew what was happening. "Visited Miss May at Brookline," he wrote on the seventh of August—

The scenery about Boston, and particularly at Roxbury, is very fine. We enjoyed it much. Our walk occupied two hours. We spent three hours in the society of our friend, and returned at 12 improved and invigorated morally, mentally, and physically by our walk and the pleasures to which it gave access—pleasures of

[130]

a pure and unsophisticated kind which are calculated
to make one feel the value of his existence. . . . I
would give more for the influence of a pure and elevated
female mind upon the improvement of society than for
all the legislative doings of men.

Landscape! Scenery! Bronson Alcott had never mentioned
uch things before, although he had always had them about him
a great plenty. And what had the "improvement of society" to
o with the matter? But Nature was attending to that too, in
er ancient, wasteful, hit-or-miss way.

Those were brave words about the scenery of the Boston
istrict, but they were spoken in his Journal. How to speak to
Miss May herself so that she would understand how he felt?
erhaps she had never thought of such a thing! How to find out?
nd so—but his own words, written at the year's end, tell the
ory:—

The hopes which I had indulged were alternating
between doubt and certainty for a time. She was not
to assist me in the infant school. I could not see her
exclusively. I dared not express the thought which I
was indulging, for she knew too little of me. It would
be a premature advance. I must, it seemed to me, wait
for favorable circumstances to disclose the truth which
I so much desired to reveal, and ascertain its acceptance. After some thought I handed my friend my
Journal, in which from time to time I had written my
opinions and feelings regarding her. This, I thought,
would lead to a disclosure. It had the very effect which
I hoped. It led to the connection in which I now so
much rejoice, and from which I have already enjoyed
so much and anticipate the fullest felicities of this existence.

It must have been at about the first of September, 1828, that
ronson Alcott and Abigail May came to their momentous un-
erstanding, for on the second of that month Bronson wrote:—

[131]

Our friend "A" returned from Hingham. Had a most
interesting interview. I do love this good woman, and I
love her because she is good. I love her because she
loves me. She has done, and continues to do, much for
me. How can I reciprocate her goodness?

One thing that she had already done, as this extract show
was to reduce his diction, for once, to plain and honest Saxon, an
another was to induce him to speak of himself not in the editori
"we" but in the first person singular. After such a beginnin
whither might she not lead him?

And he, by way of "reciprocation," decides that " 'A' shall hav
the perusal of Gisborne's *Duties of the Female Sex* as soon as
have looked it over for her."

In October, 1828, Alcott opened his Elementary School fc
Boys in Common Street, moving later to Tremont Street, ne;
St. Paul's Church. There he had some sixteen lads between thr
and seven years of age, all from well-to-do families and each pa
ing seven dollars a quarter. This second school in Boston, mo
successful than the first, attracted even more favorable atter
tion, and the throng of visitors was so great during the summ
of 1829 that the teacher began to fear they might interfere wi
the work of his pupils. His health was not uniformly good;
owed his father seven or eight hundred dollars, which was mu
more than he was earning in a year, and he wanted to be marri
as soon as possible; yet his spirits were sustained by the succe
of his teaching and the prospering of his love.

In July, 1829, the school was visited by Frances—or "Fann
—Wright, a Scottish reformer and lecturer somewhat notorio
at the time as an advocate of free love. Alcott was well-dispos
toward her because of her close connection with Robert Owe
In particular, he was pleased with the liberal views of marria
which he understood her to advocate and which he had se

[132]

resented in Owen's *New Harmony Gazette.* A little more, and
e himself might have been an Owenite—in which case he would
ever have been a transcendentalist; but it happened that toward
he end of 1829 Robert Owen was engaged in controversy with
lexander Campbell about the evidences of Christianity, and also
hat his paper, the *New York Free Enquirer,* was at the same
me attacking the Puritan Sabbath. These matters might not
ave attracted Alcott's notice if he had been alone in the world,
ut they probably interested Miss May a good deal. So also, no
oubt, did Miss Fanny Wright's views on marriage.

Alcott himself was deeply interested when, toward the end of
he year, he was asked to teach the children of the "Free En-
uirers" or Owenites, in Boston. He was offered a salary of ten
: twelve hundred dollars, more than twice what he was then
aking, with the single stipulation that he should teach only that
hich could be "demonstrated to the senses and perceptions of
e children." That is to say, he would be expected to abandon
s appeal to the soul of childhood, his effort to form character,
s constant inculcation of his idealistic faith that the things of
e senses are but shadowy emblems and simulacra of the things
at really exist. What made the situation even more interesting,
· was still, in theory, a follower of John Locke's psychology,
nich teaches that there can be nothing in the mind but what
mes to it through the senses. This proposal of the Free En-
uirers, however, would force him, if he yielded to their tempta-
n, to follow Locke in practice! He recoiled in a sort of horror.
: instantly refused the offered position. His debts, his need
money, his wish to marry, were all ignored—and one may be
re that Miss Abigail May did not urge them upon his attention.
hat were such things in comparison with the integrity of a
n's conscience and his fidelity to a holy vocation? These Free
quirers, said he "are a low party in religion. . . . I shall have
hing to do with them."

[133]

Poor as he was, and likely as he was to remain so if he allowed such whimsies of the conscience as these to interfere with his advancement, Bronson Alcott was married, on Sunday, May twenty third, 1830, to Miss Abigail May. The ceremony was performed not by the bride's brother, as has often been asserted, but by the Reverend Francis Greenwood, at King's Chapel, and the couple went immediately to live at Newall's boarding house in Franklin Street. Two months later they received from an anonymous donor—probably either Colonel May or else the wealthy merchant Jonathan Phillips—a gift of two thousand dollars.

Bronson Alcott always paid his debts when he had money. (When, as usual, he had none, how could he?) No sooner had this unexpected windfall come to hand than he started for Connecticut with his wife, going to Spindle Hill and there paying down the full sum of his debt, together with the interest amounting to about seven hundred dollars, which went back to the lamentable failures of his peddling days. There must have been some sense of relief in that action; yet the pleasure that he might otherwise have had in it was perhaps a little blunted by the fact that the kind and patient father to whom he had really owed the money had been dead for fifteen months.

Joseph Alcox had died at the age of fifty-seven, worn out by long and rather hopeless toil. He had been the father of ten children, but none had remained to help him in his last years with the work of the shop and farm. Seven hundred dollars had been to him a very large sum—far more, probably, than had passed through his hands in any year of his life. There had never been much money on Spindle Hill. Even when it reached the market the farmer's produce brought him little. Potatoes sold at retail, 1825, for fifty cents a bushel. Beef and veal cost six cents pound to the final consumer, and pork eight cents. One need not wonder, therefore, that Joseph Alcox had been obliged to sell some part of his farm in order to raise the amount of his elder son's indebtedness.

Bronson Alcott does not mention these matters. His biographer mentions them because they must have been often in his mind during that journey with his bride to the old familiar scenes. The couple visited Bristol, Plymouth, Waterbury, Cheshire, New Haven, Meriden, Hartford, and Brooklyn. It was their wedding journey. To one of them it may have been a little sad.

There was a thing that Bronson Alcott might have done in memory of his father: to keep free of debt for the rest of his life. He had not been home a month, however, before he had made arrangements for the printing, at his own expense, of a recently written essay *On the Principles and Methods of Infant Instruction*. The one thousand copies cost him about two hundred and fifty dollars, or one half of a year's income.

Yet, after all, the printing of this essay may have been judicious advertising rather than a mere reckless extravagance. It was in fact justified by its results. Among the hundreds of copies that Alcott sent out to friends and acquaintances, a few went to Pennsylvania, where they attracted favorable attention from a group of philanthropists, mostly Quakers, then deeply interested in the new schemes for "infant education." In October there came to Boston a wealthy Quaker named Reuben Haines. He visited the little school behind St. Paul's Church, talked to the schoolmaster and to William Russell, then assisting Alcott as a teacher of reading and enunciation, and admired the practical application of Quaker principles, the patient waiting for the "inner light," which he found there. Before leaving the city he invited Alcott and Russell to establish a school in Germantown, near Philadelphia, giving them to understand that he would be their financial sponsor. They accepted at once.

Upon the whole, it was a fortunate thing for Alcott, and for many others, that they did so. The exciting talk at the boarding house—Bronson and his wife had by this time moved to Mrs. Lyons' establishment in Atkinson Street—and the steadily climbing fever of reform throughout the city were drawing the school-master more and more into those external affairs in which his real strength certainly did not lie. On the fifteenth of October he had heard a young firebrand called William Lloyd Garrison lecture on slavery at Julien Hall, and had been tremendously excited. All the wise and quiet counsels on that topic that he had gathered during his long talks with the Virginian planters were swept suddenly away by the speaker's indignation. He and his brother May had rushed up, after the lecture, to shake hands with Garrison, and Alcott himself had written a glowing account of what he had heard—an account which Editor Nathan Hale of the *Daily Advertiser* had for some reason declined to print. On the eighth of November he and four or five other enthusiasts —these were Mrs. Alcott's brother Samuel May, her cousin Samuel Sewall, Mr. William Blanchard, Mr. Isaac Knapp, and the Reverend Mr. Collier—met with Garrison at Sewall's rooms in State Street and there founded what they afterwards called the "Preliminary Anti-Slavery Society." All this was most interesting, highly exciting, and in time it might come to something important; but to Bronson Alcott as a personality, a character, "Mind," it could have brought little but a steadily shallowing superficiality.

Boston, to him, was a delight and a seduction. In two years he had come to love the city—though not, indeed, for the plain dignity of her cobblestoned streets, for the charm of those Colonial houses that gleamed forth in the clear morning light as though carved out of silver, or for the embracing breath of the sea. His senses, though he had them and would one day use them even here, were not yet awakened. He loved and praised Boston as the capital of the Country of the Mind. For her he wrote a little prose-poem:—

There is a city in our world upon which the light of the sun of righteousness has risen. There is a sun which beams in its full meridian splendor upon it. Its

[136]

influences are quickening and envigorating the souls that dwell within it. It is the same from which every pure stream of thought and purpose and performance emanates. It is the city that is set on high. It cannot be hid. It is Boston!

These were admirable sentiments, in which at least sixty thousand persons, even at the time when they were set down, would have heartily concurred. And yet, for Bronson Alcott, the mood behind them was a little dangerous. His almost boyish delight in being in the thick of things would probably, if he had remained in Boston at this time, have kept him twirling every year a little more breathlessly and thoughtlessly until he had become a perfect committee-man, of the sort that "gets things done" without particularly caring what things they are. He would soon be thirty, and he had never yet enjoyed one period of quiet in which to sort and reject and choose his thoughts. His mind was still a rag bag of conjectures vivid and dim, so that, as we have seen, he could refuse, with a sort of horror, to teach in practical accordance with a psychological doctrine which, so far as he knew, he still theoretically held. His reading, slight in amount, had been done in a scrambling hand-to-mouth fashion, without regular access to any large collection of books. Not only was his mind undisciplined but he had never come into close contact with any mind that was not. He had spent some memorable evenings, to be sure, at Dr. Channing's house on Mount Vernon Street, and the talk there had struck out sparks that set his thoughts ablaze; but this had not been what he chiefly needed. Stimulus, mental excitement, the "sting that bids not sit nor stand but go!"—of all this he had experienced, like most Americans, enough. Would there come a chance for quiet thinking? If not—well, then it would not matter; for Bronson Alcott would soon be forgotten.

Reuben Haines arrived, with his attractive proposal. In two months Alcott was in Philadelphia, living at Mrs. Anstie's house,

91 South Third Street, and meeting people—Robert Vaux, Dr. Keagy, M. M. Carle, Robert Walsh, Dr. Furness, Dr. Rush, Dr. McClelland, John Vaughn, Matthew Carey, and many others. He was laying plans, writing letters to scores of correspondents, reading lectures before the newly formed Philadelphia Association of Teachers, even attending parties. This would never do. Philadelphia itself would never do. The newcomer was at first cautiously polite in the comments he entrusted to his Journal; but still, what a contrast with Boston! If that was the Capital of Mind, then this must be the Metropolis of Body.

> The subjects most cultivated here, and upon which conversation most generally turns [he wrote], seem to be the physical sciences; while those most discussed in Boston are the metaphysical and ethical. . . . The more wealthy classes dwell in expensive edifices, and form an aristocracy of which wealth, rather than intelligence, is the more prominent quality.

In February the Alcotts took lodgings at Mrs. Stuckarts' house in Germantown, where, on the sixteenth of March, their first child, Anna, was born. To the father this was an event of prime importance. Although the instinct of paternity was strong in him, it was not so much an emotional as an intellectual and spiritual event. Of its physical details he said not one word ever in the privacy of his Journal; and indeed he was seldom to refer to such things when his other children were born or expected. Mrs. Alcott attended to all such matters, leaving him free to speculate upon their astonishing results. Yesterday there had been only two of them; but now, amazingly, there were three. Oh, How? Why? Whence? And Whither?

Since the surprising advent of Cain, very much the same sort of thing has happened, on the physical level, to a large number of men, and to many of these there may have come a wild surmise or two as they have gazed down for the first time upon their first

[138]

sons or daughters. One may doubt, however, whether the birth of an eldest child has ever struck any man more "of a heap" than that of his daughter Anna did Bronson Alcott. In one sense he was prepared for it: he had been thinking about children for a long time. But he had been thinking about them, without realizing the fact, in two contradictory ways. In the first place, there was the way of John Locke's psychology, which nearly everyone in Alcott's time took for granted, just as he had done. This taught that there could be nothing in the mind which had not come through the senses; and from this it would follow that a new-born child, spiritually or intellectually considered, is a cipher, a blank, practically non-existent. As a consistent Lockian, Alcott should have said to himself as he stared at his daughter Anna, that he had before him nothing more than a small female animal which gave some hint or promise of belonging to the genus known as *homo sapiens*. But he was not, as he now began to discern, a consistent Lockian at all. How about those lines of Wordsworth's Ode—"Our birth is but a sleep and a forgetting"? How about all this eager questioning of young children—the younger the better—that he had been engaged in almost from the day he began to teach? And why had he so instantly, almost instinctively, rejected that flattering offer from the Owenites, when they had asked him to teach their children nothing but what could be demonstrated to their senses?

In something like this way Alcott discovered that his thoughts about children did not hang together. He was willing to contradict himself about many things, but not about a thing so fundamental as the nature of childhood. And so he must do some thinking. He set himself, there in Germantown, using his own daughter as his theme, for a long spell of "deep-down-diving and much-mud-upbringing thought."

Fortunately, he had the leisure. He and William Russell had forgotten to inquire whether, when they got to Germantown, they would find the educational field unoccupied, and Reuben

[139]

Haines had neglected to inform them. They discovered when they reached there that a school of manual arts and an "Academy" were already in operation, and the result was that, while Russell conducted a "female department" at the Academy, Alcott could find only some five children to teach. He had therefore a good deal of free time, even after delivering sundry lectures "On the Power of the Mind" before Russell's young ladies. Furthermore, although there was no danger of his being distracted by an excess of the world's goods, his domestic arrangements were unusually comfortable and pleasing, as Reuben Haines had given him the use, rent free, of his Rookery Cottage. Mrs. Alcott delighted in her "large grounds, with a beautiful serpentine walk shaded by pines, firs, cedars, apple, pear, peach, and plum trees, and a long cedar hedge from the back to the front fence." And then there were no reforms going on in Germantown, no committees to attend, no Unitarian ministers to hear. What, in fact was there to do, except to read and think? For the next two years Bronson did chiefly that.

One may be wrong in the conjecture, for it is no more than that, but the evidence certainly indicates that the starting point or pivot for this long bout of thinking was his daughter Anna. Whence had she come, and what was she? It was a naïve question perhaps even a stupid one. It was one of those questions to which very clever people feel quite sure that they know all the answers. But Bronson Alcott was not clever. There was something like stupor in the way he mulled his question over, dreamed about it vaporized about it in his Journal, and vainly strove to forget it. He stared at his infant daughter as stupidly, if one likes the word, as Isaac Newton had stared at the fallen apple. Yes, Newton and Alcott had this in common, had this in distinction from all very clever people, that they did not know how the two objects which had attracted their attention had got there—and they knew that they did not know.

Alcott set to work on his problem quite as scientifically as New ton had done. Before Anna was ten days old he had commenced "A Record of Observations on the Phenomena of Life as Developed in the History of an Infant During the First Year of Its Existence," his intention being to set down with the minutest accuracy every significant motion, every change of mood, every evidence of dawning mind, that his child might show. So far as he was aware, nothing of the sort had ever been done before; but thirty years later, he was to learn that a similar task was being performed by a man called Charles Darwin. The work seemed important to him chiefly because it might help him to answer his question about the origin of the "soul," but also because it should provide some substantial facts upon which to generalize about the relations between mind and body. He was, for once, a fact-finder, and he was engaged upon a task of scientific research in the field now known as psychology. Not only did he conceive the problem, but for a time he held himself to something like the patient method, which professional psychologists were not to undertake and apply for more than half a century to come.

Alcott was patient in this scientific task. The bound volumes of manuscript containing his observations on the infancy of his daughters Anna, Louisa, and Elizabeth are still in existence to show that he was remarkably accurate and self-abnegating, up to a point, in the observation and recording of fact. It is with a sort of compassionate respect that one watches him fumbling about in the chaos of a science not yet clearly defined, a student utterly without training and quite alone. The man who left school when he was thirteen and who has spent most of his adult years either in peddling "Yankee notions" or in talking to children, has no clear ideas about scientific method. Having isolated one definite problem, he finds that it leads to a thousand others and stretches out into darkness on every side. In the hope of throwing a few rays of light into that darkness he reads Broussais' *Physiology,* Jackson's *Principles of Medicine,* and George Combe's

[141]

Phrenology and *Constitution of Man*. It was at this time, in fact, that Alcott formed the habit, which lasted all his life, of reading every book of science he could get hold of and hope to understand. Yet they did not help him much. At times he was almost discouraged. Before Anna reached her first birthday he was writing in his Journal, somewhat wearily:—

> Continued Observations on an Infant. . . . Still there is much of darkness yet resting around the primal operation of the soul. I cannot report its historical progress in a satisfactory manner. Much is left to dim conjecture. There is wanting an accurate medium of psychological measurement. This, I imagine, is to be attained by the study of physiological junctions which are nearer the source and springs of vitality. As preparatory to the appreciation of vital phenomena, I intend to investigate the science of man as presented in the theories of the physiologists, and of phrenology.

These are the words of an outsider—and Bronson Alcott, wherever he went, whatever he did, was almost always to be that. They are the words of an ignorant man who is attacking, perhaps largely because of his ignorance, a problem—what is the relation between mind and body?—which has puzzled and tormented and overwhelmed all the philosophers and sages. But it is important to see, also, what these words are not. One cannot call them the words of a charlatan. They are not derived from "inner light." They do not show any of that contempt for observed fact or for solidly based induction which is often attributed, rightly or wrongly to the "transcendental" type of mind. And finally, these are not the words of a "monist." Thus far, at any rate, Alcott has withstood the temptation to solve the problem of mind's relation to matter by the simple erasure of one of the two terms. He is still convinced that reality is of two kinds, and that, as a certain friend of his was to say, "There be two laws discrete, not reconciled."

But yet, when all is said, one must admit that Alcott had very little natural ability, as he certainly had little training, in the patient humdrum of scientific observation. The facts he strove so earnestly to gather were so many seeds of thought that shot up overnight like the gigantic beanstalk of the children's fable. He might start out to see what his nine-months-old Anna would do with a doll, but before he could set pen to paper he would be reminded by her conduct of something abstract and vague and distant which could be expressed only in the most grandiloquent of capitalized Latin derivatives.

Alcott knew this foible of his mind, and occasionally deplored it.

> I sit down [he said], to make some remarks on the lives and circumstances of my children, but ere I am aware I have left the consideration of them as individuals and have merged their separate existences into the common life of the Spirit. I have left their terrestrial life, with the varied phenomena that typify its action, and am roaming at large over the domain of the celestial world—beholding not only these, my children, in the gladsome existence there, but also the unnumberable children of the Infinite Parent himself, the common Father.

Or we may take an example from that elaborate manuscript called "Psyche," into which the "Observations" finally grew:—

> Behold the babe! It is a flame of light! Behold a halo round its head! Yea, its life is as the flame when it struggles amidst the fuel. Behold how it climbs on every fibre thereof, and doth wind itself around the billets as they crackle on the hearthstone. Restless, complaining ever at the stinted material on which it feedeth, see with what greedy instinct it eats and wrestles with its prey. Nor doth it cease the consuming work till it hath wasted its fuel and vanished from sight by fitful, flickering, unwilling strokes. Restless, idle,

[143]

flapping is its flag. Even yet in its embers doth it still hold a smouldered life, and repeat the tale of its aspiring.

Emblem of the young soul that checks its action on the coarse flesh; and, while feeding on corporal things restlessly, complainingly oft in its need, strives to ascend even while yet lingering around its joys; fading from sight while struggling to hold its grasp on corporal shows. And thus, too, doth it rise from its ashes, pleading for the skies which it ascends.

In this remarkable passage it becomes quite clear that the "Observations on an Infant" could never have been published by a journal of psychological research as a "contribution to knowledge." Alcott was certainly moving on the very road the modern mind has chiefly traveled since his time, but he was moving in the opposite direction. Facts, to him, were of course good things. First and last, he gathered and forgot a quite respectable number of them. But good for what? For points of departure, and for what they symbolized. In and for themselves they had no worth. They were mere coins of the realm of thought; and, as with the coin of the economic realm, he could not treat them as though they were really important. The "Observations on an Infant" ramified and expanded enormously. First they grew into a manuscript called "The Breath of Childhood," which was later christened "Evangele," and then they were transmogrified into a manuscript called "Psyche," shot through with genius and weighted down with intolerable dullness, which even Emerson finally decided ought not to be published. Emerson was probably right, but the work which he thus condemned to oblivion was one of the most purely "transcendental" productions of the school to which Emerson was supposed to belong.

In the very changes of title which the work underwent one can see what sort of answer Alcott was giving to his original question about the infant Anna. The possibility that she was nothing more

[144]

at least to begin with, than a small female animal had been definitely abandoned by the time the title "Psyche" was adopted. Alcott's scientific observation had resulted in his discovering, as the scientist often does, only what had been from the first in his own mind. There was never a chance, from the moment that he sat down to balance the sensational against the idealistic philosophy, of his arriving at any but his own kind—that is, the idealistic kind—of conclusion.

If there had been such a chance, William Russell would have seen that nothing came of it, for he had long been convinced that children are "beings of celestial origin and destination." William Russell was a man of power and of finely trained abilities. His scholarship appears to have been both extensive and exact, and he had perhaps the most orderly mind with which Bronson Alcott ever came into close relationship. His religious convictions, which were at the same time liberal and intense, are hard to distinguish from Alcott's own, for he too was indifferent to creeds even while he was completely possessed by the thought of indwelling deity and by a passionate devotion to Jesus as an exemplary man. With the possible exception of Dr. W. E. Channing, William Russell influenced the thought and life of Alcott more than any other personal acquaintance. His influence began, through the medium of the *American Journal of Education,* before the two men met, continued during their early association in Boston, and also into the later years of Alcott's Boston teaching, when Russell was an inmate of his house. But it was during the Germantown period, when the two were engaged together as colleagues, that Russell's mind pressed continually against that of Alcott, encouraging, reproving, shaping, and directing. He taught the teacher. One might almost say that he provided the only education, in a high sense of the word, that Alcott ever had from any living man. He changed the dreamer with a streak of genius into something like a thinker, and confirmed a transcendental tendency

[145]

which might, without his support, have been worn away and lost. In certain days that were almost the darkest of Alcott's life, William Russell was a tower of strength to him. To Russell, also, Alcott probably owed no small part of the success he made in after life in the art of public conversation—a success partially due to the beauty of his voice and to the impressive clarity and music of his speech; for, besides being a teacher of children and an educational theorist, Russell was one of the better known elocutionists and public readers in the America of his time.

Full acknowledgment of his debt to this good friend was made by Alcott again and again. Writing while he and Russell were still together at Germantown, he said:—

> There is no living individual, residing in this country, with whom a connection would in any sense be desirable beside him—none with whose thoughts I could so entirely sympathize and whose plans I could so heartily espouse. Conversation and thought with him have done more for me than any other outward advantage. I look upon our speculations during the past year as among the most valuable fruits of my life —as the beginning of a new era in my career of inquiry, and as likely to exert a predominating influence over all its subsequent stages.

Alcott's intellectual gain from this association was precisely of the sort he most needed—training in the method of thought. By nature, he was the kind of man to whom ideas occur. He came from a district of inventors, where men either had nimble wits or else went hungry and ragged. But having ideas was one good thing, and the power to weld and beat them into the tools of thought was another. Bronson Alcott was not good at welding and beating. Russell was good at it. His Scottish mind, clear and logical; his training at the University of Glasgow in mathematics, theology, metaphysics; his years of teaching others how to teach, going down into the secret places of thought which were at that time

[146]

unsurveyed, unexplored—had prepared him admirably for the task he undertook of giving the powerful but unformed mind of his friend some shape. Order, system, dialectic—that was what he was good for. He delighted in working out diagrams or paradigms of thought, showing how it moved from step to step of the syllogism, how it grew and expanded from one faculty to another, how it was ever reaching up and onward from the bare necessities of the understanding to the noblest conceptions of the creative imagination. Alcott's Journals of the Germantown period are crowded with these diagrams, so different from anything that had ever before appeared in those all-inclusive pages. "Pyramids of Being," he called them—resting on the broad base of the senses but climbing among the clouds of emotion, among the planets of fancy and the fixed stars of reason, until they reached the empyrean of Spirit, the *primum mobile* of Mind, and touched the throne of God. Russell thought that the individual soul must climb the pyramid, aspiring upward step by step. That would be natural to a Scot, liking struggle, and wishing always to base his thought solidly on tested conviction. But Alcott tended to think, rather, that the soul descends "from Heaven, which is our home." Here was the chief difference remaining between the friends after their two years of close and daily association. It was a difference that was to appear again, long after, in Alcott's relations with Emerson.

Russell's main concern was with what he called "Human Culture"—a term by which he meant the progressive development of all the human powers, beginning with the physical and ranging upward into the most spiritual and ideal. He seems to have been profoundly interested, as Alcott also was when he sat down to study his infant daughter, in the relations of body, mind, and soul. As a thoughtful elocutionist and public reader, he had pondered the mysteries of that tri-unity as he saw and felt them in their most practical aspects. How was it, he had asked himself, that a mere mouthful of air, modulated by the physical organs of speech, could warm the heart, inflame the mind, and often

[147]

change the course of a human life? Could one say that they were two quite different, separate things—Body and Spirit? For, in that case, how could they tremble and sing together in so fine a unison? There were things that a public speaker knew not by argument but from experience. Ten thousand times he had known, felt, seen, so vividly, how a thought or mood of his had taken on physical body in that marvel of incarnation that we call speech, and had then been instantly transformed again into the mood or thought of his listeners. Well, it was a continuous miracle! How explain it?

The explanation worked out by Alcott and Russell together is stated clearly enough in a passage from Alcott's Journal of 1836 which shows, throughout, and not least in the new tendency to schematization, the effect of Russell's orderly mind. "I am now finding an interest," says Alcott, writing in the heyday of his success at the Temple School, "in the phenomena of the external world." Ah, that strange world of actuality, of what most men call *"real* things"! He had been so far away that he had to be introduced to it, had to struggle to convince himself of its existence like Wordsworth rushing to the side of the road to grasp a fence-post.

I have a desire to apprehend the laws of which these phenomena are the pledge and appearance. This embraces the science of physiology. I have a dim yet assured instinct that these laws, when viewed from their true point in the vision of Spirit, will appear much more than has generally been supposed. Yes, I fancy that the hour is coming when all that moved in the mind of Jesus and prompted those sublime ideas of the soul's origin and immortality—that explored Nature and mastered its synthesis, that knew men and prescribed to the healing of the human body as well as the soul—that all this shall come out as an actual distinct Idea in the mind. I imagine that it will be possible, yea, certain, that the miracles, so-called, wrought out by this faith in the spiritual and apprehension of the material, shall be made as common facts, the necessary and natural results of spiritual laws. The study of organs and functions will, I apprehend, become but another view of the Spirit's activity in the body. Physiology is none other than the study of Spirit Incarnate. We must wed the sciences of physiology and psychology, and from these shall spring the Divine Idea which, originally one in the mind of God, he saw fit to separate and spread throughout his two-fold creation of Mind and Matter. . . . Spirit and Matter, Man and Nature, are the two members of that original undivided synthesis that is the ground and heart of the Spirit of Man. These he readeth alway—sometimes out of his own form by his understanding reason, sometimes within himself by his imaginative faith. When he reads aright, the answers are *one*. He must study both, or be semi-created, half-illuminated.

Let the members of the synthesis be typified to the eye thus:

$$\begin{array}{c} |\text{ Spirit }| \\ \text{Primordial—Original} \\ Spirit \quad | \text{ taking upon itself an organic } | \quad Body \\ \text{Spirit} \quad | \quad | \text{ Body} \\ \diagdown | \text{ Man } | \diagup \end{array}$$

Man unites the two, and exhausts their function. To the clear knowledge of Body a prior knowledge of Spirit is requisite. Having this, the study of Body becomes comparatively easy. All the elements and functions of Body are included in the elements and functions of Spirit, and revealed in a simpler and more scientific form. . . . Such is the revelation made to the mind of Jesus of Nazareth. . . . Every Spirit is a Revelation, by reason of its origin and birthright. Sell it not, and depend on others! Be temperate and appre-

[149]

hend Body. Be holy and apprehend Spirit. Be thoughtful, and unite the idea of the two in one. . . . Thus
shall a man apprehend wholes, not parts; rise to principles, not resting in things; coördinating all by the law
of the Spirit.

And so it began to appear that the dualism into which Alcott's
meditations over the infant Anna had led him was not to be a final
phase of his thought. There might indeed be "two laws . . . law
for man and law for thing," as Emerson would one day assert;
but in Alcott's matured philosophy these laws were not to be what
Emerson would call them—"discrete," and "unreconciled." They
were to be the two married and complemental phases of what
Percy Shelley had already called "the One Spirit's plastic stress."
And for this development into an enriched and bi-partite monism
Alcott had his friend Russell—that clear-thinking, hard-reading,
soundly trained, and always aspiring Scot—to thank.

He did thank him, though always as one partner speaking to or
about another. And Russell himself was apparently proud to
accept such partnership. Of his own superiorities in everything
that depends upon training, external discipline, and routine effort
he must have been aware. His knowledge of books, of the world
of men and women, and of practical affairs, was much greater than
that of his friend. And yet in this pedlar who was trying to learn
to think there was something to which he paid deep respect. Even
he, perhaps, could not name it, but he knew—as Elizabeth Peabody knew already and as Emerson was soon to discover—that
it was there. No more than William Alcott, to whom in some ways
he was the successor, would he have taken all this trouble for a
person whom he thought second-rate. His estimate of his friend
so clearly implied, is most helpful to those who cannot see that
friend directly but must depend upon reflections. Russell was one
of the many mirrors that stand all along the corridor of Alcott's
years, bending back an image of the man more exact and far more
impressive than any that we could have made for ourselves.

Anna Alcott and William Russell were two of Alcott's teachers during the Germantown period. On his thirty-third birthday, November the twenty-ninth, in 1832, there was born at the Rookery Cottage, a third teacher for him. This newcomer was called Louisa May, after one of Mrs. Alcott's dead sisters. Her advent was not quite so surprising as that of Anna had been, but the father began almost on the day of her birth that same minute observation to which he had been subjecting his elder daughter for a year and a half. There was one thing about the second child, however, which may have led him to expect rather less illumination from her: Louisa, even from her birth, was dark in eyes and hair. And she remained so. He could not quite understand that fact, or reconcile it with his confident expectation that she would be a child of light.

When Bronson Alcott went to Germantown in 1830 he was not by any means a well-read man; but when he returned to Boston in 1834 he had no reason to feel himself inferior in literary experience among a body of people who were at that time giving almost too much attention to books. For three years and a half he had read fast and far and deeply, at first under the guidance of William Russell and then under that of Dr. Channing, who in 1833 spent some time at Philadelphia. There were times during this period when Alcott seemed to be "soul-hydroptic with a sacred thirst" for books and ever more books. Thus, during the summer of 1833 he left his family at Germantown and went to lodge in an attic room in Library Street, so that he might be near the Philadelphia and Loganian Libraries; and there he shut himself in for two months to read, in a sort of frenzy. His discovery of Plato at this time—"Plato I had long wished to read, but could never before find a translation"—awoke in him a strong emotional excitement. When he closed Coleridge's *Aids to Reflection* after the first of many perusals he said at once, and with exact prevision, that it would mark an epoch in his intellectual career.

[151]

Yet one might easily overestimate the importance of this long bout of reading, as Alcott himself often did in looking back upon it. In the very first of his annual Journals Alcott had reminded himself, using terms that vaguely foreshadow a familiar passage in Emerson's *Self-Reliance,* that books are always to be used with caution and independently. No book, not even Coleridge or Plato or Boehme, ever swept him out of the steady current of his own thought.

And one reason for this is that he read hardly at all to be informed, or even to be instructed, but chiefly for confirmation of what in some sense he already knew. To a book that sharpened and defined or even extended his own existing ideas, he could of course be grateful; but one that ran quite counter to his thought, and that could not be pulled over, as he tried to pull Bacon's *Novum Organum,* into at least a semblance of agreement with himself, was to him as good as nonexistent. Reading, to him, was, like his conversation, a "sharing of views"; it was never an argument or a contention. If a book agreed with him, he frequently wrote some words of congratulation to the author in the margin; and if it did not, he politely said nothing.

Alcott came to his reading in the Philadelphia and Germantown years with a mind already biassed, as we have seen, in favor of the idealistic point of view. Without clearly knowing it, he had departed from the orthodox psychology of John Locke even before he left Boston, and his associations with Russell and his meditations over the cradle of Anna and Louisa had taken him farther on the road to a pure "idealism." The discovery of Plato and Coleridge, not to mention Plotinus, Proclus, Boehme, Berkeley, and Kant, was exciting to him, therefore, less because they gave him new ideas than because they confirmed his old ones. They made him see that he was not unique and that he need no longer feel lonely, because in the past, at any rate, there had been such men as he. His experience was like that of a man who has been following a trail so nearly obliterated as to make him doubt whether he is not the first who has ever walked there, and who then discovers that the faint path underfoot was once a wide and crowded highway.

There is a degree and a kind of interest attaching to Bronson Alcott's use of books, especially during his residence in Germantown and Philadelphia, hardly to be found in the lives of other literary New Englanders such as Emerson, Longfellow, Holmes, and even Bryant, who may almost be said to have been born in libraries. Intellectual influences with which these men were familiar from their boyhood reached him only in his mature years, so that in his career we occasionally see something like the first full impact of a great writer or of a grand conception upon a mind already formed.

The spectacle has a certain fascination. One watches Alcott with a kind of compassionate envy as he blunders about among books, scarcely knowing the good from the bad at first and yet making the most startling discoveries. He comes so late into the world's intellectual treasury that one fears he may not have time to use what he finds there; but it is to his advantage that he comes with an eager mind, with a curiosity unblunted, and with none of that quite hopeless ignorance, at any rate, which is the curse of the overschooled. Like Socrates, he knows at least that he does not know. And he has also this advantage, that he comes in a mood of veneration—not, indeed, for the past as such, or even for scholarship, but for the noble minds of all nations, all ages, and for the occasional grandeurs of human nature. Certain few and mighty names have long been hanging in the sky of his imagination, scattering a faint luster not so much like stars as like dim nebulæ, upon his thought; but now, while he reads and reads in his attic room, many a new planet "swims into his ken"—Plato, Pythagoras, Boehme, Coleridge—and he greets each one as it appears with all the delight of a first discoverer. Names that the "educated man" feels it his high privilege to ignore and forget burn their way into the mind and heart of this self-made man where they are to be forgotten never. He is discovering not mere books but lifelong intellectual companions.

In his handling of books Bronson Alcott was always eager and enthusiastic, but he never became professionally expert. One may not call him a superficial reader, considering how swiftly he could pass by all the flying buttresses and outer walls of an author's thought and penetrate to its innermost secret and central shrine. One would certainly hesitate to call him a lazy reader, for the electric flash of intuition by which he pierced to essences of meaning revealed in him one of the highest forms of mental energy that we know. Evidence, however, and proof, argument, the whole apparatus of the discursive reason, interested and interrupted him not at all. He assumed that the foremost minds of the past had thought precisely as he did, by sudden and unpredictable leaps of "inspiration." Why waste one's time, therefore, upon the so-called "proofs," coldly manufactured as a mere afterthought, for something that God had said? The sublime truths that books might teach were enthroned forever in the clouds, and all that human understanding could do was to build under them a quite unnecessary foundation.

Speaking from the point of view of rigorous scholarship, one must admit that Bronson Alcott's reading habits left much to be desired. He turned over and tumbled up and down at least a thousand of the most influential books in the world, and his reading took him beyond these into many an odd corner of literature really abstruse and recondite, yet the total result never amounted to anything in the least like erudition. His faculty for ignoring and forgetting the innumerable things that he considered unimportant approached the phenomenal. So indifferent was he to matters of detail, of range, and of total structure that he never really mastered the thought of any considerable mind, ancient or modern. This being so, one is tempted to set him down as a mere tyro and fumbler, incorrigibly haphazard, inveterately opposed to hard mental toil. But then, just as one is about to reach this final decision, Alcott shows once more his power to seize a thinker's central conception, a writer's king-idea, and to hold it fast through all its transformations—as the heroes of Greek fable gripped Proteus, the Old Man of the Sea, and held to him until he returned to his proper shape and gave them an answer. Thus Alcott could not possibly have given a clear outline of Plato's philosophy, but he could make the Platonic world of pure idealism seem to Emerson "as solid as Massachusetts." The intricate subtleties of Swedenborg escaped him almost entirely, but in his own thinking there is a remarkably consistent exemplification of the great mystic's pivotal conception, "correspondence." He read the *Aids to Reflection* over and over for many years without attaining a comprehensive view of Coleridge's metaphysical position, and yet through all those years Coleridge was a guiding star of his intellectual journey.

Perhaps it is best to say, then, that as a reader Bronson Alcott had neither talent nor training, so that he was obliged to get on as best he could with a thin streak of genius.

His main defect in the use of books is clearly traceable to his almost total lack of the historic sense. He had no feeling for the literary or intellectual past as such, but lived in an everlasting now. He did not even care to know how the thought of Plato and Pythagoras had been shaped by the environment of old Athens and Magna Græcia, or how large a part of what they had said was the inevitable expression of their respective ages. Those majestic ancient voices came to him as though from the next room, and all that he valued in their message was that which taught him how to live a better life in the New England of the nineteenth century. He read them, that is to say, precisely as they would have wished to be read; and of course that was not "scholarly" at all. From the academic point of view it was both ignorant and absurd. And from the pietistic point of view this habit could become positively distressing when it caused Alcott to talk about the words of Jesus not as though he had read them in a book, quite special and sacrosanct, as spoken by some semi-mythological person said to have walked and talked by Galilee and Jordan, but precisely as though he had heard them that very morning from a man whom he had met out by Fresh Pond or beside the River Charles.

"What do these words mean *now?*" was always his question. From Jesus, Pythagoras, Plato, and all the other "Minds" of the burnt-out ages he took what he thought he might require for daily use, and left the rest to the learned antiquarians of Church and College.

Yes, it was most distressing and absurd, this incurable contemporaneity; and yet of course there was something to be said for it. There is a good deal to be said for the inflexible determination to summon all the privileged past before the judgment-seat of the present and to make it show cause why it should not be forgotten. Such has always been the true classic way, as opposed to the romantic. It was the way, for example, of ancient Athens herself. And in the America of the eighteen-thirties it was by no means confined to Bronson Alcott. One sees it also in Emerson. The transcendental movement as a whole could have had no better motto than Emerson's pregnant sentence "The sun shines to-day also." Indeed the whole country—at least outside of College and Church—was living, then, in the conviction which a certain magnificently "successful" man of our own time is said to have summed up in the serviceable phrase, "History is bunk!"

Of Alcott's steadily increasing interest in books of science something has already been said. He read them not for crude information, of course, and not primarily for new ideas about the natural world, but for suggestions of those "correspondences" between matter and spirit for which, in the central decades of his life, he was always searching. As one may study the hidden mind of Shakespeare through the works which that mind produced, so Alcott tried to examine the natural universe in quest of the

[156]

spiritual world which he believed to be its source and model. Of course there was nothing new in this. Even so early as the Germantown period some hint of the method may have reached him from Swedenborg; but it was a method quite in harmony with the cardinal theory of eighteenth-century deists, that nature is the sufficient revelation of spiritual truth. For that matter, it was in keeping with mediæval conceptions of the "microcosm" and "macrocosm," as well as with the more exalted claims put forth by certain thoughtful alchemists. There is abundant evidence, furthermore, that ancient and even prehistoric minds tended to see the universe as double—"on the earth the broken arcs, in the heaven the perfect round." However he may have reached it, Alcott was walking here too on an old worn path of thought, making those startling discoveries of things that have always been known which are open only to the self-made man.

While he was reading such books as Bartollet's *Chemical Affinity,* Erasmus Darwin's *Temple of Nature,* and Gardiner's *Mechanics, Hydrostatics, and Pneumatics,* Alcott kept pencil and paper beside him, and the product of such reading would usually be a sheaf of notes, entirely metaphysical in theme, which bore no readily discoverable relation to the book he had in hand. He did not yet know that the same method had been used for years by the English transcendentalist James Pierrepont Greaves, and also by Coleridge. He only knew that it was suited to the ways of his own mind.

The most important book in the literature of education that came under Alcott's eye at Germantown was Dr. E. Biber's *Henry Pestalozzi,* a thoughtful exposition of the Swiss schoolmaster's life, opinions, and practice. From this book alone, read within a year of its appearance in London and two years before he opened the Temple School, Alcott might have derived, if he had not already found them out, nearly all his own theories of teaching.

Since his departure from Spindle Hill Alcott had been neglecting general literature. Now he read the poetry of Coleridge, Wordsworth, Shelley, Byron, and even Keats. Shelley's life and

[157]

his social and political theories attracted him strongly, for he had not yet outgrown his enthusiasm for Godwin's *Political Justice;* but of Shelley the poet he was never, any more than Emerson, to guess the height or the depth. John Keats remained to him hardly more than a name, although it should be remembered that Keats was hardly so much as that to most book-minded Americans of the time. Byron, as one might expect, he valued not as the ribald titan who wrote *Don Juan* but as the humanitarian martyr of Missolonghi. Only Coleridge and Wordsworth were read with anything approaching a full comprehension. These poets he made his own. To both of them he owed, and acknowledged, a large intellectual debt.

During his years in Pennsylvania, as in later life, Alcott read much of Hazlitt—never learning, however, that the great essayist had spent some years of his boyhood near Boston. He read also, with keen delight, Lamb's *Essays of Elia.* Dr. Johnson's *Lives of the Poets* was recommended to him not only by his own strong interest in all biography but by the fact that Johnson was his wife's favorite author. One is sorry to record that Mrs. Alcott misled him for a time into an enthusiasm for the earlier novels such as *Falkland* and *Pelham,* of Bulwer-Lytton. Sir Walter Scott he seems to have missed almost entirely; and of other novelists, at least until the heyday of Dickens and Thackeray, he knew little. He was deeply interested in a certain anonymous writer whose articles were appearing at this time in the *Edinburgh* and in the *Foreign Review*—a writer who, he thought, might be the same Thomas Carlyle whose translation of *Wilhelm Meister* he had greatly enjoyed. In *Fraser's Magazine,* beginning in February, 1833, he found a series of papers called *Sartor Resartus,* written in an amazingly vigorous, even violent style. Were these perhaps from the same hand? He read Carlyle's *Life of Schiller,* Fuseli's *Lectures on Painting,* More's *Utopia,* and Robert Burton's *Anatomy of Melancholy.* One sees that his appetite was omnivorous. As he had done on Spindle Hill, he read whatever printed hing might fall in his way. He tried to read even the plays of Shakespeare, but could make little of them either then or later.

The most important of Alcott's reading in the Pennsylvania period was that done in the field of philosophy. Notwithstanding what has been said of his thoroughly independent and inexpert handling of books, one must admit that it was a red-letter day in his career when he first opened Coleridge's *Aids to Reflection*. A copy of that work in the edition by James T. Marsh, published at Burlington, Vermont, in 1829, had been given him by William Russell in 1830, although it was not read until August, 1832. But then, what a burst of acclaim! "In Coleridge," he wrote, "there are passages of imposing beauty and deep wisdom. He seems to have studied men more thoroughly, and to understand them better, than any previous poetic writer, unless it be Wordsworth; and his prose writings are full of splendid ideas clothed in the most awful and inspiring imagery. There is in this man's soul a deep well of wisdom, and it is a wisdom not of earth. No writer ever benefited me more than he has done. The perusal of 'Aids to Reflection' and 'The Friend' forms a new era in my mental and psychological life." Nothing is said here or elsewhere about the effect of Marsh's introduction and notes, but Alcott's copy exists to-day, sown from end to end with marginal jottings, to show that he read them as carefully as the text. This book, which might be called the Old Testament of American transcendentalism, as Emerson's *Nature* was the New, never ceased to delight and stimulate Bronson Alcott. Four years after the first perusal he was reading it for the fifth time, and fifty years later it was still in the list of his annual reading. Taking it down from the shelf to-day and finding it fragmentary, inconclusive, and rather heavily theological, one is at a loss to make out what Alcott found in it; and yet there can be no doubt that he found much. It helped to shape his mind and to fix upon him the habit of meditation. One sees the effect of it even in the paragraphic jottings, each of them under its separate rubric, of his private Journals.

[159]

Coleridge's *The Friend* and his *Biographia Literaria* were almos
equally valued, the one for its passages on philosophical metho
and the other for the chapters on creative imagination; but on
would say that *Aids to Reflection* stood next to *Pilgrim's Progres*
among the golden books of Alcott's choice.

Regarding ancient philosophers there can be, of course, n
doubt. It was in May, 1833, and in Mrs. Eaton's attic in Librar
Street, Philadelphia, that the Connecticut pedlar first opene
Plato's *Cratylus, Phœdo, Timœus,* and *Parmenides,* in the trans
lations by Thomas Taylor. When recording the event many year
after, he felt it necessary to write in red ink, as he did elsewher
only in commemorating his marriage, the births of his daughter:
the opening of the Civil War, and the assassination of Lincoln. A
about the same time he read Taylor's *Proclus* and *Plotinu*
Berkeley's *Alciphron* and *Theory of Vision* followed, with Shafte:
bury's *Characteristics* and Herder's *Outline of Philosoph*
Aristotle's *Politics* and his *Metaphysics* he had known even i
Boston, but now he reread them. Also he went through, not f
the first time, the major works of Francis Bacon, whom he i
sisted upon regarding as an idealistic philosopher who "beheld a
things in the concrete"—an opinion for which he found son
support in Coleridge's *Friend.* Toward the end of 1833 he re:
Wellick's *Elements of Kant's Philosophy* and also *A View*
Professor Kant's Principles by F. A. Nitsch, one of Kant's pupi
and professional associates. From the latter work he copied no le
than fifty-seven pages, so that he was by no means depende
upon French and English interpreters of the German fath
of transcendentalism. Cousin's *History of Philosophy* he h:
known since 1831, and had not liked. Okely's *Life of Jac*
Behmen and Swedenborg's *Treatise on the Nature of Infl:*
must also be mentioned as books read at this time which had
highly important bearing upon his later thought.

These are about one-fourth of the works that Alcott skimm
or studied during the three and a half years of his stay in Pen

[160]

ylvania. Several of them were read more than once even during
hat period, and from a number of others he made large extracts
n manuscript. A few, like the *Aids to Reflection,* were in his own
mall but slowly growing library, and some of these he was to
ead nearly every year during the rest of his life. It is clear that
e must have read rapidly. It is also clear to one who has examined
`hat now remains of his private library that he did not always feel
` necessary to read quite through even a book in which he was
eeply interested. But perhaps the most important thing to
bserve about this reading is the remarkable pertinence of almost
ll of it to the precise needs, at the time being, of the reader.
low much of the credit for this should be given to William Russell
nd to Dr. Channing there is no way of making sure; but it is
ertain that little time was lost in it and that there were few
lse starts. Alcott went at literature as though consciously draw-
g a beeline across the intellectual country that lay between his
wn mental position in 1830 and that of the "Transcendental
`lub" of 1836. Even to-day, no one with this purpose in mind
uld possibly make out for him, from the books then available, a
etter course of reading than that which he somehow found and
llowed. One is reminded of what Emerson once said about his
iend, that he could go into any strange library and lay his hand
once upon the one book that he most needed to read, even if he
d not know the language. And Alcott never knew any language
ut his own.

In these three ways, then, by the help of his infant daughters
d William Russell and a host of books, Bronson Alcott was
rrying on his education. In the meantime he was teaching; but
e little school at Germantown did not in any sense flourish. By
e death of Reuben Haines a few months after their arrival
lcott and Russell lost the patronage and support upon which
ey had counted. Alcott's schoolroom became to him more and
ore a psychological laboratory.

[161]

One of the best things he did at Germantown was to carry o
a correspondence with an eight-year-old pupil, then living in hi
home, by the name of Elizabeth Lewis. In later life he was to be
come a thorough master in the difficult and delicate art of writin
to children, but one cannot say that what appears to have bee
his first effort in that art was brilliantly successful. "My dea
Elizabeth," he begins, in terms painfully similar to those of h
boyish correspondence with Cousin William: "We have frequentl
spoken of the advantages which might be derived from epistolar
correspondence judiciously conducted. That we may participa
in those advantages, let us commence our correspondence a
once." The little girl, in her replies, stands on tiptoe as long as sl
is able, but finally, in her sixth "epistle," breaks down and cal
for "clear and simple words." She gets them; and from that poi:
the correspondence runs its course of twenty-six letters with mo
attention on Alcott's part to the true amenities of the occasic
Elizabeth writes amazingly well upon the most exalted ethic
themes, and it would be pleasant to think that she had some pa
in teaching the rather ponderous pedagogue his long and diffict
lesson in simplicity.

Alcott was to learn that lesson fairly well; but the one th
stands next to it in the Book of Life, the lesson of humor,
never mastered. Perhaps he did not have very good teachers
Cousin William, William Russell, and Ralph Waldo Emersc
And yet someone was being humorous when there appeared in t
little school that Alcott opened in Philadelphia, in the summer
1834, a lad, nine years old, by the name of Charles Godfr
Leland. A more charming and delightful misalliance has selde
been imagined by the President of the Immortals, the Spirit
Comedy, or whoever it is by whom such arrangements are ma
Leland, writing in his *Memoirs,* remembers Bronson Alcott
"the most eccentric man who ever took on himself to train a
form the youthful mind." He recalls that Alcott "read thoroug]
into us the *Pilgrim's Progress,* Quarles' *Emblems,* Northco1

[162]

ables, much Shakespeare, Wordsworth, Coleridge, and Milton—
ll of which sunk into my very soul, educating me 'ideally' as no
oy perhaps in Philadelphia had ever been educated, at the utter
ost of all real 'education.' " His words are not quite clear in
urport, for, after all, any teacher who could make the literature
ere named sink into the "very soul" of a boy who was to become
ne of America's more popular verse-writers was certainly carry-
g on, however eccentrically, an educational process sufficiently
al. From other sources we know, furthermore, that Alcott read
Leland's presence a few extracts from Spenser's *Faerie Queene*
d that the boy went forth straightway and consumed the entire
em. Alcott's real failure with Leland was that he did not correct
e flippancy and triviality which prevented that rather brilliant
an from doing much sound work. He saw this, fifty years later,
en he heard Leland read his Phi Beta Kappa poem at Harvard:
eland's poem," said he, "was right in its tone but deficient in
etic excellencies. I remember his manners when a pupil of mine
Philadelphia. He read fiction to the disparagement of his
sons, his wit running to fun and mischief."

There was not much time in the Philadelphia school, which
ted for only one term, for the proper training of a Phi Beta
appa poet, not to say of an American humorist. Alcott's mind
s working like new wine with a dangerous, intricate chemistry.
ritanism and infidelity, the French Revolution and Greek ideal-
i, Jesus and John Locke and Coleridge and Jakob Boehme,
ove together and would not mingle. Who or what should
alyze that mixture? Not Philadelphia, which seemed to know
le and care less about most of the ingredients. As time passed,
cott grew convinced that the city of Benjamin Franklin's adop-
n was not his natural home. He thought more and more fondly
the city Franklin had thought best to leave—the "city set on
h," upon which "the sun of righteousness had risen." Its name
s Boston.

Various friends were at work for him there. Dr. Channing use his mighty influence and Elizabeth Peabody her enthusiasti skill, with the result that on the ninth of July Alcott left fo Boston with a promise of thirty children for a new school. B early September he was established with his family at Mr Whitney's, 21 Bedford Street. A cabinetmaker named Georg Archibald was at work refitting Rooms 7 and 8 in the Mason Temple, Tremont Street, to Alcott's specifications. His bill wa three hundred and seventeen dollars, and the rent of the room was three hundred dollars a year. Alcott "spared no expense t surround the senses with appropriate emblems of intellectual an spiritual life. Paintings, busts, books, and not inelegant furnitu were deemed important," and he bought them out of his ow pocket. He had returned, after the exhaustion of the two-tho sand-dollar gift, to his natural element of debt, but was lookir forward—as when did he not?—to a prosperity which, accordir to the rules of average, ought not to be much longer delayed.

The Temple School was one of Alcott's three places "in t sun," and the first of them in order of time. It was there that first emerged from obscurity and became the man of note that was to remain, through good and ill report, for the half-century had yet to live. In our day it is a little hard to see how su recognition could have been won by a man who was, after all, on a schoolmaster, teaching a little group of children most of whc were under ten years of age. Our difficulty should be lessene however, when we consider that this was Boston, where forn education has always been a matter of utmost seriousness. scrutiny of the list of Alcott's pupils, coming as they did from t most prominent homes in the city, is also illuminating. A finally, there is the fact that this was no ordinary schoolmas who was taking charge of the little Shaws, Quincys, Jackso Savages, Peabodys and Tuckermans. This was Bronson Alcott. far as Boston knew when he began, there had never been s

[164]

schoolmaster before—and when he ended, there would never be, o far as Boston could help it, such a schoolmaster again.

For all that happened from beginning to end of the Temple chool, Boston, one should not forget, was quite as responsible as lcott. Ordinary pride, not only of the city but of the individual atrons, had some part in the school's very foundation, for the upils came from families that would as soon have sent them to til, as Edward Everett Hale said of his parents, as to the public hools. It was founded in 1834 at a time of unexampled financial boom," when almost everyone in the city was expecting to make a rtune by the purchase and sale of lands in Maine, and it came a close during the inevitable panic of 1837 when fortunes top-ed, banks broke, and minds that had seemed liberal were closed all innovation. It was a strange, mixed, chaotic time in Boston, at fourth decade of the last century, with the forces of con-rvatism and radicalism so evenly balanced that the shrewdest ophet should not have tried to say which would be uppermost the day after to-morrow. Boston could produce or attract the ost brilliant and most unsettling brains in the country, and also could turn against them ferociously, or, what was perhaps worse, th a cold insolence of deliberate neglect that froze the heart. ne body of representative Bostonians could follow William Lloyd arrison as a peerless leader while another group, apparently just representative, could drag him through the streets with a rope und his neck. What Harriet Martineau called "the martyr age in nerica" was beginning, in Boston, and what Horace Greeley lled "the stammering century" was getting well under way.

But this is to anticipate. In the first weeks and months of the mple School there was no hint of coming disaster. The arrange-nts, methods, plans, looked innocent enough. Dr. Channing d given his unqualified blessing to the schoolmaster and Miss abody was giving him her wholehearted assistance. Who was re likely to know a good school, a good teacher, than E. P. abody? Of this school and teacher she thought so extremely well

[165]

that after a few weeks' observation she began to take full notes—
her little hand racing down the pages for hour after hour, bu
never quite keeping up—on all that was said and done. Visitor
came in droves, from the city and the country and even fror
abroad. Miss Martineau came, very deaf and dry and matter-o
fact, hopefully directing her ear-trumpet here and there to catc
the faintest beginnings of infantile genius, but perhaps missing
few of the finer points. Dr. Channing came, and did not entirel
withdraw his blessing, although he was beginning to entertain son
doubts. "Dr. Channing's efforts," says the somewhat ungratef
Alcott to his Journal for 1837, "have been put forth to goc
purpose on many occasions—always, however, by way of quietii
and allaying. He never makes an Idea, but after these have begt
to work and have put the public mind into action . . . then do
he give his assent to them—usually with so much compromise ar
timid modification, lest he should stir up the fears and passio
of conservatives, that much of their good effect is lost." This w
rather too bad. If Alcott should lose Dr. Channing's comfort ar
support, who would take him up? Well, there was the Reverer
Mr. Emerson, who of course had not a tithe of Dr. Channing
importance, but yet, young though he was, could not be thoug
quite negligible. Mr. Emerson came and saw and was complete
conquered.

Before Alcott had been more than a year at work in Boston h
novel ideas were being advertised by Miss Peabody's hasty a
rambling but extremely able book, *Record of a School*. On eve
page of that book, which is one of the more interesting of t
forgotten documents of transcendentalism, there is evidence
the writer's highly intelligent and always independent admi
tion. One sees that a skillful practitioner of the art of teaching
watching a master of that art at work, setting down witho
extenuation both hearty praise and polite disagreement. Merely
an example of what may be called intellectual good manners a
of the complete conquest of professional jealousy, the little bc

speaks well of the two persons chiefly concerned. But, more than that, it speaks with an almost startling precision and "actuality" of the thirty children whom Bronson Alcott and Miss Peabody, his assistant, entertained a hundred years ago in that beautiful room at the Temple. One sees the tall Gothic window full of sunshine, the colored carpets, the busts of Milton, Shakespeare, Scott, Plato, and Socrates, behind the master's desk the bas-relief of Jesus,—so frequently referred to as the final arbiter of every moral discussion,—and the symbolic figure called "Silence" near the window. Each scholar has his own desk, near the wall, and his own small blackboard. The master's desk is at some distance from them, but when he wishes to talk or read to the whole school he asks them to bring their chairs, very quietly, and sit near him in a semi-circle.

Perfect order and a steady concentration upon whatever is in hand is quietly insisted upon. The children are by no means allowed to follow their individual caprice, but are constantly subjected to a rule as firm as it is kind. For although the teacher believes that each of them is a piece of divinity, he also holds that "there are other propensities, necessary to the child's present existence, which, left unguarded, will degrade its nature. There are appetites and passions which require discipline and direction." For every infraction of the rules of silence and attention the whole group has to suffer together with the culprit—although the suffering is likely to consist only in an interruption of some pleasant exercise. It is clear that the master is doing all he can to make his school a delight. He has made it as beautiful as possible, with his small funds. He speaks politely to every pupil. He is a gentleman most courteously entertaining a group of his young friends. All are kept busy enough at writing, spelling, composition of private diaries, grammar, geography, drawing with Mr. Francis Graeter and, for some of the older children, Latin and arithmetic with Miss Peabody; but everything possible is done to avoid a dull routine. There is a good deal of reading from *Pilgrim's Progress*,

[167]

Maria Edgeworth's *Frank,* selected poems, and, to name last what the children most enjoyed, the Gospels.

But no doubt the most important exercise of the day, in the opinion of the master and in the effect upon the pupils, is the defining of words, in which Alcott loses no opportunity to draw some would say to drag in, a moral, a spiritual, or a philosophical lesson. For example, he says that "yelk" is the food upon which the germ of life is nourished into the power of forming a body that may "individualize" it; and when this fairly difficult and thoroughly Alcottian conception has been grasped by the youngest children he proceeds to say that perhaps the earth is the "yelk" by which souls are nourished or born into a consciousness of the spiritual life. Frequently he tells his children that the object of the school is "to unveil the soul," and he plies them with questions meant to determine to what degree, precisely, the soul has been "unveiled" in this and that girl of three or boy of twelve. To the criticism, uttered even by Miss Peabody, that such questioning may awaken an unfortunate self-consciousness in his young charges he replies that since all are subjected to the same interrogation and all add their several mites of spiritual experience to a common pool, it should have an effect just contrary to what is feared.

One of the most unquestionably valuable of Alcott's methods as one sees them practised and exemplified—the words are hardly too strong—in the *Record of a School* was that by which he tried to build up in his pupils a strong sense of social solidarity and mutual responsibility. In his instruction, to be sure, he addresses individuals as much as possible, but all matters of discipline and many matters of taste and judgment were referred to the entire group for final decision. This was a detail of teaching about which Miss Peabody was most doubtful when she began her work with Alcott. To her the education of children meant the sedulous "drawing out" of the individual as such, but to him it was primarily the development of social beings. Her own method had

THE TEMPLE SCHOOL

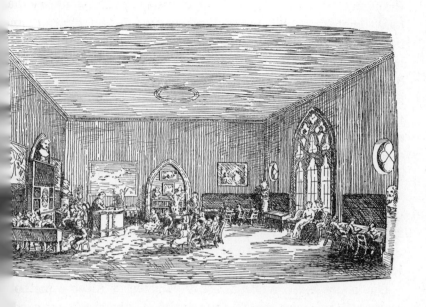

MASONIC TEMPLE
BOSTON, MASSACHUSETTS

*After an original sketch by Francis Graeter,
Alcott's drawing master*

been to deal with "stuff of the conscience" in private interviews, and she was somewhat shocked, at first, to see Alcott bring it boldly forward for public discussion. In no other respect, however, was she more completely converted to Alcott's opinion as the months went by. She came to agree with him that, whatever might be true of the girls, the conscience of a whole school of boys would be more sensitive than that of the average individual, and she also came to understand the high moral value of making each erring individual see his misdeed as by no means a private matter but as one in which the entire group was concerned.

This little controversy, although it was argued out in terms of the moral problems of children, had larger implications. Miss Peabody's original contention in favor of an appeal to the isolated and private conscience was in keeping with the whole tendency of New England Puritanism and its long struggle of souls alone with God. Alcott's disciplinary method, stressing the general truth that no man liveth unto himself alone, was in accord with his own social nature. Perhaps nothing was to set him more decidedly apart from the other chief members of the transcendental group than his belief that the moral life is one that we live not in solitude but together.

A vivid and rather familiar illustration of this belief is seen in Alcott's custom, when physical chastisement had to be administered, of having the child strike him instead of striking the child. Forty years after the close of the Temple School this detail of educational discipline was recalled by a famous preacher, Joseph Cook, as a clear analogue of the Vicarious Atonement. A considerable controversy ensued among the clergy and the newspapers of Boston. Alcott was willing to have his method of discipline so interpreted, but it is clear that in his teaching days his main purpose in using it had been to make his pupils realize the social effects and reverberations of all wrongdoing.

The strong and steady emphasis at the Temple School upon questions of morality was by no means, as we have seen, an innovation made by Bronson Alcott. Precisely that same emphasis is found in the schoolbooks of so essentially "worldly" a school-master as Noah Webster, as it had been in the teaching of New England primary schools from the beginning. For these schools had never made it their exclusive ambition to turn out ever more and better mechanics, clerks, and shopkeepers, or even better citizens. Even the moral emphasis that Alcott laid upon the defining of words was common in his day, as anyone who has in mind the curious etymologies of Carlyle, Emerson, and Thoreau must realize. Noah Webster himself, in his *Dictionary of the English Language,* had delivered himself thus: *"Swear,* v. i. 4. To be profane; to practise profaneness. Certain classes of men are ac-customed to *swear.* For men to swear is sinful, disreputable, and odious; but for females or ladies to *swear* appears more abomi-nable and scandalous."

In this regard, then, Alcott was well within the tradition of his calling. It was in his conception of what constitutes morality, in the means he used to inculcate it, and perhaps also in the con-centrated intensity of his effort, that he offered something new. The morality that he taught was so far above the cautious and calculating worldly-wisdom of Franklin and Webster as to de-serve another name—"spirituality." It was sharply distinct from middle-class "respectability." Never for an instant did he suggest to his young charges that if they were "good," as he taught them to understand that word, they would therefore cer-tainly be prosperous, respected, or even liked. He knew better, and he never lied to them. As for the means, he used always an appeal to the affections; and also he addressed the imagination, which he believed was one of the first faculties to awake in the child's mind, by means of poetry and fiction.

Highly curious and suggestive is Miss Peabody's careful de-fense of Alcott's stress upon the imaginative faculties. She is talk-ing to an audience in which the mediæval theory of imagination as a disturbing and distorting faculty is still current. She herself

[170]

can understand that prejudice, although it is improbable that, after her association with Dr. Channing and her consequent absorption of Coleridge and Wordsworth, she shares it; but she is aware that Alcott's constant use of parables and allegories and emblems, of fables and fiction and poetry, is a phase of his teaching with which the community is unlikely to sympathize. In her defense of it she shows, first, that the use of such devices for moral instruction has the most respectable authority within the Puritan, and indeed within the larger Christian tradition, and, second, that it is not a question whether children should be imaginative or not but only whether their imaginations should be soundly cultivated or left to run wild.

At least one element in Alcott's teaching seems to have been evolved not so much from an objective study of the child-mind as from a generalization upon his own mental history. To him, growing up as he did in a sparsely settled region where he could find few or none to share his thought, a gradual turning-inward upon one's own mental resources had come to seem the very law and condition of intellectual growth. His social disposition cannot, it is true, be too much insisted upon, and yet one must not forget the environment to which it had been obliged to adjust itself. Whether one decides that he thought well or badly, at any rate he was a thinker. The wish to share and compare his thoughts was always strong in him, but during the first thirty years of his life he had chiefly farmers and mechanics about him. Quite naturally, therefore, he turned to his Journals and talked to them. And although these Journals of his are less soliloquies than addresses to some imaginary second person, they involved a fairly constant introversion, introspection, and return upon the inner self.

It was this inbent habit of mind, by no means common in America and apparently even to him not so much a natural thing as an effect of circumstance, that Bronson Alcott strove to fix upon his boys and girls. If it had been good for him—and that he never doubted—why should it not benefit them also? And so, from the

[171]

beginning of his Connecticut teaching, but more and more in the years of the Temple School, he emphasized the writing of private journals, in which his pupils were expected to set down, not the trivial outward happenings of their days—Mr. Alcott, they knew well, was not interested in such things—but their "ideas." Even at Cheshire he had devised a plan whereby every pupil was required to enumerate in a special notebook the "ideas" acquired in each of his subjects of study, and it had been most gratifying to find that some of his more gifted children were accumulating these desirable coins of the intellectual realm at a rate of four or five hundred a week. At Cheshire, too, he had used a method probably suggested by Cousin William, calling for a five-minute period in every schoolday of silent and concentrated introspection during which the children were to review their intellectual history of the preceding twenty-four hours. In his defining of words and also in his interpretation of fables, allegories, fiction, and poetry he took every chance that was offered, and made chances when there were none, to enforce his own transcendental belief that the outward world of time and space exists only as God's vast allegory, forever hinting at inward spiritual truth.

It was upon this central aspect of Alcott's educational method that any thoughtful criticism, however sympathetic, was bound to pause and hesitate. Even those who were most convinced that the child's mind had but recently descended from Plato's heaven of pure ideas might doubt the wisdom, considering that it had so long a course to run in a world of illusion, of recalling the glory whence it had come. If the shades of the prisonhouse must gather about the growing boy, was it well to remind him of the universal light from which he had so recently been exiled? Or, to put the case more simply, was it kind to train a group of children who were to spend their lives in the America of the nineteenth century as if they were to live, like the Yogis of the Himalaya forests, in perpetual contemplation? Alcott was not the first, and perhaps quite the last, educational thinker to decide that it was

[172]

his function not to fit his pupils for the world as it now is, but rather, quite definitely and deliberately, to unfit them. For that belief there is not a little to be said, but its practical applications may easily be carried too far.

Dr. Channing, who certainly did not err on the side of "this-worldliness," was somewhat disturbed, when he first read Miss Peabody's *Record of a School*, by the fear that Bronson Alcott was emphasizing a sound principle beyond reason. Writing to the author with admirable tact and politeness, he said: "I want light as to the degree to which the mind of the child should be turned inward. The free development of the spiritual nature may be impeded by too much analysis of it. The soul is somewhat jealous of being watched, and it is no small part of wisdom to know when to leave it to its impulses and when to restrain it. The strong passion of the young for the outward is an indication of Nature to be respected. Spirituality may be too exclusive for its own good."

In Miss Peabody's career, this letter from a man whom she adored only a little on the hither side of idolatry may have had a considerable influence, gradually turning her away from Alcott's "inwardness" toward the more objective methods of Froebel and the Kindergarten—in the use of which she was an American pioneer. And even Alcott, although he stood up bravely against the man whom he had recently considered the wisest of Americans, was perhaps a little shaken by Channing's doubts and ultimate disapproval. "It may be," he says—and the admission is extremely rare with him—"that I have erred in some things. I cannot, however, perceive wherein. My great error, in the eyes of the community, is that of experimenting too boldly with the Human Soul. It is true that I have done with it what seemed to me good; but this I have done reverently and in faith, not in doubt, nor with profane curiosity."

The implication is obvious: whatever a man does "in faith" is one with divine guidance, and so cannot possibly be wrong.

[173]

Dr. Channing's doubts and hesitations about Bronson Alcott were not based exclusively upon what was going on at the Temple School. In October, 1835, Alcott began a series of Conversations [1] about the Old Testament, held on Sunday mornings in the schoolrooms, at which his pupils and their parents attended. These were perhaps the first Conversations, outside the regular work of a school, at which he ever officiated. In November of the following year he opened another series, held on Friday nights and chiefly for Sunday School teachers, in which the first topic was the life of Christ.

Here, then, was tinder waiting for the flame; and Alcott's intense convictions on the subject in hand were so many sparks of fire. A more cautious and worldly man, in his circumstances and holding his beliefs, would scarcely have discussed such a topic before such an audience. Certainly a man with a firmer grasp of reality would have been less surprised and grieved at the result. His group of Sunday School teachers, who had of course been selected in part for their "orthodoxy," heard with amazement the "views" of this schoolmaster, to whom the minds of Boston children were entrusted and who pretended to be so profoundly concerned about the welfare of souls, but who believed that "Jesus," as he insisted upon calling the Founder of Christianity, was no more than an exceptionally spiritual and mystically-minded man, and that Christianity itself was only one, though perhaps on the whole the best, of several quite respectable religions. They were shocked. They began to talk rather more about the heretical schoolmaster, among themselves and to their friends, than they did to and with him.

Disquieting rumors came to Channing's ears. There were interviews at Channing's house, by no means so pleasant as those which had marked Alcott's first months in Boston with letters

---

[1] Alcott himself regularly spells the word with a capital letter when referring to that form of public discourse of which he was the chief practitioner in his time.

of red. For Alcott was no longer the almost unquestioning admirer, the humble aspirer, sitting at the feet of a man all-wise.
He was a teacher himself now, and a preacher into the bargain.
He had listened patiently to the Boston preachers, and most of
all to this one, only to find them bound by tradition, fettered
and shackled by ritual and creed and dead men's thoughts. He
talked with Channing now as at least an equal, confronting one
'inner light" with another.

There is something about these interviews, as one pictures them,
that twitches the corners of the mouth; for both of these good
men were listening most earnestly for the Voice of the Spirit, and
yet were hearing, or believing that they heard, quite contradictory
things! One may smile; but the smile should be compassionate.

"Sadly did I hear of the distrust with which Dr. Channing regarded my Friday Evening Conversations," Alcott wrote to himself,—

> Is it not unworthy of him? Whence this pusillanimity
> of mind in one whom the nations deem the brave and
> bold defender of sacred truth? Truly might I pause,
> were I not assured by instinct more authentic than
> another's, however vile, that my doctrine is from
> heaven, and that, with my friend and brother, even
> Jesus, I am a meek and humble follower of the Divine
> Word within—which I must announce and interpret in
> the face of all obstacle. I must and shall speak as I
> feel. I shall preach the Gospel as it is revealed to my
> own soul. By so doing I must exert the right of my
> nature.

Ah, the terrible meek! Oh, these utterly humble souls, so hard
to distinguish from the insanely arrogant, whose humility consists
in a perfect assurance that they are told by messages direct from
the throne of God what to think, what to say, what to do! Rise
up, then, Joan of Arc, Francis of Assisi, Apollonius of Tyana,
Martin Luther, John Huss, Bernard of Clairvaux, and John Brown

[175]

of Osawatomie; for all of you, by your own unimpeachable testimony, have heard from God—albeit such remarkably inconsistent things! Nor do you stop there. "The simplest person who in his integrity worships God," says Emerson, "becomes God." Beyond that assertion, it is clear, humility and meekness can no farther go.

Bronson Alcott went that far. Recording one of his less and less satisfactory talks with Dr. Channing, he says:—

> We conversed mostly on the connection of the divine and human natures. I attempted to show the identity of the human soul, in its diviner action, with God. At this he expressed great dislike, even horror. He felt that doctrines of this character undermined the very foundations of virtue, confounded the nature of good and evil, destroyed human responsibility, and demolished free will.—Singular perceptions this man has. He seems unable to take the views of another; and though professedly free and declaring the doctrines of freedom, he binds himself to an imperfect creed and denies to others the assumption of views contrary to his own. . . . He is a disciple of the understanding, despite his professed reverence for reason and spirit. He is not disenthralled from the slavery of sense and the visible. He asks demonstrations, where self-affirmation declares the truth to a nature in harmony with itself. He came too early to be the clear and lucid seer of the spiritual domain. . . . He cautions me as if I were a rash and sense-driven youth, liable to dash out my brains against the dogmas and formulas that I encounter. He fears for me.—I told him this evening that a good purpose, sustained by purity of life, always supplied the wisdom and the skill to carry its purposes through every conflict with the powers that be.—Virtue endows the intellect with wisdom, and wisdom is valorous. It heeds not dogmas or conventions. It drives over their ruins to its own divine end.

But these outcries and self-assertions of a mind at bay were of a later time, 1837, when Alcott had lost the assurance that he was performing a task not only necessary but desired. In 1835, to which we may now return, he was standing "on the top of golden hours," associating upon terms equal, free, and brotherly with just those persons whom he most wished to know—persons who would have seemed to him, five years earlier, quite beyond his reach. It was not that he had in him the slightest ingredient of the "climber." The people he sought out were not, for the most part, socially prominent, but thinkers, writers, talkers—people who made things instead of merely owning them. They belonged to that "large number of peculiarly interesting and valuable persons" always to be quite sharply discriminated from the "broadcloth vulgar," whom even Miss Martineau had to admit that Boston did contain. They were those "Minds" that Alcott had set out to find during his first days in the city. He had found them. He was one of them. The terrible loneliness to which almost every creative intellect has been doomed in American life seemed to him to be lifting. The outsider began to think that he was inside. He was very happy.

The Temple School was prospering. Miss Peabody was taking all the afternoon classes, now, leaving Alcott more freedom; and no less a person than the senior Richard Henry Dana—poet, essayist, and rounded scholar—was lecturing there on English literature. Dr. Channing was still benignant. An acquaintance with the "Reverend Mr. Emerson," recently begun, was ripening swiftly into an intellectual and mutually deferential friendship. There were calls, in company with Miss Peabody and Mr. Dana, upon Washington Allston at Cambridgeport; and there was wonderfully rich wide-ranging talk there with America's foremost painter, who seemed to have combined the best of Europe with the best of the American North and South. Even better than Channing did, this man knew Coleridge. What had Coleridge said of Allston? That he was surpassed by no man of his age

[177]

either in poetic or in artistic genius. And one could easily believe that statement, sitting there in the crowd of pictures that brought Italy's sunshine into the gray little town while this accomplished man poured out the cornucopia of his thoughts. Bronson Alcott, the schoolmaster from Spindle Hill, talked with Washington Allston, from South Carolina, Harvard College, London, Paris, Venice, and Rome, as one creative artist to another.

An artist he was now, at least in his own opinion, this man whose first creative effort had been to fashion a violin out of a maple tree in the barn at Spindle Hill. He did not work in color, wood, stone, words, or any of those swiftly perishing things, but in lives, in souls. He was molding minds. He carved the contours of the everlasting. He was an architect of the future. His was the "holy art." Why should he not hold up his head in the company of Washington Allston? With Coleridge himself, whose long misery had just come to an end over there at Highgate, he would have felt at home. If Plato had come to Boston—and to what other city of the modern world would an avatar of Plato more certainly proceed?—Bronson Alcott, very bashful but not in the least abashed, would have been the leader of the reception committee.

Lesser artists used lesser tools—brushes, chisels, pens, and the like. Bronson Alcott used the Conversation. He had not invented this tool. Miss Peabody, he understood, had used it to some extent in her teaching before she came to know him; and he was aware, too, that the art of conversing had been a good deal cultivated during the eighteenth century, before Jefferson's introduction of the Argand lamp had made it easy for people to read in the evenings. The fact that it had been cultivated chiefly by women—as he, at any rate, believed—was in itself a strong recommendation. But these were trivial matters in comparison with the fact that Pythagoras, Socrates, and Jesus, the three greatest teachers of all time and therefore the three foremost creative artists, had used the Conversation as almost their only pedagogical method. The time for Socrates and Pythagoras had not yet arrived in Alcott's thinking, but his mind and mood were obsessed by the thought of Jesus, that almost perfect teacher and all but perfect man who had best exemplified the divinity which is in all men.

Bronson Alcott went up and down Boston talking about Jesus as though He had been in every sense an actual human being. He used no special, set-aside, sanctified language in speaking of Jesus. The name "Christ" had been dropped from his vocabulary, and the name "Our Lord," although he was an Episcopalian, had never been there. In talking about Jesus he reached for the simplest words he could find, probably because he saw that Jesus had done the same thing—and the effect upon his prose style was most wholesome. He would drop the startling name "Jesus" into almost any talk at any time, on Monday as well as on Sunday. Was it not blasphemous? Certainly it was most disconcerting to respectable people, who felt that they had relegated all that 'Jesus" stood for, if not to a special day and a particular building, at least to a special mood or state of mind, and that they had insulated it from all contact with the actual by thick wrappings of ritual and theology. What was worse, Alcott evidently believed that anyone who really cared for Jesus ought to talk and act and think differently on that account. What was perhaps worst of all, his own speech and thought and conduct seemed to be a vivid and positive illustration of this belief.

He did not mouth on Sunday those curious Biblical remarks about the blessings of poverty and then spend the rest of the week in the service of Mammon. He remained poor, and yet was cheerful. His very consistency was a rebuke. The prosperous Philistines of Boston might have said of him, as their forerunners in ancient Alexandria had said of the poor religious hermit: "He professeth to have knowledge of God, and he calleth himself the Child of the Lord. He was made to reprove our thoughts. He is grievous unto us, even to behold, for his life is not like that of other men. His ways are of another fashion. He abstaineth from

[179]

our ways even as from filthiness."—Oh, it was an ancient and inveterate, almost a natural, antipathy.

Alcott liked best to talk about Jesus with children, thinking that they were best able to understand that essentially childlike mind. Such talks had, for him, a triple value: they were instructive to the children, they helped him to understand the nature of childhood, and they taught him about Jesus. He expected to learn from them more than he taught, and the probability is that he did so.

In this spirit of the student Alcott began, in the autumn of 1835, a series of Conversations on the Gospels with the children of his own school. It was one of the most characteristic things he ever did. His whole personality and character went into it, as one piece. The conception and the execution show the boldest reach of his mind. Some contemporaries thought that God was with him and others that the Devil was in him, but all agreed that he was like a man possessed. And so it was appropriate enough that, in its effects upon his public standing and professional career, this series of Conversations on the holiest theme should have been his most disastrous failure. Having soared highest, he fell farthest. The fall broke his life in two, and brought his work as a teacher of children to a close.

There were thirty-seven children in the Temple School while these Conversations continued, nine of whom were between ten and twelve years of age, eighteen between seven and ten, and the rest six years old or less. One of the most profound, little Josiah Quincy, who certainly spoke very like Wordsworth's "mighty philosopher," "seer blest," and "eye among the blind," was six. The children came from homes of various sectarian affiliations: Universalist, Unitarian, Baptist, Episcopalian, Methodist, Swedenborgian, and Free Enquirer. There were twenty-nine boys and eight girls—just enough to ensure that "purity" which the teacher considered so important, but enough also, alas, to make it seem

[180]

particularly horrible that the teacher himself should have allowed and even promoted the discussion of themes about which "female children," at any rate, should never speak, never hear, and never even think.

These Conversations were in fact what their name implied. They were not lectures or monologues, for Alcott talked far less than the children did, and most of his contributions were questions. "I ask and ask till I get something fit and worthy," he said one day. "I am not thinking, generally, of any particular answer. Sometimes I ask because I do not think myself, and hope that you will find some word that will embody the spirit of the Conversation. Sometimes—always, indeed—I seek to assist you by my questions in finding the answer, by the free exercise of your own minds. All truth is within. My business is to lead you to find it in your own Souls."

In a language which had at last become admirably simple, using images drawn from the common fund of childhood's experience, Alcott followed along the thin clue of his pupils' thoughts, with extraordinary skill and unmistakable reverence, as far as that thread could lead him. There he stopped. For he was not trying to tell his children anything. Rather, he was hoping to be told. The whole manner of the man and all his words—set down by Miss Peabody or by her sister Sophia, soon to be Mrs. Nathaniel Hawthorne, or by Miss Margaret Fuller—suggested that as he moved onward into the penetralia of a child's mind he felt that he was approaching a shrine. And yet he had also a scientific purpose in mind. It was a psychological investigation that he had on hand, as it had been a few years before when he had gazed interrogatively down upon Anna and Louisa in their cradles. They had been less articulate philosophers than these of the Temple School, and so had obliged him to contribute more than his share to the Conversation. He was still contributing to it in that manuscript, now called "Psyche," which Mr. Emerson was reading with mingled joy and pain. But the question in his mind, or rather the hypothesis, had not changed.

"You all appear to think," he said once, "that you have something within you godlike, spiritual, like Jesus, though not so much. And what is this?"

"Spirit, Conscience," piped a dozen young voices in chorus. And one boy added, "Conscience is God within us."

One smiles, at first, to observe how Alcottian were the answers that Alcott drew from his young friends. "If you call Jesus God, and God God," said a six-year-old boy, "then I think there would be two Gods, and that is the same as worshipping statues." When the teacher asked whether there were any idolaters in Boston, the prompt answer was "Yes; a great many of them. They worship money." When Alcott asked what person in history had "kept his babyhood," several children replied that Jesus had done so, and one lad volunteered the startling remark that "God is babyhood." At this answer, however, Alcott showed some hesitation. One can almost see him think. "I believe," said he, "that there is truth in that; and yet it is a language so liable to be misunderstood that it had better not be used."

If Alcott's cautious and skillful questioning did elicit, too frequently, no more than a reflection and an echo of himself, it was certainly against his will. Again and again he told the children that he did not wish to control their minds or even suggest their answers. More than once he declined to state his own opinion on a question which had led to disagreement among them. One of his pupils remarked to him, with the polite freedom which he always cultivated in the classroom: "I don't think it has been much of an argument on your side, for your side was only asking questions." And Alcott replied: "No; it is my object to make you argue, make you reason, by giving the terms. I have not sought in these Conversations to present my own views of truth, but to call forth yours; and by so doing to make you conscious of your own powers of finding it. It is the part of a wise instructor to tempt forth from the minds of his pupils the facts of their

[182]

inmost consciousness, and make them apprehend the gifts and faculties of their own being. Education, when rightly understood, will be found to lie in the art of asking apt and fit questions, and in thus leading the mind by its own light to the perception of truth"—in which remark there was perhaps more of Socrates than of Jesus. Once more in his Journal for 1836 Alcott says that good instruction is always the lending of one's own mind to another, so that he may see how truth looks through that prismatic glass.

Like every other good teacher, Alcott was aware that it was his business to set his pupils free—and free, perhaps most of all, from himself; but he must also have known the extreme difficulty of this final achievement. Had Jesus succeeded in it? He had hardly even tried; and that would mean that He was not, after all, quite the perfect teacher. Had Socrates succeeded? He tried, and with some success; yet there was much of Socrates in Plato, as there was of Plato in Aristotle. The wisest and most loving father could not avoid leaving some mark of his own mind upon a son. The most cautious and careful scientist would always reach a result in his experiment strongly warped by the bias of his own mind. Alcott did all that the most thoughtful scientist, parent, or teacher could do to escape or erase his "personal equation." As much as possible he strove to be not Bronson Alcott but the smooth clear pipe for the breath of the Spirit. Of a session in which he felt that he had failed he said: "It is remarkable that this is the only instance in which I have premeditated one of these Conversations. I studied this passage beforehand, and in no instance have we succeeded so ill. It is better to give the subject up to the children and let them lead us where they will."

Yet of course it was impossible for Alcott to exclude himself entirely from the Conversations. More than once, to illustrate the soul's contrition for sin, he told a story about his three-year-old Louisa, not mentioning her by name, and her swift oscillations between passionate anger and love. And again, to show what might be the effect of nature's beauty and peace upon the soul, he recalled his own hours of vision on New Connecticut Hill: "I knew a boy once who lived in a small farmhouse under the brow of a hill covered with trees and beautiful retired coves and solitudes; and he used to rise early in the morning and go out and choose one of these beautiful places, when the dew was on the ground and the trees and the birds were singing and the sun was glittering, and there he would say his prayers; and he found it easy to be good and kind all day when he practised this. I knew this boy very intimately."

Yes, in spite of him, the Conversations were full of Bronson Alcott. There was more idiosyncrasy in his way of asking a question than in most men's emphatic statements. Little by little he drew and deepened an indelible image on those young minds that would last through their lives and go on to their children's children. He taught, or at any rate he enforced, no theological system, no sectarian doctrine, no Christology. He was content to set Jesus of Nazareth in those young minds and hearts as an unforgettable example and ideal, to bring Him near, to make Him dear, to draw Him down to Boston. And, for his own share in the profit, he felt when he was through that his children had told him many a thing he had not guessed before. Also he felt that his long-standing belief in the Platonic theory of "recollection" had been confirmed. The children had said such wonderful things! They amazed even him by their wisdom, which could never have been learned in this dark and forgetful world; and others were impressed as much as he.

Mr. Emerson came on the fifteenth of June, 1836, to hear Conversation upon the Gospel of St. John. The next day he wrote in his Journal:—

I felt strongly, as I watched the gradual dawn of thought upon the minds of all, that to truth is no age or season. It appears, or it does not appear; and when

[184]

the child perceives it he is no more a child. Age, sex,
are nothing. We are all alike before the great whole.
Little Josiah Quincy, now six years six months old, is
a child having something wonderful and divine in him.
He is a youthful prophet.

One week later, Emerson wrote in the same Journal:—

Mr. Alcott has been here with his Olympian dreams.
He is a world-builder. Evermore he toils to solve the
problem: Whence is the world? The point at which he
prefers to begin is the mystery of the Birth of a Child.

Yes, ever since the advent of Anna and his long brooding beside her cradle, Alcott had preferred to begin there. The mystery
of birth was to him what the "flower in the crannied wall" would
soon be to Tennyson—a central and symbolic mystery which,
if he could solve it, would help him to the further solution of
"what God and man is." For it involved, of course, the multiform
question how the soul takes on a body, why it needs one, what
it does with it, what it was and did before it had one, and what
it will do when it has that strange encumbrance no longer.
A good place to begin such inquiries was with the mystery of
birth. When he came to the birth of Christ in his discussion of
the Gospels, Alcott asked his children what they thought about
the matter—supposing, perhaps, with his sometimes astonishing
naïveté, that they might have more authentic opinions than
adults about an event which was in their own experience so recent.
He found, or thought he did, that the children were absolutely ignorant about the physiology of birth. On that subject he did not
attempt to enlighten them, but merely said that it was a matter
with which they were "not acquainted," and passed on. One lad,
he discovered, believed that bodies came out of the ground and
lay about upon it here and there, waiting for souls, which came

[185]

directly from God, to inhabit them. Such a theory suited Alcott's purpose well enough, for he wished his pupils to understand that "the deliverance of the spirit is the first thing. . . . The physiological facts, sometimes referred to, are only a sign of the spiritual birth. You have seen the rose opening from the seed with the assistance of the atmosphere. This is the birth of the rose. It typifies the bringing forth of the spirit by pain and labor and patience. . . . And a mother suffers when she has a child. When she is going to have a child she gives up her body to God, and He works upon it in a mysterious way and, with her aid, brings forth the child's Spirit in a little Body of its own; and when it has come she is blissful."

These are the only recorded words in which Bronson Alcott ever called the attention of his children to the physiology of reproduction. Not only are they delicate and gentle words in themselves, but, like a cloud in the sunrise, they are caught up into a context of thoughtful beauty that suffuses and all but erases them in the splendor of Spirit. Alcott could not have avoided saying as much as this without leaving one of those fearful *lacunae* over which most parents and teachers of his time were wont to "draw a veil." What he said, moreover, though certainly slight in amount, was sufficient to place and to leave the whole matter of sex where he always thought it belonged, in the Shekinah glory of holiness.

Cousin William was saying far more on this subject, in print and on public platforms; and so was Sylvester Graham, also from Connecticut, who was at this very time fluttering the Boston dovecotes by the most alarming veracities. In those few circles quite "unmixed," where such matters could be mentioned at all it may almost have seemed that Connecticut was conspiring against that "purity of the home" which Boston had silently maintained for a good two hundred years.

Miss E. P. Peabody, who had recorded most of the Conversations, was in a position to know what whispers concerning them

were beginning to be heard in the parlors of the "best families."
She became alarmed, and in the summer of 1836 she left the
school. But this was not enough. Alcott had in his possession,
and intended to publish, all the records that she and her sister
Sophia had made of the talk between teacher and pupils about the
life of Jesus. There were things in those records, both questions
and answers, which had seemed unexceptionable, even beautiful,
when she set them down, but which now she had come to feel
ought not to be associated with the name of a respectable maiden
lady of a certain age. The situation was extremely awkward. Not
only had she written down these passages with her own hand, but
she had made no protest about them at the time—although she
had, as the record would show, doubted the wisdom of several other
procedures. What made her position all the more uncomfortable
was the fact that in her *Record of a School,* now before the public,
she had taken the attitude of an incorruptible reporter who must
set down everything—somewhat as though she had seriously accepted as her model Chaucer's half-humorous apology:—

> Who-so shal telle a tale after a man,
> He moot reherce, as ny as evere he can,
> Everich a word, if it be in his charge,
> Al speke he never so rudeliche and large.

Yet now, there was no help for it, she must insist that Mr. Alcott
make certain deletions and suppressions which would at any rate
relieve her of all responsibility for what, she feared, was about
to happen. Writing from Worcester on the seventh of August,
1836, the anxious woman delivered herself in these perplexed
and somewhat perplexing words:—

Dear Sir:
The very day after my letter to you I received a
communication from a friend; by which I learn that
much more extensive than either you or I were aware
of is the discussion of such subjects as it is known were

[187]

discussed in connection with the birth of Christ censured even by friends of your system and of yourself, and that something of an impression was gratuitously taken up that I left the School on that account—an impression for which I can in no ways account, except it was thought I ought to leave it. For I have been *very wary* what I said about it—generally leading off from the subject when it was mentioned, but turning attention upon your purity of association being so much like that of children. For I always wanted the plan to succeed in this particular of it especially, so sure I am that it is impossible to keep children ignorant and that it is better to lead their imaginations than to leave them to be directed by idle curiosity. And yet I do not think I should ever have ventured so far myself. And a great many questions I thought were quite superfluous, and what was to be gained by them was not worth the risk of having them repeated and misunderstood abroad. A great deal is repeated, I find, and many persons, liking the school in every other respect, think it is decisive against putting female children to it especially.

I have told you this in the spirit of friendship, and hope you will not despise it. I am conscious of the effect of a few week's freedom from the excitement of being a part of the School, or taking down that exaggerated feeling which made every detail of it seem so very important to the great course of Spiritual Culture; and I never was under half the illusion in this respect that you were.

But with respect to the Record: whatever may be said of the wisdom of pursuing your plan as you have hitherto done in the school-room, where you always command the spirits of those around you (only subject to the risk of having your mere words repeated or misinterpreted) I feel more and more that these questionable parts ought not to go into the printed book, at least that they must be entirely disconnected with *me*.

In the first place, in all these conversations where I have spoken, I should like to have that part of the conversation omitted, so that it may be felt that I was entirely passive. And I would go a little farther: there is a remark of Josiah Quincy's about the formation of the body out of *"the naughtiness of other people"* which is very remarkable. Please to correct that in my record. But if you wish to retain it, you can add a note in the margin saying: 'the Recorder omitted Josiah's answer in this place, which was &c. &c.'—putting Josiah's answer in your note.

There are many places where this might be done, and thus the whole responsibility rest upon you. I should like, too, to have the remarks I made on the Circumcision omitted. I do not wish to appear as an interlocutor in that conversation either. Besides this, I must desire you to put a preface of your own before mine, and express in it, in so many words, that on you rests all the responsibility of introducing the subjects, and that your Recorder did not entirely sympathize or agree with you with respect to the course taken, adding (for I have not the slightest objection), that this disagreement or want of sympathy often prevented your views from being done full justice to, as she herself freely acknowledges. In this matter yourself also is concerned.

Why did prophets and apostles veil this subject in fables and emblems if there was not a reason for avoiding physiological inquiries &c? This is worth thinking of. However, you as a man can say anything; but I am a woman, and have feelings that I dare not distrust, however little I can *understand them* or give an account of them.

Yours, etc.

E. P. Peabody

[189]

To this curious compound of fear, duplicity and chaotic language, Bronson Alcott, we may be sure, bent his patient and quite unresentful attention. He had supposed that, whatever happened, he might depend upon E. P. Peabody to understand him, and also to stand by him; but apparently he had been mistaken. He could not laugh at her, although that would have been the best solution; he could not put her present conduct in its exact category with a round curse; he could not even recall to his own mind what particular species of animal it is that is always first to leave a sinking ship; above all he could not, he simply must not, abandon in the face of any evidence his conviction that women, as compared with men, are always remarkably "pure." One thing was clear to him from the start, however, as he studied Miss Peabody's tangled phrases: he was not going to tell any lies. He would not assert, in a Preface or elsewhere, that there had been a "disagreement or want of sympathy" on the matters in question between him and his Recorder while the Conversations were going on, for that simply would not be true. He could however, and he did, relegate to footnotes and to the back of the book he was editing a number of passages that had to be marked "Omitted by Recorder" or "Added by Editor" or simply "-Ed." The total effect of these passages, when read together, does not, it is hardly needful to say, suggest anything but the loftiest spirituality on the part of the man who first spoke them and who finally decided that they were to be included. It does suggest, however, some highly interesting reflections upon those "feelings" which, as a woman, Miss Peabody dared not distrust, however little she could understand them.

Miss Peabody understood her Boston, at any rate, thoroughly well; and no more complete vindication of her anxieties could have been imagined than the storm that soon broke over Alcott's head. On the twenty-second of December, 1836, James Munroe and Company of Boston published, as an "author's book he first volume of the *Record of Conversations on the Gospels held in Mr. Alcott's School, Unfolding the Doctrine and Discipline of Human Culture*. Considering that this publication was costing he editor seven or eight hundred dollars, one is glad to say that he book was admirably printed and bound. The auspices do not eem quite so favorable, however, when one has taken time to bserve that the contents of the book are exactly, one might say tudiously, calculated to antagonize three strong bodies of public pinion: that of the clergy, that of educators, and that of all those vho guard the "purity of the home." For, in the first place, the ook was obviously and intensely religious from beginning to end, ut in a direct, unmediated and untheological way that was likely o seem more detestable, because it was more insidious and under- utting, than downright atheism. In the second place, it was an mplicit condemnation of those theories and practices of teaching hat were based, consciously or otherwise, upon the "limb of atan" or "young viper" school of thought. Lastly, and of course nost interestingly, it was a book that had been Bowdlerized al- nost under the reader's eyes—all the passages to which Miss eabody's purity had somewhat belatedly objected having been arefully lifted out of their contexts and segregated for a separate nd delightfully horrified examination. This was unusual, to ay the least. Most expurgators of that industriously expurgating ra had recourse to the modesty of asterisks when they thought it ecessary to "draw a veil." Dr. Bowdler himself, when he had ut forth his purified Shakespeare eighteen years before, had resumably consigned all the peccant passages, once and for all, to is wastebasket. But to print such things as footnotes and in an ppendix—was it not to point them out, to underscore them ith a sort of leering salacious glee?

Bronson Alcott, having written his Introduction—Emerson lled it "an admirable piece, full of profound anticipations"— d having paid as much as he could borrow of the printer's bill, t down to await the grateful acclaims of the community. He

[191]

did not expect an immediate success, and indeed he was a littl
anxious about the first reception of his book, yet he coul
modestly confide to his Journal that the work would "date a ne
era in the history of education, as well as a prophecy of th
renovation of philosophy and of Christianity." However thi
might turn out to be, the whispers that Miss Peabody had hear
months before in the parlors of Tremont and Beacon Street—
feminine whispers only, no doubt accompanied by lowered eye
and crimsoned cheeks—were deepened soon by the rumble c
masculine voices until the clamor culminated in the authoritativ
thunder of the Boston Press. There was going to be a storm.

Alcott's answer to the first flashes of premonitory lightning wa
to issue, in February, the second volume of the Conversation
After that he sat silent—listening, thinking, suffering, and watch
ing his beloved school go to pieces. No mob shouted at the door c
the Temple School, demanding that he give up the keys or tha
he retract his devilish book. That would have been a relief, bu
it was denied him. He made no impressive speeches to mobs or
irate parents, and neither did his five-year-old daughter Louis
One denies these things because they have been asserted. Bu
there was drama going on, not histrionics. There was the inwa
tragedy going on of a slow and silent heartbreak. The mo
imaginatively one enters into and shares the man's sorrow, tl
more one will wish to say of it only the sober truth.

The first bolt from Olympus aimed at Alcott's little book w
launched by Nathan Hale,—brother-in-law of Governor Edwa
Everett, father of Edward Everett Hale, Bostonian Federali:
soon to be a railroad president, for forty years owner and edit
of the Boston *Daily Advertiser,* and a Deacon of the Brattle Stre
Church. The fact that he was the nephew of another Connectic
schoolmaster who had regretted that he had but one life to gi
to his country did not incline him to mercy toward this or
Almost anywhere in Boston it would have been enough merely

[192]

now that Mr. Hale did not approve of the *Conversations on the Gospels,* but it was soon common knowledge that Mr. Hale disked that book extremely. His keen nose had scented four or ve different kinds of heresy in it, but he summed up his remarks ith the scathing sarcasm: "These conversations appear to be the rst fruits of the new attempt to draw wisdom from babes and icklings."

After this there followed certain voluble and abusive inanities The Boston Courier, signed by "A Parent," which one would esitate to quote even in part if they did not so clearly reveal the ort of mentality with which every man who thinks a little in advance of his generation has to contend. Accusing Alcott of "diving eep into solemn mysteries," the Parent bursts forth:—

> We cannot repress our indignation at the love of notoriety, for it can be nothing else, which will lead a man to scorn the truth & the best interests of society— & boldly defying public opinion & the sentiments of the wise & good, to pollute the moral atmosphere, throw a stumbling block in the path of improvement, & say to the travellers therein "Thus far shalt thou go, & no further!" . . . It were a venial error in Mr. Alcott had he simply published the crude remarks of his pupils, but he has gone further. He seemed to delight in his own person in directing their attention to the more improper subjects—& when they appeared with intuitive perception to shrink from contact with them, he has forced their minds to grapple with them. . . . Mr. Alcott should hide his head in shame.

Thus encouraged, the Editor of the *Courier,* Mr. Joseph T. ickingham—probably with the intent of disinfecting the moral nosphere and removing the stumbling-block from the path of provement—gave it as his opinion

> . . . upon the honesty of a man, that the *Conversations on the Gospels* is a more indecent and obscene

[193]

book (we say nothing of its absurdity) than any other we ever saw exposed for sale on a bookseller's counter. Mr. A. interrogates his pupils on subjects which are universally excluded from promiscuous companies of men and women. . . . We doubt, too, whether the clergymen who are so ambitious to outdo each other in the force of their puffs upon the *Conversations* would deem it wise or expedient to read in their pulpits some of those portions of the Gospels which Mr. Alcott reads to his pupils as containing topics of juvenile conversations and discussions; or if they should read such passages and offer to their congregations the remarks that would naturally be suggested thereby, we apprehend it would be among their last readings in any pulpit.

Having thus charged the Gospels themselves with obscenity —and certainly they are quite as obscene as Alcott's *Converse tions* upon them,—Mr. Buckingham rested for that day. But then were noble powers of indignation in this man. He it was who, few years before, had poured the vials of contempt upon "tw natural and experimental philosophers" who were trying to g up a project for a railroad from Boston to Albany—a projec he said, "which every one knows, who knows the simplest rule i arithmetic, to be impracticable . . . and which, if practicabl every person of common sense knows would be as useless as railroad from Boston to the moon." Some practical jester it ma have been—one rather suspects that transcendental humori James Freeman Clarke—who inserted in the *Christian Regist* a letter in which Alcott was defended and praised, citing as t letter's source the *Boston Courier*. If it was done in order see how Mr. Joseph T. Buckingham would perform, the perp trator was not disappointed. On this occasion the editor ended h diatribe by saying: "We are told that a clergyman living no gre distance from Boston, when asked his opinion of the *Convers tions on the Gospels,* said that one-third was absurd, one-thi

[194]

lasphemous, and one-third obscene. And such, we apprehend, will
e the deliberate opinion of those who diligently read and soberly
eflect."

All of these vilifications Alcott pasted very neatly and me-
hodically in his commonplace book, making no comment of any
ort upon them. Beside the remark quoted from "a clergyman
ving no great distance from Boston," however, he wrote in the
argin, in lead pencil, the name "Rev. Andrews Norton, D.D."
t was the name of transcendentalism's most redoubtable foe.

Not all the comments upon Alcott's book, by any means, were
dverse. There came comforting letters from the mother of
osiah Quincy and from the famous and influential fathers of
emuel Shaw and Emma Savage. James Freeman Clarke wrote
vo highly favorable notices of the book in the *Western Mes-
nger,* that brilliant little forerunner of the *Dial.* Clarke it was,
o, who made the gravely ironical suggestion to Editor Bucking-
am:—

> We perceive that the Boston *Courier* recommends
> that Mr. Alcott be presented to the Grand Jury on
> account of his book. We respectfully suggest, in ad-
> dition, that the indictment be in the words of that
> formerly found against Socrates, the son of Sophronis-
> cus. In Xenophon's *Memorabilia,* chapter 1, it runs
> thus: "Socrates is accused of not believing in the gods
> in which the city believes, but introducing other new
> divinities; he is also accused of corrupting the minds
> of the young." The two cases would then be exactly
> parallel.

The *Christian Register,* most influential of Unitarian journals,
o defended Alcott's book with warmth and ability; but by far
e most important of all the comments, favorable or adverse, was
e long and brilliant article entitled "Alcott on Human Culture"
ich appeared in October, 1838, in the *Boston Quarterly Re-*

view, written by the religious stormy petrel of those days, Oreste
A. Brownson. The article runs to some five thousand words. I
is a thoughtful and highly intelligent discussion of Alcott's edu
cational, religious, and philosophical theories, written from th
inside by a close personal acquaintance—Alcott and Browr
son believed, indeed, that they were distantly related—who know
not only his man's present opinions but how he reached then
Few men in America at that time had been so elaborately e
plained to their contemporaries as Alcott was in Brownson
study. This was, in fact, the first sympathetic, deeply co
sidered, and fully informed examination ever made of an Amer
can transcendental thinker.

To Alcott himself praise was hardly more disturbing tha
blame. What he wanted, now as ever, was a friendly association,
sense of coöperation with "worthy" men and women toward son
"worthy" end. This end or goal might be ever so vague, di
and distant; he cared less than perhaps he should have care
about that, because what he really desired—in his teaching, h
reforming, his conversing, and in all the travel of his later yea
up and down the land—was the warmth of human sympath
He had of course read the brokendown translated version
Zimmermann's *Einsamkeit,* or "Solitude," now in its twentie
American edition. What reading man of his time had not? I
liked to think and speak of himself as a "solitary" because it h
long been established, partly with Zimmermann's help, that eve
man of "genius" must be that. Yet nothing could have be
farther from the truth. From the earliest years of his bashful bo
hood he had been an outsider, looking in; and now what w
worst about this calamity of the School and the *Conversatio*
was not the public hue and cry, the loss of pupils, the incre
of poverty, the forced auction of his school furniture and of 1
busts of Socrates and Plato, the sale of his books, the threat
a mob, or even that the children pointed at him as he walked
the street and called out derisive names. The worst was that

[196]

who had been for a little while definitely inside was now thrust forth again into a world either hostile or indifferent, a world that knew him not and had no wish for his gifts or for his service.

And yet, was the night quite so dark as that? In the very deepest of his trouble he had received, on the twenty-fifth of March, 1837, a letter from Mr. Emerson:—

> . . . I hate to have all the little dogs barking at you, for you have something better to do than attend to them; but every beast must do after his kind, and why not these? And you will hold by yourself, and presently forget them. . . . You are so deeply grounded in God that I shall not fear for you any loss of faith in your ends by opposition; but I do not want these people to shut the school for the moment. But you will bide your time, and, with views so large and peculiar, can better afford to wait than other men.

Emerson had written to Editor Nathan Hale, moreover, a letter in defense of Alcott's book which Hale refused to publish, but which did appear in Buckingham's *Courier,* heavily swathed in editorial disclaimers of any responsibility for the opinions expressed. Emerson called upon Alcott whenever he could in Boston. More and more often, he invited Alcott to visit him at his new home by the fork of the roads in Concord. As Dr. Channing drew away, Emerson came nearer, until Alcott was writing in his journal:—

> Only Emerson, of this age, knows me, of all that I have found. Well, every one does not find *one* man, one *very man, through and through.* Many there are who live and die *alone.*

Ah yes, he thought, if his trouble had done no more than to bring this one great friend, it would still have been a blessing. The hemlock, though bitter, might yet be found a healthful and invigorating drink.

It was a mysterious thing, this law of "compensation" as his new friend called it, which had brought him, just at the time of his most disastrous outward failure, his deepest inward joy In the dark hours of April and May, when all the world except his faithful wife and daughters and one friend had turned, apparently, against him, Alcott found escape from misery in the continual thought, the always warmer and more loving thought of Emerson. He remembered the time far back—on the twenty eighth of September, his Journal told him, in 1828—when he had first seen that tall, slim, boyish figure with the oddly sloping shoulders and beautiful head, and how he had called the Reverend Mr. Emerson's sermon on that occasion "a very respectable effort." Respectable! Of course he knew, now, that it must have been a work of genius. And then there had been those many lectures, some of them about science and others on abstruse themes of philosophy and ethics. He, Alcott, took no great stock in lectures. They deceived people into the belief that they were growing wise, whereas true wisdom must be always the spontaneous outgrowth of one's own nature. No man, not even Emerson himself, could do more than suggest to another what must always be found within. Yet Emerson's early lectures, delivered here and there in Boston before small groups of people, usually the same people and most of them rather young, had been a rich experience. It was not so much that they brought new ideas for the greater part of what the lecturer had said was already familiar to one, at least, of his listeners. Something of their effect would be due to the bold splendor of their style, which often suffused the homeliest words and images with a sudden glory. In addition, there was the wonder of that versatile voice; there was the light of innocent wisdom that always shone from the clear peering straightforward eyes; and, most of all, there was the constant realization, while Emerson was speaking, that one was in the presence of essential nobility. Whatever he might say, and even when he said nothing, Emerson showed an inward grandeur

[198]

These lectures had been an experience of beauty to Bronson Alcott; and yet, perhaps on account of his bashfulness, he had never spoken to the lecturer until one evening in early July of 1835, when Emerson had come to his chambers at 3 Somerset Court to meet Mrs. Harrison of Philadelphia. That was less than two years ago; but now it was hard to think what his life had been before this beloved friend had come into it. Three months later Alcott had paid his first visit to Concord, while the maples were aflame along the village street. What talk, what marvelous talk there by the fireside in the study, with wise and learned George Bradford for a listener! And Emerson had listened too, with that strangely beautiful light shining in his eyes. Emerson listened, so to say, creatively, making a man utter things he had never known were in him—wonderful things, never to be remembered or set down.

And this had been only the first of many visits at the square white house by the forking of the roads. Oh that they might continue, and that he might live a long life to enjoy them! When the outer world was coldest and when the shadows all but hid his path, oh that there might always be a light for him in that one window, and fireside warmth and a welcome! But even while he breathed that prayer Bronson Alcott knew, with almost a young lover's sensitive prescience, how much it would cost him never by word or deed or unguarded glance to endanger this delicate gift of heaven. For the spirit of Emerson, he saw, was as shy as a faun of the woods. It was cold as a snow-maiden. Emerson must never know that where he had given only his admiration, his strong and faithful help, his wise counsel, and the partnership of his deep poetic mind, Bronson Alcott had given no less than his whole heart.

Thinking with the head alone—though of course that was always bad thinking—Alcott could find much serious fault with Emerson. He summed it up by calling his friend a "rhetorician." There were times, he thought, when Emerson seemed to love a

[199]

fine phrase better than a brave deed. He reminded one a little of
what people were beginning to say about Governor Edward
Everett, who had been his instructor at Harvard. Beauty, charm
grace, and all the accomplishments of the consummate stylist he
had in overflowing measure; but one must wonder now and then
how these were to be brought to bear upon the crude and gross
America of the present. As Emerson himself very well knew
America did not stand in need of more graceful penmen, or o
more eloquent men of the platform, so much as she did of more
stalwart and self-reliant and downright *men*. But Emerson, one
sometimes felt, was hardly American at all. There was much o
the Englishman in him, and more of the Greek. He looked back
ward, whereas America was of the present and the future. He
lived too retired. When the Temple School began to break Emer
son thought that his friend should abandon all practical wor
and retreat to some quiet village such as Concord, there to wor
out his destiny as a mere writer. To be sure, if one could write a
well as Emerson. . . . But no; even then writing would scarcel
fill out a manly life.

Emerson had thought decidedly well of some of his friend
manuscripts. Indeed, he had thought so well of certain passages i
his Journals for 1834 and 1835 as to paraphrase them under the
heading "What a certain Poet sang to me," at the end of h
marvelous little book on *Nature*. He had not liked the "Psyche
manuscript quite so well, and had said some severe things abo
that product of many months of toil. No doubt it was all tru
what he had said—so true that perhaps one had better give up
hope of ever writing well. And yet Emerson did make too mu
of books, of writing, of mere paper and ink. If he had gone
school on Spindle Hill instead of attending Harvard College,
he had loaded several tons of Connecticut boulders upon a sto
boat every day for months, or if he had walked ten thousand mi
carrying tin trunks from house to house in the Carolinas a
Virginia, he might have seen such matters somewhat different

—But these were things that one said with the head. They had nothing to do with love.

Those days and nights in Concord, sitting with Emerson by the fireside in the book-lined study, walking with Emerson through the fields and across Mill-Dam Brook to the Walden woods and the clear blue water, were different, unaccountably, from all other nights and days. They were themselves like so many clear blue lakes of time lying out under a serene heaven where no wind came. Going forth from Boston to Concord, that fair small country of the mind, was to leave the obscure and meaningless trouble of this shadowy world unnumbered leagues behind one, and to emerge as it were in a remote and golden cloud-land where two disembodied spirits might sit forever, discoursing upon "fate, free-will, and knowledge absolute."

There was no metaphor bold enough to express the quietly ecstatic happiness of those interviews in which two minds that had been made for each other before the beginning of time met and married. They took him, Alcott said, to the stars. When back in Boston again he would remember them as something astral, as though he had been sitting with his friend upon some far-off planet and looking down from thence upon all mundane anxieties and concerns. Days would pass before the wonder and strangeness wore away, and before he could bring his mind to bear again upon these little things, these tiny people.

But then the minute troubles of the transitory and phantasmal world came creeping back, one by one. There seemed to be no armor of mood, no steady courage of the mind, that could entirely resist them. And yet he could escape. He surrendered the outward walls and gatehouses of his castle—solvency, social honor, fair-weather friends—and retired as cheerfully as he might into the tower of his memories. Rather touching it is to see him sitting at his desk day after day, while Boston was talking his school to pieces, remembering the times when he had been happiest in his

[201]

boyhood on Spindle Hill. Fifty pages of reminiscence he wrote while the storm of public denunciation was at its height. He went in vivid recollection from house to house, from one log cabin to another, visiting the simple-minded and kindly people he had known long years before. He went down, in memory, to the old bathing-place above the mill. It was not sentimentalism or self-pity that drove him, but the need of escape from a present that seemed to be crushing his heart. He could do nothing more, now than he had done; he could, or he would, say nothing whatever to his adversaries; but he could think, he could remember, and, best of all, he could hope. In the central keep of his mind there was a well of perennial water always springing. The world had never poisoned that well. Often he said over to himself, or wrote out on paper, those lines of Samuel Daniel's "Epistle to the Countess of Cumberland" which he and Emerson greatly loved:—

> He that of such a height hath built his mind,
> And reared the dwelling of his thoughts so strong,
> As neither fear nor hope can shake the frame
> Of his resolvèd powers, nor all the wind
> Of vanity or malice pierce to wrong
> His settled peace, or to disturb the same—
> What a fair seat hath he, from whence he may
> The boundless wastes and wealds of man survey!

Yet was not this making too much of very little?—for, after all it might be said that nothing new to Alcott's career was happening, but that an ill-educated and troublemaking teacher who had by this time acquired almost the habit of failure was simply failing again. The answer is, of course, that all failure—and, for that matter, all success—depends for its interest and significance upon the mind to which it occurs. To an ordinary man failure is no more than a misfortune, but to one in the million it may be tragedy. One man can fail more grandly in a schoolroom than another upon a throne. In fact, it matters not in the least how small the stage, how poor and bare the properties, there are some minds in which a failure like that of Bronson Alcott at the Temple School awakens the noblest reverberations, extending out and on through all the skies of thought. Was his mind such a one? For there is no more searching question to be asked about any man than whether he is capable of a really tragic suffering—a suffering which involves the whole man, shaking him to the base of his being, and which either destroys or transforms him.

In the tragedy of Bronson Alcott, supposing for the moment that he had one, the failure of the Temple School was not the close but only the climax, that point at which the force and fortunes of the hero first came to deadly grips with hostile forces at least as strong as they were. For the final catastrophe, and for the decision whether such a man as this was to be allowed to go on living at all in a world so hostile, we shall have to wait. In the meantime it will be well to show, in a bald narrative of events, just how hostile that outer world had already become.

The financial situation of Boston in the spring and summer of 1837 was an environing circumstance which Alcott never mentioned and of which he may not have been clearly aware. The "Eastern Land Speculation" of 1833–1834, when the Temple School was founded, had made many New Englanders, and in particular many Bostonians, rich—at least to all external appearance—overnight. By 1837 hundreds of large fortunes were crumbling and three banks in Boston itself were under grave and justified suspicion. Bronson Alcott's perfect innocence and even ignorance of all this did not save him from its inevitable results. His novel and even radical ideas about education, mildly interesting to the prosperous Boston of three years before, had now come to seem positively dangerous if not wicked; and debts, too, which had been contracted in a boom-time for school furniture, books, busts, and *Conversations on the Gospels,* had now to be paid.

The newspaper attacks upon Alcott's book began late in March

[203]

of 1837. In April the Alcotts moved from 26 Front Street to a cheaper house at Cottage Place, South End. At about the same time Alcott sold some three hundred volumes of his private library, most of which had been collected for the adornment of his schoolroom and for the use of his pupils, for one hundred and fifty-eight dollars. The furniture and decorations of the school room were disposed of in the same vendue. His enrollment of pupils, which had reached forty, declined during the "whispering campaign" of the autumn of 1836 to twenty-five; and during the cannonade of the press in the spring of 1837, to ten. In May of that year Alcott moved his school from the handsome rooms of which he had been extremely fond into the basement of the Temple. In May, also, his friend George Ripley informed him with all possible kindness, that the Unitarian clergy of Boston regarded him as "an interloper into the theological field," and that they considered the present occasion the best opportunit for making their sentiments known. At about the same time the schoolteachers of the city expressed, informally, a similar opinio about his educational theories and practices. In June, when Alcot was invited by his admirer and imitator, Hiram Fuller, to dedicat the Greene-street School at Providence, which had been closel modeled after the Temple School, he felt obliged to decline i favor of Emerson lest the obloquy surrounding his name should in jure the new establishment. Dr. Channing was still polite, thoug distant and disappointed. E. P. Peabody, though she did what sh could to defend the school in the pages of the *Christian Register* had done far more toward its ruin by leaving it as soon as she ha smelled danger. Margaret Fuller, who had for a time taken h place, was going to Providence to teach in the Greene-stre School.

At one time, early in April, the public animosity against Alco rose to such a pitch that mob violence was threatened. This w becoming a favorite method, in Boston, of expressing patrio sentiments upon questions of the day. In 1834 a large compa of Boston men, mostly truck-drivers, had destroyed by fire and pillage the Ursuline Convent in what is now Somerville. Boston "gentlemen of property and standing" had dragged William Lloyd Garrison through the streets with a halter round his neck in 1835, and had threatened the life of his friend George Thompson, an English lecturer against slavery. In 1836 Alcott's friend Sylvester Graham narrowly escaped a mob which gathered to attack him just before a lecture intended "for married women only." In June, 1837, there was to occur the great anti-Catholic riot in Broad Street in which fifteen thousand persons were engaged. Alcott's own particular mob, which had been planned for his entertainment at one of his Friday evening Conversations with Sunday School teachers, did not, for some reason, establish connections, and was postponed *sine die*. Nevertheless, this whole series of popular movements might have suggested to him certain drastic revisions in the prose-poem he had composed some years before: "There is a city in our world upon which the light of the sun of righteousness has risen. There is a sun which beams in its full meridian splendor upon it. Its influences are quickening and invigorating the souls that dwell within it. It is the same from which every pure stream of thought and purpose and performance emanates. It is the city that is set on high. It is Boston."

During July and August, as one should not be surprised to learn, Alcott had the second long and serious illness of his life. So far as the record shows, he had no malady that a physician might have named if a physician had been called. It seems probable that, as he himself says, he was simply "prostrated," and that for a time there was some obscure question in his mind whether it would be worth the effort to go on living. The same question was to recur six years later, with the same temporary cessation of whatever small engine it is in a man that keeps him going on. At these two periods in his life Bronson Alcott touched rock-bottom and experienced something like ultimate despair, although on this first occasion he did not sink quite so deep, perhaps, as on the second.

[205]

He was to learn, however, that "there is a budding morrow in midnight." Before he was well out of bed he had a letter from Emerson saying "Come out here instantly to spend a fortnight with me." He went, in fact, to South Scituate, where Samuel May was then preaching, and then to Concord, where Emerson was writing his great Phi Beta Kappa Day Address. On the thirty-first of August he was a member of that breathless audience at Cambridge that listened to "our intellectual Declaration of Independence . . . as if a prophet had been proclaiming to them 'Thus saith the Lord.'" He was never to forget "the mixed confusion, consternation, surprise, and wonder" with which those professional scholars heard one whom they had thought a brother scholar cry down, apparently, their special craft. Here was a company of bookmen gathered to hear one more chapter in the annual praise of books; but what they really heard, from a man whom they could not possibly call ignorant, was the calm assertion that "Books are for the scholar's idle times." Here was a gathering of eminently respectable persons who had built up a barricade of books and paper between themselves and the scramble, the trade, the labor, of the vulgar outer-world. Was it pleasant to be told by this slope-shouldered son of seven generations of preacher that "there is virtue yet in the hoe and spade, for learned as well as for unlearned hands?" It was not pleasant. It was shocking. Here, finally, was a group of more or less learned men who had been given to suppose that scholarship consists in accumulating and then retaining, not unlike any ordinary miser, the largest possible collection of facts about the past; but now one of their own guild and brotherhood was telling them that an American Scholar, at any rate, is to be known not by what he can hold but by what he can think, promulgate, and do in this present American time. It was a sort of treason.

Nothing of all this, except perhaps the glory of the utterance, was in the slightest degree new to Bronson Alcott. For ten years he had been saying all this, and much more of the same sort, his Journals. As always with him, even when he first looked into Coleridge and Plato, what he found for himself in the Address on "The American Scholar" was chiefly corroboration. Now and then he may have thought that he detected even a reflection of his own mind, an echo of his own words. Toward the end of the address Emerson quoted "the melancholy Pestalozzi" as saying that "no man in God's wide earth is either willing or able to help any other man." Why, were not those the very words that he, Alcott, had quoted to Emerson only the other night beside the study fire? Not that it mattered—and not, thank Heaven, that the words were true! Pestalozzi had spoken them during his bitter failure at Yverdon, so strangely like the whole misery at the Temple School; but they were not true words. When a man's heart is broken he should be silent. Other words there were in the address, however, that seemed to be levelled directly at his condition. Were they not meant for him alone? Take those special words, spoken in a clarion voice before the multitude, but ringing through the innermost chambers of one lonely listener's heart: "If the single man plant himself indomitably upon his instincts, and there abide, the huge world will come round to him. Patience,—patience; with the shades of all the good and great for company; and for solace the perspective of your own infinite life; and for work the study and the communication of principles, the making of those instincts prevalent, the conversion of the world."

Ah, brother of one's inmost soul—understanding, comforting, strengthening, counseling, pointing to the onward road! Who could despair, having such a companion? Who could think ill of a world that held one such man? Who could doubt the beneficence of that Providence which had brought one, along the tangled ways of space and time, to the one mind that could greet and prize one's boldest thought and speak it forth with the tongue and voice of an angel? What was it that Aristophanes had said about Love in Plato's *Banquet?* That each of us is only the half of a whole man, forever seeking the other half that belongs to

[207]

him. And now and then, when the gods are kind, that other half might be found.

So, now; to go back to Boston, to "defer never to the popular cry," never to quit one's belief "that a pop-gun is a pop-gun, though the ancient and honorable of the earth affirm it to be the crack of doom." In silence, in steadiness, in severe abstraction, to hold by one's self. To be henceforward, if never before, "Man Thinking," and a "Dedicated Mind."

Alcott went back to Boston early in September to discover that he had now six pupils to teach in the dismal little basement room. It would appear, then, that he must be a very poor teacher and that Boston had found him out; yet in October there came an enormous letter from James Pierrepont Greaves of London—the friend and correspondent and translator of Pestalozzi, no less!—in which *The Record of a School* and *Conversations on the Gospels* were lauded almost fulsomely. How perplexing! And these books had been given to Greaves by Harriet Martineau, who had certainly not been enthusiastically favorable in her remarks about the Temple School. In the second volume of her *Society in America,* just received in Boston, Alcott had found himself held up to ridicule as a schoolmaster "who presupposes his little pupils possessed of all truth in philosophy and morals, and that his business is to bring it out into expression, to help the outward life to conform to the inner light and especially to learn of these enlightened babes with all humility. Large exposures might be made of the mischief this gentleman is doing to his pupils by relaxing their bodies, pampering their imaginations, over-stimulating the consciences of some and hardening those of others, and by his extraordinary management, offering them every inducement to falsehood and hypocrisy."

Thus Miss Harriet Martineau, that rather mediocre Minerva. But J. P. Greaves, a friend of hers, had apparently reached a different conclusion—perhaps because he had not had her ac vantage of spending half an hour in Alcott's classroom, listening to what went on there with the help of an ear trumpet. In any case, one could not be seriously grieved or vexed at Miss Martineau's remarks. They might be severe, but they were not so abusive as those of the Boston *Courier*. And, besides, that gallant and superb Margaret Fuller had pounced upon the English woman like a bird of prey: "Many passages in your book," she had said, "are deformed by intemperance of epithet. Would your heart, could you investigate the matter, approve such over-statement, such a crude, intemperate tirade as you have been guilty of about Mr. Alcott—a true and noble man, a philanthropist, whom a true and noble woman, also a philanthropist, should have been delighted to honor; whose disinterested and resolute efforts for the redemption of poor humanity all independent and faithful minds should sustain, since the 'broadcloth vulgar' will be sure to assail him? He is a philosopher worthy of the palmy days of ancient Greece,—a man whom the worldlings of Boston hold in as much horror as the worldlings of ancient Athens held Socrates. They smile to hear their verdict confirmed from the other side of the Atlantic by their censor, Harriet Martineau." In vigor of expression, at any rate, the American Minerva triumphed.

But the heart had gone out of Alcott's teaching. In June, 1838, finding that he had only three pupils left at the Temple, he closed that school and, four months later, opened another at his new home, 6 Beach Street, with fifteen pupils. There William Russell came to live with the Alcotts, renewing an old intellectual influence of utmost value. More and more time was given to thought, to reading, and to the public Conversations which Alcott had now begun to conduct in adjacent towns—Hingham, Lexington, Medford—and also in his own home. Schoolmastering grew irksome. He kept recalling the sad lines from Coleridge:—

> Work without hope draws water in a sieve,
> And hope without an object cannot live.

[209]

In June, 1839, Alcott admitted to his school a Negro child by the name of Robinson. He knew right well what the result of this action would be—if for no other reason, because he had heard how the good people of Canterbury, a few miles from Brooklyn in Connecticut, had recently wrecked the school of the Quakeress Prudence Crandall and had lodged the teacher in jail merely for proposing to teach Negro children. The parents of Alcott's white pupils demanded that the black child be dismissed. Alcott's Journal-entry reads: "Decline dismissing the child and, June 22nd., have five children remaining as pupils—my own, Wm. Russell's, and Robinson's."

It was the end. Always careful in the keeping of his accounts Alcott made this note:—

Receipts for teaching in Boston—

In Temple	1834–5	. . . .	$1784.00
" "	1835–6	. . . .	1649.00
" "	1836–7	. . . .	1395.00
" "	1837–8	. . . .	549.00
In Beach Street	1838–9	. . . .	343.00
			$5720.00

If he had wished to complete the record so as to bring his financial situation clearly before him, he might have added that he was at this time about six thousand dollars in debt.

How good a teacher was Bronson Alcott? It is impossible to say. That he taught with a passionate devotion, with creative imagination, and with the utmost reverence for a task which he regarded as holy, there can be no doubt whatever; but to the ultimate question concerning his results there is, of course, no answer. The teacher's work is unlike that of the lawyer who estimates his success in the number of cases he has won and the fees he has been paid, or that of the physician who thinks in terms of the bodies he has saved from disease and death. The teacher, in the words of Saint Paul, "planteth a vineyard and eateth not of the fruit thereof." He is like Johnny Appleseed, traveling on and on with a gunny sack for a garment, sleeping under the trees of imagination and feeding chiefly in fancy upon the apples that his children's children may some day eat. No teacher ever fully knows the depth of his failure or the height of his success, and assuredly no one can tell him. His pupils themselves cannot tell him, even when they try. Those of them who contend most vigorously against him, and seem all their lives to be describing an orbit quite different from his, may give the best proofs of his power; just as those who never pass beyond praise and imitation are certainly among his worst failures. Under such circumstances it is well for school superintendents, college presidents, experts in "education," and biographers to recognize their ignorance and hold their peace.

We have seen that Miss Peabody, who knew something about teaching in general and a great deal about Alcott's in particular, considered Bronson Alcott the greatest teacher she had ever known. Horace Mann, on the other hand, when Alcott once offered to address a convention of schoolteachers meeting at Concord, declined the offer without thanks. Henry Barnard, a Connecticut schoolmaster whose influence upon education was at least as great as Mann's, seems to have wavered between these extremes of opinion—first calling for an article dealing with Alcott's teaching career and then failing, without expressed reasons, to publish it. The probability is that Alcott's reputation as a teacher would stand to-day on a higher level if it had not been to some extent obscured by the intervention of those kindergarten methods to which Miss Peabody turned in later life. He himself could never see that Froebel had added anything of value to his own methods and principles.

Something, perhaps, though certainly very little, might be deduced from the fact that Alcott taught Josiah Quincy the third, Charles Godfrey Leland, William Furness the artist, and Dr. Owen Wister; but much more emphasis should be laid upon the fact that he was by far the most influential if not quite the only teacher of Louisa May Alcott. There are, besides, a good many letters to bear testimony in his favor, like the one written by his friend William Russell, in 1848:—

> I have laid aside a few drawings of our dear William to be conveyed to you. . . . I felt assured you would be interested in such mementoes of one who enjoyed so much in being your pupil. . . . If ever teacher had a grateful and revering pupil, you had one in William. He would often revert with delight to the relation in which he once stood to you, and frequently draw his illustrations of sentiment and character from your teaching and example.

Here there is a hint of the only assertion that can be made with confidence about the ultimate effect of Alcott's teaching. One sees how that teaching was woven into the life of William Russell' son, who died in youth. Let us suppose that ten other pupils among the three or four hundred that Alcott taught were affected to the same degree. In their lives, and in the lives of many thousand whom they touched, the teaching of Alcott would be immensel amplified—would be woven, in fact, into the total fabric of American life. One may be quite sure, therefore, that the spirit is little richer, that the wealth of mind and heart is a little mor treasured in America, because Bronson Alcott made clear to som few boys and girls, just one hundred years ago, the differenc between the foolishness of this world and the wisdom of Go He may have been wrong in his Platonic theory about the sourc of those young minds and spirits. He was not wrong in his belie that in such a land as ours and in such a time as was coming o they would need all the faith he could give them in the world c things unseen. It was against the money-changers, the Man monites, and the hard crass worldlings of every description tha he contended, striving to keep alight that glimmer of the ide which, when it goes out, will leave this country America no mor

The last words of Russell's letter remind one that Alcott's teaching and his example were one and the same thing. He taught chiefly by virtue not of what he knew but of what he was. It was not so much from the Tree of Knowledge that he plucked the fruit for his children as from the Tree of Life. Noah Webster would certainly have classed him among those "illiterate men" who in his belief had no right to be schoolmasters because they had enjoyed "no instruction in grammar"; but, upon the whole, one is glad that the learned and bellicose lexicographer was never in a position to pass upon Alcott's scholarly attainments and to find them, as he would have, insufficient. As to Alcott's learning: It is interesting to recall that in the year 1831 a farmer's son called Theodore Parker went up to Boston to teach in a private school. He was twenty years old. He was expected to teach mathematics, French, Greek, Latin, and philosophy. Bronson Alcott's important teaching in Boston began three years later, when he was thirty-five; but even then he could not have taught one of the subjects that the young man from Lexington handled with perfect ease. And yet Alcott's work as a teacher is still going on, while Parker's—no doubt partly because it was obscured by the blaze of his later fame—is forgotten.

Bronson Alcott closed the last of his regular schools—containing, as we have seen, three children of his own, the son of a close friend who was then living with him, and a young Negress —when less than half of his life was spent. Yet it is true to say of him that he never ceased to be a teacher. He always kept as close to children as he was able. From the first there were his daughters to be taught, then their pupils, and finally, as a kinglelight, the children of Anna and May. Some of the happiest years of his life were those that he spent as Superintendent of Schools in Concord, when once more he could talk to children directly. And when he was shut away from children, as often happened, he did as much for them as possible by instructing their parents in those Conversations that began in the smaller towns about Boston and finally took him many times into the Western States. In his last years his teaching career was crowned by the success of the Concord School of Philosophy.

But there came a change in the theory of Alcott's teaching which corresponded with a change in the whole man. One may call it a quieting, a deepening of faith, a slow realization of the forces that were working on the teacher's and parent's side. During his years at Cheshire and even at the Temple School he had pushed, he had meddled, he had interfered and domineered, leaving too little to the normal tendencies of growth. In educating his own daughters, however, he avoided this. In facing that supreme task, he must have thought back to his own childhood and youth, seeing and feeling at last not only how little school had done for him but also how little, comparatively, it can do for any child. A good school, he felt, could never be more than an imitation of a good home. What need of any school whatever if the home itself could be provided?

And so it happened that the four children of this schoolmaster had little to do with school in the ordinary meaning of that word. This was due not to parental poverty or indifference but to a thought or intuition which underlay all their father's educational theories. There was a sense in which Alcott fundamentally disbelieved in schools and schooling; and when it came to a decision for those whom he most deeply loved, the schoolmaster was defeated by the teacher and father. He felt down to some wisdom that lay deeper than his professional beliefs. Again and again he wrote in his Journal such passages as this:—

> My children are so much more interested in the Book of Nature, whose pages are ever fresh and fair and teeming with new meanings, that they care little about the mere literature of the same. They are unwilling to pass their time within doors, or fix their thoughts on formal lessons. I spend an hour or more in the morning daily with them, but to small profit. Their thoughts

[214]

are on the distant hill, the winding river, the orchard, meadow, or grove; and so I let them have the benefit of these. I would have them fill their fancy with moral images and their hearts with high associations. The country is much to every young soul. . . . It was discipline and culture to me. I dwelt amongst the hills; I looked out upon rural images; I was enshrined in Nature; God spoke to me while I walked the fields; I read not the gospel of wisdom from books written by man, but the page inscribed by the finger of God. The breath of that mountain air, that blue and uncontained horizon, not less than my mother's gentle teachings . . . were my teachers. Nature was my parent, and from her, in the still communings of my solitudes, I learned divine wisdom even when a child.

These words show that there had been some profound and no doubt progressive change in Alcott since he chose as the motto of his "Cheshire Pestalozzian School" the words "Education Is All." Before he could write them he had to conquer an obsession that had ruled his thoughts for fifteen years, making him believe that the chief, perhaps the only, means of culture lay in books, schools, and direct formal instruction. The same obsession had already ruled in the culture of New England for two hundred years, and since Alcott overcame it in his own thinking it has domineered there for a century more.

The reign of the book in New England has been in some ways beneficent, though not in all. Certainly it has been inevitable. New England was founded upon a Book, and before she had conquered the wilderness this one Book had bred ten thousand more. New England was governed during her first two hundred years by a set of men whose culture was almost exclusively bookish. In that long period she made few songs of her own and composed no pure music. She invented no dances whatever, wrote few plays, produced few actors. When she built well she looked to the old home for her models. Such good painters and sculptors as she had were either imported or else trained abroad. She made swift and sound and often beautiful ships, but there her chief motive was utilitarian. It was only in the carving of her beautiful gravestones that she struck out an indigenous art—and the gravestone itself was a book of granite or slate to be read out of doors. The seed of New England had been sown from the start upon paper and that is a soil which produces little but brains.

To understand the conditions is to condone the results. Take a body of people, mostly middle-class, in whom for various reasons the deep instincts and traditions of the peasant and craftsman and landowner have been broken, and for whom at the same time the old stratifications of society have been destroyed. What is to be expected? A general scramble and strain away from every sort of toil and craft and association that seems plebeian to middle-class minds. The result is a pseudo-culture based upon fear of things falsely regarded as low and vulgar rather than upon love of things really high and fine. The outcome is not true gentleness but only the "genteel." The intellectual mark of such a society is not that real knowledge of things which can only come of doing and making, but only a superficial knowing *about* things. And in such a strain and scramble the book provides the readiest means, the school the nearest ladder.

Bronson Alcott did not escape this tendency of his time and place. He had his own genteel period, as we have seen, during which he strove to clamber chiefly upon books out of the almost illiterate environment of his youth. One sees the effect of the effort in certain permanent traits of his prose style. In the exaggerated emphasis that he laid during his younger manhood upon schooling one detects the same pervasive obsession. And yet concerning all this there are two important things to be said. In the first place, Alcott's use of book and school alike was always directed toward real and inward knowledge rather than toward external

[216]

show. In the second place, in fifteen years Alcott went through a complete arc of thought and feeling which is ordinarily traversed in not less than three generations. From the basic simplicities of Mother Earth into the loftiest abstractions and then back again, in three lustrums—the speed of the round trip is amazing. Thesis, antithesis, and synthesis: why should not the Saint Louis School of Philosophy claim him as a brother-Hegelian? It was the normal movement of his thought, and the very pattern of all his teaching. The water rose and the water fell, but always it was a fountain.

No one of Alcott's associates, early or late, had quite this range of experience. Theodore Parker, coming also from a New England farm, plunged early into books, and through all the remainder of his furious fifty years he kept on plunging farther. Emerson, born among books, found that devotion to vines and trees and corn-hills was "narrowing and poisonous." Thoreau, of course, had at least as strong a passion for Nature as Alcott was ever to show, but then he had never left her; and there is a kind of wisdom, a kind of love, that is only to be gained by departure and return. Hardly even in Henry Thoreau at his bean-hoeing do we find quite that marriage of earth and heaven recorded in some of Alcott's Journal jottings of the Concord years, where the gardener and the philosopher jostle each other on the same page.

But this was in the future. In June, 1839, Alcott felt that he would never endure the stifling air and the imprisonment of a classroom again. A great yearning for the soil from which he had so long been sundered flooded his senses and filled his heart. Were not the teachings of earth far wiser than those of any school? Did they not reach deeper than any book? Was it not the Great Mother who had taught him the best of what he knew? Had even Coleridge and Plato done more than confirm what he had guessed on New Connecticut Hill? There was a solid rock-bottom truth, after all, in Wordsworth's bold lines:—

[217]

> One impulse from a vernal wood
> May teach you more of man,
> Of moral evil and of good,
> Than all the sages can.

It was high time for Bronson Alcott to make up his mind on these questions. He had closed his last school in complete failure, but his main task as a teacher was just beginning. There were his three girls, and what he did with and for them would be the supreme test of his educational theories and powers. Was he to bring them up by the forcing process which had produced Margaret Fuller as a showpiece, or would it be better to let them grow naturally in sun and shower like Wordsworth's Lucy? The decision must not be postponed. Anna, to be sure, could never be a problem, and Elizabeth was still an infant, but Louisa—a dark-eyed, vivacious, and perplexing hoyden, thoughtless of books and loving to run in the wind—would soon be seven years old.

TRANSCENDENTAL
TALKER

Pains of solitude—Unable to write—Ascending and descending
to meet—The need of action and living speech—A phrenologi-
cal report—A conversation at Lynn—The Transcendental Club

LOUISA'S father would soon be forty years old, yet he was
without an occupation. On the twenty-second of June, 1839,
after he had dismissed the little Negress and had sent young
William Russell and his own three daughters out to play, he
might feel that the world demanded, asked, even wanted, nothing
more from him. He too had been dismissed. The thread of his
life was broken.

> Now am I visibly idle [he wrote]. My hand is
> without service. The Age hath no work for me. I stand
> with folded arms, desirous of doing some work for
> Soul; but the Age hath nothing of that sort in hand. It
> hath handsful for this of Body, and, unheeded, I gaze
> on the labourers around me. All hands, how busy!

What noise of instruments! What roar of elements!
"Fool!" saith the Age, "did'st thou think the Soul, of
which thou talkest, and for which thou wouldst fain
labour even unto death, hath aught like this? Thou
speakest mystically of instincts, faculties, whose needs
these arts shall never supply. Behold, all nature labours
and lends her stores to supply all needs."

The phrases are ponderously rhetorical. There is an echo in
them of the abrupt and clangorous rhythms that Carlyle of
Craigenputtock had attributed, ten years before, to his creature
Teufelsdröckh of Weissnichtwo. Odd enough it is to hear those
rhythms caught up now in Boston, and still more strange to observe how the romantic Weltschmerz of a Scot writing about an
imaginary German has infected not the style alone, but the very
mind and heart of a Yankee from the Connecticut hills. Alcot
"dramatizes" his own situation in terms suggested by *Sarto*
Resartus, and one can even guess that he has especially in mind
the sonorous passage beginning "Two men I honour, and no third,"
in which Carlyle distinguishes work for Body from work for
Soul and yet binds them together in the holiness of all toil. But
while observing this let us not make the common and stupid
blunder of supposing that an emotion which uses a borrowed form
of expression must be on that account any the less sincere.

Bronson Alcott's pain was real enough, and it was the pain of
isolation. Well equipped to do that "work for Soul" which has
always been the more important half of the American task, he
found "nothing of that sort in hand." The clatter and din of the
new factories was calling New England down to the watercourse
from all the old villages and farms. He had answered to quite another call. In the ear of fancy he heard the crack of axes and the
thunder of falling trees in the American forest. He heard the
thudding pick and scraping shovel of the roadmakers, the rattling hammers of bridge-builders, and, under all, the steady onward rumble and creak of the Westward-going wagons. And ye

[220]

although an American as typical as any, he had no part in that huge effort of concerted hands and brains. While the men of his place and time were streaming out once more on the trail that stretched from the Punjab to the Pacific, he had emigrated into the Western lands of the mind and soul. And why not? Did America think that there was nothing ahead for her but wider lands, taller corn, loftier mountains? Nay, but there were endless prairies of thought to be crossed, Sierras of the spirit to be scaled, and Californias of dream to be made real. If America did not know this, he must tell her. He was a spiritual pathfinder—a Daniel Boone, a Marcus Whitman of the mind. What wonder that he found himself alone?

Of course Bronson Alcott should have known from the start that such pioneering has always been lonely, but the necessary solitude of the thinker was a price which he could never cheerfully pay down. No way of earning a bare livelihood, no part in the common task, no place for him among companions working shoulder to shoulder—was it not unmercifully hard? He scanned his motives, his purposes, and the whole course of his conduct since he had begun to teach in the Connecticut villages. Why this succession of failures following upon the most confident hopes, with the last failure the most dismal of all? He could not lay them to any lack of fidelity on his part. No merchant in Boston, no scholar in Cambridge, no minister in Massachusetts, had been more instant in duty than he in his work for children. No one, not even Channing or Emerson, had listened more intently for the unerring voice of the Spirit, telling him what to do. Was it not clear, then, that the fault must lie not with him but with the world? Quite against the grain of his joyous and optimistic nature, he began to suspect that the world was out of joint and that he had been born to set it right.

This may require further explanation. We have watched Bronson Alcott, from the time when he turned from the peddling of Yankee notions to the teaching of children, showing an ever more

[221]

fierce and exclusive concentration of all his powers upon the tas[k]
in hand. At first it seemed to him almost as good a task as th[e]
preacher's, toward which it may be that he had unconsciousl[y]
aspired in his boyhood. Before long he had decided that it was [a]
better one, because it dealt with souls as yet unspotted from th[e]
world and took hold on what was coming instead of drowsing i[n]
the un-American past. That would mean that it was a holy task[,]
and that any man who performed it faithfully was no less tha[n]
a priest, a prophet, a holy man—in short, a man sent from God, [a]
messiah. But of course one knew how messiahs had commonl[y]
been treated in the past. Ill-treatment was almost proof of me[s]-
sianic standing.

Here was a line of thought that would take a man rather fa[r.]
But there were other lines. We have seen that Alcott was usuall[y]
an outsider looking in—and looking in, too, with a wistfulnes[s]
which those who have been born inside and have never lost the[ir]
unearned advantage can imagine, if at all, only with utmost diffi[i]-
culty. He was the son of a poor and barely literate man, bor[n]
in a backward district of a State from which the aristocracy [of]
Boston were accustomed at that time to import chiefly their ta[ll]
coachmen. His schooling had been brief and poor. He had do[ne]
his first work, very badly, among a class of men who, howev[er]
popular they may have been as a laughingstock, were rated [by]
substantial citizens not many notches above the criminal cla[ss.]
Such dignity as there had been for him in his position as a scho[ol]
master was what he had brought to it, and this had certainly n[ot]
been increased by his repeated failures. And such a man, with su[ch]
a background, had married into one, or rather into several, of t[he]
older and more respected families of Boston. He had come up [to]
New England's capital to live, with much the same hopes a[nd]
trepidations that a provincial Frenchman feels in going up [to]
Paris. Greatly daring, he had essayed to teach the scions of B[os]-
ton's "first families." Nearly all the men with whom he had ass[o]-
ciated in Boston were graduates of Harvard College, and he h[ad]

[222]

ot even graduated from the little gray school on Spindle Hill. everal of them were men of considerable wealth, and he was inking deeper every year into the quicksands of debt. A few of hem were accumulating influence and fame. So far as the world new him at all, he had accumulated for the most part disgrace nd obloquy.

To be sure, Alcott did not want fame in its cruder forms. He as so far from desiring what is ordinarily understood by "social ecognition" that he more than once refused kind offers of hositality from persons of the highest social prominence solely beause they were not the sort of persons with whom he cared to ssociate. No sane man, it seems probable, has ever shown a ore complete indifference to money than he did. He could uite cheerfully do without all of the coarser goods that are in ie world's gift; but he did want, intensely, to have a place, to belong," and not to be shut out. Even more, he wanted to get is sacred work done. If Boston shut him out, as Boston was so ever at doing, he might just possibly endure that; but if Boston ied to keep him from his holy task, then something might sudenly snap.

It is not surprising that Alcott grew, in these circumstances, mewhat morbidly intense. His Journal took on a new stridency tone. "Save me, O ye destinies," he cried, "from idleness, from me and servile engagements, from compliance with the vulgar ms and pursuits of my age. Lift me above its low maxims, and ake me a light shining amidst darkness!"

One must remember, in reading these words, that Alcott had) games to play. He had little play of any kind except with his vn children. He had never learned to laugh. A child of the hills, r more dependent than he had yet found out upon earth and air d open sky, he had been for ten years pent in city streets. He as not entirely well. He owed money to many persons, and had prospect of paying them. His wife, though faithful utterly, had own perhaps a little bitter during the eight years of steadily

[223]

increasing debt, and her words, though she meant less by then than might seem, were sometimes harsh and jarring.

And so Bronson Alcott turned inward. If he could not work or laugh or play, if no one came to see him, if his coat was so green with age that he could hardly go to see others, he could at least read over again, for the fourth or fifth time, the few books he had saved from the Temple School auction; he could write longer and ever more abstruse entries in his Journal; and, finally, he could think. He became something like what Emerson must have meant by the grand phrase "Man Thinking." Through no conscious choice of his own he had been set aside as a "Dedicated Mind."

But ah, it was cold and lonely work! Had Emerson known how lonely it would be, this dedicated thinking? How did he manage to keep off the terrible chill of solitude, sitting alone there among his books in his bare white house, or walking across the fields to Walden? Emerson was taking much pleasure just now, he said, in the company of a young fellow-villager, one Henry Thoreau—Alcott did not yet know how to spell the foreign-sounding name—who had recently come home from Harvard. Well, he would need all the companionship he could get after that fierce outbreak of all the orthodox against his Divinity School Address of last summer. How similar it had been to Alcott's own experience after the appearance of *Conversations on the Gospels!* The same people, even to Andrews Norton, had said much the same things. And then Alcott had written fondly, affectionately, but of course for his own eye alone:—

> I propose spending a few days in Concord with Emerson. We have much, I fancy, to say on the present aspects and tendencies of the times. A day of controversy is coming over our heads. . . . Persecutions fierce and unrelenting are to be waged against us. Our tempers are to be tried. I shall like to learn the mood of this my brother as he looks out from the seclusion of

[224]

his rural retreat.—"Brother!" That is a kindling name. I feel the sentiment of kindred quicken within me as I write it. He *is* a brother of mine, and an only one. All other men seem strange to me when I think of him; for none other knows me so well, and I value none so dearly. I may confide in him. Bravest of my contemporaries, he walks the earth magnanimously. I behold his front and despair not of men.

As for Emerson, he showed what it was that made the solitude f thought comparatively easy for him when he wrote in his own ournal:—

How can I not record so fair a fact as the visit of Alcott and Margaret Fuller, who came hither yesterday and departed this morning? Very friendly influences these, each and both. Cold as I am, they are almost dear. I shall not, however, fill my page with the gifts or merits of either.

These are the words of a man who said on another occasion at "We descend to meet." An equally characteristic remark Alcott's was that "Wherever two persons hold conference with ch other, an invisible though implied person is ever prior to e concert, and to this third person deference is always had, as a common arbiter." The contrast is sharp and clear, and all the ore so because Alcott tended to think that this implied "third rson" is divine. He consistently believed, at any rate, that every al "marriage of true minds" involves an ascent, a sanctification, en a sort of temporary apotheosis, for each and all of those concerned. It was with an interpretation peculiarly mystical and inase that he read the great text: "Where two or three are gathed together in my name, there am I in the midst of them." The two friends differed in many superficial opinions, but in other respect were they so radically, almost instinctively, opsed as in their thought and feeling about human association.

[225]

To Emerson—although one must certainly not forget his many close friendships, his clubs, or his pleasant relations with neighbors—it was a thing to be used sparingly, with caution, and for purposes ulterior to itself. To Alcott it was holy, besides being the main happiness of life if not the very reason for our existence. He did not "utter the word *en masse*" with Whitman's enthusiasm, but he could make almost a prayer out of the simple word "together." All his life, apparently, he was groping toward a conception of social relationship which would have given it the highest and deepest religious sanction. He seems to have felt, vaguely and yet strongly, that the vehicle or medium by which mind communicates with mind is nothing less than divine spirit. He seems to have believed that the binding element which unites friends, lovers, families, and all larger social groups, is spiritual. If he were living to-day and were conversant with recent scientific thought, he would certainly find a startling "emblem" of his belief in our theory of the material universe as a vast system of integration, partnerships, societies, and coöperative groups ranging all the way from the atom to the nebular vortices and held together in every part by a power of which even yet we can hardly guess the essential nature. During long periods of his life he was apparently convinced that the most direct approach which the human consciousness can make to the Supreme Being is not by what may be called the vertical ascension of prayer and worship but by a horizontal going-forth into the lives of others. Thus he escaped those agonies of uncertainty concerning the salvation of the individual soul with which so many generations of Puritans were tormented. He tended to think that we are either to be saved together or else not at all. Thus it was, too, that he came by his unquestionable religious attitude toward the teaching of children, and, in later life, toward the Conversation. To Emerson, from first to last, the "ecstatic moment" came in solitude; but with Alcott it was more likely to be a shared experience, made possible by the sharing. To him it seemed natural and right that the Apostles were "filled

ith the Holy Ghost and began to speak with other tongues as the
pirit gave them utterance" at a time when they were "all with
ne accord in one place."

Emerson was so well pleased with his own cool distance from
ie world that he thought his friend would do well to adopt a
milar way of life. He wrote to Alcott, at the time when the Tem-
le School was manifestly failing:

> In the few moments broken conversation I had with
> you a fortnight ago, it seems to me you did not ac-
> quiesce at all in what is always my golden view for you,
> as for all men to whom God has given "the vision and
> faculty divine"; namely, that one day you would leave
> the impracticable world to wag its own way, and sit
> apart and write your oracles for its behoof.

These words were written, it should be said, before Emerson
ıd seen that final revision of "Psyche" which convinced him,
·rhaps somewhat prematurely, that Alcott would never be able
· succeed as an author. As for Alcott himself, the proposal did
ıt tempt him precisely for the reason that it involved a retired
not a lonely life. What seemed to Emerson a chief advantage
the writing-man's career was to Alcott a main defect. After a
scussion of the problem which seems to have filled a visit to
ıncord of unusual length, he wrote in his Journal:

> My week's intercourse with Emerson has done me
> good. It has classified me. I define my theatre of action
> the better by comparison with his.—He is a scholar. He
> lives to see and to write. He looks abroad on Nature
> and Life and sketches their features with his pen. I
> act, rather than observe; foresee, rather than live in
> memory. . . . I am of a temper too earnest and in-
> tense to rest in contemplation, to observe, describe
> merely. I must think, and set my thought in the dra-
> pery of action and living speech.

[227]

"Action and living speech"—both would lead him out of soli
tude; but, of the two, he certainly had more talent for the second
Some might say, and indeed Emerson did say with emphasis, tha
Alcott could not really act at all, but no one was ever to asser
that he could not talk. With his admirable voice and enunciation
with the large and various vocabulary that came so much mor
readily to his tongue than to his pen, and with a mind store
with images, analogues, correspondences, drawn from book:
society, nature, and manual toil, Bronson Alcott was an ine>
haustible fountain of talk. The waters of his thought had bee
stored in the high hills of his youth, and they had lain quietl
there under the suns and moons of many a year's lonely medita
tion; but now they came racing down into the crowded city by th
sea to leap and dance and play before the weary people, to aspi
and to mount once more, in a splendor of morning lights, towar
the serene heaven whence they had come. What though the top
most spray of the fountain's spire was often dispersed into a mi
so fine that the eye lost it? Always the most ethereal thoughts (
the supreme talkers—Coleridge, Socrates, Jesus—climbed so ne;
to heaven's gate that they were lifted in and did not return. L
the world listen and be thankful for what it could get—and than!
ful even more for all that escaped and was swept away upwar
He, Bronson Alcott, listened and was filled with gratitude, for I
never supposed that these words were entirely his. They were al
the words of the Spirit that had sent him.

But whatever might be the reason, talking was a thing th
Alcott could do. It was a thing he loved to do, perhaps part
because it committed him to nothing. It was like that writing
the snow in his boyhood, beautiful to-day and gone to-morro
Like music, it died almost in the moment of birth, and all its k
ing was a farewell; and yet it was most lovely to remember. U
like painting, sculpture, and even most men's writing, it was ne\
the imitation of an external model, an outward law, but the fi
and spontaneous putting-forth again of a law that a man b

[228]

drawn inside himself and reënacted there. Though never wild or licentious or uncontrolled, it was one continuous improvisation, free in that good true sense of a willing subjection to the laws of the inward senate-chamber. The fountain sprang in the air with always the same fixed form, as though it were a tree of rushing and falling water, yet every particle of spray that rose and fell had all the liberty of a wind-blown raindrop.

Talking, moreover, was a social art. Even when it did not pass beyond monologue, it involved a partnership. Compared with writing, in which at best one could speak only to dimly imagined faces, it was warm and human and real. Good writing was itself no more than a distant imitation of good talk. In *Sartor Resartus,* what was the secret of that amazing style? Simply that the writer had been listening to the cadences of some actual voice—perhaps his father's, or his own. Emerson thought, did he, that one should stand away from the world and speak with the pen? Well, the pen was a poor stiff tool, looking too much like the capital letter I." The pen was a sort of pike, intended to hold people off. A man could not really think with pen in hand; he could only imitate and remember. Thinking occurred when minds met in the air and carried.

Emerson was a somewhat hesitant talker, often fumbling too long, as writers will, for the exact and unique word. All the more on that account he wondered at the profusion and the frequent splendor of his friend's talk, in which he took a pure æsthetic pleasure like that of a man watching a fountain. In the course of a long passage about Alcott in his Journal for March, 1848, Emerson says:—

He delights in speculation, in nothing so much, and is very well endowed and weaponed for that work with a copious, accurate and elegant vocabulary; I may say poetic; so that I know no man who speaks such good English as he, and is so inventive withal. He speaks truth truly, for the expression is adequate. Yet he

[229]

knows only this one language. He hardly needs an antagonist—he needs only an intelligent ear. When he is greeted by loving and intelligent persons, his discourse soars to a wonderful height, so regular, so lucid, so playful, so new and disdainful of all boundaries of tradition and experience, that the hearers seem no longer to have bodies of material gravity but almost they can mount into the air at pleasure, or leap at one bound out of this poor solar system. . . . He has moreover the greatest possession both of mind and temper in his discourse, so that the mastery and moderation and foresight, and yet felicity, with which he unfolds his thought, are not to be surpassed. This is of importance for such a broacher of novelties as he is, and to one baited, as he is very apt to be, by the sticklers for old books or old institutions. He takes such delight in the exercise of this faculty that he will willingly talk the whole of a day, and most part of the night, and then again tomorrow, for days successively; and if I, who am impatient of much speaking, draw him out to walk in the woods or fields, he will stop at the first fence and very soon propose either to sit down or to return. He seems to think society exists for this function, and that all literature is good or bad as it approaches colloquy, which is its perfection. Poems and histories may be good, but only as adumbrations of this; and the only true manner of writing the literature of a nation would be to convene the best heads in the community, set them talking, and then introduce stenographers to record what they say.

For the art of conversation Alcott had a definite and conscious theory which was woven into the whole fabric of his thinking. And he was curious, too, in the history of this art, carrying back to the teaching-methods of Jesus, of Socrates, of Pythagoras, and bringing it down to the writings of Walter Savage Landor

whom Alcott considered one of the foremost of contemporary
prosemen for the simple reason that he dealt in the Conversation.
A main charm of this art to the man from the Connecticut hills
was that all its materials were, so to speak, home-grown. A talker
did not depend upon the quarry for marble or upon the shop for
paints and canvas. His work was more like carving a violin out of
the maple tree that one had felled in the back-pasture, and then
stringing the bow with hairs from the tail of the family horse; but
it was even better than that, because all the substance of talking
was really insubstantial and was brought down from the upland
pastures of the mind. And another charm of it was that it involved
the partnership of women. One could not recall any woman to
place beside Raphael, Michelangelo, Milton, Beethoven, or Chris-
opher Wren, but in the art of conversation one could find women
of genius in any New England town. They were bringing a new
quality, a Sibylline wisdom, into the treasure house of American
life. They did not argue and contend and ask for definitions like
Garrison or Parker or Henry James. They saw truth directly, and,
without waiting for reasons, they said what they saw; or else they
sat and listened, helping a man up and on with their trustful
sympathy—and that was better still. In the mere silence and ac-
quiescence of a good woman there was more wisdom than in the
volubility of a brilliant contentious man.

And so, while he still remained "Man Thinking" and a "Dedicated Mind," Bronson Alcott went forth from the solitude of
thought to meet and talk with men and women in the towns and
villages of the Boston region. Once more he took to the road as a
pedlar of "Yankee notions," although that phrase had taken on a
somewhat more ethereal sense for him in the course of fifteen
years. Some clerical friend, perhaps the Reverend S. D. Robbins
of Lynn, would advertise among his parishioners that Mr. Alcott
would conduct a series of Conversations, for the next eight or ten
Wednesday evenings, upon some such loose and ample topic as

[231]

over

"Self-Culture" or "Human Life." When the first Wednesday came Alcott would walk from Boston to Lynn, partly in order to save the coach fare but partly also because he found that the best preparation he could make for a long talk was simply a long walk. Usually he made no other preparation, unless it might be to read for an hour or two in some book that seemed congenial with the topic of the evening. Upon reaching Lynn he would go at once to the home of the Reverend Mr. Robbins or of some other sponsor of the series. Hotels and taverns were loathsome to him. He did not like the noises or the smells of them, the talk that he heard in them, the absence of women, or the bills that they presented for immediate payment. A hotel did badly for pay what any good man should delight to do well for mere love of his fellow man. During his peddling journeys in the South Alcott had always preferred to sleep in the slave quarters rather than at inns and taverns, and now he had the added reason for shunning such places that he had been for several years a vegetarian. Emerson, when on his lecture tours, nearly always refused proffered hospitality and went to the hotel, because he wished to be alone. Alcott, when he went out conversing, always sought hospitality in private homes for just the opposite reason: he wanted companionship. And if it be said that he might have found this at the tavern as even Nathaniel Hawthorne could do at North Adams or in Parker's bar, one must answer that Hawthorne did not really find companionship in those places but only a spectacle of crude virility to feed his hunger for facts.

At seven in the evening, after the early supper, there would be some twenty or thirty persons gathered in one of the Lynn "Parlours," sitting on sofas and Hitchcock or Windsor chairs round a mahogany table on which an Argand lamp was burning. On the hearth would be a fire of driftwood. The room itself, its proportions and appointments, its decorations and lighting might seem a little stiff and cold and bare to a visitor from our own day, and yet there would be at least the relics and reminders in it of a taste distinctly better than that into which New England was slowly settling down. The faces of nearly all those present would be of the sort called "Mayflower faces," now that they are so rare that the search for one of them in the streets of Boston or Hartford is like looking for a four-leaved clover. An irreverent caricaturist of today might well decide to draw the whole group as a mere assembly of noses. To our ears, moreover, the voices of these people would not be remarkably musical, and their speech would show an almost conscious avoidance of musical range and pitch; yet when the whole roomful was talking together one might at least say that these reshapers of the English language were making full use of their extraordinary nasal equipment. Seldom, however, would many be speaking at once. The tendency would be, rather, to give each individual a respectful and silent hearing—and then, not infrequently, to disagree.

On the first evening of the series Mr. Alcott would be introduced to each of his interlocutors; and one of the more surprising observations made by a twentieth-century eavesdropper would be the fact that every name spoken was what we now call, somewhat amusingly, an "American name." The mild and graceful dignity of Alcott's bearing would also surprise, and possibly amuse, an onlooker of our day, born and bred since the old race of gentlemen died out. Emerson, an expert in such matters, was soon to write of his friend Alcott:

> He is very noble in his carriage to all men, of a
> serene and lofty aspect and deportment in the street
> and in the house. Of simple but graceful and majestic
> manners, having a great sense of his own worth, so that
> not willingly will he give his hand to a merchant,
> though he be never so rich,—yet with a strong love of
> men.

There was something in Alcott's manners that was faintly strange to his New England audiences, but nothing that could be called exotic. They had been learned, as we have seen, among the plantations of Virginia, so that they were American sufficiently, and were as democratic as good manners ever can be, without belonging to his exact time and place. They had been practised for many years, moreover, in the schoolroom. He who had played the courteous host to hundreds of American children—inviting them to partnership, inciting them to common effort, leading them as groups and yet loving them one by one— why should he not be courteous now to their elders? It was no new thing that he was doing. Among children he had learned to be patient and hopeful and kind. In talking to children he had dropped away from his speech, if not from his writing, all that tasteless pomposity of the pseudo-genteel. In association with children he had learned the better part of what he now had to say. Put it thus: He was the interpreter of childhood, the spokesman of childhood's heaven-sent wisdom, reminding grown people now of the truths that they once had known but had long, long since forgotten.

In Alcott's physical presence there was a strong suggestion of personal dignity and of power quietly controlled. He was not a man with whom persons of any discernment in character would be tempted to take liberties. People might turn to look after him as he walked down the street in Boston, New York, or London, but they would scarcely do so in a mood of derision. He wore unusual hats, and yet it was always clear to persons with half an eye for such matters that these hats were abundantly justified by the unusual quality of the brain beneath them.

But how, more precisely, did Bronson Alcott look to those conversational audiences before whom he appeared, when about forty years of age, at Lynn, Salem, Lexington, Hingham, and other towns of the Boston district? He was nearly six feet tall and his lithe slenderness gave the effect of a greater height. The years of physical activity in his boyhood and youth had left their mark in a figure of good proportions, in strong shoulders, and in rather large but well-shaped hands. He held himself easily erect and walked with a step remarkably light and springing. It was the shape of his body and head rather than his features that might have caused some persons—he himself not among them—to regard him as a handsome man. His skull was nobly arched and domed, with a brow rather high than broad. Any deficiency that it may have had must have been in the region of the cerebellum.

As one of the early American readers of Lavater, Alcott was interested all his life in physiognomy and consistently held that "the body is a type of the soul." In phrenology, one of the minor "crazes" of his time, he had no faith whatever, and only just enough interest to make him record the findings of the three or four practitioners for whom he sat—apparently at their request—during the eighteen-thirties. The last of these, a certain "Mr. Fowler of New York," found in 1838 that the volume of Alcott's brain was "full, with great activity," and that his temperament was "nervo-sanguineous." Concerning Alcott's "organs" he reported that those to be classified as "very large" were Philoprogenitiveness, Adhesiveness, Approbativeness, Veneration, and Ardor, and that those to be considered unusually large were Amativeness, Inhabitiveness, Circumspection, Firmness, and Self-Esteem.

This craniological description, however exact it may have been, does not help us to imagine the appearance of Bronson Alcott as he came before his first adult audiences. What they probably observed first of all was the serene azure of his eyes, which Henry Thoreau was one day to commemorate by calling him a "sky-blue man." The gaze of his eyes was steady but it seemed to be fixed on the far distance, like that of a sailor or a mountaineer. It was as though he looked through all things near at hand rather than at them. His mouth was large, firm, accurately chiseled, and the long thin upper lip was slightly indrawn like that of a horse. The chin was curiously knotted or puckered round a central depression. From the well-shaped nose—unmistakably of the Yankee sort and yet not unduly large—two deep wrinkles, not unlike those to be seen in the later portraits of Emerson, swept laterally downward beyond the corners of the mouth. Alcott's face, indeed, was already heavily furrowed. Perhaps on account of his troubles at the Temple School, he looked at forty much older than his years, as he was to look far younger than he was at the age of eighty. His perfectly straight hair was fading from its natural reddish hue toward the color of corn tassels. Already thin on the top of his head, it fell in long lank strands behind and over his large ears; and although it did not yet cover his coat collar one could see that this was its aspiration.

Such was the general appearance, then, of the "Mr. A. Bronson Alcott" whom we are to imagine as seated in the center of a crowded parlor at Lynn, about one hundred years ago, beginning an evening's entertainment with a simply worded declaration of his faith in conversing. There was nothing hard or strange about it, he would be saying. It was an art in which all of those there present had already acquired much experience, and quite possibly some of them were far more skillful at it than he. And yet he had used it a good deal—perhaps most successfully with children. He had not invented it. On the contrary, he had found it almost perfectly exemplified in the Gospels and in the Dialogues of Plato. If it was a finer thing, as he believed, than the lecture which his old friend Josiah Holbrook was spreading through the land by means of the American Lyceum, that was because a group of people made it by working together in concert, each individual contributing to a result more valuable than any one could have produced alone. There was not much value in merely being told things, even by the wisest minds. The truths that were to be entirely ours we must always discover within us, and the Conversation was no more than a ship on which every separate mind and heart might set forth on a voyage of self-discovery, inward bound. Yes, self-knowledge, that goal of all the wise men ancient and modern, was their goal too; but he thought that they might most profitably seek it not in solitude, as so many had believed, but as a company of kindred minds and hearts. And simple though it was, the Conversation seemed to him a chief means of that "civilization" and "culture" about which there had recently been some talk and inquiry in New England. Above all others, it was a "humanizing" art. Those "humanities" which his friends over in Cambridge thought were to be discovered chiefly in Latin and Greek he thought he could find more readily in the parlors of New England towns, in converse with men and women—but chiefly with women; for it was a main article of his creed that women excelled in this art, or at any rate that no Conversation was likely to prosper without them.

An effect of mild hypnosis would be spreading by this time through the group. Many would resist it, but a few would succumb with a glad sense of release from their shyness and inhibitions. They were being asked, most courteously, for their assistance in a common effort. Some were being told for the first time in their lives that their opinions were of worth and would be valued. And certainly it should not be hard to speak one's deepest, highest thought in the presence of such a man. One could tell that he had never sneered at any human being. The power of ridicule simply was not in him. All the time he was speaking the faintest imaginable smile would hover not so much upon as above his face, as though it were a halo or a reflection. It was not a smile of amusement or of disdain. Rather it seemed to be a sort of spiritual light, a nimbus of serenity. And his eyes, although they gladly met the gaze of any single interlocutor, were for the most part upward cast while he was talking with the group, as though he were addressing that one composite mind to which each individual had contributed his share. The inflections of his finely modulated voice were more versatile and wide-ranging than those to which New England was accustomed. One would say that his voice, and his face as well, had been trained not for the hiding of emotion, in the New England way, but actually for its revelation. And every sentence that he spoke, although it was obviously springing up in his mind for the first time, had a sort of preordained finish and beauty. A careful student of style would have observed that his characteristic sentences were long and loosely flowing, with many tributaries of subordinate clauses feeding into them, so that when he was halfway between capital and period there might be some doubt, even a little anxiety, as to whether he would not lose his way among the many islands and estuaries of his thought before he came to the full round close. He seldom did so. Neither was there any difficulty in following what he said. About Mr. Emerson's lectures people differed, some asserting that they were quite simple and others frankly declaring that they could not catch their drift at all. But Mr. Alcott was never permanently cryptic or dark. If you did not understand, or if you disagreed, you said so, and he usually tried to meet your difficulty. You could not do that with a lecturer. And there was something about Mr. Alcott's way of rounding off his periods by the inflection of his voice that was in itself an accenting and clarification of what he meant. At least he always started from the common ground, however his thought might wheel in ever-widening gyres and spirals as he went upward like a hawk into the summer sky. If he disappeared, that was because he was lost in light.

A strange experience it was to see him sitting there so quietly with eyes uplifted—only his hands moving, moving incessantly, drawing diagrams of his thought on the table, clasping and unclasping, or stroking his knee as though it were a kitten whose fur must not be rubbed the wrong way—while his thoughts were all the time plunging up and upward into Plato's heaven of ultimate being and pure idea.

Yes, a strange experience it must have been, but during almost fifty years of the nineteenth century it was one with which many

[238]

hundreds of Americans, East and West, became familiar. Bronson Alcott was never to become so famous as General Tom Thumb or Barnum's elephant "Jumbo," nor was he ever to be so highly remunerated for his services to the country as Jay Gould or John D. Rockefeller, and yet he was quite as representative of America's essential spirit as any of these figures. No one who wishes to understand the decades on either side of the Civil War can afford to disregard his Conversations.

It was frequently said that they were in fact monologues. The same thing was said, perhaps correctly, about the talk of Carlyle and Coleridge, and Alcott himself said of Carlyle that he could not converse but could only talk. For the two British giants we have no sufficient records, but of Alcott's Conversations the records are abundant, full, and completely trustworthy. They show just the opposite of what is commonly asserted, proving that his main effort was not to domineer but to elicit, and that in this effort he showed remarkable quickness of wit and fertility of resource. When he found that he had to do most of the talking himself he invariably marked down the Conversation of that evening as a failure.

There was one kind of rejoinder, however, that Alcott could not or would not meet. The contentious spirit, the mood of debate, the mind that was forever lying in ambush to leap upon the slightest exaggeration or warmth of statement, simply silenced him. He asked people to come together to share their affirmations, not their doubts and fears and hesitancies, certainly not their egotisms. He asked them to add, not to subtract. It was the greatest common denominator, and not the least, that he was always seeking. This was the reason why, when Henry James, but at Emerson's on a famous occasion, tried to heckle Alcott, or when William Lloyd Garrison, on another, made himself thoroughly obnoxious not only to him but to every other sensitive person by questioning his facts and his logic, attacking him from below, Alcott simply took refuge in the uppermost silences. In-

[239]

deed, that was always to be his mode of escape from every perplexity, even from "family straits"—to soar above it into that intense inane of overarching blue where he found always plenty of room. When the hunters tried to pierce him with a fact or snare him in a syllogism, there would always come that sudden strong beat of wild wings, and, looking up, they would see him easily floating far, far above.

Many Bostonians remembered for many years an occasion when Alcott was conversing about "Angelic and Demonic Man." They had been somewhat amused to hear the former described as contemplative, withdrawn yet kindly, intuitive, blond, and with blue eyes. The speaker was too evidently describing himself. But when he went on to describe the demonic man as physically powerful, with dark eyes and hair and unusual energy and strength of will, his listeners began to cast sidelong glances at the Reverend William Batchelder Greene, who was sitting just before the speaker and was evidently becoming restless. His hair was raven black, his eyes were fiery, and he was a man of exceptional strength both of body and of mind. Moreover, he had made trouble for Alcott on other occasions.

"This demonic man," Alcott was saying, "is sternly logical. He loves argument and disputation. He smokes tobacco."

"But has not the demonic man his value?" asked the Reverend Mr. Greene with a deceptive humility of tone.

"Oh, yes," said the converser. "Yes, the demonic man is good in his place, very good. He is good to build railroads; but I do not like to see him in pulpits, begging Mr. Greene's pardon."

And then there came a swift succession of further questions, each of which drove the intended victim a little farther toward the verge of a manifest absurdity—until at last, when he had been left "without a leg to stand on," Alcott took sudden flight into the splendors of the loftiest philosophic abstraction.

As for the demonic Reverend Mr. Greene, he soon after resigned his place in the Christian ministry.

[240]

It may well be that Alcott could not have met on their own level these more agile wits and better-stored heads than his own. What is certain is that he would not. That would have been to wreck the work of art for which he, as coryphæus, was responsible. He, the conductor, was trying to draw forth a symphony from a band of harmonious minds. When a member of the orchestra burst into a solo that was not set down in the score, there had to be a complete pause in the music—after which the concerted playing might perhaps begin again. Many tales and rumors about these interruptions were once current in the Boston region. They pleased a people whose experience of intellectual conflict was deeper than their knowledge of spiritual peace; but they were all of them quite beside the point. For the most part the interrupters were persons too clever and too self-centered to understand what was going on. Ensemble playing was simply beyond their comprehension. Each of them was a soloist, and supposed that Alcott must be trying to be one too.

Emerson once told George Frisbie Hoar about a Conversation at his own house at which Theodore Parker had attacked Alcott for his vagueness of statement. He said that "Parker wound himself around Alcott like an anaconda. You could hear poor Alcott's bones crunch." No doubt this must have been exhilarating to watch and hear, but, after all, the main purpose of the occasion had not been the crunching of Alcott's bones.

Contemporary opinions differed widely about the worth of Alcott's Conversations. Women liked them best, as he would have expected and hoped. Emerson seldom thought that Alcott did himself full justice in them, although he often felt that they were wonderfully good. Daniel Ricketson of New Bedford complained that they rambled too much, and was of course told that they were not to be tested by the standards of the lecture. O. B. Frothingham, a close observer of things transcendental who often attended the Conversations in Boston, spoke of them with unqualified praise. "The unfailing serenity of the leader," he said,

[241]

"his wealth of mental resource, his hospitality of thought, his wit, his extraordinary felicity of language, his delicacy of touch, ready appreciation of different views, and singular grace in turning opinions toward the light, made it clear to all present that to this special calling he was chosen." What is a little surprising is the not infrequent testimony that Alcott's part in the Conversations was remarkable for humor. Wit and audacity were certainly not lacking, and the talk was seldom positively dull. The somewhat scornful attitude of clever critics such as T. W. Higginson and J. T. Trowbridge is hard to reconcile with the fact that Alcott's Conversations continued for more than four decades to attract Boston audiences ranging from thirty to seventy persons. Perhaps the final truth about them was best indicated by Trowbridge himself, although he did not like them:

> Do you care to meet Alcott? His mind is a mirror
> Reflecting the unspoken thought of his hearer.
> To the great, he is great; to the fool he's a fool—
> In the world's dreary desert a crystalline pool
> Where a lion looks in and a lion appears,
> But an ass will see only his own ass's ears.

One need scarcely say that Alcott's Conversations were by no means uniformly successful. As every teacher and public speaker will understand, he often had to deal with groups of persons who sat like so many blocks of wood—and of wood, too, as heavy and hard as teak, utterly uninflammable. They could not even be warmed. Graven images would have been as voluble, and stones of the field as enthusiastic. After an evening with a group of this kind, an evening that had seemed an eternity of torment, the converser would go home in profound melancholy, wondering what was wrong with him.

And indeed there was something seriously wrong with him, and the responsibility for these ghastly failures did not lie with his collocutors alone. The fact is that there were two Bronson Alcotts, and that no one could ever make the least guess which one of the two would turn up on any given occasion. First, there was the Alcott whom Emerson eulogized as "a profound insight, a power, a majestical man, looking easily along the centuries to explore his contemporaries, with a painful sense of being an orphan and a hermit here"; and then there was the Alcott of whom Emerson spoke in the same sentence as "very tedious and prosing and egotistical and narrow." Such contradictory statements are highly perplexing to the student until he suddenly realizes that both the favorable and the unfavorable comment are perfectly true. There really was in the strange compound called Bronson Alcott a certain impecunious, down-at-the-heel, wool-gathering chronic failure of a man about whom Emerson quite justifiably remarked: "I do not want any more such persons to exist." When this man took charge of a Conversation, things did not go remarkably well. But then there was that other Alcott, so amazingly and utterly other, whom Emerson called "the most remarkable man and the highest genius of the time." When he took hold, things might be said which every auditor would remember as long as he lived. Occasionally the two would show themselves on the same evening, as they did in a Conversation recorded by Emerson in 1855:

> I was struck with the late superiority he showed. The interlocutors were all better than he; he seemed childish and helpless, not apprehending or answering their remarks aright; they masters of their weapons. But by and by, when he got upon a thought, like an Indian seizing by the mane and mounting a wild horse of the desert, he over-rode them all, and showed such mastery and so took up Time and Nature like a boy's marble in his hand, as to vindicate himself.

It is evident from these quotations alone that Emerson was fascinated by the swift or slow oscillations that he saw in his friend between almost a feckless imbecility on the one hand and a demonic force and drive of intellectual energy on the other. Why should he not have been, considering that he had known from his boyhood precisely the same soarings and sinkings in his own mental life? How many times had he called himself "a God in nature" on one day, and on the next been obliged to say "I am a weed by the wall"! The fated, necessary seasons of stupidity and ineptitude out of which our few supreme moments are painfully and precariously born were well enough known to him. Whether Alcott also recognized them as inevitable is not certain. He inclined toward an explanation of his alternating successes and failures in the Conversation which was somewhat more flattering. "Talent," he said, "strikes conviction, but genius does not convince. To whom it is imparted it gives forebodings of the immeasurable and infinite, while talent sets certain limits; and so, because it is understood, it also maintains."

The topics of Alcott's Conversations—"On Man," "On Character," "On Temperaments and Pursuits," "On Social Life," and the like—were of course by far too large and vague and general. One may see, however, in glancing through the titles of Thoreau's or Emerson's Essays, that this was a common fault of the time. So also, if it was a fault at all, was Alcott's frequent direction of the talk toward moral and spiritual edification. Although he regarded the Conversation as unquestionably an art, he saw no reason why its ends should be exclusively æsthetic. It differed from the sermon by only one degree more than the lectures of the day. One might call it a sermon made by "communal composition," having the advantages of improvisation and spontaneity and yet always, like the talk of Chaucer's Clerk, "sownynge in moral vertu."

In the respect that they were entirely spontaneous and were improvised upon the spot, Alcott's Conversations were better examples of transcendental method and theory than the carefully elaborated lectures and essays of Emerson. Like his friend.

[244]

Alcott listened patiently for the "one accent of the Holy Ghost," but he interpreted its oracles instantly, without editing or deletion. He was the Over-Soul's passive spokesman, its "pale-mouthed prophet dreaming," as Emerson was its all but perfect scribe. Perfectly evident it is that Emerson, for all his praise of a spontaneous rhapsodism, was consciously the master of a superb rhetoric which he had won by hard purposive toil. Alcott, on the other hand, reminds one of the unlettered peasant Cædmon, who sat wistfully silent while the many skillful singers were chanting their lays, but to whom the Angel of the Lord appeared, after he had gone to the stable for the night, and said "Sing!" Or he is like Moses, who hung back from the divine errand and said: 'O my Lord, I am not eloquent, neither heretofore nor since thou hast spoken unto thy servant; but I am slow of speech, and of a slow tongue.' And the Lord said unto him: 'Who hath made man's mouth? . . . Now therefore, go, and I will be thy mouth and teach thee what thou shalt say.' "

In these Conversations, then—welling up in the Temple School, spilling over into Boston and the adjacent towns and villages, after some twenty years lifting across the Adirondacks in jets of lofty cloud, and at last flowing down in annual freshets and floods of talk into the Great Valley—Bronson Alcott escaped the loneliness and separation of the "Dedicated Mind." He was "Man Thinking," but he was Man Talking too. Thus it was, not for the first and certainly not for the last time, that he turned an apparent defeat into unquestionable victory. Boston had tried to sneer and shout him down, and his answer was an inexhaustible torrent of "living speech." Boston had told him that he was no longer to teach her children, and he set forth to teach the parents of America. Even Emerson had tried to shut him up somewhere with pen and paper for companions. Emerson, in most ways so good a general, had advised a retreat. Alcott's answer was a charge.

[245]

The military metaphor, however, does not suit this man wh
always made the threat of force look foolish. Instead of turnin
back into solitude he walked abroad in the hearts and minds o
men; he moved out of his own misery into other lives. It was
perfect strategy, when the world was shouting "You shall not d
that," for him to answer "Let us do this thing together." So h
met the doubled fist with open arms.

Not all the world had joined in the shouting. In Boston itse
there were at least a few persons who understood Bronson Alco
and who stood by him. These were the "Minds" that he ha
sought out from the beginning, related not distantly to tl
"Brahmins" of a somewhat later day. In spite of their stror
liking for independence they had a way of standing together, a
they felt an increasing need to do. It was a time of loosely o
ganized social groups, circles, *cénacles,* many of them witho
officers or dues or rules, that met for general conversation whe
and where they found it convenient. One of these was the s
called "Symposium," which, to use Alcott's own words about
"was a company of earnest persons enjoying conversation on hi
themes and having much in common."

The casual and offhand character of the little group cann
well be exaggerated. Composed of persons who strongly d
trusted all institutions and organizations, it drew itself togeth
as loosely as possible. It had no chairman or president, no settl
place or time of meeting, and no definite name. Alcott sometim
called it "the Club," and at other times "the Symposium," reg
larly misspelling the word. Others called it "Hedge's Club" b
cause it was likely to meet when F. H. Hedge, then preachi
at the Unitarian Church in Bangor, happened to be in Bost
The outside world soon came to speak of it as "the Transce
dental Club," using the adjective with about the same tinge
sarcasm that was present in the early use of "Methodist"
"Quaker." Partly on account of his infirm health but also

[246]

:ause of his lifelong preference for working behind the scenes,
he man to whom it chiefly owed its existence, Dr. Channing,
ttended its meetings scarcely at all. Some precedency was given
o Dr. Convers Francis of Watertown, but only because he was
he oldest member of a group composed for the most part of
ersons still rather young.

The public, unable to understand or unwilling to believe that
he group was so nearly formless, regarded it, Emerson tells us,
s a "concert of doctrinaires to establish certain opinions or to
naugurate some movement in literature, philosophy, or reli-
ion." Of any such definite purpose it was at first entirely inno-
ent. The general public, too, always looking for a convenient
andle, was convinced during the period of Alcott's deepest dis-
race that he was the ringleader of the "Transcendental Club."
he public was wrong. And it was no less wrong when it shifted
he alleged leadership, during the uproar against Emerson's Divin-
y School Address, to the shoulders of Emerson. The group had
o acknowledged leader. At the time of the first meeting Alcott
as probably the most famous, or perhaps one should say the most
otorious, member, and it is reasonable to suppose that from first
last he did a large share of the talking. He was also the most
urely "transcendental" of the group, and seems to have been so
garded. With the possible exception of Emerson, he was the
ost regular in attendance. Yet it was in no sense peculiarly
s club.

There had been a preliminary meeting in which Dr. Channing—
often, in spite of what Alcott had said of him, the originating
rce behind the forward movements of the time—had urged
on young George Ripley and a few others the founding of
me association for "mutual inquiry." On the nineteenth of
otember, 1836, Ripley brought five persons together at his
use in Boston "to see how far it would be possible for earnest
nds to meet." These five were Alcott, Emerson, Hedge, Fran-
, and James Freeman Clarke. They issued invitations to Dr.

[247]

Channing, Jonathan Phillips, James Walker, N. L. Frothingham J. S. Dwight, W. H. Channing, and C. A. Bartol, of whom only the last three later appeared with any regularity. This, however was primarily a business meeting, and it adjourned with an agree ment that the first real discussion should be held at Alcott's hous in Beach Street on the third of October, at three o'clock.

At the second session there were present, besides the host Emerson, Hedge, Francis, Ripley, Orestes Brownson, Clarke, an Bartol, and they discussed the topic "American Genius—th Causes which Hinder Its Growth Giving Us no First-Rate Pro ductions." The theme had already been worn threadbare by doz ens of Commencement-Day orators—by young Henry Wadsworth Longfellow among them, up at Bowdoin, eleven years before We may doubt whether anything new was said on the topic b the gentlemen gathered in Alcott's parlor, but it would be interes ing to know what old things were repeated, for this was just th topic that Emerson was to handle ten months later in his P Beta Kappa Day Address on "The American Scholar," treating with such memorable mastery and force as to make all his liste ers and readers forget that it had ever been handled before. O would like to know what Alcott contributed, and what Emerso thought of his contribution. Would he not use all the advantag of his ignorance, and tell these scholars of Harvard College th a main deterrent to American genius was its subserviency to t European past? If he did not, then he must have fallen belo himself on this occasion, and failed to represent Connectic One would like to think that he recalled certain words from t Preface to Noah Webster's Speller which he had been oblig to learn by heart in the school on Spindle Hill, and that Emers listened with fascinated attention while he spoke them. I the words were these: "Europe is grown old in folly, corrupti and tyranny. In that country laws are perverted, manners licentious, literature is declining, and human nature is debas For America in her infancy to adopt the present maxims of

[248]

ld world would be to stamp the wrinkles of decrepit age upon
he bloom of youth and to plant the seeds of decay in a vigorous
onstitution. American glory begins to dawn at a favorable pe-
iod, and under flattering circumstances. We have the experience
f the whole world before our eyes; but to receive indiscrimi-
ately the maxims of government, the manners and literary taste
f Europe, and make them the ground on which to build our
rstems in America, must soon convince us that a durable and
.ately edifice can never be erected upon the mouldering pillars of
ntiquity."

The topics discussed at later meetings of the Symposium were
kely to be related in some way to theology, and this not pri-
arily for the reason that nearly all the members of the group
ere either actual and practising or else reformed clergymen.
he reason was that they were really interested in theology,
:ough in ways that would have won them little approbation
om the orthodox of any religious sect. How could they fail to
: so interested? They were living toward the end of an epoch,
•vering more than two centuries of American history, during
hich the nature of God and His dealings with the human soul
.d seemed to almost every serious New England mind by far
e most absorbing topic of thought and discussion. Profound
anges of belief had come about during that period, and the
embers of the Symposium were intellectually the products of
ose changes. Strict Calvinism had gradually relaxed its grip,
ring the eighteenth century, upon the more liberal minds, and
d been succeeded in the Boston district by a Unitarianism
iich, in the opinion of its enemies, made its creed chiefly out
what it did *not* believe. All the early transcendentalists were
itarians in some sense, but nearly all of them had come to feel
it the doctrines of this Church which had always been essen-
lly liberal were too restricting, and that a movement which had
vays been individualistic in its nature was too binding upon
: individual. Alcott's early disagreements with Dr. Channing

[249]

had shown that one of them, at least, was passing beyond the theological position of the very man whom they rightly regarded as the champion of their liberties—although it should have been clear that when they fled from him he was the wings on which they flew. Channing had been the instigator of this very association which was now to transcend him. He was indeed the "Bishop" of the group, as Emerson was to call him; but it is the duty of a good bishop to hold himself always somewhat in the rear of his more aggressive and younger clergy.

Dr. Channing was in complete sympathy with another complaint, quite untheological, which these younger men were bringing against Unitarianism. When Emerson called it "pale" and Alcott called it "puny," they referred to an unquestionable predominance in it of head over heart, of logic over imagination, of cold thought over warm feeling. In a word, they found it anæmic. Religion according to the old Calvinism had been too much a matter of holding the right opinions—but was there really much advance in making it consist primarily in not holding the wrong ones? Channing would have been the first to admit and he had been one of the first in New England to assert, that religion is by no means exclusively a doctrinal matter, an elaborate game in which the Divine Being proposes a puzzle to the soul and offers huge rewards and punishments for success failure in the solution. He had long realized that, in his own half frozen New England at any rate, Christianity needed as much as anything to be warmed up. And warm it he did—or rather being himself an invalid, he suggested to a few of the youngsters standing about that it might be well to lay a stick or two of fresh wood on the smoldering fire.

The student who goes beating about in the thickets of New England life of the half-century preceding the Civil War is likely to be amazed at finding how many trails run back to the hermitage where this frail little man, Dr. William Ellery Channing, sat thinking and husbanding his strength. As much as possible he "hid

ife." He preferred always to work through others. He was often
blamed for withholding sympathy and support from movements
which, in fact, he had set going. His way was to suggest and hint,
to nod and to nudge, and seldom or never to urge anyone toward
anything. But a smile from him might turn the course of a life-
me, and a letter might precipitate a wide-spreading reform.

So carefully hidden was the work and influence of Dr.
Channing that even Alcott, who did not make many mistakes of
the kind, never quite found him out and never fully realized—
r, at any rate, acknowledged to himself—how much he owed to
his quietly pervasive, enormously seminal mind. It may well be,
indeed, that too little emphasis has been given in the foregoing
pages of the present book to Channing's influence upon Alcott;
but if so, that is because Alcott himself gave too little. What was
who was it, that made the Connecticut pedlar ready, in ten
ears' time, for membership in the "Transcendental Club"? We
nnot have been entirely wrong in attributing the speed of that
ansition, as Alcott did, in part to William Russell. But what is
be said of the many sermons that Alcott heard at the Federal
reet Church soon after his arrival in Boston? What of those
ng and intimate conversations in Channing's study? How much
to be attributed to the fact that just when Alcott was beginning
Marathon-run of reading at Philadelphia, Dr. Channing,
eady his close acquaintance, slipped into that city for a visit of
eral weeks?

When Channing had been for thirty years in his grave, Bronson
cott, then living at "Orchard House" in Concord, had a dream
night about his old friend—a dream suggesting a subconscious
lization, never squarely faced by his conscious mind, that
anning had been from the first the awakener, the guide, and
informing purpose of his intellectual and spiritual life. And so
may have been; but if Alcott himself was not aware of it, how
we do more than surmise? "The heart of another is a dark
st."

[251]

Considering how many trails lead out from Channing, it is well to know how he himself had reached the somewhat lonely habitation of his mind. By hard thinking, of course, for one thing—and thinking in terms of that same theology which he was to transcend. He was made possible, in part, by the huge propulsive force still pent up in dying Calvinism. It was as though a rocket about to fall had released and set on fire another that should flare still higher against the dark, and then, in its turn, send forth a third. But theologic lore, and the subtle brain that could take John Calvin as it were between finger and thumb and look him through and through, made only the lesser half of Channing. In order to know him and to comprehend his influence one must keep in mind two things: first, that mystic experience, that "ecstatic moment" which came to him in his Harvard days while he was walking under the willows by the Charles and his heart was suddenly flooded by the sure and inexpugnable conviction of God's everlasting love; and second, the fact that he was the first ambassador plenipotentiary of the English Romantic Movement who was accredited to the American people. We are still talking, in Barrett Wendell's words, about our early "transplanters of culture," and the phrase does suit such cool-headed students as Longfellow, Irving, and Lowell well enough. Channing's service, however, was more like that of Prometheus, carrying the seeds of fire in a hollow reed. It was not the legend and lore of a dead or dying Europe that he brought us, but the sparks of thought and feeling that were then setting all Europe and England alight.

Channing's two-year residence in England during the early eighteen-twenties had an importance of the first magnitude the transcendentalism of later decades. His association there with Wordsworth and Coleridge and his complete conversion to Romantic School had the effect of inspiring his rather cold New England theology with the warm breath of life. Or rather to wove his theology together with philosophy, poetry, history, social enthusiasms, into a fabric that could never again be

aveled. Thus it was not of versemakers alone that he was think-
ng when he wrote the often-quoted words:—

> The poetry of the age has a deeper and more impres-
> sive tone than comes to us from what has been called
> the Augustan Age of English literature. . . . Men
> want and demand a more thrilling note, a poetry which
> pierces beneath the exterior of life to the depths of
> the soul, and which lays open its mysterious working,
> borrowing from the whole outward creation fresh
> images and correspondences, with which to illuminate
> the secrets of the world within us.

Just this it was that the transcendental movement, half-theo-
gical and half-romantic in its origins, was to do for us. It was to
·ing "a more thrilling note" into our literature, our philosophy,
d our religion by piercing "to the depths of the soul."
When the Symposium began its sessions in 1836 Unitarianism
as obviously triumphant in the region of Boston. The Reverend
yman Beecher, that Calvinistic tyrannosaurus from Connecticut,
d recently gone away westward, convinced that in the country
und Massachusetts Bay, at any rate, his tribe was practically
tinct. But the transition was only from King Log to King Stork,
d the "party of the future" within the Unitarian ranks found
at they still had a "party of the past" to contend with. They
und a doughty antagonist, to choose only one example, in Pro-
ssor Andrews Norton of the Divinity School,—a sound scholar,
een thinker, and a man who loved to give and take hard blows,
who was teaching the psychology of John Locke to the young
n who would be the preachers of to-morrow. That psychology,
nfining all our knowledge to the experience of the senses and
ereby denying the validity of innate ideas and intuition and in-
iration, had come to seem hatefully materialistic and irreligious
a few minds, and particularly to those minds that had been
erated and illumined by Dr. Channing. It was, in fact, this

[253]

"sensationalism" of Locke, together with the skepticism of Hum
which was its inevitable outgrowth, that the transcendentalist
of Germany, England, and America strove to transcend. Kant an
Schelling and Schleiermacher opposed it in Germany, Coleridg
and Wordsworth and Carlyle in England, and now in Americ
there rose up against it this unobtrusive little "Transcendent:
Club." In opposition to Locke, and somewhat more consciously i
conflict with Professor Andrews Norton, Locke's disciple, it a
serted the reality of innate ideas, the actuality of intuition, th
validity of inspiration, and the universal immanence of God.
held and taught as a central tenet that God speaks to the huma
spirit not solely, and not primarily, by means of any speci
tradition, creed, Bible, person, or Church, but that He speal
directly, speaks to all men, and speaks now. This, of course, w:
only Protestantism carried to a logical extreme; but some membe
of the group went farther still in their more excited moments a
declared, as Emerson put it, that "the simplest person who in h
integrity worships God becomes God"—and in this article
belief, although it had the most venerable authority in the r
ligious literature of India, orthodox New England saw n
Protestantism so much as crude blasphemy. However that m:
have been, it is clear that in their almost violent emphasis up
the primacy of Mind and Soul the transcendentalists were co
fronting the already boastful materialism of their time and count
with an idealism at least as confident and self-assertive. They c
not intend that, merely for the lack of an opposition, Ameri
should be run away with by capitalists, merchants, enginee
politicians, and scientists who had lost their minds in developi
their brains. In those classes, roughly speaking, was the enen
although of course they made a few finer distinctions. They w
comed every triumph of true science, for example, as anotl
mark set up on the long march of mind into the realms of Ch:
and Old Night. Science at its best, they believed, was their frie:
not because it could ever find out anything essential about mat

ut for the reason that it was constantly finding out the most
mazing "correspondences" and "emblems" of spiritual truth.

None of these men, one must remember, had ever been sub-
ected to any rigorous scientific, logical, or mathematical train-
ng; and in their consequent lack of intellectual patience and
aution they did not show the mental qualities which we have
arned in recent decades most highly to respect. Upon a first
nd superficial acquaintance we can scarcely be fair to them, for
ey were not wholly of our kind and time. The natural habitat
f their thought was that period of profound and exalted mysti-
sm, unquestionably one of the supreme epochs in the history of
'estern mind, which immediately preceded Sir Isaac Newton's
emonstration of what might be done by a closely reasoned
rutiny of the observed facts of nature. Newton and his follow-
s, including John Locke, have thus far drawn the main body of
'estern thinkers all one way, and not even yet have we fully
timated how much has been lost or forgotten as the price of all
at has been gained. But the members of the transcendental
oup did not march with this main body, and that is the chief
ason why the very word "transcendental" has come to suggest
a erratic and irresponsible kind of thinking, almost impossible to
mprehend. As a matter of fact the essential principles of their
dealism" were quite simple, and far more susceptible of clear
monstration than the principles upon which the materialistic
eeds are supposed to rest. Our difficulty is not that their thought
as insane, and certainly not that it was in any sense new—for
d it not float in the central current of the Platonic tradition?
but only that it has gone out of fashion for a time. It will
urn. It is returning. The leaders of contemporary science, what-
er may be said of the rank and file, grow more transcendental
ery year.

Bronson Alcott, Ralph Waldo Emerson, and their little circle of
anscendental thinkers, found themselves less at home in the
ierica of their time than with the Platonizing poets and phi-

losophers of the seventeenth century such as Henry Vaughan and Henry More. They accepted the conclusions of modern science without accepting its method. In the midst of the world's greatest inductive effort they turned back to the pre-Newtonian, even the pre-Baconian methods of deduction. Believing that every mind is a microcosm of the universe, they held that all natural law should be discoverable by mere introspection, so that their indifference to external fact amounted at times almost to contempt. In making such a statement one immediately thinks of Henry Thoreau, of course, as an exception. Thoreau was indeed an indefatigable observer and collector of natural phenomena, and yet it was precisely he, of all the transcendental fellowship, who strove most mightily to put and to keep mere observation in its properly subordinate place. It was he who said:—

> Packed in my mind lie all the clothes
> Which outward nature wears . . .

As for Emerson, his delight in keeping nature underfoot and always "ancillary to man" is familiar enough. "The astronomer the geometer," says he, "rely on their irrefragable analysis, and disdain the results of observation. The sublime remark of Euler on his law of arches, 'This will be found contrary to all experience yet is true,' had already transferred nature into mind, and left matter an outcast corpse." And Alcott is not to be outdone. A characteristic remark of his asserts that "not the forms merely but the materials of natural things, are preconceived in man's mind, and put forth as the Nature we survey externally. Nature is mind in solution—the waste or spent man. Without man matter were not, nor Nature."

In all this there is an air of rash and unconsidered affirmation which reminds one somewhat too strongly of the "tall tales" that were even then springing up along the frontier into an American mythology. It was a little as though the transcendentalists had decided that America must have a metaphysics to match

plendor of Niagara and the height of the Rocky Mountains. They
how a careless ease in their speculations, a noble disregard of
vidence, which somehow recalls the mood of the pioneer. Ex-
loratory and tentative, perfectly foot-loose among the centuries,
lost of them unimpeded by any excess baggage of erudition, and
yperbolical always, these men, one sometimes suspects, are
apable of saying almost anything that can be said in a suf-
ciently violent and startling phrase. They betray their literary
nd rhetorical training by an almost unquestioning dependence
pon phraseology. They think in a fog of metaphor and are con-
nually misled by the will-o'-the-wisps of analogy. Promulgating
ws of their own enactment, they walk up and down in Nature
ith all the freedom that Adam felt in the Garden, naming the
imals out of his own head.

But one is to consider that they were living all the while in a
ate of strong intellectual excitement. With the help of Plato, Plo-
us, Boehme, Berkeley, Swedenborg, Kant, Coleridge—the list
ight be indefinitely extended—they had taken hold upon an an-
er to the most fascinating problem that has puzzled the wit of
an: What is the relation or linking of thought to things? To this
ey gave the idealistic answer, as Locke had given the material-
ic. Locke had said that things come first, and they said that
ought does. Mind, Soul, and Ideas were to them the primary
lities, and all the solid-seeming remainder of the Universe—
dies, planets, solar systems, and the like—was but their Brocken-
adow. This answer had been an exciting one for thousands of
ars before they found it, but it had never been more so than it
s amid the roar and rush of American life in the nineteenth
tury. In the wildest of their exaggerations they could never out-
st the captains of industry and the exploiters of the continent.
ey had to talk at the top of their lungs in order to be heard
ll.

The root-idea and central doctrine of American transcendental-
was that God is present in his whole nature and being in

[257]

every part and particle of the universe, including the soul of eac
individual man. From this it follows that every particle of th
universe, including the individual soul, is not only divine but ;
a complete microcosm of that universe—holding all that it hold
being all that it is, and potentially knowing every truth and la
upon which it is based. It follows also that knowledge of God
identical with the soul's knowledge of itself, and, again, th;
knowledge both of self and of God may be won by the contempl;
tion of that visible Nature which is at once the creation and tl
"emblem" of the World-Soul. To these we may add the furth
consequence that in a world so constituted the moral and tl
natural law must be in their final analysis identical, so that eith
one is deducible from its counterpart.

When these tenets are taken together with their corollaries a
implications they amount to a body of doctrine quite sufficient f
the founding of a "school." The Symposium was drawn and he
together as a social unit, however, by something more than a s
of common beliefs. All the members were products of the sar
national, intellectual, and spiritual past. Behind them all lay tl
whole history of American Calvinism and Unitarianism, besid
the powerful influence of Dr. Channing. Most of them we
graduates of the same college. When they first came together th
were saturated, one and all, with Coleridge's *Aids to Reflecti*
and the comment that President James Marsh of the University
Vermont had recently written upon it. They all knew that p
found twelfth chapter of Coleridge's *Biographia Literaria* w
its English glorification of Schelling's idealism. Alcott had bou;
the book at Matthew Carey's shop in Philadelphia in 1831, a
had read the chapter through in every succeeding year. All
them knew the solemn little druggist Sampson Reed and had re
his brilliant book, soaked in Swedenborg, inadequately cal
Observations on the Growth of the Mind. All of them had re
Carlyle's *Sartor Resartus* when it first appeared in *Frase*
Magazine, and would soon be reading it again in the Ameri

[258]

lition that Emerson was to put forth before any had been published in England. They were all acquainted with men who had
sunk transcendentalism, during their student years, directly
from its German source—men such as Edward Everett, George
Ticknor, George Bancroft, and Emerson's brother William. They
knew the German exile Charles Follen, now a professor at Harvard, and the German scholars Charles Beck and Francis Lieber.
Frederic Hedge had studied in Germany, to good purpose. Ripley
and Francis and Bartol were hard and close students of German
literature. When Margaret Fuller and Theodore Parker had been
added to the group it was clear that there could be no lack of German in the Symposium. And finally, the group had a Bible. In that
very month of September, 1836, when they first met, Emerson had
published his oracular and darkly refulgent little book called
Nature. There, in a hundred pages, nearly every important thing
that Emerson or any other American transcendentalist would
ever say was either said or implied.

What else there was to hold the transcendental group together
can only be discovered by reading and vividly imagining the whole
history of its period—and this in its social, industrial, and political
bearings as well as in those directly related to philosophy and
literature. At present one can only say that it was sufficient. There
has been too much uninformed assertion that the members of the
group were of "like minds" only in the respect that no two of
them thought alike. Considering the centrifugal tendencies in the
very essence of their doctrine, what impresses one is their unanimity. But perhaps this also can be explained by their environment. They were pushed and cemented together by the pressure of
a materialism which grew every year more arrogant, more self-
assured, and apparently more determined to crush the last breath
of idealism out of American life. What they thought and said and
wrote may be regarded, if one likes, as no more than a minority
report. It was one of their many heretical opinions that minorities,
in the long run, rule the world.

[259]

To follow the history of the Symposium or "Transcendent Club" through the three or four years of its existence would lea too far from the course of Bronson Alcott's career, though nc from that of his interests. The group met four or five times a yea and he was always present, whether the meeting was called fc Watertown, Newton, Concord, Milton, Chelsea, or Boston. Th topic for discussion was usually decided upon at the previous mee ing, so that those who cared to do so might prepare themselve but there is nothing to show that Alcott or any other member ev did so. The simple order of events was that Convers Francis, tl senior member, called upon the other members in turn for such r marks as they cared to make upon the topic, and when all had be heard from in this way the discussion became general.

A difference of opinion which provoked much debate througho the history of the Club was that concerning the "Personality" God. Several of the members, and Emerson among them, had go so far in their revolt against the old Calvinistic dogma as to de consciousness, purposive will, and selfhood to the Supreme Bei although this was not, as Andrews Norton called it, "the late form of infidelity," but rather, as Emerson said, in sober truth t result of "a Saturnalia or excess of faith." Bronson Alcott ne went so far. Such cold abstractions as "Impersonality," "Lav "Right," "Justice," "Truth," left him cold. He wished to kn what the one Power was in which these abstractions inhered, t Power that gave them all their vitality and related them one another. It seemed to him the chief deficiency of the Tra cendental School, and also of Emerson's theological thought, t it said nothing of a personal relationship between man and Maker. The difference of belief on this subject developed betw the two friends almost at the beginning of their acquaintance, i it remained a difference and a perennial topic of discussion tween them for the following forty years.

Intellectually, Alcott was independent to a remarkable deg He lived in the Emersonian atmosphere for two thirds of his I

[260]

ime without taking on more than the faintest tincture of thought
eculiarly Emersonian which he had not previously attained or
ould not have worked out independently. We have already seen,
owever, that in everything related to what may be called the
ocial emotion Alcott was much more susceptible than Emerson
o his surroundings. The general mass and mob of human beings,
o be sure, did not much sway him. He always held that "the
egasus of the multitude is a mule." It was a society of Minds
at he was always seeking, and in the "Transcendental Club" he
ound it. If he had ever been asked to explain his half-instinctive
aning toward such associations he would probably have said,
omewhat as he defended the "social conscience" of the Temple
chool against Miss Peabody, that a group of such minds as the
lub brought together was likely to be a better thinking unit
an any single mind it contained.

THE CONTAGION
OF REFORM

*Public ferment—The antislavery movement—Come-Outer.
Chardon-street Convention—Concord meadows and Orphic Sa
ings—What shall the man DO?—A kind letter from Emers*

THE Conversations and the "Transcendental Club" provid
Alcott with sufficient opportunities for dressing his thought
"the drapery of living speech," yet there still remained the qu
tion that Carlyle was screaming across the Atlantic at his frie
in Concord: "Why not *do* something?" To be sure, it was ne
quite clear just what Carlyle himself was *doing,* in the gri
heroic and probably violent sense that he seemed to give the wo:
but his question was not on that account the less disquieting.

It will be remembered that when Emerson decided against
publication of "Psyche," Alcott made up his mind to pub!
himself to the world not by means of the pen, as his friend
previously advised, but by "living speech" and "action." By
word "action" he had come to mean almost the opposite of w

e saw Emerson doing in his Concord seclusion, and something
ike what Garrison and Ripley were discussing in their plans for
n association of reformers. It was not that he felt the slightest
ense of pique against his friend for not liking his manuscript,
r for any other reason. Neither was it that he felt any need of
sserting his own independence. Emerson was to him, and would
lways remain, unquestionably the kindest, the wisest, and the
reatest of living men; yet that was no reason for imitating
merson. The only way to be truly Emersonian was to be one's
lf. Furthermore, there were certain qualities of Emerson's mind
nd character which Alcott could honor but from which he wished
hold himself aloof. Emerson's life, so cool and distant, seemed to
governed by the Goethean ideal of self-development and per-
nal culture. Emerson stood away from the dust and heat of the
orld's struggle, not selfishly but because he thought he could be
ost helpful in that way. Alcott preferred to live within hearing
the hammers. Upon the whole, Emerson was averse to the spirit
d the methods of reform. It was not that he denied the abuses
hich the reformers were striving to correct. His theory was that
ective improvement can be brought about in human affairs not
organizations, associations, or legal enactments but only by a
ange in the individual mind and heart. Alcott's assent to this
eory was not enthusiastic. With his mind he saw that it was
obably true; but all his heart, so eager for partnership in some
orthy" effort, was pulling him in the opposite direction.

We have more than once observed that Bronson Alcott did not
turally belong to the class of which reformers are made. He
s incorrigibly optimistic, thinking far better of human nature
n it deserves. His lack of interest in political, economic, and
ial problems was in keeping with his almost complete ignorance
them. He was much surprised, for example, after he had been
ing in and near Boston for more than twenty years, to hear
eodore Parker speak as though there were a good many

[263]

prostitutes in the city; and when he was over seventy the revela-
tions made by a young man from New York named Anthony
Comstock left him simply aghast. He could somehow manage to
spend three years and a half in the slaveholding South without
acquiring any particular aversion to slavery, and he could spend
half a lifetime in a poverty that would have crippled and crushed
most other men without ever guessing that there might be some
thing radically wrong with capitalism. One hears it said—though
not, to be sure, correctly—that Emerson was insufficiently aware
of the world's evil and woe. By comparison with that of his friend
Alcott, Emerson's knowledge of wickedness was encyclopædic

How, then, did Alcott become a reformer? He was pushed and
pulled and enticed into it. He caught reform from the epidemic
contagion of his time. He had been forced from his calling, he was
disengaged, he was lonely, and Reform offered an opportunity to
work with others in an effort sufficiently vague and grandiose to
command his utmost enthusiasm. As for a "cause," there would
never be any difficulty about that. Nearly everything needed re
forming. There was slavery, drink, the tyranny of men over
women, diet, Puritanical notions about the Sabbath and the
Bible, money, capital punishment, the treatment of the insane
schools, war, and any number of other "causes." Some reformer
concentrated upon a few of these, and others, seeing how all the
evils of the world were interrelated, assailed them all at once
There was a great deal to be done and not much time in which
do it, for, strangely enough, the very persons who were pointing
out the manifold evils in the world were also firmly convinced tha
the inevitable millennium was near at hand.

Although in most respects the very antithesis of a reformer
Alcott was a man who liked, as Whittier confessed of himself, "
turn the crank of an opinion-mill," and by 1839 he was the so
of person from whom opinions might reasonably be expected. He
secreted opinions, though not in the sense that he hid them away
or kept them to himself. His notion of heaven, one would say, mu

[264]

have been to sit forever in loose and slippered ease in some
celestial summerhouse, "sharing views" with all comers, but pref-
erably with those of the Platonic persuasion. And for fifty years
before he got to heaven he did very well at this more amateur kind
of reforming in nineteenth-century America.

Even before the failure of his Temple School Alcott had made
some progress toward the mental and emotional attitude of the
reformer. His teaching had been done, from the early Connecticut
days, in defiance of custom and tradition. Actuated at first by the
motives of the British reformer Robert Owen and then by those
of Pestalozzi, it had always acknowledged the clear and conscious
intent of renovating society by enabling children to recover and
retain their divine nature. Godwin's *Political Justice,* read during
his first residence in Boston and again at Germantown, had been
working in Alcott's thought through all the intervening years. His
turn against the prosperous and conventional Unitarianism of
Boston, which he saw ever more closely interlocked with business
and politics and the conservative forces of society, was itself re-
ormatory; and his increasing antagonism toward certain of the
local clergy was not less so. Finally, in his determination to bring
the teaching and example of Jesus down to date and to apply them
in contemporary Boston, he was positively and unmistakably a
"radical."

This mood and interest may have gone farther back. It was pre-
sely during the years of Alcott's youth on Spindle Hill that the
democrats" and dissenters of Connecticut made their long,
arduous, and finally triumphant struggle against an established
clergy in league with a set of strongly entrenched politicians. He
himself had been a "dissenter" because he had belonged not to
the Congregational but to the Episcopal Church, and he was,
without knowing it, inevitably a "democrat," in a time when that
word meant something not very different from "republican." Inwardly and essentially, he was a dissenter from all established
authority and opinion. By nature rather than by political affilia-

[265]

tion he was a democrat in the sense that what he wanted from government was the least possible interference with local and individual rights. He had seen the reverend gentlemen of the Established Church refuse, year after year, the request for the incorporation of the Cheshire Academy, and he knew how the efforts to found an Episcopal college in his State had been thwarted by Congregationalists if not actually by Yale men. He had read the *Connecticut Courant* from the time when he could first read at all, and had discerned in it some of the less charming aspects of extreme conservatism. And finally, when he was eighteen years of age, he had shared in the enthusiasm of all Connecticut dissenters and democrats at the overthrow of the Established Church and the ratification of a Constitution somewhat more adjusted to modern needs than the Royal Charter of 1662. It had been a triumph of "reform."

In tracing the gradual process by which a mind naturally disposed to go along with any decent existing order was converted to revolutionary and at last even to anarchistic programs, one is more and more impressed with the importance in it all of the mind's changing attitude toward the Christian church and clergy. We have seen that Bronson Alcott went up to the Capital of New England with the deepest respect for preachers and with the highest hopes for what they, he believed, were soon to do in fulfilling the prophecies of the Nazarene and bringing God's Kingdom to America. During his first months in Boston he became acquainted with the foremost of these preachers, whom he instantly recognized for what he really was, one of the most powerful and beneficent minds of the day. And yet even Channing, found to his dismay, was hesitant and timorous and loath in his application of Jesus' teaching to the Boston scene. Channing never "made an idea." Channing waited for the popular voice and chimed in with the majorities. Channing's nerves, as Garrison was to say, were very delicately strung. The blare of a ram's horn was

o him most painfully distressing. In his opinion, the dulcet tones
f a silver trumpet should be enough to sing down the walls of
ericho; and so he played, very sweetly, upon his own. The walls,
owever, stood.

If gold shall rust, then what shall iron do? What had to be said
f Boston's lesser clergy? What did it mean that, when Garrison
ame up to Boston from the Baltimore jail and proposed to talk
here about the horror of slavery, not one Christian church in the
ity would allow him a platform, and he had to speak in a hall
onated by a condemned infidel? Just after Garrison had been
aled through the streets by a Boston mob, Bronson Alcott, re-
urning that day from his first stay with Emerson at Concord, was
he first to call upon him in Leverett Street Jail. No ministers had
een there, or were to go.

And Alcott often went down to the office of the *Liberator*, where

> In a small chamber, friendless and unseen,
> Toiled o'er his types one poor unlearned man;
> The place was dark, unfurnitured and mean,
> Yet here the freedom of a race began.

e saw on the floor of the dingy room the bed of the editor,
ublisher, printer. To go from that poor room of Garrison's to the
arsonage of some prosperous clergyman, paid to do the work of
od but not—in Alcott's opinion—doing it, was to arouse many
oubts and questionings.

The animus against the existing order, then, that was slowly
cumulating in Bronson Alcott's mind, was decidedly anticlerical
tendency if not in origin. One might almost say that he turned
ward reform because the preachers—not quite all of them, but
e greater number—turned away from it; but a more accurate
atement would be that from beginning to end he held to the
ample, as he understood it, of the Founder of Christianity. In
ch uncompromising and unmediated imitation of Christ there
s always been, from Saint Anthony of the Egyptian desert to

[267]

Count Tolstoy laboring the soil among his peasants, a large
element of radicalism leading directly to schemes for reforming the
world. In every Christian epoch there have been Christians so
simple and naïve as to suppose that because their Master was unquestionably a radical and a reformer, they also should be. Bronson Alcott was one of these. Another was his friend George Ripley
who in 1841 read himself out of his pastorate at the Purchase
Street Church because he found that "the liberal churches have
begun to fear liberality," because he had come to think that
"the purpose of Christianity . . . is to redeem society as well
as the individual," because he intended thenceforth "to aid the
overthrow of every form of slavery," and considered it his duty
to visit not only "the abodes of fashion and luxury but the dwellings where not many of the wise and mighty of this world are apt
to enter." A few months after the delivery of this philippic, which
was none the less devastating because it was so gently phrased,
George Ripley founded Brook Farm.

Transcendentalism was in essence a philosophy and a religion
of reform. Over against all the puny and man-made institutions
and constitutions of the world, it heard the Voice of God speaking
directly to the soul, uttering there a doctrine remarkably different from that of the preachers and politicians. Against the
shortsighted children of common sense who pointed out that man
is nowhere free in fact, it asserted that however the body may be
bound the soul of man is everywhere free by nature because it is
divine. Transcendentalism, moreover, cut its followers loose from
the moorings of the past, setting them free to drift or sail on the
strong tides of progress toward a millennium regarded as inevitable. One and all, those followers believed in "progress," though
they knew not why. Like their forerunners in Revolutionary
France, they assumed that human nature is "perfectible." They
lived in confident expectation of some vast Event, certainly
"divine" though not "far-off," toward which the whole creation
moved. They could not guess what this Event might be, and they

had no way of making sure what particular Man—for they commonly used the capital letter in referring to this modern Messiah —would bring it to pass. Any one of them might be that Man, and Bronson Alcott was by no means the only one to entertain a strong suspicion that he himself might be chosen. Thus the transcendentalists of a hundred years ago lived, one sees, in an air electric with expectation. Like the early Christians of the Mediterranean cities in this as in not a few other respects, they were sure that some tremendous Change was coming, and that it behoved them to make ready.

A transcendentalist could scarcely fail to be a reformer in some sense. Emerson found it necessary to write several lectures to explain why he, at least in the ordinary sense, was not one.

In that New England of a century ago, moreover, and most obviously in the neighborhood of Boston, reform was a contagion. It was the American Revolution still going on. For the War of Independence had secured not more than half of the objectives of 1776; and now, having won our freedom from England, it was a question whether we could also put down our domestic tyrants. That innocent-sounding little phrase "all men" in the Declaration of Independence was now to be interpreted. For some fifty years we had tacitly assumed that it referred primarily, if not exclusively, to men of property and position; but this was now being doubted. Dr. Gallaudet, in Hartford, thought that it should include the hopelessly deaf; Dr. Howe, in Boston, was extending it to include the blind; Dorothea Dix had determined that the insane should not be left out; and Bronson Alcott was certain that even children came within the sense of the phrase. These beliefs, though it might take many a long conflict to get them definitely established in practice, were already on the way toward triumph. When William Lloyd Garrison came forth, however, with his notion that black slaves also had a right to the "pursuit of happiness," and when the Grimké sisters asserted that women had a right, if not to happiness, at least to speak on public platforms,

[269]

then many persons of utmost respectability and unimpeachabl
standing felt that the time had come to call a halt.

Emerson once remarked that "there are always two parties—
the party of the past and the party of the future." Both of thes
were well represented in the New England of a hundred years age
If there were still Puritans in that New England, there were als
plenty of Yankees. If one of the main products of the region wa
the New England conscience, another, at least according to th
popular belief in other districts, was the wooden nutmeg. Almo
any prophet with half an eye upon the future could foresee tha
there was going to be a pretty fight.

The struggle was remarkably similar to that which went on ?
England between the time of Burke's *Reflections on the Frenc*
Revolution and the Reform Bill in 1832. Here as there, the even
in France awoke wide reverberations. They divided friend fro
friend and father from son. On the twenty-third of January, 179
Boston had roasted a thousand-pound ox in the public stree
and consumed it, together with two hogsheads of punch, at a gre
banqueting table as "a peace-offering to Liberty and Equality
In this expression of revolutionary fervor the city had been alm
unanimous, feeling that what was going on in France was hard
more than a continuation of the American Revolution. At t
time of its public feast, however, Boston was not aware of the ?
teresting fact that Louis the Sixteenth had been executed in Pa
just two days before the roasting of its ox. When the news of t
regicide finally did arrive, by sailing-vessel, many a dignifi
house in the city put out signs of mourning, and a profound char
was worked in many of the more sober and responsible minds fr
which they were not to recover for several decades. From t
day, if never before, Boston had its own conservative party,
"party of the past," which would long be numerous and power
enough to make life interesting for reformers. It is signific
that Edmund Burke and Dr. Johnson were the most valued

[270]

British authors on Beacon Hill when the members of the "Trans-cendental Club" were shaping their thought and lives upon such incendiaries as Wordsworth and Coleridge.

Underneath most of the reform movements of Alcott's time, of course, lay the dark and terrible fact of slavery. The Church was reviled as a "whited sepulchre" because of what seemed its hypo-critical attitude toward this evil thing. "Come-outerism" was a refusal to have any part or lot in an institution so corrupt and cor-rupting as the Church was thought, by the more extreme spirits, to be. It seemed to make all other institutions suspect, decidedly including the institution of the State. What was widely considered the betrayal by the Church of all righteousness and righteous men threw the New England Protestant back upon his last line of defense against the forces of evil—his own conscience. And did not all the merchants, the manufacturers, capitalists, bankers, and rich people in general, toss up their silk hats and shout for slavery with one unanimous voice? Therefore money was an evil thing, corroding the soul, which must be put down and abandoned.

When this fact is understood, that slavery was the main foe they had in view, one does not feel contemptuous toward those eager, hasty, and often very ignorant enthusiasts who first flung themselves into the little army of reformers a hundred years ago. They were indeed a motley and miscellaneous crew, but they were one at heart. They struck rather wildly at this and that external and often trivial symptom, yet they were well aware of the main disease. They knew that there was really a black core of corrup-tion in Church and State which, if not cut out, would soon destroy all.

One grows weary of the assertion, more and more fashionable in recent years, that slavery, after all, was only an economic error which was rapidly working out its own cure when the Abolitionists took hold and precipitated a national disaster. If the slave States recognized this error they concealed their knowledge with re-

[271]

markable skill and vigor. Taken as a group, they certainly did not recognize it. During Abolition days slavery was steadily tightening its hold, like a boa-constrictor, upon the South and upon the Nation. But even if they had recognized it the assertion would still be nothing to the point. What the Abolitionists and the Anti-slavery people knew beyond a peradventure was that slavery whether good or bad for the agriculture of the South, was extremely bad for New England.

One tires of the iterated assertion that these reformers knew nothing about the South. The assertion is not true, as Bronson Alcott's three years and a half in the slave States and Moncure Conway's birth and breeding in them may remind one. And if it were true it would have no bearing. We must grant to these people at any rate, a certain knowledge of their own North; and they felt that slave-catching in the streets of Boston was not an edifying sight for their children or a worthy occupation for the deacons of their churches. Descendants of *Mayflower* and *Arbella* men could not cheerfully turn themselves into man hunters. Docile and timorous as we Americans have grown in recent decades, we ough still to understand and to honor the stern sentence that Emerson set down in his Journal one night after he had come home from Boston with a copy of the Fugitive Slave Act in his pocket Emerson was not a profane man; and when he seemed to be so he was more likely to be praying. What he wrote that night was this: "I will not obey it, by God."

But the conscience of New England was aroused most of all by the sins of Yankees. Even criminal statistics were showing that the denial of education to the Negroes of New England, where they were taxed, indeed, but for the most part could not go t school, was dangerous. All New England knew the tale of Prudence Crandall. Let the South save itself as best it might sensitive minds suffered for the North when they heard that in certain Christian church at Hartford the pews where the Negro sat had been screened away with boards, so that the souls o black folk had to snatch what salvation they could through slits in the planking not entirely unlike the lepers' squints of the Middle Ages.

These reformers did certainly say many wild and violent things, inaccurate and misinformed if not utterly without foundation, about conditions in the cotton fields and slave quarters of the South; but they never imagined worse conditions, because they could not, than did actually obtain in many places. Their mistake was the common one, inevitable in times of passionate excitement, of generalizing upon sporadic instances. Let only those blame them who are quite sure that they maintained a perfectly cool, critical, and impartial judgment while professional propagandists were flooding the press of America with lies about German atrocities in Flanders; or, if that is too far off in time, let only those find fault with them who are quite confident that they will keep their own heads when the next open season for professional lying begins.

One has heard more than enough about the "bigotry" of these "Puritans" who are said to have insisted upon making a moral issue out of an unfortunate economic situation. For we must consider that they had not our advantages. The "economic interpretation of history," which tends to crowd moral questions quite out of every picture of the past, leaving only the law of demand and supply, had not yet been invented. In their ignorance, they had to think in terms of old-fashioned right and wrong; and as to wrong—that is to say, sin, wickedness, the "ways that take hold upon death"—they were simple-minded enough to think that they found the marks of it in slavery. A certain Boston clergyman had the task of finding a home for a fugitive slave woman. She looked entirely white to Boston eyes, unskilled in such nice discriminations, but she was in fact the daughter of a planter by a slave, and she had been living for years with that same planter's son, her half-brother, as his mistress. People who knew nothing about the Southern States could not tell, of course, how very exceptional

[273]

this was; but they did not need to be Puritan bigots in order to feel that a moral question, rather than one exclusively economic was involved.

And, all the while, there was that bold and fearless bugler William Lloyd Garrison, blowing on his ram's horn. It made a raucous sound. It rasped on the people's nerves. It aroused even those who were most at ease in Zion, and would not leave them even a little more folding of the hands for sleep. No one could ignore Garrison, or forget him. "I am in earnest," he had said quite unnecessarily, at his very outsetting. "I will not equivocate; I will not excuse; I will not retreat a single inch; and I will b heard!" His sentences were like the short sharp blows of a fighting man going in to kill. They were like rifle shots. They hurt the ear. There was something vicious in him, as well as something visionary. There was a fire in him that had been kindled ages before in the hearts of the seers of Israel and had never quite gone out. The breath of those ancient prophets, which had blown the little *Mayflower* across the sea, was living still in this son of a drunken sailor and a heroic, ignorant woman; and still it cried, like Jeremiah: "O earth, earth, hear ye the word of the Lord!"

One might hate Garrison; he had rather expected that. One might try to fight him; that was what he liked. One might prove that he was a pestilential nuisance, a stench in all respectable nostrils, and a menace to the peace of society; he modestly hoped so. What one could not successfully do was to pretend that he was not there. Neither could anyone think or feel or speak about him with moderation. People took him either for a fiend or for a demigod. In those blazing eyes behind the little spectacles, in the long lean face and interminable brow, some read the marks of the madman and some of the messiah. He was all male. He saw every moral question in black and white. A thing was either perfectly right or else it was utterly wrong for him; and if it was wrong then of course it must be immediately righted, at any cost. In the old Calvinistic way, he thought of every sin as infinite because was an offense against the Infinite Being, and if the retribution fell even a little short of an infinite loss and destruction then that was mere good fortune. He was quite cheerfully willing, therefore, to pull down the total structure of the nation and destroy a myriad of lives if one human soul, though it were of a black slave, might thereby be enlightened. After the remanding of Anthony Burns in 1854 he stood up before ten thousand people on the Fourth of July in Framingham and publicly burned a copy of the Fugitive Slave Law, then a copy of Judge Loring's decision, and finally the Constitution of the United States; and each time the flames shot up the huge concourse cried "Amen!" Even to-day it is almost impossible to speak or write about Garrison moderately. The force and fire of the man is still exciting. He was an axeman, striking furious blows at the roots of a poison tree. He was a gadfly, setting the whole herd in motion until there should be a stampede. For years he saw much of Bronson Alcott.

If we are to understand how the mild-mannered gentleman from Connecticut ever became an Abolitionist and a reformer,—he who had been so hospitably entertained by the Southern planters and had seen no horrible evil in slavery,—we must first try to imagine those many interviews, all the way from Garrison's first appearance in Boston to the verge of the Civil War, in the dingy little office of the *Liberator* or else at Alcott's house. Garrison was a close friend and associate of Alcott's brother-in-law, Samuel May, and also of Mrs. Alcott's cousin, Samuel Sewall. He was Mrs. Alcott's friend as well. Even if Alcott had wished to confine his thought to ancient Athens and never to hear of what was going on in Washington or on Capitol Hill, he would not have been able. Garrison was a man of one idea. Alcott saw this. He saw quite through Garrison and saw him "in the round," as very few other men of the time ever did. He saw and said that Garrison was only the more violent half of a true reformer. And yet he could not live in close and prolonged association with such a fire—and without being at least heated.

[275]

> Garrison [he wrote] is far from catholicism and comprehension of the whole truth. . . . The most intolerant of men, as trenchant as Ajax, he has not yet won self-victories. . . . He has perfect skill in the use of his weapons, nor has he ever lost a battle. He cannot give quarter even, and is as unrelenting to friends as to enemies. Mercy is no attribute of his justice. He knows all the manners of the snake, and, were he self-freed, might crush his head; but as it is he will only scotch the hydra and play with its tail.

Alcott's thought overleapt the present. His natural tendency was to brood upon a few periods of the past, chiefly the early Christian and the Athenian, not at all in the mood or with the purpose of the historian but with the hope of transmitting that human treasure into the good time coming. But Garrison drove and dragged him into the passions of that present hour. And there had not been Garrison there would still have been Samuel May, "God's chore-boy" and Alcott's own good friend. He was always saying "Here am I, Lord, send me!" and the Lord was sending him into the most uncomfortable places. He had been mobbed five times in one month during a lecture tour in Vermont and he told about it all with the cheerful, rancorless simplicity of a saint.

And if there had not been May to keep Alcott in mind of the present world, then there would have been that wonderful farmer's son at Roxbury, Theodore Parker. Alcott walked over there to the parsonage a month or two after he had closed his last school. He found a powerful stump of a man, twenty-nine years old but already growing bald, and with the tired eyes of a mighty reader. Was he not mighty in all things—in learning, in laughter, in force of thought and passion, even in physical toil? He too, like Alcott, and unlike most of the thin-wristed paper-turners of Boston, had loaded granite boulders upon stone-boats and had helped to build the stone walls of New England. It made a deep

[276]

ference, that brotherhood in toil. Now he was at work in much the same spirit upon books in half a dozen languages—books in which his visitor could not have read a word. Alcott failed to comprehend this passionate hunger for mere knowledge and ever more knowledge, valued for its own sake and about almost anything. It was strange to think of Parker as a transcendentalist; yet he undoubtedly was that in almost every particular except his antlike scurrying about after bits of information and dragging them home into his voracious memory. Apparently he had not learned that "books are for the scholar's idle times." Perhaps a main trouble with him was that he had no idle times whatever. Fifty hours a week he had over his books after his pastoral duties had been attended to. He was growing at all points at once, like a lusty young poplar rushing upward and pushing outward in a New England pasture. Poplars grow swiftly, but do not live long. It was clear at once to the prophetic Alcott, however, that here was a man of "genius" who would leave his mark on the times. Back at home that night Alcott wrote: "He will be found on the side of freedom when the hour comes that shall try men's faith. I deem him one of the true men of the age."

And Margaret Fuller was one of the "true men" too. At least she had the brain of a man, with something precious, something mysterious, added. Alcott walked out to Jamaica Plain in August to talk with Margaret—for so her friends loved to call her even in that stiffly formal time. She was planning a series of Conversations, more or less in imitation of his own, to be held with women only, and she wanted his advice. Margaret had grown since she had given up her place as his assistant at the Temple School and had gone to Providence to teach. He had not known how large, how regal a person she was becoming, or what a commanding talker. Always eagerly on the lookout for a special wisdom among women, he gladly attributed it to her. He thought, as Emerson did also, that she had some secret which even her great powers of speech could never quite reveal. There was something labyrinthine, glamorous, Egyptian about her, that led one on and on. Symbolisms, mysteries, mythologies, grew clearer in her presence. Her voice had undertones of sorrow. Most significant was that recurring dream of hers that she was a long-lost princess for whom the people of some dim realm were evermore in search. She seemed to live in the shadow of a sad impending fate. What was it that she wanted? Men gave her admiration.

Yes, nearly all men admired the distressingly homely Margaret, and somehow felt assured, while they watched her large, heavy features and rapidly blinking eyes, that they were in the presence of beauty. Yet they could not help thinking, too, how much she was like a man. Had not her father and her uncles made her as much as possible after their own kind, and to be admired? What a host of languages she could read! How profoundly she could talk, even as a child, about art and metaphysics! But not one of the brilliant men she knew ever guessed how much she was like a woman. They gazed at her and talked with her and heard her talk by the hour; they read her laborious articles in the *Dial* and the *Tribune,* and her brave little book on *Woman in the Nineteenth Century,* wondering why they were not better; but not one of them understood her. It was a time of heated brains indeed, but of hearts perhaps a little cold. Margaret gave Bronson Alcott parts of her Journal to read; and yet not even he ever guessed her open secret until it was too late—until she had become, in his own lovely phrase, "the great and noble lady gone down into the sea." Or did he guess it even then, after the Princess had returned to the dream-people who loved her? One cannot make sure that even Alcott, with the guidance of his own lonely heart ever knew the injustice that Cambridge and Boston and Concord had done to this warm and vivid woman, feeding her with admiration and abstractions when what she had wanted was love.

With Garrison, Parker, Margaret, Edmund Quincy, Dr. Follen and Horace Mann, Alcott filled his days and nights as well as h

[278]

could after the close of his last school. He went to Concord with Margaret on a visit at Emerson's house, and he conducted Conversations in many places. In September there was talk at the meeting of the Symposium about the founding of a literary and philosophical magazine, and Alcott proposed a name for it which he had recently been giving to some parts of his private Journal— the *Dial*. Little by little he accumulated interest in his own time. He stepped down toward "the actual." By the beginning of October in 1839 he could say: "Let no man despise his age. He thereby degrades himself; he confesses to his own infirmity. Let him nobly bestir himself and make his age minister to the maturing of the order of things which preëxists in his own Idea!"

Writing to his brother Junius at about this time he said:—

> Last week I attended a convention of Non-Resistants in Boston, where much was said, and more implied than said, on questions of reform. I left with the conviction deepened that a few years will bring changes in the opinions and institutions of our time of which few now dream. All things are coming to judgment, and there is nothing deemed true and sacred now that shall pass this time unharmed. All things are doomed. The eye of justice searches the hearts of men, and the secrets of all evils and wrongs are made known. . . . A band of valiant souls is gathering for conflict with the hosts of ancient and honorable errors and sins. These shall assuredly overthrow the Ideas now standing in our High Places and do somewhat to restore the worship of the True and Living God in the hearts of men. I would be of and with these in their work.

The words are vague enough, but they show that Bronson Alcott had almost completed his transition from the philosopher to the reformer. He was beginning to feel that Armageddon was at hand. He had no clear notion, to be sure, what Armageddon

[279]

was to be, and he did not yet know what particular sins and errors he was going to assail, or who were to be the other assailants; but at any rate he hoped to be one of them and to attack something, mightily, before long.

Alcott's uncertainty of direction was by no means peculiar to him. One sees the same thing even in a mind so logical, exact and narrow-gauged as that of Garrison, who was always concerned in a dozen or more reforms at the same time. One could not foretell which side he would be on, and it was only certain that when once he had made up his mind he would be extremely bitter. Garrison, in fact, whom many now think of as eager above all else to plunge the country into civil war, was the leader of those very Non-Resistants whose convention Alcott had attended. Now that miscellaneity and confusion in reform of which Lowell, imitating Emerson, was to make such brilliant play in his essay on Thoreau, was as widespread as it was inevitable, because every sin and error that flesh is heir to was seen to be entangled with all the others. In recognition of this fact, most of the reforming organizations of the day began in the thirties to hold their annual meetings at the same time. During one of these so-called "Anniversary Weeks," in June, 1837, Alcott had attended the meetings of the American Unitarian Association, the Social Meeting of the Sunday School Teachers, the Boston Sunday School Society, the Book and Pamphlet Society, the Anti-Slavery Society, and finally—one suspects that he must have named it himself—the Meeting of Gentlemen Friendly to New and Worthier Views of Men and Things. In comparison with the gatherings of the clan in later years this was a poor and thin Week, but it shows how the mind of New England was moving.

What is most apparent in Bronson Alcott's attendance upon these conventions, and even in the speeches that he habitually made at them, is not so much the strength of his conviction, though he never said anything that he did not at the time firmly believe, as the delight he took in breaking forth into human as

[280]

ociation, at least temporarily, from the solitudes of thought. More than one of his contemporaries recorded the opinion that he "loved to sit on platforms" and "delighted in the sound of his own voice." This was probably true, but the reason for it was something other, or at any rate something more, than simple vanity. Alcott's behavior on these occasions did indeed suggest the moods of adolescence; but that is what one must say of the whole national period in which he was living. The reform movement itself was adolescent in temper. What was particularly youthful, and in a way somewhat pathetic, about Alcott's reforming period was its eagerness, as of a mind and heart socially famished, for companionship in a common effort. "Oh, my brother!" he wrote to Samuel May, "hardest of trials is this one, of being sundered from my kind, and left to tread the solitudes without an approving voice or a kindly smile from any one." Anniversary Week did for him what the camp-meetings of the West were already doing for thousands of lonely men and women.

Probably Alcott never had a better time at any convention, at least in a social way, than at the gathering of the Millerites and come-outers at Groton, Massachusetts, in the midsummer of 1840. Early in the morning of an August day he met George Ripley, Theodore Parker, and Christopher Cranch at Emerson's house in Concord—they had walked from Boston on the day before—and proceeded from there, on foot, across the hills through Acton, Boxboro, Littleton, and Ayer, to the Groton tavern; twenty-five miles. The walk through the beautiful summer land was itself a delight to him, and the talk of his three companions, all of them learned men and all members now of the "Transcendental Club," was no doubt worthy of the landscape. But the company at Groton itself was of a kind to warm his heart—and also to turn his head. Indeed, there was not much chance left of his escaping the Fruitlands adventure when once he had seen and fraternized with that strange company. They all seemed to agree with him. The Millerites agreed that Armageddon was near, and, what was even more satisfactory, they were telling their friends that it would involve the second coming of Christ and would occur on the twenty-second of October in 1843. (Parker groaned that this was "too long to wait!") The Come-outers, a vigorous lot of natural mystics from Cape Cod, agreed that the Bible, though a good book, was overrated, that churches and ministers and creeds were quite unnecessary, and that the only authentic source of divine truth was what God said in the heart. Two of their preachers, said Parker in his diary, "were as rough-looking men as you would find in a summer's day—rough, I mean, in their exterior, for their countenance was full of the divine. Their hands, their dress, their general air, showed they belonged to the humblest class of society." They came, that is, from a class of society not unlike that with which Alcott had been familiar on Spindle Hill, but they were much more self-assertive than the neighbors of that region had ever been. They had a way of standing just outside of churches and shouting the preachers down and they sometimes entered the church and trampled across the cushions before the pulpit in the midst of the sermon, by way of homiletic criticism. Bronson Alcott knew how they felt and just what they meant by these vigorous methods, although he never expressed himself in quite that way. He seems to have liked the Come-outers, and in later years he was to apply their name, half-humorously, to himself. The Come-outers and the Millerites disagreed violently with each other and there were plenty of other deep thinkers present who disagreed with both of them. Among the lot was the sturdy Joseph Palmer from No Town, famous throughout the countryside for his majestic beard and for the sufferings and persecutions he had been through in defense of it. Probably he had come to the Convention looking for someone to insult him. Palmer, as a usual thing, agreed with no one, but he liked Bronson Alcott and Alcott liked him. They were to meet again.

[282]

Messrs. Ripley, Parker, and Alcott were almost as much amused by the Groton Convention as the always irreverent Cranch, but they were also a good deal excited. They had a sense of sudden and delightful liberation in hearing simple-minded men speak out, in the vigorous Doric which was mother tongue to all of them, precisely those heresies about Church and Priest and Sabbath which had long been yeasting in their own minds. Boston was far away. They were three country boys in the country, listening to country people. Anyone could say what he thought up there in the breezy hills, where there was never a Boston merchant or any other respectable person to overhear. It was most refreshing. After the excursion to Groton no one of these three men was ever quite the same again. Within a few months each one of them had taken a sharp turn in his career.

Back at home once more, all three began to think that Boston, and especially its smug and airless churches, would be the better for a little of that country breeze. They laid a plan. In September the Friends of Universal Reform, at their instance, agreed to call a Convention which should "examine the validity of the views which generally prevail in this country as to the appointment of the first day of the week as the Christian Sabbath, and to inquire into the origin, nature, and authority of the institutions of the Ministry and the Church as now existing." All three questions bore the Come-outer stamp. Edmund Quincy was appointed Chairman and Bronson Alcott was appointed to issue the call.

The great Convention thus prepared for met at the Chardon Street Chapel in three separate sessions, each of which lasted three days. At the first session, meeting in November, 1840, it discussed the Sabbath; at the second, held in March of the following year, it considered the Church; and in the third, called in the next November, it dealt in vigorous fashion with the Ministry. The meetings were largely attended. "Everybody," as Alcott said in his Journal, "was there." Dr. Channing was there, a silent and retiring man with only a few months more to live, perhaps

[283]

wondering a little at this noisy result of his silent hour beneath the willows at Cambridge so long ago. Emerson was there as an absorbed spectator and listener, half-amused and half-sympathetic, taking notes for a brilliant report finally published in the ninth number of the *Dial*. Bronson Alcott was there at every meeting, and at every meeting he spoke. Contemporary records indicate that he was the foremost man in the Convention and that it was he who "taught the doubtful battle where to rage." Amid the numberless speeches, debates, resolutions, votes, and shows of hands, with those delightfully exhilarating cries of "Infidel!" and "Atheist!" flying up and down, and in the surge and crowd of "madmen, madwomen, men with beards, Dunkers, Muggle tonians, Come-outers, Groaners, Agrarians, Seventh-Day-Baptists Quakers, Abolitionists, Calvinists, Unitarians, and Philosophers," Bronson Alcott rose to his seventh heaven. Here indeed was a "sharing of views" on a majestic scale. "By no means the leas value of this Convention in our eye," said Emerson in his *Dial* report, "was the scope it gave to the genius of Mr. Alcott, and not its least instructive lesson was the gradual but sure ascendancy of his spirit, in spite of the incredulity and derision with which he is at first received."

Ah, yes; Bronson Alcott was showing the proud old city that he was not quite the only person who doubted some of its most cherished orthodoxies, flouted some of its most honored respectabilities. It had taken its children away from him, had reviled him, had tried to starve him, and had left him very lonely, but here now were his reinforcements—this motley crew from the farm and the forge and the mill, from the hermit's cabin and the shoemaker's bench and the salt-caked fishing fleet. He was not ashamed of their uplandish raiment, for he had worn homespun himself. He was not ashamed even of Joseph Palmer's beard There had been a considerable outcry and pained protest against that beard at the beginning of one session; but Alcott had quietly risen to inquire, in the first place, whether in the opinion of the

[284]

ssembly there was anything in the essential nature of a beard
which prevented its wearer from becoming a Christian, and
econdly he had wished to know whether they had really come
here to discuss beards or, as he had been led to suppose, to con-
ider certain fundamental questions of the spiritual life. As for
Palmer himself, his simple contention had always been that God,
in his inscrutable wisdom, had given him his beard for reasons
past man's finding out, and that he, Joseph Palmer, was not going
o undo a work of God. He had already lain in jail for several
months on account of his beard, and he was to wear it all his
fe, even arranging to have a realistic representation of it carved
pon his tombstone.

The absurdities of the Chardon Street Convention lie on the
urface, but the significance of that gathering in the life of
ronson Alcott and of America is not so easily seen. Although the
cal clergy were present in a body, and did what they could to
ifle and stultify the expression of heretical opinions, the gather-
g was largely composed of persons to whom, however illiterate
d incoherent they might be, the things of the spirit were dear,
d to whom the professional control of those things had become
teful. Like the Come-outers at Groton, the rank and file of
em wanted to cleave down through the thickly accumulated
yers of gentility, respectability, orthodoxy, ritual and creed
d customary observance, the palaver about miracles and
enary inspiration, the pious and learned prattle about the
liness of the Bible and the divinity of Jesus, until they came
the warm and pulsing quick of the spiritual life. That is to
y, they wanted precisely what Alcott had sought from the
ston clergy when he first came to town, what he had never
ased to look for, though he had looked in vain: a practical
plication of Christian truth to the immediate facts of life in
merica. The Convention showed that thousands of Americans
ught and felt as he did. It showed that, far from being an
centric or unique figure, he was almost normal. Against the

[285]

somewhat narrow and exclusive backdrop of Beacon Hill alone he might indeed look singular enough to invite the persecution of herded orthodoxy. No sooner was America called in to stand beside him, however, than he was at once seen to be profoundly representative of that radical idealism and heretical spirituality which has kept America alive at heart through all the steadily mounting materialism of her three hundred years.

Emerson, born and reared in Boston, was an absorbed spectator So far as the record shows, he said nothing. He was studying his Bronson Alcott and his America at the same time; and he was seeing, perhaps a little to his surprise, how the two of them swam together. "The composition of the assembly," he said in his ample report for the *Dial*, "was rich and various"—

> The singularity and latitude of the summons drew together from all parts of New England, and also from the Middle States, men of every shade of opinion, from the straitest orthodoxy to the wildest heresy; and many persons whose church was a church of one member only. A great variety of dialect and of costume was noticed; a great deal of confusion, eccentricity, and freak appeared, as well as of zeal and enthusiasm. If the assembly was disorderly, it was picturesque. . . . The faces were a study. The most daring innovators and the champions-until-death of the old cause, sat side by side. The still living merit of the oldest New England families, glowing yet after several generations, encountered the founders of families— fresh merit emerging and expanding the brows to a new breadth, and lighting a clownish face with sacred fire. The assembly was characterized by the predominance of a certain plain, sylvan strength and earnestness, whilst many of the most intellectual and cultivated persons attended its councils. . . . If there was not a parliamentary order, there was life, and the assurance of that constitutional love for religion and

[286]

religious liberty which, in all periods, characterizes the inhabitants of this part of America. . . . These men and women were in search of something better and more satisfying than a vote or a definition, and they found what they sought, or the pledge of it, in the attitude taken by individuals of their number, of resistance to the insane routine of parliamentary usage, in the lofty reliance on principles, and the prophetic dignity and transfiguration which accompanies, even amidst opposition and ridicule, a man whose mind is made up to obey the great inward Commander, and who does not anticipate his own action but awaits confidently the new emergency of the new counsel.

And in what follows Emerson shows that the man he is thinking as exhibiting this "prophetic dignity and transfiguration" is ronson Alcott.

A good many people in Boston who could recall the attacks of ree or four years before upon the *Conversations on the Gospels* ust have been mildly surprised at the serene reappearance of man who, they thought, had been disposed of forever. They d supposed that he had gone down for the third time, and here : was calmly ruling the waves. Certainly not all of them had rgotten the severe, or rather the contemptuous, handling of this an by the eminently respectable editor of the *Boston Advertiser,* r. Nathan Hale; so that it must have been confusing extremely read an article in that same paper highly praising one of cott's speeches at the Chardon Street Chapel—and an article, , written by Mr. Hale's twenty-year-old son, Edward Everett le, then just out of Harvard.

There were one or two very able and interesting addresses [wrote the young reporter]. A most impressive and happy one from A. Bronson Alcott, exhibiting his peculiar sentiments and explaining his transcendental doctrines . . . was listened to with great attention.

[287]

We very much regret that it was not taken down in short-hand, word for word and comma for comma, for we are satisfied that the speaker, by his utmost efforts, could never in his closet commit to paper anything equal to it. Everything was methodical, clear, and explicit—not a word misplaced or superfluous or equivocal—all in excellent taste—delivered clearly, calmly, and distinctly, and with the utmost modesty and candor. We have never heard any exposition of the transcendental doctrines so intelligibly made or placed in so favorable an aspect.

But were the Come-outer questions that were mooted a Chardon Street in any way related to reform? Bronson Alco rapidly becoming one of the most uncompromising radicals the time, would have answered that they were related as the ro is to the tree. What was the use of discussing even slavery, he would have said, until it was decided whether to give impli obedience to the Bible, Church, and Clergy, all of which we then quoted in slavery's support, or to that "Inward Commander who had never breathed a syllable in defense of any such loat some thing? Let us get first principles settled and the rest w follow, would have been, as always, his word. To the win shouters of Anniversary Week he would have said, in the wor of Emerson: "Nothing can bring you peace but the triumph principles." That was the fault he found with most of the radic about him, that they were not radical enough. They did not pie to principles but stopped short with symptoms. That was wh he had meant in saying even of Garrison that he would not se the head of the hydra but would only "play with its tail."

In order to place Alcott exactly in relation to reform one to see that he emphatically did not belong to what may be cal the Ben Franklin—or perhaps one should say to the Poor Ri ard—tradition. In all his writing, apparently, he never once m

[288]

ioned Franklin. For that matter, he scarcely mentioned Noah
Vebster, that brilliant example of the Franklin tradition who was
ɔ near him in time and place and even in superficial interests.
Vhy was this? They were farther from him in spirit than Py-
1agoras or Lao Tsze. Concerning both he would have said, as
e did of Brook Farm, that they were "not sufficiently ideal."

These men—and one might as well group Robert Owen, Alert Brisbane and Fourier with them—were Lockians. They
1ought that mankind was to be improved inch by inch, although
1ere were a million miles to go. They thought that the heart
to be addressed through the senses, through self-interest and
e lower understanding, and by means of moral maxims exactly
1 the spiritual level of the counter and the till. Theirs was a
opkeeping morality, and a philosophy merely prudential. They
ed to tempt men to be decent by asserting, with a wild dence of the facts of which even Alcott was never guilty, that
is would make them prosperous. The largest claim they cared
make for honesty was that it would turn out in the long
n to be "the best policy." "In the affairs of this world," said
or Richard, "men are saved not by faith but by the want
it." And the blue-backed Speller drummed into the minds
a hundred million American children the degrading maxim:
e kind to all as far as you can. You know not how soon
u may want their help." The Spelling Book and poor Rich-
1 left an impress upon American life and upon the surface of
1erican character that is still clearly discernible, even though
 simple economic theories on which some of their maxims were
ed are gone with the great auk. So pervasive has been their
oble influence that it has shaped our very notions of ourselves.
d yet we are wrong in thinking that America is a nation comed of Poor Richards and of boys who have learned to steal
les without being caught. There are now, and there have
ays been, fundamental motives at work in American life that
non-prudential and that do not emanate from the shop. Bron-

son Alcott represents them. In so doing he is at least as typica[l] an American as Noah Webster or as Benjamin Franklin himsel[f].

Not to comprehend this is not to see Alcott at all, and to b[e] unable to understand him is to miss a main fact about America[.] He was a dreamer, yes; and so is every true son of his fatherlan[d]. He cared little for money. Neither does any true American car[e] much. He hitched his wagon to a star. We, at present, prefer t[o] hitch our trailer to a car; but we shall get over that, and recogniz[e] at last, that he was a man of our own kind.

If Bronson Alcott were now living he would clearly see ho[w] transient is our present passion for automatic toys. We ma[y] rightly call him adolescent, as all his time was, but at lea[st] he had passed his puberty. Were an avatar of Alcott to vis[it] America in this twentieth century he would be amazed to fi[nd] how rapidly we have gone backward in mental age, and towa[rd] not innocence but ignorance, during these hundred years. A[nd] yet he would have so clear an intuition of what lies deepest [in] us that even this retrogression would hardly dismay him. [He] saw it coming, or already going on, and yet was not dismaye[d]. Even in the affairs of this world, in spite of Poor Richard, [he] was saved by faith, the evidence of things *not* seen.

It was to what lies deepest in Americans that Alcott a[d]dressed himself as a reformer. The lesser and superficial tas[ks] none of which can be permanently finished until the great ta[sk] is done, he left to other men. He saw, for instance, how ho[pe]less was the effort to argue, convert, or legislate America o[ut] of intemperance. That would be like plucking a dead leaf [or] two from a tree that was rotting at the core. He had no hope t[hat] the battle against vice and ignorance and misery would e[ver] be won by guerrilla tactics. There would be no perman[ent] good, for example, in reclaiming this or that city slum. W[hat] was the cause of slums? Greed. And what was the cause [of] greed? Emptiness of heart and mind. What had emptied the[m?] They had shut God out.

[290]

No; mankind would never reach the Holy City by "inching along." Against John Locke and Benjamin Franklin he set Plato and Jesus, those really bold gamblers for the human soul who ventured all on a single throw. And he said, as Jesus did to Nicodemus in the night: "Except a man be born again, he cannot see the kingdom of God."

Bostonians, of course, hardly liked to take the risk of being born again, lest they might not appear a second time in Boston. But Alcott was discovering what the native sons so seldom guessed, that there were other places elsewhere. For example, there was Concord, whither he moved his family in the spring of 1840 and set up the twentieth or so of his homes in the Hosmer family's "Dove Cottage." And also, most surprisingly, there was England. For several years he had been receiving enormous letters from a Pestalozzian enthusiast, then living in London, called James Pierrepont Greaves; but now, in this same springtime, before the rest of his Concord gardens was well planted, there came a letter from an unknown Charles Lane, telling him the most exciting things about an establishment that Greaves had made at Ham Common, near Richmond, in England, and had called "Alcott House." There appeared to be a school there, closely modeled after the Temple School. It was intimated that if Alcott could manage to get to England he would find at Alcott House a considerable circle of highly enthusiastic and transcendental Englishmen who had for some time been regarding him as their master. This was a most agreeable announcement.

If those Englishmen knew anything about the cost of intellectual leadership, however, they ought to realize that a man whose chief distinction lay in three or four successive failures in teaching school would scarcely possess the sinews of travel. Alcott answered Charles Lane's letter. He answered still more enthusiastic letters from John A. Heraud, a third-rate poet, an acquaintance of Coleridge and Wordsworth and Carlyle who, as editor of *The*

Monthly Magazine, had recently attributed to Alcott Emerson';
Nature. He answered further letters from J. P. Greaves and sen
him copies of all his own printed writings together with those o
Emerson. There was nothing more that he could do. It would b
pleasant to see these English friends and this English school tha
bore his name—and yet what, after all, was England? Englan
was the past, and lay eastward. His thought was for the future an
the West. England was the country that had burned Washingto
in the War of 1812. He had read all about it in the *Connecticu
Courant,* and it was hard for even the most pacific of men to forge
such things. In July his fourth daughter, named Abby May, wa
born at Dove Cottage. He owed several thousand dollars. H
would never see England.

He toiled with spade and hoe in his garden, delighting in tl
half-forgotten sleights of hand that he had learned beside his fath
in the years at Spindle Hill. Ah, the dear smell and sight ai
warmth of the good brown earth once more! Health poured in
him from the ardent sky and seeped from the sod below. He to
his place in the summer mowing, Connecticut against Mass
chusetts, and swung and rested and swung and rested until tl
rhythms of the ancient sun and stars were singing in his ve
bones. What wonderful grass in those old meadows of Concor
The grass of Spindle Hill had been good, but wiry, and alwa
while one mowed up there one would be expecting a hidden ro
or a stone. Here it would be only the nest of a mouse or a mead
lark that one might uncover among the waving timothy. Was th
not something in mowing almost magical, certainly mysteriou
How was it so beautiful, this singing the grasses to death?
could take a man who was sad and almost defeated, and in a d
an hour even, it would return him to the land of the living. I
Emerson know how good a thing mowing is, how lovely, h
heartening?

In the midst of the mowing season there appeared the f
number of the *Dial,* excellently printed by the Cambridge Pi

and "pure, ethereal as the voice of the morning," but still, as he thought, no more than "a twilight Dial." Pallid and thin as it was, the Boston newspapers promptly fell upon it with shrieks of delight. In their hilarious opinion the fifty "Orphic Sayings" by A. Bronson Alcott were like "a train of fifteen coaches going by, with only one passenger." Try as he might, A. Bronson Alcott himself failed to see any resemblance. But let them say what they would. Let them see what they could. The "Orphic Sayings" had come easily, as though from on high, and Margaret, the editor, thought they read well. There was one good passage in them, at least—the thirty-fifth:—

Nature is not separate from me. She is mine, alike with my body; and in moments of true life I feel my identity with her; I breathe, pulsate, feel, think, will, through her members, and know of no duality of being. It is in such moods of soul that prophetic visions are beheld, and evangels published for the joy and hope of mankind.

That was what a man learned at mowing.

The best answer to the public ridicule of "Orphic Sayings" seemed to be the composition of more "Orphic Sayings," and also the cradling of grain for the neighbors. Alcott went here and there conversing, always taking without a word whatever fee was offered for his services, and frequently taking no fee whatever. He was a pedlar, yes; but he was a gentleman too. With Margaret Fuller and George Ripley he discussed at Emerson's house the plans for communal living which were soon to develop into Brook Farm, but he was not personally drawn toward that enterprise. In October he harvested his crops and dined with Dr. Channing. "Mr. Alcott little suspects," the great preacher wrote soon after Miss Peabody, "how my heart goes out to him. One of my dearest ideas and hopes is the union of Labor and Culture. I wish to see labor honored, and united with the free development of the

[293]

intellect and heart. Mr. Alcott, hiring himself out for day-labor and at the same time living in a region of high thought, is, perhaps the most interesting object in our Commonwealth. Orpheus at the plough is after my own heart; there he teaches a grand lesson,—more than most of us teach with the pen."

Emerson too liked to think of Alcott as a laboring philosopher or philosophic laborer. Miss Anna Thaxter of Hingham wrote: " do rejoice that you are hiring yourself at daily labor. You are thus rendering a most essential service to the community and the age. It was remarkable what æsthetic pleasure it could give to scholarly persons, sitting quietly among their books by their study fires, to think about Alcott at work in the fields or the woods all day and then coming home to think and write and read. It reminded them, no doubt, of Carlyle's essay on the peasant-poet Robert Burns but not, presumably, about Phœbus Apollo tending the sheep of Admetus. And Alcott was thoroughly living up to what was expected of him. When his autumn crops had been gathered he went into the wood lots of his wealthier neighbors and chopped wood for a dollar a day throughout the winter, writing more "Orphic Sayings" the while and reading Hesiod's *Works and Days,* Henry More's *Poems,* Cudworth's *Intellectual System,* Xenophon's *Memorabilia* of Socrates, Jamblichus' *Life of Pythagoras,* Porphyry *On Abstinence,* Newton's *Return to Nature,* Goethe's *Theory of Colors,* Greene's *Vital Dynamics,* and Coleridge's writings in general. Meanwhile, he was teaching his three older daughters, meeting the poor children of the village once a week, and doing, as usual, a considerable part of the housework.

In January of 1841 Emerson proposed—whether before or after consultation with Mrs. Emerson is uncertain—that the entire Alcott family should move at once to his house. Wiser counsel prevailed. In the following month Alcott wrote in his Journal:

Family straits. Read Eschylus' Prometheus and Law's Way to Divine Knowledge.

[294]

In March Mrs. Alcott's father, Colonel May, died, leaving to his daughter a legacy of three thousand, one hundred dollars. The legacy was at once attached by creditors, and Alcott found that if he were to apply it all to his debts and were also to sell all his personal effects and the five hundred copies of *Conversations on the Gospels* that were undisposed of he would still owe thirty-four hundred dollars. The *Conversations* were in fact soon to be sold—to trunk-makers, at five cents a pound; but the general outlook remained somewhat gloomy, however interesting an object "Orpheus at the plough" may have been to Dr. Channing and others in the Commonwealth. Many a man would have brooded over it. Alcott, immediately after sketching his financial situation, wrote in his Journal:—

> Converse at Lexington, Hingham, Boston, and at Emerson's; also with poor children. Read Plutarch's Morals and Grotius on Property.

Although continually occupied, Alcott had not yet found an occupation. In that he was like all America. The indefinite number of things that a man might do, and the unlimited time he had to do them in, kept the problem from assuming any urgency. He could never quite bring his mind to a focus upon that problem. To be sure he had applied for one of the Concord schools, but the unaccountable failure of his application had seemed to relieve him of all further responsibility. Still, he was mildly and hopefully curious about the future of Bronson Alcott. Vague, majestic proposals, usually a little fantastic and seldom tainted by any hint of sordid gain, floated in and out of his thoughts like golden voluminous clouds on a summer horizon. He never walked over of an evening to sit by Emerson's fire, he never stood for a five-minute chat while young Thoreau leaned on the fence-rail, straw in mouth, he never walked out to where Edmund Hosmer was resting his

horses in mid-furrow and waiting to drop some acrid maxim
of rural philosophy, without offering his latest guess at the
mystery of his own future career. He took the thing so easily
that it soon became a public problem, exercising the wit and
imagination of the village: "*What* shall Alcott do?" As the
seasons came and went people began to ask "What, after all
can Alcott do?" Finally, however, the problem lay clear and
plain: "What is to be done *for* Alcott?"

One of the most charming of all his own ideas about the
matter was the one that had come to him two years before
in the summer of 1839, just after he had done his last teaching in Boston. Why not get him a pedlar's pack again and go
out into the villages of New England, as he had once gone
among the Southern plantations, drifting from door to door
and talking with women and children, talking with the black-
smiths and carpenters and plowmen, occasionally spending several days or even a week in a single place to hold Conversations
in the town hall or the vestry of the church? It had been a
most alluring plan, and all the more attractive because it was
in some way related to Wordsworth's Pedlar in the *Excursion*
which he had just been reading. He felt that he would have been
entirely happy, going always on and on without a goal, wading
through seas of talk, carrying a few trinkets for sale, perhaps, but
chiefly ideas to be given away; and then always to be with
people, with simple people, not graduates of Harvard, and
occasionally to discover a Mind. . . . Yes, an almost perfect
plan. It would have drawn his mind together into unity; for
there would have been the countryman, the pedlar, the teacher,
the converser, and the lover of mankind, all in one. But Mrs
Alcott had not liked it. She had asked awkward questions.
"Family straits" had been narrowly avoided. Cousin William
who had been living with them at the time, had not liked it
either. William never had liked peddling. He seemed to think
it lacking in social respectability. But what of that? A man

[296]

should carry his respectability inside him, so as to dignify any occupation. Nevertheless, the good plan had been abandoned—or postponed. It lingered on the outskirts of thought. Some day, perhaps, when the girls were older and the debts not quite so large—well, who knew? Surely it was a broad basic rule for right living, never entirely to abandon any phase of experience that one's life had brought, but in maturity to retain one's childhood and even in old age never to forget one's youth. Once a pedlar, always a pedlar. The time might yet come when he would buckle on some kind of actual or metaphorical pack and walk out again into the world's weather, along strange new roads—the westward-running roads it might be, this time—to meet many new strange people.

And in the meanwhile he would edge as close to that good scheme as he could get. As the spring of eighteen hundred forty-one came on he went out again to his "parlour parishes," speaking and conversing wherever people would have him, taking for his services whatever they cared to give and never thinking it too little. In May he conversed at Hingham, Scituate, Marshfield, Providence, and in the newly founded community at Brook Farm. In the same month he visited Theodore Parker at Roxbury, Edmund Quincy at Dedham, Adin Ballou at Mendon, and Abby Kelly at Millbury, while caring for his garden at Dove Cottage, writing more "Orphic Sayings," and carrying on correspondence with at least thirty persons in Old and New England. Adin Ballou asked him to join the community at Hopedale, as Ripley had invited him to join Brook Farm, but the one was even less "ideal" than the other. Alcott did not take long in deciding that he would scarcely feel at home in a phalanstery where everyone, including the nursing mother, was to receive exactly fifty cents a day for services and was to pay one dollar a week for board and room. The plan was intolerably arithmetical and had no clear relation to the home—always the source and model of every sound institution. Thomas

[297]

Davis, in this same month, invited the Alcotts to share his home near Providence, and Samuel May suggested that they take a farm near him at Scituate.

However it might have been in Boston, Alcott was no longer being neglected. Along a score of different channels at once he was moving out into other lives—mingling with, one might almost say bathing in, the social stream; and wherever he went he was welcome. When one remembers his rather lonely boyhood and the stark, bleak solitude of some of his middle years —remembers, too, the deep need that he always felt for companionship—it is pleasant to set down the names, though most of them are now forgotten, of the many men and women whom he visited, talked to, corresponded with, and worked beside in this period of his career. The ship of his life was moving through the doldrums now, one day scurrying far out of her course before a squall and, on the next, stuck, becalmed; but there were many other sails in sight, far-off and near.

Chiefly, of course, there was always Emerson, the nearest the dearest of all. Then there was Henry Thoreau, who took just a little understanding at first, but was clearly worth the effort. Emerson said so. That young man came at one like a hedgehog, bristling with heretical opinions and confidently expecting conflict; but when he found that the person he had selected for an antagonist was something of a heretic too, he could grow more charmingly mild and gentle. Henry Thoreau came more and more to Dove Cottage. Never "too soon made glad," never wearing his heart on his sleeve, he liked Alcott from the start. "He is the best-natured man I ever met," he said. "The rats and mice make their nests in him." Henry was a hero and teacher and elder brother all in one to Anna and Louisa and little Beth.

And other people of quite other kinds were coming to the Cottage now and staying a day, a week, a month, as it might please them—people that Henry Thoreau could not endure. Those bearded Essenes from the back-country, Abraham Ever tt and Joseph Palmer, came and stayed a week. (Did they ravel in couples, one asked, the better to protect each the other's beard?) Mrs. Alcott thought it might be well to hang up a shingle reading: "Come-outers' Haunt." Those two roistering companions from Providence, William Chace and Christopher Greene, came and stayed and confounded the people in church on Sunday morning by ribald shoutings from Barrett's Hill. Half transcendental and also half Come-outer, these young men were so intensely religious that they were constantly trying to shock the unco' guid by the most outrageous blasphemies against "the Nazarene." "What a pity," Emerson was writing, "that we cannot curse and swear in good society!" These young men could. Like J. F. Clarke and Christopher Cranch, they were making transcendentalism, among all the other things that it might or might not be, unquestionably a lark. Why not? It was chiefly a lark that Bronson Alcott had when he walked from Concord to Haverhill with John Wattles, another guest, and there conversed in a church with a congregation of Come-outers. In June he spent two weeks at Braintree in the Green Mountains, preaching all kinds of reform at once and distributing *Plain Speakers, Dials* full of "Orphic Sayings," *Health Journals,* and Emerson's Essays to the mountaineers, many of whom were unable to read. That was larking too.

But it did not last long. Back at home the debts were growing, and Mrs. Alcott was often despondent. There were even Concord debts now, and some difficulty in getting food for the children. Food for oneself did not matter. Clothing for the girls came mostly from Mrs. Alcott's Boston relations and friends, but it was almost always old clothing, made for adults. Alcott designed and cut the dresses for his daughters; he taught them and talked to and played with them, he wrote them charming letters, and often prepared the family meals. But none of this brought in money. In November he took his axe to the woods again to earn his dollar a day. Once more there

Emerson sends Alcott to England

appeared in his Journal the eloquent phrase "Family straits," surrounded by a list of the books he was reading—Pufendorf and Grotius and Pestalozzi and the Gospels—and by the names of his many correspondents.

This, he said, was "the winter of his discontent." On the twenty-ninth of January he was stricken by the news that little Waldo Emerson, "that beautiful boy," had died on the night before. He could faintly guess what this terrible blow would be to his friend, not only because he had known and loved the wonderful child—as who had not?—but also because the only son he himself had ever had, or ever would have now, had died, almost as soon as born, two years before. He mourned with Emerson, although it is likely that he dared not say a word to show that he was mourning. All the stronger on that account seemed the proof of his friend's fidelity when there arrived, before little Waldo had been two weeks in his grave, a letter from Emerson, then lecturing at Providence, saying:—

> It seems to me . . . you might spend the summer in England and get back to America in the autumn for a sum not exceeding four or five hundred dollars. It will give me great pleasure to be responsible to you for that amount; and to more, if I shall be able, and more is necessary.

One sees how this magnificent offer, from a man who was by no means in easy circumstances when he made it, had come about. Ever since the failure of the Temple School Emerson had been suffering for his friend, had even been feeling guilt or inept because he could not help him with anything but counsel and companionship. Moreover, he had been not a little impressed by the exalted tones of praise for Alcott that came across the Atlantic from the circle at Alcott House. How well he knew that no man is a prophet in his own little provincial town, and especially if that town be in New England! His fee

[300]

ing had always been that people would not see Alcott rightly, for he was "like a piece of Labrador Spar, which is a dull stone enough until you chance to turn it to the particular angle where its colors appear, and it becomes a jewel." But now more than ever, in the thick of these present perplexities, it had seemed to him that what Alcott most needed was "a pure success." He believed that if the men and women whose good opinion was fame could see Alcott as he was, and could express as heartily as these English correspondents their joy in his genius, then the spirit of his friend "would be exalted and relieved of some spots with which a sense of injustice and loneliness had clouded it."

How kind and generous a thought! In some ways it was also a wise one. Emerson himself had been in Europe and England, and his travels had done him much good, even though a certain stanch and proud Americanism in him had prevented a full surrender to the shows of the past. He scarcely knew that Alcott was more American than he, with a mind definitely faced toward the West and the future. That would make a difference for which he could not allow.

And there was another chance of error which he did not realize, in a matter more nearly concerning him. It would have given Emerson a deep pleasure to bring together in bonds of friendship the two friends of his for whose minds and characters he had the profoundest respect, and this it was, no doubt, that he promised himself by way of a private reward. Yet something told him that he must be cautious. Nothing could well exceed the caution with which he wrote to Carlyle on March 21, 1842:—

> I write now to tell you of a piece of life. I wish you
> to know that there is coming to you a man by the name
> of Bronson Alcott. If you have heard his name before,
> forget what you have heard. Especially if you have
> read anything to which his name was attached, be
> sure to forget that; and, inasmuch as in you lies, per-

mit this stranger, when he arrives at your gate, to make a new and primary impression. I do not wish to bespeak any courtesies or good or bad opinion concerning him. You may love him or hate him or apathetically pass him by, as your genius shall dictate; only I entreat this, that you do not let him go quite out of your reach until you have seen him and know for certain the nature of the man. And so I leave contentedly my pilgrim to his fate.

ALCOTT HOUSE

{ 1842 }

*The voyage–"Horned and sanguinary Britons"–Carlyle–
Strawberry juice and potato juice–A lay monastery–English
reformers–An English transcendentalist–Plans for Paradise–
America preferred–Book-buying in London–Joyous return*

ON THE eighth of May, 1842, the ship *Rosalind* set sail
from Boston Harbor with Bronson Alcott on board, bound
for England. Among the very few other passengers was the
son of Alcott's old acquaintance Dr. James Walker, already a
professor and destined to be the President of Harvard College.
There was also the son of the Scottish historian and philosopher,
Sir James Mackintosh, together with his wife, a daughter of
the great Boston merchant Nathan Appleton.

How dangerous a companion Alcott was for these young
scions of rank and riches and academic dignities, one of the letters that he read in his berth on his first night out would have
shown them. It was addressed to Dr. John Bowring, M.P., and

was, allowance being made for the writer's point of view, a fairly accurate portrait. The letter ran thus:—

Boston, May 8, 1842

Esteemed Friend,

You will not require of me an apology for introducing to you an esteemed friend of mine, the bearer of this (A. Bronson Alcott, of Concord, near Boston) for I am sure you will greatly admire the sweetness of his spirit, the independence and originality of his mind, and the liberality of his soul. . . . Mr. Alcott is a true man on the Anti-slavery and peace questions, an enlightened and warm-hearted philanthropist, a resolute and uncompromising foe of priestcraft, bigotry, and sectarianism under every guise, a Reformer who is for laying the axe at the root of the tree and not for pruning its branches, and a philosopher who is determined to think for himself. Though not harmonizing with him in all his speculations—religious, metaphysical, and social—yet I hold him in high esteem for the purity of his life, for the many virtues which adorn his character, and for the rare moral courage which he has displayed in giving utterance to "heretical" doctrines and unpopular thoughts. He is the bosom friend of Ralph Waldo Emerson, and both are well known to Thomas Carlyle. I have no doubt that his intercourse with the free, educated, reformatory minds with which he will probably come in contact on your side of the Atlantic will be mutually instructive and delightful. May his visit be greatly blessed to the promotion of "peace on earth, good will to men," and to the demolition of all those national and geographical distinctions and prejudices which alienate and curse our race! I write in great haste, etc. etc.

With great respect, I remain
Your admiring friend,
Wm. Lloyd Garrison

The voyage of the *Rosalind,* three weeks in length, was a prosperous one with few events for the "pilgrim." He took due note of the "stately icebergs, from Labrador, probably," he read Wordsworth's *Excursion* for the second or third time and was again impressed by the similarity between the opinions of certain characters therein depicted and his own. He read Emerson's Essays, and said of them: "Divine poems, these, having the exalting effect of poesy on the mind. 'Tis like the fragrance of woods and fields—so sylvan, so balmy. Delicious, these improvisations on Love and Friendship, reviving all my ties at Concordia. Again am I a youth, and after long wonderings in the solitary wilds of thought I am a denizen of the realms of affection, a dweller in the courts of humanity." He had much spirited conversation with his fellow passengers on topics of reform, and although his radical doctrines "were at first taken as pleasing fables," he felt assured at last that he had made some impression. Most of all, he thought about home.

> As yonder needle at my ship's helm inclines [he wrote], so doth the heart of a friend, in all the latitudes of life's drifting interests, incline with constancy to the hearts it loves.

For the thirtieth of May the Journal says:—

> We are in the English Channel. A water-man with provisions comes on board. Several others in sight. It seemed like meeting neighbors to see these bluff hardy persons and hear them speak in their rude brogues. . . . I took my berth late, but sleep forsook me. Troops of gentlest, fairest, sublimest thoughts usurped my brain all night. I slept not, but was planting Edens, fabling of worlds, building kingdoms and man, taking the hands of lovers, of wife and babes. So, at four, it being light and a most magnificent morning, I arose to write.

On the following day Alcott wrote to his wife:—

Most propitious of breezes! Bravest of ships, this *Rosalind!* Here we lie in this faerie water on this breezy May morning, in full sight of the British Isles . . . and this without reefing a sail nor scarcely an adverse wind during all our passage. Fortunate man! Solidest of ships! But that Atlantic queasiness I did not escape during the first days. Still it left me a most vigorous appetite, and the cottage bread kept sweet and good till devoured. It lasted a week or ten days, the applesauce some days longer with the steward's scalding and sugaring; and an apple or two remains in prime condition in my wallet at my berth's head. Apples I shall henceforth and always recommend to all my friends who may try this brine. Mine were most grateful at all times, and a treat to my fellow passengers. With potatoes, which were most excellent in kind and well-dressed, I did very well.

A separate book, even of considerable length, could scarcel exhaust the interest and significance of Alcott's four-montl stay in England, the story of which must here be told in a fev pages. Alcott did what he could, one might say, to simplify th account, for he saw but little of England, and most of what h did see he did not like. He went to London much as he ha first gone to Boston fourteen years before, with his head dowr his eyes upon the road, and his thoughts bent inward. It wa as though he were drawing a beeline from Dove Cottage to A cott House and back again. And this was not because he was bad traveler, for he was in fact a good one. Neither was it du to ignorance, for by this time he was decidedly a well-read ma The truth is, simply, that he was once more on the hunt fc Minds, and in this period of his career that word had come t mean Reformers.

Why did he not like England? One reason was that he did not see it. Rural England, so exactly suited to his taste for a landscape controlled and mastered, would have charmed him if only once for a moment he had opened his eyes to what lay before them; but the fact is, to choose a single example, that he lived for the greater part of his stay within two or three miles of the lovely and famous prospect from Richmond Terrace without ever quite becoming aware of that view. In London, to be sure, upon his first arrival, he did make a few observations and pay a few perfunctory visits to places of note. On his first night there, lodging at the London Coffee House in Ludgate Street, he walked up to St. Paul's, which he considered "over-wrought with ornament," and stood gazing; but it is clear that he did not really see even that building, for all that he said of it that night in his Journal was:—

> I found myself transmuting the material into the spiritual architecture instantly, and St. Paul, with the other Apostles, seemed to emblem the fortunes which their doctrines had had in the world. There they stand above the din and smoke of the town, their voices spent ere they reach the multitude below, their sublime inspirations all hardened into dogma and ritual, their prophet a mystery even to the few who tread the aisles within. Effigies and echoes of the Everlasting Word— its Christ a ghost, and its priests ossified at the heart.

This is hardly the mood or the mental focus that allows for accurate observation of the outer world. There is a tone of intellectual arrogance about it, suggesting a mind convinced that its own private thought is more significant than even the most imposing external fact. And yet this mind is not wholly unobservant. On that same evening, his first in England, Alcott wrote: "London seems a rare union of the costly, elegant, magnificent, with the useful, convenient and plain. All is solid, substantial, for comfort and use. But all is for Body."

The comment upon Westminster Abbey, if less shrewd and true, is no less revealing:—

> Prayers were being chanted, with responses from the choir, as I entered. The service is imposing, but derives its interest from historical associations altogether. It is a spectacle merely. There is no worship in it. A pantomimic ritual. A masked show. . . . All seemed ignoble to me, and the Abbey and its Gothic architecture, its cloisters and tombs, its chapels and aisles, but an eulogium on the desecrated genius of man, a monument of his fallen greatness.

Little by little it grows clear what sort of judgment the stranger from the Western World, descended from a man and woman who had left England only two hundred years before, was passing upon the mighty town. He thought its religion a sham. He thought it was living for material things and that its spirit had departed. But he had another charge to make: London, he believed, was brutal. At St. Paul's, when he finally entered that building, he was horrified at what seemed to him the desecration of a shrine by the tombs and effigies of men whose fame had been won by the slaughter of their fellow creatures. He went to the Tower, and found it "a most melancholy place, a Golgotha. . . . It is a relic of barbarity, and could have been designed and executed by the sanguinary Britons alone." At the Royal Academy he saw "only portraits of horned and sanguinary Britons, of the pride and folly of England. The statuary was best, but the subjects were chiefly busts of royalty, of the nobility and gentry, and held no attraction for me." After this visit he cried out: "My eye is pained, my thought revolts at portraits and originals, and I sigh to be back in the land of my birth."

As coming from Bronson Alcott, these are violent words. They express a feeling of strong disgust. In order to understand them at all one must remember that the London of a century ago, that is

o say the London of Charles Dickens, was in many ways really
a disgusting place, as Heinrich Heine had recently found it. The
carnivorous habits of the English and their glorification of slaugh-
er, whether of men or beasts or birds, were to Alcott simply
epulsive. Among American visitors to England he was apparently
ne of the first to become aware of the broad red streak of bru-
ality that really does run through the history of the English
eople, strangely contrasting with a delicacy of refinement such
s no other Western people can show. He for whom "the roast
eef of Old England" had no particular charm was the man to
e this phase of the truth more clearly than Cooper or Irving.
nd he too, the single-minded idealist, was the man to discern
ost clearly and to detest most heartily another tendency, by no
eans confined to the English but one in which they have shown
emselves unusually adept: the tendency to attempt the simul-
neous service of God and Mammon.

The fond American husband was saddened, furthermore, by
hat he saw, and still more by what he surmised, of the treat-
ent of Englishwomen by their lords and masters. How could
not have been, coming from a land in which women were
garded as extremely precious creatures and, above all things,
ure," into one in which it had long been suspected that they
e merely human? He saw and talked with Jane Welsh Carle—but what those interviews with the Scottish Sibyl meant
him he never set down in writing. There were things that he
uld never say to anyone, unless it might be his wife; and
en her he must ask not to tell Mrs. Emerson, for Emerson
ed England, and it was a questionable independence for Al-
t to be disliking it so intensely on Emerson's money. He
ght perhaps tell Mrs. Alcott about the throng of prostitutes
tling and thrusting for trade in the London streets— a sight,
him, perfectly heart-rending. How was he to know that his
n little Boston had even at that time more than two hun-
d brothels? Well, he might tell her or he might not. At any

rate, he gave her the effect of it all in a letter written in early
August:—

> My thoughts are all Occidental now, and I shall not
> find rest till I tread that land again and give myself to
> those ministries which are ours. I am not at peace in
> this Lion's den, amidst beasts of prey. I would dwell
> in quiet with husbandmen, repose in gardens, and tread
> fields unstained with blood. I have no love of England,
> nor England's sons or daughters. There is here no re-
> pose nor gentleness nor grace. Strife and violence mar
> all things, all men. Hercules stands at every corner
> with sanguinary club, grim in iron mail. . . . I will not
> turn on my heel to see another man (Beast I meant).
> And the women are tragic all—Mrs. Carlyle, Fox,
> Heraud, all are tears of sorrow.

A manifest fault in these passages is that of hasty generali-
ation upon slight knowledge and few instances. One might a
most suspect that Alcott, in writing them, was trying to outc
the wild absurdities of Mrs. Trollope's *Domestic Manners of tl
Americans,* which everyone in Boston had been reading wit
mingled rage and glee, ten years before. But no; it was a hab
of his mind to leap at once from the single fact, or suppose
fact, to its interpretation. And, once he had fixed in mind tl
idea that Englishmen were violent, "sanguinary" creatures, cru
to their women and living by force and rapine for the Bo
rather than the Soul, he had little difficulty in discovering exa1
ples. It seems probable, moreover, that as he walked the Stra
and Fleet street and Cheapside Alcott's mood may have be
exacerbated by ordinary hunger, for the "cottage bread"—ma
by himself of nothing but unbolted meal and water—was
gone now, and there was not a good apple to be had. Few thin
of course, lay a greater strain upon amicable international re
tions than the universal ignorance of foreigners—no matter v
the particular foreigners may be—about food. Wherever Alc

[310]

went for food, whether to the Cock, the Mitre, or the Cheshire Cheese, he was revolted by the sight and smell of viands which were to him simply dead animals in various stages of decomposition. It was not bigotry so much as a physical repulsion that turned him against all this and made him think of Englishmen—perhaps with an unconscious recollection of Porphyry *On Abstinence*—as walking sepulchers and perambulating tanks of beer. He had long been what he called "Pythagorean" in his diet, but he would be more so as soon as he got the chance. It may have been while he was rummaging about in Covent Garden Market looking for an edible apple that he composed the maxim: "Pluck your body from the orchard bough; do not snatch it from the shambles."

But there was something more at work than a gnawing stomach, or even that international antagonism to which the near-of-kin are especially prone. The spirit of reform knows no country, and Alcott was disapproving of Englishmen not as Englishmen, in the shallowly "patriotic" way of Cooper, for example, but rather, in the way of Shelley or of Cobbett, with the conviction that as mere human beings they left a great deal to be desired. He felt that they stood in desperate need of reform, just as the English lecturer George Thompson had felt about Bostonians during his recent ill-starred adventure in their city. For this belief he could have quoted much excellent British authority; and indeed the bitterest of his denunciations were mild in comparison with what Englishmen had long been saying about themselves. Probably he did not allow enough, or at all, for the pride that the English have long taken in putting their worst foot foremost. Hitherto he had accepted at face value what he had read about the Englishman in the writings of Thomas Carlyle, a Scot, and in those of Robert Owen, a Welshman, and now he had about him a group of professional reformers who would gladly have turned England upside down if they had been able. He believed what they told him, and he felt what they were feeling, not knowing how they had come to feel and believe in that way. For it was a major defect in Alcott's mind, and a characteristically American defect, that he had little historical knowledge and still less historical sense. A person, a mind, an event, a social or political or economic situation, stood forth bare and stark, in his thought of it, without cause or temporal background. He could not see any of these things as the contemporary aspect of an endless continuum. He saw them all as though they were suddenly exploding out of nowhere. And it was partly for this reason that he, as a reformer, underestimated the difficulty of thrusting them back into the region whence they seemed to have come.

Alcott entered at once into the social antagonisms that had been building up in England through a millennium of history, but he did not know that history, or care to know it. He adopted the whole program of Chartism as though it had been of his own invention. He saw no difference between reform in London and reform in Boston—except of course that London was afflicted with a past and that Boston was mostly a glorious future. He did not and could not comprehend either the thousand-year-long patience of the English masses or the old-experienced skill of the masters of England who knew to a nicety when to stand firm and when to yield. So when he wrote, on the third day of July, that "the growling, hungering multitude will bear their wrongs no longer," he was simply mistaken. They would and they did bear them, very much as they had been doing since the days of Wat Tyler, or those of Boadicea.

The blunder is not to be laid at Alcott's door alone. Many persons far better informed than he was, many Englishmen in and out of Parliament, were convinced in the summer of 1842 that a revolt of the laboring classes would soon overturn the throne and lay the whole aristocracy low. Most of the people he met—George Thompson, Robert Owen, W. J. Fox, J. M. Morgan, Joseph Hume, Daniel O'Connell, Joseph Sturge, idney Smith—believed this. They ought to know. And, besides, hat were those words learned in boyhood from the Preface the blue-backed Speller and never quite forgotten? "Europe is own old in folly, corruption, and tyranny. In that country laws e perverted, manners are licentious, literature is declining, and man nature is debased." Very well, then. What Alcott saw out him in England, or thought he saw, was simply a corrupt d moribund aristocracy rapidly crumbling to its fall. Standg on the dome of St. Paul's and looking out over London, he ote:

A huge den this, truly, wherein Beelzebub whelps, the roar of whose voice reverberates throughout the civilized world. But the reign of the Beast is near its end. London, with its gaudy glories, its cruelties and enormities, its thrones and hierarchies lording it over the souls and bodies of men, shall become the footstool of a nobler race of kings.

merson sent him to England

In London as in Boston, Alcott went about expecting some mendous, almost immediate change. Many people in both nispheres were expecting this. William Miller, who had told Groton Convention exactly when the "Second Coming" uld occur, was only giving precise statement to a widespread ling. Those who had this dim premonition made, of course, y one mistake—that of supposing that the change would be astrophic instead of gradual and steadily accelerating. Al- t expected an explosion, and he went up and down looking the Man who was to light the fuse.

Vould it be Carlyle? For surely, if one could judge at all from printed word, there was and could be no more explosive peron earth. Carlyle the mighty, Carlyle the peasant-scholar, the Preacher and the Prophet of the Act and the Instant d—oh, certainly now, in these last ebbing moments of the

[313]

old bad world, Carlyle must be meditating and making ready
for some world-shattering performance that would make the
old things new! It was not "What hast thou thought, felt, read
known or dreamed?" that he was always asking, but rather, an
in tones of uttermost indignation and clamorous outcry, "Wha
hast thou *done?*" This man Carlyle had so wrought upon th
nerves of a few thousand Americans, and Alcott among them
that it was only by main force of will that they could refrai
with this battering alarm bell beating in their ears, from rush
ing headlong into the street and throttling the first millionair
who came to hand.

Well and good. On the twenty-fifth of June, Alcott felt tha
the time had come for him to find out what the Scottish tita
was planning to do.

One can see him standing there on the little landing at 5 (no
24) Cheyne Row, with Emerson's kind but cautious letter in h
pocket—a tall, lean man with hair already gray and a prem
turely furrowed face. It was for him really a great occasio
In a moment he would be in the presence of one of the for
most Minds on earth. One can see him admitted by the serva
and watch him glide with his light and silent step into the lit
parlor to the left of the entry—a parlor not unlike Emerso
study in Concord except that it was not so large and that t
fireplace was absurdly smaller. Emerson himself seemed w
him there, in spirit. One must remember that this great m
was Emerson's dear friend. And then there would come
heavy shuffling step on the stair and—Carlyle!

A lifetime of reading, years of talk, verbal descriptions and i
tations, portraits, daguerreotypes even, could not prepare one
that apparition. Alcott saw a man as tall as himself, and bu
There were still in him, as it were, the ruins of physical pow
That would be the strength of the peasant, which can stand a
thing for one generation. His eyes were tired. His face, tho
he was only forty-seven, was seamed. His iron-gray hair, th

nd heavy, was tumbled and tossed about. He hoped that Mr.
Alcott would not mind if he lit his pipe.

Yes, Alcott would say in answer to the first inquiry, he had
eft Mr. Emerson well, though terribly saddened and shaken
y the recent loss of his boy. Perhaps Mr. Emerson would
ever quite get over that. And soon the man who had never had
child other than those of his brain would be saying, in reply
) a question, that he had now ready for press a little book
alled *Past and Present,* but that the real labor, the gruesome
rudgery, the ghastly toil that was bringing his gray hairs in
orrow to the grave, was a *Life and Letters of Oliver Crom-
ell.* Had Mr. Alcott ever, in expiation of ancestral sins or per-
aps of the original curse upon Adam, been obliged to burrow
r year after year through dusty tunnels of tomes forgotten and
egible manuscript intolerably dull? No? Then Mr. Alcott's con-
ption of the lengths to which human stupidity had been allowed
' the All-Wise to extend itself, was inexact. *Past and Present*
d written itself. The whole thing stood there ready to one's
nd in the mediæval chronicle on which it was based. But the
omwell was buried deep in the most incredible rubbish heaps
lies upon barefaced lies, in which a man might often drudge
d droil for a week without sifting forth one tiny grit of a
t.—Why, then, did Mr. Carlyle spend his precious time and
ents upon Cromwell, who, one understood, had lived a goodly
e ago? For the living breathe with the living, nor prowl
ong the sepulchres by the sweet light of day. The living are
r intent upon charities, the humanities. From this present
ir, and not from past centuries, they would dispel the dark-
s and drive the spectres forth.—In replying to which in-
ry, set down here in almost the exact words that Alcott
rwards attributed to himself, Carlyle must have let himself
in a splendor of rhetorical denunciation of all things con-
porary that left the professional talker from across the seas,
once in his life, speechless. The substance of Carlyle's re-

[315]

marks would be that one burrowed in the past because, false an
stupid and ignorant though one must acknowledge it to be, ye
it was fair and true and wise compared with these moder
times.

But Alcott's own record of the visit is sufficiently revealing:-

> Ride to Chelsea and spend an hour with Carlyle.
> Ah, me! Saul among the prophets! 'Twas a dark hour
> with him, impatient as he is of any interruption, and
> faithless in all social reforms. His wit was sombre as it
> was pitiless; his merriment had madness in it; his
> humor was tragical even to tears. There lay smoulder-
> ing in him a French Revolution, a seething Cromwellian
> Rebellion; nor could the deep mellowness of his tones,
> resonant in his broad northern accent, hide the restless
> melancholy, the memory-fed genius, the lapse of proph-
> ecy into the graves of history, whereinto, with his
> hero whom he was disinterring, himself was descending
> —the miming giant over-mastered by the ghosts he
> evoked from their slumbers, the dead dealing with the
> dead dolefully enough. . . . His conversation was cyni-
> cal, trivial, and gave no pleasure. He needs rest; must
> get this book off his brain to find his better self and
> speak sanely to his contemporaries. I know his trouble;
> also his cure.

Perhaps intending to administer this "cure," Alcott trie
second time, in July. "Again at Carlyle's," says the Journ

> . . . and pass the night there. But we sped no better
> than at first, he the Cynic and I the Paradise-Planter,
> together. "Work, Work!" his creed and motto; toil
> of brain, dire draughts on memory, the sacrifice of
> sentiment to intellect, devotion to thought at the cost
> of affection. Woe is me!

And on the second of August Alcott wrote to his wife
have seen Carlyle once more, but we quarrelled outright a

all not see him again. Greatness abides not here; her home is
the clouds, save when she descends on the meadows or treads
e groves of Concord."

Which of the two was responsible for this quarrel one may be
rfectly sure; but it is not clear—partly because of certain
letions in Norton's version of the Carlyle-Emerson corre-
ondence—just how the quarrel began. Twenty years after, the
ler Henry James was saying in Boston that Carlyle had been
xed at Alcott's refusal to eat what was set before him at
eakfast. He had sent out for some strawberries for the vege-
rian's special benefit, and when these were put on the table
cott was said to have taken them on the same plate with
potatoes, so that "the two juices ran together and frater-
ed." Carlyle was made almost ill, apparently, by this revolt-
spectacle, so that he could eat nothing himself "but stormed
and down the room instead."

Manifestly, there remain some ingredients of truth in this
e even after one has made the proper deductions for each
the masterly narrators. As a breakfast is involved, however,
eems to refer to the occasion early in June when Alcott had
nt the night at Cheyne Row, and not to that later visit when
two men had "quarrelled outright." Of that visit or call
re appears to be no record.

But much is to be read between such lines as we have. There
no difficulty in recognizing Alcott's disappointment in the
at man to whom he had been looking for ten years as the
ler of all reform in England, and whom he now found buried,
he thought, in the past. He had come seeking a hero in the
ng flesh, and he found a man who could not digest his din-
Carlyle, with a hero in the flesh before him, had long since
le up his mind that all the heroes were dead, and also that—
erson always excepted—no good thing could come out of
rica. The Connecticut prophet and the Scottish historian

[317]

had much in common—friends, social origins, intellectual an
cestry—and yet each of them thought the other a little mad
As the two transcendentalists stared at each other across th
breakfast table, three thousand miles of sea roared betwee
them, and a widening gulf of time. The American, ignorant o
the past, wanted to know how the gospel according to Carlyl
could be applied in action to the world of here and now. Th
Scot, hating the present world with a black and furious hatre
plunged indignantly backward into history. *Past and Prese*
—what a significant title! Potato juice and strawberry juice
and never the twain should meet!

Surely it was a sad, strange, ludicrous colloquy, full of laug
ter for devils and full of tears for all kind and lonely hearts.
there was a definite fault on either side it lay with Carlyle, for
was the host and was receiving the friend of a friend who was a
ways the soul of courtesy. One may feel fairly certain that Carly
was guilty of some rough egotism, some irritable intransigean
some derision of the hare-brained scheme for "Paradise Pla
ing" that was then growing at Alcott House. Later, no dou
when his dyspepsia was a little better and when the "dem
fowls" next door had been somewhat less vociferous during
night, he was sorry.

In spite of the resolution recorded in the letter to his wife,
cott did call upon Carlyle for what appears to have been the fou
time—but found him gone from home. There is even a legend,
ported by Frank Sanborn, that the two men went walking in M
fair, and that the one peasant's son said to the other, pointing
the expensive magnificence of the houses: "Do you see this, m
This has stood for a thousand years, and will stand when you
your dom'd Potato Gospel have gone to the dogs." One incli
to believe that story, for it would have been hard for anyon
invent a remark so characteristic of Carlyle's manners or of
crass materialism with which, in his later years, he tormented
own hypersensitive mind.

However that may be, Carlyle wrote a farewell letter to Alcott
that was at least kind; and to Emerson, for the loss of whose hopes
he must have been genuinely sorry, he wrote in a way perhaps not
intended to convey all his feelings. Alcott, he said, "is a genial,
innocent, simple-hearted man, of much natural intelligence and
goodness, with an air of rusticity, veracity, and dignity withal,
which in many ways appeals to me. The good Alcott; with his
long lean face and figure, with his gray worn temples and mild
radiant eyes; all bent on saving the world by a return to acorns
and the golden age; he comes before one like a venerable Don
Quixote, whom nobody can laugh at without loving."
Every stroke in that miniature portrait, drawn as it was by
the hand of a master, is a revelation; and yet the effect of the
whole, chiefly because of the patronizing condescension that per-
vades it, is somehow false. Emerson saw this. For once he did
not even try to reply in kind to Carlyle's clever phrases. In his
response there is an uncompromising fidelity to his American
friend which does him honor: "Alcott is a great man, and was
made for what is greatest . . . As you do not seem to have
seen him in his pure and noble intellect I fear that it lies under
some new and denser clouds."

If Carlyle did not admire Alcott, the rest of England—so far
as it had the chance—was doing so to an almost embarrassing degree. At Alcott House in particular, whither the eponymous parent of that institution betook himself at once and where he
remained during most of his stay abroad, he was given full
measure of that "pure success" of which Emerson had thought
he stood in need. The house itself, he found, was a commodious
and handsome structure with many dormer windows looking
out among old trees across a beautiful countryside. It contained
a schoolroom conducted—as Alcott thought, with wisdom and success—by a certain young Henry Gardiner Wright, whose methods
showed a judicious mingling of Alcott with Pestalozzi. Also there

[319]

were two older men in the house, of a fiber less delicate and mo
virile. William Oldham, the manager of business affairs and pate
familias in general, was an imperfectly educated but an extreme
earnest and soulful aspirant toward the heights of Spirit ai
Mind. Charles Lane, with whom Alcott had long been correspon
ing, had for some time been editing the *London Mercantile Pric
Current*.

Alcott House was a lay monastery, of a sort with which En
land has never been unprovided since the Reformation broug
the old religious brotherhoods to an untimely close. Compar
with the group of brilliant men whom Viscount Falkland h
gathered about him at Great Tew in the seventeenth century,
was far less pious and intellectual. As compared with the Hell-F
Club in which John Wilkes and Bubb Doddington disported the
selves beside the Thames more than a century later, it was
more decently behaved. Some remnants of the monastic spi
however, it certainly contained. For one thing, it was unquesti
ably religious—and its religion was reform. It had a str
penchant toward celibacy, which, however, was not due
much to abstract preference as to sad experience in the mar
relation. And also it had its sacred books. They were
Record of a School and *Conversations with Children upon*
Gospels.

What Alcott House chiefly lacked, one feels, was laugh
gaiety, and a sense of relative values. Perhaps the religior
reform has never kept its votaries sufficiently aware that it is I
pleasant and proper to play the fool, as Horace said, on the r
occasions, and that if one does not do so then one is likely to
the fool on all occasions whatsoever. At Alcott House, one
pects, that grievous penalty was paid. At any rate the three
brothers were at all times excessively earnest and sober.
took themselves with utmost seriousness as at least the pote
saviors of a society otherwise lost and damned, and they did
than nothing to alleviate the profound seriousness with which

isitor from New England had long been accustomed to regard the
ocial mission of Bronson Alcott.

Besides the three monastic brothers already named, other men,
nd also a few women, came and went—each bearing his or her
tle pot of frankincense and myrrh. There was John Abraham
eraud, who had managed to fail in more things, as poet and
amatist and editor and philosopher, than a wise man would
er have attempted, but who was a first-rate enthusiast for
muel Taylor Coleridge and Bronson Alcott. There was James
Smith, a mystic primarily, but also the editor of Robert Owen's
isis and author of *The Divine Drama of History and Civiliza-
n*. There was the astronomer and mathematician George
ancis, said to be the master of forty languages. There was
:s. Wheeler, famous for her numberless heresies, for her beauti-
daughter, and for being the mother-in-law of the novelist
rd Lytton. There was Richard Henry Horne, critic, epic poet,
amatist, and friend of Mrs. Browning. There was Dr. Henry
nsell, some day to be Dean of St. Paul's. There was John
estland Marston, famous as a dramatist and as the father of the
nd poet Philip Bourke Marston. There was Newton Crosland,
o had written *The New Principia* and *Transcendental Vagaries,*
d also his wife Camilla, who translated Victor Hugo and wrote
ular novels. There was Francis Barham, author of *The Death
Socrates, A Tragedy.* Most conspicuous of all, there was
n Goodwyn Barmby, editor of a penny magazine boasting a
which was alone worth at least a shilling: *The Promethean
Communitarian Apostle.* "A radical poet," Emerson called him,
h too little fear of grammar and rhetoric before his eyes, and
as little fear of the Church or of the State." A taste of the
's quality—and a hint, too, of the way in which the entire
p received their sage from the Western World—is given in a
thless note that he dashed off to Alcott early in July.

have a prophetic hope in my heart," he exclaims, "that
r days for society and myself are at hand. The swallow-heart

[321]

tells of the advent of Summer, and I hear a voice call 'Home
Home!' May the Cincinnatus-spirit in you evolve other Cir
cinnati! Good Agrarian, temple and sanctity the field! Why d
you say that the way to the East is by the West? The Family
good; the neighborhood is *better;* the Communitorium is *bes*
You are an older man than I am. When you want blood I will l
a vein. Take it! For in Blood there is redemption!"

After which outcry of self-revelation it is only needful to a
that John Goodwyn Barmby entertained the most exalted opinio
of the general salubrity of cold baths.

In a book narrating the progress of a Yankee pedlar one ca
not turn aside for a full consideration of this highly interesti
English group, which had been drawn together by the magnet
a single mind. That mind, or at any rate the body it had inhabite
had recently been withdrawn, but here were still the iron-filin
so to speak, arranged about the vacancy it had left. Or one mig
say that here was still the swarm, looking for another queen b
And a strange swarm it was, bringing in nectar from orchards a
fields and meadows amazingly distant and diverse. If Bost
was amused at the miscellaneity of her own reformers—"wild-e
enthusiasts," as Lowell was to call them, "rushing from all sid
each eager to thrust under the mystic bird that chalk egg fr
which the new and fairer Creation was to be hatched—one
only wonder what she would have thought of these Engl
"Apostles of the Newness." All of them in some sense "tr
scendental" and affected at the second or third remove by
thought of Coleridge, all riding on the English backwash of
French Revolution, they had one thing in common: that extr
and perhaps excessive "tender-mindedness" so likely to be p
duced in a time and place primarily "tough-minded." For the r
their enthusiasms were dietetic, hydropathic, spiritualistic, c
munistic, economic, "Alistic," Fourieristic, metaphysical, ed
tional, political, religious, vegetarian, and what not. As at Br
Farm and Fruitlands, but not at quite all of the American c

[322]

unities, almost the only kind of enthusiasm not overtly mani-
sted among them was the erotic. And yet even there it was re-
embered, it would never be forgotten, that Mr. Henry Gardiner
Iright himself had broken the Founder's heart, perhaps short-
led his life, by marrying a yeoman's daughter and actually
getting a child.

These good people, early Victorians, some of them not only good
at quite as intelligent as their great-grandchildren, were ac-
istomed to gather at Alcott House on a few gala occasions of the
ar for a sharing of views. London's *Morning Chronicle* for the
th of July, 1843, bore the following Public Invitation:—

> An open meeting of the friends to human progress
> will be held to-morrow, July 6, at Mr. Wright's, Alcott-
> House School, Ham Common, near Richmond, Surrey,
> for the purpose of considering and adopting means for
> the promotion of the great end, when all who are in-
> terested in human destiny are urged to attend. The
> chair taken at Three o'clock, and again at Seven, by
> A. Bronson Alcott, Esq., now on a visit from America.
> Omnibuses travel to and fro, and the Richmond steam-
> boat reaches at a convenient hour.

We are fortunate in having a report of this meeting, apparently
m the hand of Alcott himself, as published in Margaret Fuller's
l for Ocotober, 1842. The reporter begins:—

> A very pleasant day to us was Wednesday, the sixth
> of July. On that day an open meeting was held at Mr.
> Wright's, Alcott-House School, Ham, Surrey, to define
> the aims and initiate the means of human culture.
> There were some sixteen or twenty of us assembled
> on the lawn at the back of the house. We came from
> many places; one 150 miles; another a hundred;
> others from various distances; and our brother Bron-
> son Alcott from Concord, North America. We found

[323]

it not easy to propose a question sufficiently comprehensive to unfold the whole of the fact with which our
bosoms labored. We aimed at nothing less than to speak
of the instauration of Spirit and its incarceration in a
beautiful form. We had no chairman, and needed none.
We came not to dispute, but to hear and to speak. And
when a word failed in extent of meaning, we loaded the
word with a new meaning. The word did not confine
our experience, but from our own being we gave significance to the word. Into one body we infused many
lives, and it shone as the image of divine or angelic or
human thought. For a word is a Proteus that means
to a man what the man is.

At this meeting Wright, Lane and Alcott presented th:
"scriptures," respectively dealing with "Reformation," "Tra:
tion," and "Formation." Wright made the point that all hun
institutions are "so wreathed together that one reform com
a hundred, and of course every attempt to reform in one par'
resisted by the establishment in all parts." In his opinion, the
fore, "an integral reform" must comprise not only an amendm
in the Corn Laws, monetary arrangements, the penal code, ed:
tion, the Church, the law of primogeniture, and divorce,
should extend to questions not yet publicly mooted such as
common reliance upon a mere commercial prosperity, the b:
in representative government, the right of man to inflict pain :
man, the need of a purer generation, the need of substituting
principle of love for the strife of opinion, the abrogation of pri
property, and the substitution of "divine sanction" for civil
ecclesiastical authority over marriage. Charles Lane summe:
his remarks, which were primarily an attack upon pr:
property, with the statement: "We ignore human governm
creeds, and institutions; we deny the right of any man to di
laws for our regulation, or duties for our performance; and de
our allegiance only to Universal Love, the all-embracing Jus:

Bronson Alcott chose as the motto for his closing "scripture" the words "Behold I make all things new," and began: "In order to attain the highest excellence of which man is capable, not only is a searching Reform necessary in the existing order of men and things, but the Generation of a new race of persons is demanded." He declared that "the elements for a superior generation consist in an innocent fertile mind and a chaste healthful body, built up from the purest and most volatile productions of the uncontaminated earth, thus removing all hindrances to the immediate influx of Deity into the spiritual faculties and the corporeal organs." Working upon this premise, he went on to lay the utmost emphasis upon marriage and family life, upon housewifery and husbandry, and upon "the relations of the neighborhood."

Thus far one recognizes the social, the filial and paternal Alcott of former days, but in what immediately follows there is evident a profound change, or at any rate the rather sudden emergence of a new principle. "We propose not to make new combinations of old substances," the speaker continues. "The elements themselves shall be new. The great enigma, to solve which man has ever labored, is answered in the one fact, Birth. The discipline, the loves, the wishes, the sorrow, the joys, the travail of many years, are crowded into conception, gestation, and birth. If you ask where evil commences, the answer is, in Birth. If you ask what is the unpardonable sin, the answer is, an unwise Birth. The most sacred, the most profane, the most solemn, the most irreverent, the most godlike, yet possibly the most profane of acts, this one stands as a center to all extremes; it is the point on which God and Devil wage most irreconcilable warfare. Let Birth be surrendered to the Spirit and the results shall be blessed."

One sees that Bronson Alcott, who had been in England exactly a month when he read this scripture, had somehow acquired since he arrived there a new idea or principle looking in the general

[325]

direction of what is now called "eugenics." It was not an America
idea either in origin or in nature. In fact one may say that it wa
definitely opposed to certain basic beliefs or prejudices—inherite
from the French Encyclopædists, but ultimately from the ancie
Stoics—of American life. It flew directly in the face of th
doctrine or feeling that "all men" are, or can in any sense b
"equal." One would expect it to arise, as in fact it did, in a count
of aristocratic rather than democratic backgrounds. Nevertheles
Alcott accepted, and never forgot or abandoned, this idea. It w
one of the two chief gains of his English journey. The other, n
so much an idea as a plan, was clearly indicated in the same spee
before the group at Alcott House: "It is proposed to select a sp
whereon the new Eden may be planted and man may, untempt
by evil, dwell in harmony with his Creator, with himself, his f
lows, and with all external natures. On a survey of the prese
civilized world, Providence seems to have ordained the Unit
States of America, more especially New England, as the fi
wherein this idea is to be realized in actual experience; and, tru
ing in the faith which inspires, the hope which ensures, and
power which enacts, a few persons, both in the new country a
the old, are uniting their efforts to secure, at the earliest possi
moment, and by the simplest possible means, a consummation
sublime, so humane, so divine."

There was one central doctrine advanced at this meeting,
Alcott and Wright and Lane alike, which was certainly of fi
rate interest to Emerson, who edited all three of these spee
for the *Dial*. This was the doctrine that reform begins at hc
with the individual—precisely what Emerson was to say in
addresses on "The New England Reformers," "The Trans
dentalist," and "Man the Reformer." In some parts of these
dresses, but especially in the first of them, Emerson seem
glance at Alcott as one who has violated, if he is not ent
ignorant of, that principle. But Alcott was in fact so far

[326]

gnorant of it that he may even have been the first person to call
t to Emerson's conscious attention.

The difference between Alcott and Emerson in this regard may
e stated, with some exaggeration, by saying that Alcott thought
ll reform should begin with the individual and that Emerson
nded to think it might end there. Characteristic of Emerson are
ich remarks as these: "Dear heart, take it sadly home to thee,
iat there will and can be no coöperation"; and again: "All
ie fine *aperçus* are for individualism. The Spartan broth, the
ermit's cell, the lonely farmer's life, are poetic; but the
halanstery, the 'Self-supporting Village' are culinary and
ean."

To much of this Alcott would have agreed, but he would have
ished to add that there is a middle term between the extremes
the hermit's cell and the intolerably public phalanstery of
ato's, Sir Thomas More's, and Fourier's dreaming. He held
at this golden mean is the Family, into which the individual
urs his life and out of which issue all the lower but more in-
isive institutions such as the State, the School, and the Church.
nerson seems never quite to have grasped this distinction, and
; later disapproval of the experiment at Fruitlands did not allow
ough for Alcott's unwavering determination to maintain the
nily life there as the basis and model of all that was done. In
y case, Emerson had no reason to charge Alcott or his two chief
idjutors with the failure to see that no reform can ultimately be
ter than the reformers; for he himself had copied out and
ted these clear words of their manifesto:—

> However extensive and grand or noble may be the
> ultimate measures proposed, it is . . . the imperative
> duty of the sincere reformer at once to commence that
> course of conduct which must not less conduce to his
> own than to the universal good. . . . A personal re-
> form of this kind, humble as it may appear, is obviously
> the key to every future and wider good. By reformed

[327]

individuals only can reformed laws be enacted, or reformed plans effected. By him alone who is reformed and well regulated can the appeal fairly be made to others.

The three speeches delivered at Alcott House on the sixth o July were in large part a posthumous expression of the though of a rather remarkable man. Alcott's keenest regret during hi English journey was due not to his failure with Carlyle but t his discovery, upon his arrival in London, that James Pierrepoi Greaves, the founder of Alcott House and his own corresponde for several years, had died three months before. But yet one made to feel that if Greaves had lived on he could scarcely hav exerted a deeper influence upon the American visitor by the livir voice than he did by means of those heavily annotated books ar manuscripts of his with which the house was crowded, by tl thoughts and sayings which his surviving associates were alwa; eager to communicate, and by something more intangible b more pervasive still—an aura of mind and personality with whi Alcott found himself from the first in accord. It was a stran experience for him, always too deeply a participator in Spi to have the faintest interest or belief in "spirits," to sit there the sofa where his dead friend had spent his last days, readi that friend's books, reading his manuscripts, and looking out the little sunny churchyard where his grave was still covered w flowers. Alcott wrote from that room to his wife:—

Mr. Greaves was the soul of the circle—a prophet of whom the world heard nothing but who, it seems, had quickened much of the thought now current in the most intelligent circles of the Kingdom. He was acquainted with every man of deep character in England, and with many in both Germany and Switzerland; and Strauss, the author of the Life of Christ, was a pupil of Mr. Greaves when he held conversations in one of the colleges of Germany after leaving Pestalozzi. A most remarkable man. Nobody remained the same after meeting him. He was the prophet of the deepest affirmative truths, and no man ever sounded his depths.

James Pierrepont Greaves, born in 1777, had spent his young manhood in the management of a prosperous mercantile concern. Ruined by the Berlin and Milan decrees of 1806, he abandoned all his property to creditors and began again, but in 1817 he became so much interested in educational reform that he left his growing business and went to live with Pestalozzi at Yverdon, where he remained for four years as an assistant teacher and as pupil to the master. A strong affection grew up between the two men, neither of whom could speak—or, apparently, made any effort to learn—the other's native language. Greaves spent four years more, as a tutor in English, in the Universities of Basel and Tübingen, after which he returned to England and founded the Infant School Society. For a time he wandered about the country, living with friends and relatives and interesting himself in various reforms, most of which seem to have been related to the ideas of Robert Owen. About the year 1835 he established, at his lodgings in Burton Street, London, what should probably be called a "salon," attended by most of the persons who have been named above as loosely connected with Alcott House. *The Record of a School* and *Conversations on the Gospels,* presented to him by Harriet Martineau upon her return from America, were received by him with such enthusiasm that he gave the name "Alcott House" to the establishment he was then setting up near Richmond. It had been his hope and plan to visit Alcott in America, and at one time in 1838 he had actually paid his passage money, but the trip was prevented by increasing ill-health. He left Burton Street for Alcott House only some five months before his death, which occurred on March 11, 1842.

[329]

There were many things in common between Greaves and Alcott besides the Pestalozzian tinge of their educational theories. Greaves, for one thing, appears to have been a thoroughgoing transcendentalist. He had certainly an acquaintance with Coleridge, with whose mind his own showed at least a superficial resemblance. It seemed a curious fact, when Alcott discovered it, that Greaves also had been for many years in the habit of reading scientific books in order to jot down the metaphysical suggestions that came to the mind during the perusal. Twelve quarto volumes of minute manuscript produced by the English transcendentalist in this way finally came into Alcott's possession. But it was what the man had said, and the brief maxims that he had written down frequently on the margins of his many books, that convinced Alcott of his consanguinity with this now silenced Mind. "I hear every one crying out for association," Greaves had somewhere written:—

> I join in the cry; but then I say: associate first with the Spirit,—educate for this Spirit-association, and far more will follow than we have as yet any idea of. Nothing good can be done without association; but then we must associate with goodness, and this goodness is the Spirit-nature, without which all our societarian efforts will be turned to corruption. Education has hitherto been all outward; it must now be turned inward. The educator must keep in view that which elevates man, and not the visible exterior world.

These words Alcott himself might have written at any period within the preceding ten years. At some time before he made speech on the sixth of July, however, he had come upon another and a much more compact statement in the Greaves papers which must have caused at first a considerable upheaval in his thought: "As Being is before knowing and doing, I affirm that education can never repair the defects of Birth."

[330]

It was in this statement, apparently, that the dead master of Alcott House had brought his whole doctrine to a burning focus. Certainly the sentence burned into Alcott's mind. Within a few weeks, at most, he was putting it forth in elaborated form, as we have seen, in a public utterance. It recurs again and again in his own manuscripts. What is more, it seems to have deflected the current of his own thinking, perhaps even of his life. Most reformers worked with adults. Alcott had felt from the opening of his active career that this was beginning too late, and so had done his work with young children—thinking to forestall in that way the shades of the prison house. But now a mind whose wisdom he had come to regard as positively oracular and infallible was telling him that what is done for children is always done too late, since everything has been decided at birth and long before it. One can readily see that such a belief, once accepted, would decidedly tend to dampen the enthusiasm of a professional teacher. Alcott did accept it. In consequence, though he never lost his strong interest in teaching, he never again made any such claims for the teacher's task as one finds in his early Journals. More and more, in his later thought and public utterance, he insisted upon what he was pleased to call a "pure Birth," emphasizing the necessity that the divine Existence be—in the words of Greaves—"developed and associated with man and woman prior to marriage."

Greaves himself, apparently, had come to the sad conclusion that although this sanctification of marriage was necessary it was so practically impossible; and so he believed, as a logical consequence, that there ought not to be any marriages whatever. He himself never married. The two elder men at Alcott House had done so, but deeply regretted it. Great consternation was felt and expressed in that celibate establishment, therefore, when it was learned that Henry Wright had entered into a clandestine marriage. Oldham left the school at once, though he returned after protest. Lane was reconciled with the utmost difficulty. Greaves wrote to Oldham, exactly in the spirit of an aging

[331]

bachelor, that he was grateful at least for not having to live in the same house with this designing woman, ending with the words "Thank God I can close my room-door and lay me down in peace to die." Shortly after, he did so.

Just how deep and sound a mind James Pierrepont Greaves possessed it is impossible, at this distance of time, to make quite sure. There is an abundance of dithyrambic praise of him from his immediate associates, but there is a dearth of evidence that he was, or could have been, quite the sage they took him for. No man, it seems safe to assert, has ever attained the heights of the intellectual life who has constantly remained in business, as Greaves did, up to the age of forty—and even the fact that Greaves twice failed in business need not convince one that he was profoundly wise. In most of the remarks of his that have been preserved there is a suggestion of vapidity, not to say emptiness, that goes beyond Bronson Alcott at his most platitudinous and worst. His strength, like Alcott's, seems to have been in conversation, for he did undoubtedly hold together for some time, in his Burton Street salon, a group of rather brilliant people. It has to be considered that Wright and Lane and Oldham, who were chiefly responsible for what little we know of him, were not educated men. All three of them were business men, like Greaves himself—and it is perhaps worthy of remark that when the man whose training has been almost exclusively in practical affairs gets a faint glimpse of the idealistic point of view, he is often more extreme, because less experienced, in his idealism than those who have been living all their lives in the world of thought.

One is inclined, therefore, to make some mental reservations reading the obituary notice of Greaves drawn up by the three survivors at Alcott House.

We believe [they say] that very few individuals of the present era have exercised upon their contemporaries an equal degree of modifying influence to that

[332]

which marks the career of our venerable friend. All those lofty previsions to which the attention has been directed in the prophetic revealings of Wordsworth, Alcott, Emerson, and others, were anticipated and pre-declared by the deceased.

They were particularly eager to set their friend above Coleridge, with whom, for some reason, they frequently compared him. The dramatist Barham said explicitly that he considered Greaves very much the intellectual superior of Coleridge, and possessed of "much higher spiritual attainments and experience." But this is a moderate statement in comparison with the words of Charles Lane, who always gave to Greaves the credit for converting him from infidelity. Lane considered Greaves "a gigantic mind, bestriding the narrow world of literature like a colossus." He regarded him as one of those "men of intelligence so living and so penetrating that they seem to have the key in their own minds to every book." After such adulation it is a relief to turn to the savage condemnation of Carlyle, although this is probably no nearer the truth on the other side. "I knew old —— myself," he wrote to Emerson, almost certainly with reference to Greaves, "and can testify, if you will believe me, that few greater blockheads (if 'blockhead' may mean 'exasperated imbecile' and 'the ninth part of a thinker') broke the world's bread in his day."

Carlyle, one sees, was at any rate consistent. He was not fond of Paradise Planters. But after all the question is not so much what Greaves really was as it is what Alcott thought him to be. Had he ever seen the man we might well have trusted his opinion, for in his hundreds of judgments upon men and women he made surprisingly few mistakes. Without the advantage of a personal contact, he believed Greaves to have been a great man, though not, to be sure, on anything like the level of Coleridge. What Greaves had said he believed to be true, partly because he had long been saying identically the same things himself. In everything, in fact,

[333]

except the new doctrine of "pure Birth," the effect of Greaves upon Alcott's mind was in the nature of corroboration. The outline of the English transcendentalist's fundamental teachings, a drawn up by Lane and Wright and Oldham, would serve almos as well for the American's. They tell us that—

> The peculiar characteristics of his philosophy . . . lay in the dogma that there subsists an eternal, sensibly realizable connexion between the human soul and Deity; that God ever impregnates it with new seeds . . . that the development of these seeds is . . . an awakening of divine nature in humanity, and the fostering influences best adapted for such an awakening are the object to be contemplated in all societarian arrangements. Association on a high basis was his ideal for the present conjuncture. . . . The peculiar practical doctrine which his whole life tended to explain and illustrate is the eminent superiority of Being to all knowing and doing. . . . Out of this feeling he constantly inculcated not so much that practice should coincide with theory as that a depth of Being should be realized capable of supporting both theory and practice.

If one adds that Greaves was a vegetarian for the last thir six years of his life, and this not for physical but for intellect and spiritual reasons, that he was a strong believer in the th apeutic value of cold water, and that he was an enthusiastic "I thagorean" in all the senses that vague word may contain, it comes clear that one might call him "the English Alcott" with much exaggeration. And yet in one important respect, as we h seen, his thought differed radically from the American's. Al had always supposed, without spending any particular thou upon the matter, that human beings are potentially equal at bi and that only opportunity makes the differences in their att ments. This belief had long been inconsistent, to be sure, ertain basic principles of his thinking; but he was not one of those completely logical, and also excessively rare, persons who rearrange all the furniture of their minds whenever they move in a new article of opinion. The assumption that the potentialities of the mind are approximately equal at birth among all individuals had lasted throughout the eighteenth century, when it was held, for example, by such level heads as those of John Locke, Thomas Gray, Dr. Johnson, Rousseau, Helvetius, and Condorcet. For that matter, it has endured down to the present time in the minds of most Americans, although it has long been confronted by the ndings—also firmly believed by the same persons—of so-called intelligence tests." Greaves made Alcott see that this opinion was at variance with the observed facts, and also that it harmonized far less readily with Platonic teaching than with those doctrines of John Locke which he had long since abandoned.

Alcott deduced the consequences and corollaries swiftly enough. If the education of a child could not "repair the defects of birth," then one must educate the future parents of the race. This, of course, would involve a much broader program of reform than Alcott had thought necessary when he began his effort to regenerate mankind in the Infant School alone. It would involve an even stronger emphasis upon the sanctities of the family life than he had made hitherto. And one of the most direct results of Greaves's doctrine, highly amusing to Boston and Concord people, was the profound genealogical research into which Alcott plunged as soon as he was able—all of it conducted, in defiance of strictly American theories if not of American feeling, in the effort to find out precisely of what sort of "Birth" he himself was the result.

One is glad to see that Alcott was untouched by one of the nobler phases of the work going on at Alcott House. This was adequately represented by a little magazine called the *Healthian*, published in London and bearing on its title page a quotation from Alcott himself: "Greater is he who is above temptation than he who, being tempted, overcomes." In spite of its display of met-

aphysical terms and pretensions, the magazine was thoroughly materialistic. It was vegetarian, teetotalarian, "chaste," hydropathic
phrenological, physiognomical, Pythagorean in so far as it understood the term, and much given to the citation of ancient authorities which it did not understand. It was still more inclined to deny
the reality of those same diseases, and the actuality of those same
bodies, which it spent nearly all its space in discussing. There was
in fact, a most ludicrous contrast between its lofty spiritual o:
"ideal" claims for itself and its actual preoccupation with food
viscera, teeth, drinks, drugs, and baths. It took a very high mora
tone with people who enjoyed the coffee bean and the leaves of te;
and tobacco. In short, it represented the not uncommon but as
suredly loathsome type of pseudo-religion, really a belated form o
magic, which tries to use "Spirit" chiefly as a pain-killer. Whe
Bronson Alcott used the word "Spirit," however, he meant some
thing sufficiently vague but never a cheap substitute for th
apothecary's shop. He did indeed edit one issue of the *Healthiar*
contributing to it a brief paper on "The Pythagoric Life," but :
seems likely that he was partly responsible for its discontinuanc
and for the substitution of another and better magazine, writte
chiefly by Charles Lane, called the *New Age, Concordium Gazett.
and Temperance Advocate.* The second item in the title is a r
minder that the group at Alcott House was calling itself, by 184.
the *Concordium,* probably in honor of Alcott's town. In th
magazine, mainly devoted to education, the word "Spirit" w;
more properly employed.

It should be clear, then, that Alcott at Alcott House four
himself in a maelstrom of reform. When he arrived there he mig
well have been in some doubt, in spite of what Garrison had wr
ten about him, whether he was a reformer at all, but by the tir
he came to leave he might have doubted whether he was anythi
else. Vegetarian societies claimed him; associations advocati
"Total Abstinence from Intoxicating Drinks" (must he then gi

[336]

up his beloved cider?) snatched at him; advocates of bathing even as much as once a day greeted him as a brother; and all the enemies of private property saw that here was a man after their own hearts. Alcott was asked again and again to preside at meetings and to "sit on platforms," and one is happy to record, against the later allegations of Father Hecker and J. T. Trowbridge, that he usually refused. The whole experience, however, rather turned his head. In spite of Emerson's opinion, a "pure success" was never good for him. An earnest lady of Islington wrote to ask whether he intended "to do altogether without government," modestly feeling that perhaps there might be something to be said for it. She had read the *Record of a School,* and had "revelled in the *Dial*" but had not been able to satisfy herself that all private property ought to be abolished. Would Mr. Alcott be so kind as to give her his considered opinion upon this matter? One sees that whatever his opinion turns out to be she is prepared to accept it implicitly and to act accordingly. Mr. Alcott is to her a sage, a pundit, an oracle.

And Alcott's success was not with women only. Toward the end of his stay he wrote in his Journal:—

> Mr. Birch, a gentleman from Derbyshire and friend of Mr. Greaves who has done much for Alcott House, called on us again to-day. He is deeply interested in the New Ideas, is curious about Emerson, reads every thing of his, and does all he can to promote a better state of things. *The Conversations on the Gospels, Record of a School,* the *Dial,* he admires. On leaving he tempted me to visit him, and put into my hands a ten-pound note. So I shall go into Derbyshire soon.

Alcott did, in fact, take this journey, the only one that gave him more than a glimpse of rural England. He was gone two weeks in the second half of August, visiting the town of Derby and returning through Gloucester, Cheltenham, Cirencester, and

Windsor. But there seems to be no record of the impression the trip made upon him. In later years, so far as one can tell, he never recurred to it in memory. Once more he was absorbed in thought. The actual scene, even though of Derbyshire Peak and the Cotswold Hills, could not break in upon his vision of the "Ideal." He was now, as he believed, on the direct road to Paradise.

At Alcott House, when he returned thither on the first of September, events and plans were beginning to take a definite course. Lane and Wright, after much eager discussion, had resolved to return with him to America. They had come to agree with the firm belief expressed in one of his Journal-jottings:—

> Britain, with all her resources and talent, is not the scene for the education of humanity. Her spirit is hostile to human welfare, and her institutions averse to the largest liberty of the soul. Nor should an enterprise of such moment be endangered by the revolutions to which all things are here exposed, and which threaten, as I think, the speedy downfall of the realm. Our freer, but yet far from freed, land is the asylum, if asylum there be, for the hope of man; and there, if anywhere, is that second Eden to be planted in which the divine seed is to bruise the head of Evil and restore Man to his rightful communion with God in the Paradise of Good.

It was an old, old conviction of weary Europe, that Paradise was to be found, if anywhere, in the fair young West. This conviction had driven the Spanish conquistadors on their terrible blood-soaked trails, it had lured the French Jesuits deep into Canada and other Frenchmen down the Mississippi, it had sustained the Pilgrim Fathers in their hungry toil, and had inspired the beautiful eloquent lies of Chateaubriand. There was nothing at all new in the vision which finally came to earth in the life ed farmhouse on a Massachusetts hill. In England particularly, ver since the opening of the French Revolution, romantic minds ad been yearning westward. Just fifty years before it was decided at Alcott House that Wright and Lane and Alcott should o West to find their Eden and that William Oldham, faithful nd unselfish soul, should remain to carry on, two youths called outhey and Coleridge had been planning a "Pantisocracy" for e banks of the Susquehanna—chosen, no doubt, not so much or its good supply of mosquitoes as for its mellifluous name— here they hoped to bring in the reign of brotherly love and the d Saturnian calm. Not to have felt these Occidental longings as to be incompletely romantic—a charge that could not reaonably have been brought against the brothers at Alcott House.

There were busy days in that House during the last three eeks of Alcott's stay. On the seventh of September a convenon of serious thinkers assembled to discuss the problem prented by Alcott's lady-correspondent in Islington, whether prite property ought to be entirely abolished. No final decision ems to have been arrived at, unless we may infer one from the ct that Alcott accepted from another English admirer on that casion the gift of another ten-pound note. A third admirer ve him busts of Pestalozzi and Socrates. A fourth, apparently, d him to go into London and buy himself books to the extent twenty pounds.

This he did. And if anyone is ever interested to decide at just at period in all of Alcott's eighty-eight years that essentially ppy man stood on the pinnacle of happiness, such an investitor ought not to ignore the days in London, in mid-September 1842, when his hero loitered and lounged, blew dust from Elirs, and gazed at books in half a dozen languages he could t read, at Brown's bookshop in Old Street, at Elkin's in Lomrd street, and at Baldock's in Holborn. Just what his purpose s is uncertain. He may have been thinking, partly, about the n that he and Emerson and Margaret Fuller had discussed a year before—a plan of Alcott's hatching for a "university" at Concord, in which the leading transcendentalists were to conduct courses. But this does not seem probable. The truth appears to be that he was engaged in filling the gaps in the private library of J. P. Greaves, which it was planned to take to America, and that he went to London with some list of the books that were missing from that collection. However this may be, his purchases as recorded by himself, were a remarkable index to the literary and philosophical interests of the Transcendental Movement. In a record of the months spent in England which Alcott drew up in later life there is included a

List of Books Bought by Me in London, 1842

Epictetus	2.0
Hack's Grecian Stories	2.0
Antoninus	5.6
Howel's Original Pilgrim	1.0
Macanin on Perfection	1.6
Muret's Rite of Funerals	3.6
Penn's Biography	1.6
Blondel on the Sibyls (folio)	12.0
Medica Artis 2 vols. (quarto)	1.05.0
Philostratus (folio)	8.6
Poetical Translations 3 vols.	16.0
Spinoza Opera (quarto)	10.0
Boccaccio's Decameron	5.6
Diodorus Siculus (folio)	16.0
Tacitus	3.0
Ovid	1.0
Lucretius	1.6
Horace	2.6
Porphyry	1.6
Juvenal and Persius	1.6
Quintus Curtius	1.6
Theognis	1.6

[340]

Hesiod	1.6
Catullus	1.6
Martial	1.0
Apuleius	2.6
Marcus Antoninus	5.6
Homburg's Mythologica	12.0
Fichte's Vernunft	4.0
Fichte's Bestimmung	3.0
Schelling's Bruno	5.0
Novalis Schriften 2 vols.	7.0

Sir. Ken. Dibgy On Nature of Bodies	1645
Confucii Sinarum Philosphus (fol.)	1787
Laws of Menu by Sir W. Jones	
The Desatir Persian and English	1818
Theosophia Revelata of Behmen, with Life	1715
Behmen's Life, by Okley	1780
Theologica Pacifiae itumque Mistiriae	1622
Mad. Guion's Life 3 vols.	1791
Fenelon's Account of Mad. Guion	1759
Man before Adam	1656
Sargeant's Trans-Natural Philosophy	1700
Hartley's Paradise Restored	1764
Plotinus on Suicide T. Taylor	1834
Sterry on Freedom of Will (fol.)	1675
Norris Amoris Effigies	1744
Norris Matrimony	1739
Tryon's Averroeana	1687
Tryon's Way to Health	1697
Newton's Return to Nature	1811
Sir J. Flowers on Bathing Places	1732
Magia Adamiae Antiquity of Magic	1650

With these books and several hundred others of the same general nature, Alcott and Wright and Lane, together with Lane's on William, embarked at London on the twenty-eighth of Sep-

[341]

tember, 1842, and set sail in the ship *Leland* for Paradise. They had a slow but prosperous voyage.

Far away in the cottage beside the Concord River Mrs. Alcott was writing a prayer in her Journal:—

> May gentle gales and gentler waves bear him and his dear treasure of lives and loves home to us safely! May no dangers affright them, nor perils assail them! Hold this precious casket, God of waters, in the hollow of thy hand!

On the twenty-first of October the good woman's prayer was changed to a pæan. "Good news for Cottagers!" she scrawled in her swift and ugly script across the page:—

> Happy days, these! Husband returned, accompanied by the dear English-*men*, the good and true. Welcome to these shores, this home, to my bosom!

Was her rapture somewhat premature, and the expression of it a little too reminiscent of her favorite novelist, Bulwer-Lytton? At any rate it lasted at least two days, for on the twenty-third she wrote again:—

> After dispatching the duties of the morning, walked with friends and children. I was deeply impressed by Louisa's ebullition of feeling: "Mother, what makes me so happy?" Mr. Lane relieved me from replying, for a big prayer had just then filled my breast and stifled utterance. I wished to breathe out my soul in one long utterance of hope that the causes which were conspiring just then to fill us with such pure joy might never pass away—the presence of my dear husband, the gentle sympathy of kind friends, and the inspiring and exhilarating influence of Nature. . . . We have planted and watered in our natural life. May we reap and garner in a divine love!

[342]

PARADISE PLANTER

{ 1842-1843 }

A hawk in Dove Cottage—Heart versus head—A severe discipli-
narian—Suffocation—Purchase of Paradise—Idyllic beginnings—
A serpent in Eden—The Shaker village—Farmhouse tragedy

THE "pure joy" with which Mrs. Alcott had greeted the advent of the "dear English-*men*" was not of long duration.
October was hardly out before it was clearly understood at Dove
Cottage that Louisa's "ebullitions of feeling" were only a little
less distasteful to the visitors than were those of Louisa's mother.
Also, there had been certain clarifications about the visitors
themselves. Mr. Henry Wright, the nearly perfect teacher of Alcott House, was not standing transplantation at all well. He had
been heard to grumble at the "Pythagorean diets" of the Cottage and he showed no delight in manual toil. Bronson Alcott
would soon be crossing out with a pencil those words of a letter
to his wife in which, only six months before, he had described
Wright as possessing "a wisdom and love incarnate in no man,
save Lane, that I have ever met." And as for Mr. Charles Lane

[343]

himself, the mistress of Dove Cottage would try to believe wha
Mr. Emerson had said about him in the *Dial* for October, tha
he was "a man of ideas," and that "deep opened below deep in hi
thought." Abigail Alcott was inured to philosophers and had lon
been accustomed to making all the possible allowances for then
but now she was discovering that this particular philosopher o
her husband's recent importation was an almost intolerable pe
son to have about the house.

Before the dim and enigmatic figure of Charles Lane ever
thoughtful biographer of Bronson Alcott, every conscientious hi
torian of the Fruitlands adventure, must be brought to a stan
Too obscure and paradoxical for a full explanation, he is by fa
too important in Alcott's life to be ignored. We see him at a
clearly for only a few months of his career, and it is not eas
to harmonize those months with what we know about the yea
of his life that preceded and followed. "What was he, and wh
was he not?" An old daguerreotype portrait of him shows a thi
lipped, wry-mouthed, and stubborn face, with undistinguishe
jaw, prominent nose, small eyes that may have been somewh
shifty, and a high square brow—the whole by no means sugges
ing the kind of man that one would care to bring back from fo
eign parts, or, at any rate, to introduce into the bosom of one
family. And about this man one has to decide upon the eviden
presented in certain letters that he wrote home to William Ol
ham, in the not entirely dispassionate testimony of Mrs. Alcott
Journal, and in such glimpses of truth as may be found in *Tra*
scendental Wild Oats, written by a woman in whose childhood
had played the part of an ogre. Obviously, the chances of goir
entirely wrong in one's estimate of Lane are considerable.

How did it happen that an expert reporter of the London sto
market invested nearly all his available funds in the purchase
a Massachusetts farm, for purposes purely "ideal"? What was th
nature of that "immorality" which, according to a letter writt
by Oldham to Alcott in 1866, caused the expulsion of this exce

ngly "moral" man from Alcott House and the ruin of that House tself? With what consistency could so stern an advocate of the elibate life enter into a second marriage and proceed to the be- etting of five more children? What is to be said of a man both nthusiastic and cold, humanitarian and cruel, a player of the vio- n and yet fit for something very like "treasons, stratagems, and poils"? If the last suggestion seems too severe, one is to recall lat within a month of his arrival on American soil Lane began) advocate the overthrow of the American Government, and that, oming as Alcott's friend, he set himself to wreck Alcott's home. 'he temptation is strong to call him simply Satanic and to cast im for the rôle of the serpent in Eden, but then one is confronted y evidence that he was in some ways definitely a good man. It ould be easy to account for his paradoxes by calling him a hypo- ite, if only he were not so obviously, even painfully, sincere.

On the whole, the best that one can do with and for Charles ane is to say that he was temporarily ridden, to the verge of sanity, by an idea. While in America, at any rate, he showed e humorless, live-or-die, neck-or-nothing intensity and concen- ation of the uncompromising zealot. He believed that he had st one task to perform; and that was, to save the world. To this d he must first of all save Bronson Alcott from two contaminat- ; influences: Emerson and Mrs. Alcott.

We move a little closer to Lane's mystery when we realize that thought habitually in general terms. Emerson himself had inted this out when he remarked, in his article on "The Eng- h Reformers," that "Mr. Lane does not confound society with :iableness," and then proceeded to quote Lane's own words: "It when the sympathy with man is the stronger and the truer that ﹕ sympathy with men grows weaker and the sympathy with ﹕ir actions weakest." One knows that sort of person, so tender vard abstract humanity, which does not really exist, as to be lost indifferent to every concrete man, woman, and child. And ﹕erson's brief statement and quotation—both given, strangely enough, as though in praise—hold true for all that we know about Lane. He was a man who could bestrew his written and spoken discourse with such words as "Love" and "Wisdom" without ever pausing to love any individual or to do one wise thing. This being so, the contest that went on at Dove Cottage and at Fruitlands was inevitable. By a slight exaggeration in the interests of clarity one may say that that contest was waged between the feminine tendency to think in terms of the concrete and the male tendency toward abstraction. We need not wonder, then, that to Bronson Alcott, who in this and many other ways was both male and female, the contest was almost fatal.

Between the strongly emotional mistress of Dove Cottage and the cold, abstract ex-editor of the *London Mercantile Price-Current* there began, in the first days of their acquaintance, an obscure and silent struggle. Mrs. Alcott felt about family as her husband thought about it. To her it was a divine institution, which all others would do well to imitate. To Lane it was a relic of barbarism, soon to be displaced. In his Preface to an English translation of Madame Gatti de Gamond's *Phalansterian*, a French book of the Fourier school, he had recently said that Family Union had already given way to National Union and that this must soon disappear into that Universal Union which would obliterate all lesser relationships. In this he went beyond even Fourier himself, who had not insisted upon the abolishment of the family although he had suggested certain licenses in the marriage relation which were repugnant to English and American feeling. Having made a miserable failure of his own first adventure in matrimony, Lane was at this time convinced that all such adventure should be discouraged. Bronson Alcott he admired, but he deplored Alcott's wife and children.

One's sympathies are strongly on the side of Mrs. Alcott; for even if the family was not quite a perfect institution it was at any rate nearly all she had. She was by no means a perfect woman; her temper, as she was painfully aware, left much to be desired ut she was fighting for something upon which for many years she had spent her entire strength and devotion. With little except a wife's and mother's instinct to support her—reinforced by a well-sharpened tongue, one must admit, for use upon extreme occasions—she gathered her four children about her skirts and bravely faced this "dear English-*man*," who, upon his side, to be sure, had only a set of rather sour and doctrinaire ideas emanating from France.

Once more it is easy to smile at the paltriness of the setting; but undoubtedly there was drama going on. There was a hawk in Dove Cottage.

Bronson Alcott hardly knew at first what was proceeding, hardly guessed that one strong force was tugging at his heart and another at his head. Certainly he had both of these things, and why, then, could not both parties be satisfied? But his wife's terrible fear was, all the while, that her husband's head, with Lane to help, would overcome his heart's affection. She did not know—as how could she, herself so flawed and disintegrated?—that this man of hers was rapidly becoming one of those rare persons whose thoughts and feelings are of the same piece. Yet he was to have his struggle, too. The battle for Bronson Alcott, waged at first by significant silences and averted eyes, was to enter the man's own mind and will and was to bring him right to the door of death.

A pitiful note in Mrs. Alcott's Journal, written little over a month after the arrival from England, clearly shows how matters were going.

Circumstances most cruelly drive me [she writes] from the enjoyment of my domestic life. I am prone to indulge in occasional hilarity, but seem frowned down into stiff quiet and peace-less order. I am almost suffocated in this atmosphere of restriction and form. Perhaps I feel it more after these five months of liberty and option. My diet, too, is obviously not enough diver-

[347]

sified, having been almost exclusively coarse bread
and water—the apples we have not being mellow and
my teeth very bad, my disrelish for cooking so great
that I would not consume that which cost me so much
misery to prepare. All these causes have combined to
make me somewhat irritable, or morbidly sensitive to
every detail of life. . . . They all seem most stupidly
obtuse on the causes of this occasional prostration of
my judgment and faculties. I hope the solution of the
problem will not be revealed to them too late for my
recovery or their atonement for this invasion of my
rights as a woman and a mother. Give me one day of
practical philosophy. It is worth a century of speculation and discussion.

One sees that the auspices for the planting of a new Eden wer
not highly favorable, with Eve already making trouble. Yet Mr
Alcott continued to go about in the surrounding country, seekir
a fertile site, neither too small nor too costly, for Paradise. Tw
months before her husband's return she had begun this ques
so that she was able on his return to report, unfavorably, upc
the Hosmer Farm at Stowe and the Codman Farm at Lincol
She was, in fact, almost as much interested in the "adventure" .
Alcott and Lane.

A serious injustice has been done to Abigail Alcott in the tr
dition that she endured the harebrained schemes of an impra
tical husband solely because of her personal fidelity to him a
not at all because she had any belief or part in them. Of her pe
sonal fidelity there is not, of course, the slightest question.
shines on every page of the little diary which she traced out
candlelight with a tired hand during her husband's absence
England. The vulgar and bourgeois view, however, that what s
chiefly wanted was domestic comfort for herself and her ch
dren, will not stand for a moment against the testimony of I
diary, her letters, or her life. Such an opinion ignores the f

hat she was at least as much a reformer as her husband—an ardent worker for "Women's Rights," a close friend of Garrison, a cousin of Samuel Sewall, and a sister of Samuel May. It is true that she had been born and bred a "lady," and that during most of her life she was a rather hard-working woman; but it was certainly one of the most ladylike things about her that she did not mind that. She worked hard with her hands at Dove Cottage and Fruitlands and twenty other places of the family's long pilgrimage; but it was part of her clear-eyed assertion of women's rights that women had not only the right but the obligation to work as hard as men. She never shared the sentimental American notion that women should be merely the coddled wasters or conspicuous spenders of worldly goods. Material things meant hardly more to her than to her husband.

The pity that has been lavished upon Mrs. Alcott, not so much in print as in gatherings of old wives and elderly spinsters male and female, would have aroused nothing but instant and voluble wrath in her vigorous mind and heart. Her objection would not have been that such pity does her a gross injustice but that it is unjust to the man whom she loved and honored above any other creature. She was a shrewd judge of persons, and she lived with Bronson Alcott for forty-seven years. Every shred of the evidence, which is large in total amount, goes to show that from end to end of their friendship, companionship, lovership, partnership, she thought him the kindest, wisest, bravest, and altogether the greatest man she had ever known. "Dearest, best of men," she wrote once in her diary, "I ought to know that you will live here in the confidence and reverence of your age as well as in the remembrance and eternal honor of posterity. . . . Few know you now; but there are those coming up to the true perception of all that is divine and sublime in your principles and life. Patience, yearning soul!"

We are bound to accept Mrs. Alcott's many statements of this kind as the expression of her settled conviction, enormously out-

[349]

weighing the few harsh words about her husband that she may
have let fall on her weary and distracted way—words that idle
and irresponsible gossips have set rolling like snowballs down the
generations. Like her daughter Louisa, she had a most unfortunate habit of relieving the strains of life by sharp and wounding
words. Her husband, who had no such tendency, could never fully
comprehend it. He could only forgive it, and see how little it
really meant. To be sure, he made several ingenious efforts to explain it, most of them based upon Jacob Boehme's declaratio
that persons of dark complexion—and Mrs. Alcott was very dark
—were of "demonic" origin. And yet this, he felt, was not quite
satisfactory, so that he was a good deal cheered and relieved when
he discovered while reading a book of English genealogy that the
Mays were thought to be of Portuguese descent. That, he considered, was much better, and he accepted the explanation
eagerly.

Of course it did not cover quite all of the difficulties involved.
There was that painful occasion, for example, when he had gone
over to Hawthorne's to inquire, after a considerable period of
coolness and distance, whether there was anything wrong between the two families, and Hawthorne had replied that it was
in his opinion quite impossible to live on neighborly terms with
Mrs. Alcott. Hawthorne had been most kind and gentle, but there
had not been much to say. Alcott had thought it better not to ask
for any special forbearance either on the ground that his wife
was "Portuguese" or on the alternate theory that she might be a
"demon."

At Dove Cottage, now, in this winter of 1842–1843, events were
in the rapids and were racing toward the cataract. Bronson Alcott
had returned from England a reformer unafraid, and he had with
him at least one English reformer to see that he did not waver.
Henry Wright, to be sure, seems to have begun wavering when
he first tasted the corn bread of New England toward which

[350]

ven ascetic Englishmen appear to have a natural antipathy. In
December, at any rate, he removed to Graham House in Boston,
om whence he drifted away to Lynn. Finally he returned to
ngland and soon died—going, if we may accept William Old-
am's dispassionate statement, "to Hades." In the meanwhile
lcott and Lane were lecturing and conversing on Community
ife in Boston, Providence, Dedham, Brook Farm, Lynn, and at
merson's house. Lane was writing busily for half a dozen papers
England and America, but especially for Garrison's *Liberator*,
xplaining "the Newness." It is indicative of the good time they
ad that in December the two reformers found themselves shut
ut of the Marlborough Chapel in Boston, where they had been
pecting to speak, and discovered that a mob was gathering
gainst them in the streets. They were able, however, to hold
eir meeting at Ritchie Hall, stoutly supported by Orestes
rownson and other advocates of the millennium.

During this month of December, indeed, Alcott and Lane con-
acted three series of Conversations in Boston, notwithstanding
e fact that Alcott was preparing all the family meals and was
lping Lane with the instruction of the children. The entire
mily at Dove Cottage was being subjected to a severity of
scipline such as it had never known before. Its diet had previ-
sly been simple but was now positively ascetic. Not only the
aster of the house went without meat, as he had done since 1835,
t all did. And in many other respects spontaneity was giving way
an iron rule. Another mind was taking hold. The Alcott family
s being conducted by a representative of a race with long ex-
rience in the management of subject peoples.

In a letter to Junius Alcott written at Dove Cottage in mid-
nter Lane says that the whole family is up between six and seven
lock and has "a cold-water sponging all over, and a rub with the
arse crash linen towel." The water, he tells us, is often frozen
inch thick, and after it has been broken it sometimes freezes
in at the edges while they bathe. Breakfast, prepared by Al-

cott, consists of bread, apples, potatoes, and cold water, eaten b
the fireside and without plates. "Conversation of a useful and in
terior kind," says Lane, "is generally mingled with our physica
increment," and after breakfast there is "a singing lesson by ai
of the violin," played by Lane. Thereafter, Lane returns to h
little chamber to write in "much God-like quiet. . . ."

Mrs. Alcott proceeds to her domestic duties. Mr. A.
saws and chops, provides water, bakes some days, pre-
pares all the food, in which he tries new materials and
mixtures of a simple character. From 10 to 12.30, study
for the children—consisting of diary, reading, spelling,
conversation, grammar, arithmetic, etc. etc. . . . The
school, having been in existence nearly three months
now, goes on as quietly and serenely in the teacher's
absence as when he is present, and the improvement in
all students, young and old, is quite manifest. At 12.30,
dinner. Except on Sunday, when it is also taken round
the fire, this meal is spread on the table, there being
generally some preparation which requires a plate,
etc. At 1, I return to my chamber and there is a general
dispersion to play, read, or work. At 2 P.M. Anna
comes to me for French and William for Latin. From
3 to 4 Anna, Louisa, and William have geography,
drawing, or geometry. Mr. Alcott thus secures an undisturbed hour or two. From 4 to 6.30 the children
sew with Mrs. Alcott, or play; I write or go to the village for letters, or to Mr. Emerson's. Then at 6.30,
supper at the fireplace, the same as at breakfast, with
conversation more prolonged; or, at 7.15, another singing lesson, followed, frequently, by a dance. At eight,
bedtime for the young folks, and about an hour later,
for the adults. Thus have passed away many happy
days—happy to me, and I believe none of us would
like to return to a more complicated diet of molasses,
milk, butter, etc., all of which are given up. The disci-

pline we are now under is that of abstinence in the tongue and hands. We are learning to hold our peace, and to keep our hands from each other's bodies—the ill effects of which we see upon the little baby.

One can readily understand that Mrs. Alcott was feeling "almost suffocated in this atmosphere of restriction and form." She spent the Christmas Holidays in Boston, "to try the effectiveness of a short absence from home," but returned at the first of the New Year, 1843, "glad to resume the quiet duties of home and love." She had left home, as she said, toil-worn and depressed, but she returned feeling quickened by a new spirit. One reason for the change was that she had received a note from her husband, which she records in her Journal as another illustration of his trust in Divine Goodness. He had written:—

> I sincerely believe that you are in the arms of a benignant Providence who shall do for yourself and us more than we can conceive or ask. Let Him guide. Relinquish all self-wilfulness. Be willing to be used as He shall direct. I am in the hands of a Holy Destiny that shall make me be, and do, better and wiser than I can do for myself.

It was probably the utterance that came closest, of all that Bronson Alcott ever said or wrote, to the language of piety.

Ever since his arrival in America Charles Lane, of course an Abolitionist, had been shouting defiance at the national Government and advocating, chiefly in the *Liberator*, the complete and immediate secession of every right-minded man. The editorial articles and public speeches of Garrison himself had long tended toward the same advice, and behind Garrison stood the fiery young mystic of Vermont, John Humphrey Noyes, with his paper called "the Perfectionist."

"My hope of the millennium begins," said Noyes, "at the over
throw of this nation," and he declared to Garrison that he had sub
scribed his name "to an instrument similar to the Declaration
'76, renouncing all allegiance to the government of the Unite
States, and asserting the title of Jesus Christ to the throne of th
world." It will be seen, therefore, that when Bronson Alcott r
fused, at the opening of the year, to pay his poll tax, and w
taken to jail on January 17 by the Concord Deputy Sheriff, Sa
Staples, he was not doing a thing startlingly original. (Whe
Henry Thoreau did the same thing four years later it was becor
ing almost conventional.) Alcott had hoped to be incarcerated
least for the night, but his tax was paid by Squire Hoar witho
his knowledge or consent and, to his great disappointment,
was released. A year or two later he seems to have tried once mo
to get into jail in the same way, but by that time Mrs. Alcot
more respectable relatives in Boston had apparently made sor
arrangement with the Concord constabulary which made it i
possible, and Alcott was obliged to request them that he be
lowed "the privilege of the non-payment of his taxes." The pri
lege was not accorded. When Henry Thoreau in 1846 did succe
in being jailed for a few hours, Alcott defended him with cc
siderable vigor against Emerson, who, says Alcott, consider
Thoreau's conduct "skulking and mean and in bad taste."

The winter passed with much assailing of the national gove
ment on the part of Charles Lane and much conversing in Bos
and elsewhere by Bronson Alcott. In the *Dial* for April there
peared an article by Lane on Alcott's books and the Tem
School, tedious enough to sink the reputation of any man
roundly damned by Ellery Channing. Alcott dictated to Lane
story of his early life and adventures. He took pleasure in the
signing and cutting of dresses for his daughters. He helped
the entertainment of the many visitors who were being attrac
to Concord quite as much by his own fame as by that of En
son. Occasionally he did a day's work in the woods, but his d

[354]

ere steadily accumulating. As always when he was poorest himelf, however, he was most thoughtful of those who were poorer han he, and some part of the meals he prepared for the family t Dove Cottage was frequently sent out to a hungering neighor. Emerson, ignoring his own claim to that title, called Alcott ie most munificent man in Concord.

Mrs. Alcott, during the winter, hit upon an ingenious device or staving off "suffocation." On the fifteenth of January she rote in her Journal:—

> Established today a household post-office.—I thought it would afford a daily opportunity for the children, indeed all of us, to interchange thought and sentiment. Had any unhappiness occurred, it would be a pleasant way of healing all differences and discontents. It is to be opened every evening after supper, and the letters, notes, or parcels to be distributed to the respective owners. A budget-basket hung in the entry is the receptacle for all communications. No child or person is to open the budget during the day, but the postmaster is to do so and distribute in the evening, each child taking turns to be postmaster.

This device, which must have reminded Alcott of the days ien he corresponded with Cousin William from across the road, s not only ingenious but wise. It did indeed tend to heal differces, and the letters written to Mrs. Alcott by Charles Lane re among the most creditable productions made by his pen ring his stay in America. The domestic post office gave valu-e training in the arts of narrative to the three elder daughters, l especially to Louisa, who was by this time becoming a "prob-i." Alcott himself, remembering the lessons he had taken from e-year-old Elizabeth Lewis in the art of writing to children, ned out many a little masterpiece of simplicity, a few of which still to be seen on the walls of Orchard House in Concord.

With the spring there returned in all its urgency the problem of discovering a site for the new Eden. Alcott and Lane looked at estates in Milton, Roxbury, Brookline, Watertown, Southborough, and Stowe, besides visiting Thoreau's two favorite haunts at "Hallowell Farm" and the "Cliffs" in Concord. They moved about with all the dignified leisure of philosophers. One of them had done enough farming to know at least that the time for planting corn and vegetables, if not of Paradises, would soon be over, but he took two weeks of the sowing-season for a visit to his mother at Oriskany, New York, and to his friend Benjamin Dye at Braintree, Vermont. On the twentieth of May, however, Alcott and Lane walked from Concord to the village of Harvard, some fourteen miles to westward, and there saw for the first time the "Wyman Farm," on a beautiful hillside overlooking the Nashua River. There were ninety acres of land, fourteen of them in wood and the rest arable. The land was good, and the view, looking out towards Wachusett and Monadnock, was superb. Alcott, be sure, who wanted to live near Emerson and had set his heart upon "the Cliffs" above the Sudbury River, did not much like the place; but Lane, who had come to the conclusion after eating several dinners at the Emerson house that the master of that house was not sufficiently ascetic to have a good influence upon Alcott, did like it. He bought the land for eighteen hundred dollars, and was given permission to use the house and barn for one year rent-free. At the same time Lane paid all of Alcott's Concord debts—recorded by Lane as amounting to three hundred dollars and by Alcott as only one hundred and seventy-five—so that the family might leave the village. On the fourteenth of June the Alcotts and the Lanes moved to Wyman Farm, taking with them in a wagon what few poor chattels remained after many previous movings, and called the place "Fruitlands"—no doubt, as the wits of the time never wearied of saying, because it had no orchard.

[356]

Fruitlands was Alcott's second "place in the sun," and it was so the scene of his most conspicuous failure. Probably most of those who have any knowledge of Bronson Alcott whatever regard him as the shadowy projector of an experiment in communal living which failed in seven months, and in every way deserved to fail. And perhaps the Muse of History, if she can afford only one brief chapter to this man, could scarcely do better than to choose that episode in which he did indeed draw something like his total self together, both his weakness and his strength, and in which, certainly, a biographer must find the pivotal event of his career. There need be only this caution, which of course the Muse of History will not require, that if we are to let Bronson Alcott stand or fall by the test of Fruitlands, then we shall wish to see not only what he did there but why he did it, and with what results, more accurately than we have hitherto done.

The greater number of those who have glanced at the Fruitlands episode at all have been primarily interested in persons other than the man chiefly concerned. Students of Emerson and Thoreau have pointed out, with varying degrees of accuracy and critical acumen, how wise those two friends of Alcott's were in having as little to do with the adventure as possible. Chivalrous defenders of Mrs. Alcott against her husband have condemned the whole affair because they have believed, mistakenly, that she was against it from the start. Thousands of Louisa's ardent lovers have made sure that the whole effort must have been ridiculous because she, in a sprightly piece of fiction, seemed deliberately to hold it up to ridicule. And even Alcott himself, in his old age, came to smile indulgently at the adventure and to say things about it, forgetfully, that were not quite true. Fruitlands, therefore, is not yet understood.

The first thing to be made clear is that Fruitlands was made, in large part, in England. One means more by this statement than that an English reformer provided nearly all the money for the adventure and was constantly consulted in the laying and worl ing-out of plans. One refers to the fact that Bronson Alcott thought and mood had been profoundly modified by his fi months in England, during which there had been such a fever ar uproar of reform all about him as Boston had never known. A cott had gone to England a fairly modest man, with a set of n unreasonable notions—notwithstanding Garrison's exaggerat remark about his root-and-branch radicalism—about the wa in which human affairs might be improved. After a few mont of adulation at Alcott House, of "sitting on platforms" here a there, and of gifts of ten-pound notes, he had come home aga with somewhat less modesty than he had taken abroad and wi his never-extensive stock of common sense considerably deplet At Alcott House and elsewhere in England he had been associati with persons of lower intelligence than those who in Boston a Concord had held him for several years in check. There is a n tone, almost of arrogance, in some passages of his English lette as where he says on the tenth of August that he must make a c lection from the writings of J. P. Greaves "for *The Dial,* or i own 'Janus,' which I hope to issue on my return to the U.S. organ I must have, an instrument wherein my thought shall be lost amidst the confusing discords and witlessnesses of popu letters." In this opinion, he adds, "both Lane and Wright ag with me." Indeed it would appear that during his entire s' abroad all the members of the Alcott House group agreed w nearly everything that he said. Had not the late Mr. Greaves h self expressed the utmost admiration for this American seer? doing honor to Alcott they honored their dead master.

The fact is, then, that Bronson Alcott, naturally a modest n and by no means naturally a reformer, temporarily mislaid modesty during his stay in England and took on in its stead tain theories about the routes leading to the millennium wh were, for him, remarkably definite. Without these two chai he might never have gone to Fruitlands.

In his *Dial* article on "The English Reformers," already re-
erred to, Emerson makes it clear that during the summer of 1842
Alcott House had been in ferment with plans for some kind of
association" or "community" which would enable a few per-
ons, at least, to lead an ideal life and would serve as a model
or others. Most of these plans showed some vague reminiscence
: Christian monastic discipline, but all of them were related
ore or less closely to the "socialism" of François Charles Fou-
er, the contemporary inventor of the "Phalanstery." Fourier's
eas had been brought across the Channel, and considerably
odified in transit, by Robert Owen, by editor Doherty of the
ndon Phalanx, and by many others, including J. P. Greaves.
Thus it came about that Emerson could write as follows con-
rning the pamphlets that Alcott was sending him from Alcott
ouse:—

> Many of the papers on our table contain schemes and
> hints for a better social organization, especially the
> plan of what they call a "Concordium, or a Primitive
> Home, which is about to be commenced by united
> individuals, who are desirous, under industrial and pro-
> gressive education, with simplicity in diet, dress, lodg-
> ing, &c., to retain the means for the harmonic develop-
> ment of their physical, intellectual, and moral natures."
> The institution is to be in the country, the inmates are
> to be of both sexes, they are to labor on the land, their
> drink is to be water, and their food chiefly uncooked by
> fire, and the habits of the members throughout of the
> same simplicity. Their unity is to be based on their edu-
> cation in a religious love, which subordinates all per-
> sons, and perpetually invokes the presence of the Spirit
> in every transaction.

lthough written while Alcott was still in England, the words
d almost like a description of the Fruitlands community.
nd yet if England was the bow, the arrow was Bronson Al-

[359]

cott. Not in five months nor in five decades could England hav
changed the essential traits of character and belief that Connect
icut and Boston and Concord had worked into him. Fruitland
was not Fourieristic. It was not like any other of the many exper
ments in communal living that were contemporary with it i
America. It was not even like Alcott House. It was like Bronso
Alcott. Fruitlands was true to Alcott's central conviction tha
all effective and enduring changes in society must originate, as I
said, "within the individual and work outwards. The inner beir
must first be organized. . . . Hence reform begins truly wit
individuals, and is conducted through the simplest ministries
families, neighborhoods, fraternities, quite wide of associatio
and institutions."

"Families," "neighborhoods"—one thinks not of Fourier's Ph
ansteries, of Robert Owen's New Lanark or New Harmony,
even of Brook Farm; the words make one remember Spindle Hi
And "individuals"—what had the French Revolution, stead
hardening and freezing into new conventionalisms, really do
for them? No; Fruitlands was conceived as something new. Sm
and even paltry though it may have been in its extent, its inte
was daring and novel. In plan and purpose, at least, it was a co
scious departure from all the schemes for communal living a
all the paper Utopias that had been devised or dreamed since t
time of Plato's *Republic*. Made in England on a French mo
it bore the Yankee stamp in this respect, that it was planned
begin and to end with the individual—although between the
ginning and the end all society was to be renewed and reform
Must we really "descend to meet," as Emerson said? Well th
said Alcott, let us descend and draw all men up to us.

There were several outward and patent reasons, too obvious
enumeration, why Fruitlands could scarcely have been expec
to succeed. From the common-sense point of view it was a cra
brained scheme, attracting only such brains as were themse
a little flawed. What could be expected from an experiment ba

pon agriculture that was to be carried on by two such men as ane and Alcott? The one had gained his knowledge of farming hiefly by sitting at a desk in the City of London and recording ie market price of edible grains. The other had some little praccal knowledge of country matters, but this had now been overid by a set of puerile sentimentalities about releasing the domestic iimals and even the soil itself from "bondage." The fact is that lcott ignored at Fruitlands that basic rural wisdom which he ust have had, the wisdom that reminds a man proposing to live i and by the soil that either he will coöperate with Nature's ays or else, if he chooses, starve. Was there not something argant in the attempt to foist his puny will and way upon the and eternal scheme? But perhaps it is better to call his fault mply an "excess of faith." He was doing his best to serve the >irit—and why, then, should not Spirit help him by a slight adjustment in the natural course of things? Jehovah had held ick the sun and moon in order that Joshua might finish his bat-:. Why should he, Bronson Alcott, be obliged to sow and reap the same time as any ordinary farmer? Perhaps he might be iny miles from Fruitlands and deeply engaged in conversation >on spiritual themes at the moment when the tedded hay was engered by a thunderstorm or on some day when the rye was idy for the sickle. What then? To use one of his favorite exessions, he "doubted not that some arrangement would be ide." It was a miracle that he was always expecting, but what usually got was the law.

Yet the mere failure on the land was not the thing that ike Alcott's purpose. So far as that was concerned he might ssibly have survived the first winter on his bleak hillside, and n in the Spring there would certainly have been reinforcents to carry the battle onward, perhaps to a sound success. t no; the thing that really wrecked Fruitlands was the internee strife that went on there from the beginning between two ids, two wills, or rather, two ideas. On the one side was the

[361]

socialistic, ultimately communistic idea represented by Lane—French, Mediterranean, old as Plato's *Republic,* a product of th city-state, submerging the individual and resting upon the ph losophy of the anthill. Pagan in source, it was pagan too in i present nature, and utterly at odds with that religion which ha always held, in the words of Saint Theresa, that a single soul worth all the rest of the world. And on the other side was the ind vidualism of Christianity, of Puritanism, of New England, of th American wilderness, trained and hardened by innumerable lone wrestlings with the Spirit and solitary conflicts with death in man forms. This did not come from any city-state or constitution cleverly thought-out human scheme. It was the opposite kind thing. One can see it in Saint Anthony of the Egyptian desert an in Daniel Boone of Kentucky. It had come to Alcott not out of an book but chiefly from Spindle Hill. Two things he had know there that were holy, against which he never would turn. One them was the family life, with his mother's smile at its cent And the other was that Presence of which he had been n vaguely and then vividly aware on New Connecticut Hill, spea ing to him, alone.

In the everlasting strife of ideas all considerations of me magnitude and number sink away. Communism and individuali met and grappled in the little red farmhouse above the Nash River with the same deadly intent that they are showing at t hour in their battle for the control of Europe. But of course, future historians may have to say about the European bat neither the one idea nor the other was slain or defeated or e endangered. It was Fruitlands that died.

The story of outward events at Fruitlands has already b told with such accuracy and sympathetic justice by anot pen [1] that a brief outline of them may here suffice.

During the first few weeks there was much eager activity

[1] See *Bronson Alcott's Fruitlands,* by Clara Endicott Sears, Boston, 1

[362]

lowing, planting, and sweeping. The old farmhouse was not in
t condition for occupancy and needed many repairs. Against the
igher principles of the projectors, who hoped eventually to free
omestic animals from all activities "beyond their natural and
leasurable exertions," a hired horse was used in the first plow-
ig, and an incongruous team of an ox and a cow was surrepti-
ously introduced—not, however, without ultimate detection.
.nimal manures were dispensed with entirely because they were
onsidered filthy in both idea and practice, and also because they
ere thought too stimulating to the soil. Some eleven acres were
ultivated and sowed to maize, rye, oats, barley, potatoes, beans—
it what was to become, then, of "Pythagorean diets"?—peas,
elons, squashes, buckwheat, and turnips. This was well enough,
:cept that most of the planting had been done too late in the
ason. Mrs. Alcott worked busily, and at first cheerfully, in the
ouse with her elder daughters. In the field, besides Lane and
lcott and a local farm-hand hired by the month, there were two
w recruits. One was twenty-year-old Samuel Larned, a tempo-
ry convert from the fleshpots of Brook Farm whose main title
fame is the fact that he had subsisted for one whole year upon
ackers and then for another year upon an exclusive diet of
ples. The other was Abraham Everett, a cooper by trade, pro-
undly serious, and a man, said Lane, "of rather deep experience,
ving been imprisoned in a mad-house by his relations because
had little property." Even with this advantage, however, he was
t, in Lane's opinion, "a spiritual being—at least not consciously
d wishfully so."
There was no sign, as yet, of any deep disagreement between
: leaders of the community. Lane wrote to Oldham: "Mr. Alcott
as persevering in practice as last year we found him in idea.
do better and better, to *be* better and better, is the constant
me. His hand is everywhere like his mind. He has held the
ugh with great efficiency, sometimes for the whole day, and by
straightness of his furrow may be said to be giving lessons to

[363]

the professed plowmen, who work in a slovenly manner." Yet i
this plowing Alcott was obliged to abandon a task which he woul
have enjoyed even more and would have performed more skil
fully: the building of a hundred feet of shelves for the Greave
library. He was still preparing meals for the now enlarged famil
and baking his simple "cottage bread" in the shapes of anima
so that it might be more palatable for the children. Lane too
charge of the little school—for some reason it had been decide
that he was a better teacher than Alcott—and of the accounts an
the extensive correspondence.

There is an air of idyllic and almost Arcadian serenity ov
those first few weeks at Fruitlands. "Would that you were he
for a month!" exclaimed Secretary Lane in a letter to Oldham:-

> We have now the most delightful weather you can
> conceive. We are all dressed in our linen tunics, Abra-
> ham is ploughing, Larned bringing some turf from the
> house, Alcott doing a thousand things, Bower and I
> have well dug a sandy spot for carrots, the children
> and the Lady are busy in their respective ways, and
> some hirelings are assisting.

Busy though they were, the Fruitlands people had their times
relaxation. On the twenty-fifth of June Alcott arranged a mer
making, "with odes and music," in honor of his daughter Eli:
beth's seventh birthday, for which the whole community reti
to the fourteen-acre woodlot which they preferred to call "
Grove." No severe critic could assert that the Odes written
this occasion by the same hand that had just been driving
straight a furrow were of a high order of literary merit, but t
showed that combined affection and reverence for childh
which was one of the amateur poet's most amiable traits.

And then there were the noonings and the long summer e
nings of philosophic talk, which was always to Bronson Alcott
best thing that life affords. There was talk in a noble sett
such as Plato of the Academy or Pythagoras of Crotona mi

well have envied. No one, indeed, who has ever stood on Prospect Hill in the town of Harvard and looked out over the richly wooded miles that roll toward Mount Wachusett can ever believe that Fruitlands was utterly a failure. For always there must have been beauty there, in every season, at every hour of the day or night, to exalt aspiration and to hallow the bitterest defeat. It is a place as beautiful as New Connecticut Hill, and as fit for transcendental musings. And when one walks down to the little farmhouse on the hillside, so perfectly restored and preserved by a care as learned as it is deeply respectful of the past, one sees again that here, in spite of all, there must have been some fine and high success. Even for Charles Lane to have come here out of London's turmoil, out of that crass and brutal England of Macaulay's description, and to have sat here on this "philosopher's settle" during the evenings of six months, sharing views with one of the best talkers in America—was that failure? All things are comparative, and before we make sure that the Fruitlands adventure was one long defeat we should do well to inquire what a few of the most prosperous merchants in Boston were making of their lives from June to January of the Fruitlands year. Were they surrounded night and day by the noble companies of the stars and the journeying clouds? Were they always quietly assured that, however their plans might fail, their hopes were high and their purposes pure? Were they living in thought continually with the best minds in the past or present of which they had ever heard? And were they working steadily all that while not for their own gain but for the good of humankind present and to come? If so, then they were no doubt as successful and as happy during those months as Bronson Alcott, who was hopelessly in debt and was heading straight toward the most overwhelming disaster of his life.

Visitors began to come from over the hills to the lonely farmhouse which had not even a road leading to its door. Theodore Parker, who would soon be going to Europe in search of health and of more books to read, came from West Roxbury. George Ripley came from Brook Farm, that sharply contrasting community, so prosperous and populous and gay, now making rapidly in the direction of the Phalanstery. Brook Farm was succeeding in the way of the world, but Ripley would have been one of the first to recognize that it was far less transcendental, and therefore less successful, than Fruitlands. The trouble with Brook Farm was that the good people there—as they would one day admit to themselves—had "no thoughts." To Fruitlands came also William Russell, who was now a prospering teacher at Andover. Isaac Hecker paused there for a few weeks on his long religious pilgrimage, and perhaps he would have remained if he had not found the community deficient in "the Everlasting." Young Henry Thoreau came and peered here and there with his beak and eyes of a hungry hawk, finding the place well stored with old books that he had to read, but short on common sense. Emerson came early in July—Emerson, whom Alcott would rather have pleased than all the world beside.

"The sun and the evening sky do not look calmer," he wrote "than Alcott and his family at Fruitlands. They seem to have arrived at the fact—to have got rid of the show, and to be serene. Their manners and behaviour in the house and the field were those of superior men—of men at rest. What had they to conceal? What had they to exhibit? And it seemed so high an attainment that I thought—as often before, so now more, because they had a fit home, or the picture was fitly framed—that these men ought to be maintained in their place by the country for its culture. Young men and young maidens, old men and women, should visit them and be inspired. I think there is as much merit in beautiful manners as in hard work."

So much he said by way of wholehearted approbation; but then came the cautious Yankee afterthought: "I will not prejudge the successful. They look well in July; we will see them in December."

[366]

FRUITLANDS FARMHOUSE

PROSPECT HILL
HARVARD, MASSACHUSETTS

And even at this high tide of the year, when all were hopeful, Fruitlands would have been good hunting ground for any humorist whose respect for the "Ideals" involved had not overcome his sense of the ridiculous. For the good sort of laughter that is both thoughtful and kind, without any ingredient of Mark Twain's arrogant crudity or of Holmes's metropolitan cleverness, one does not know that American life has ever afforded a better chance. The Muse of Comedy must have hovered for a long time in the air over Fruitlands farmhouse before her darker sister took her place. One does not need to accept any of the myths and legends that have grown up about the adventure in order to be amused. The mere record of Alcott's planting proves that he had no intention, such as the quidnunc gossips attributed to him, of confining his family's diet to the vegetables that "aspire," or grow above the ground. There seems to be no definite evidence that Fruitlands boasted a "nudist"—that is, a person who had taken it into his head "that clothes were an impediment to spiritual growth." Fruitlands did not stand in need of any such incitement to gaiety, for did it not possess, and even flaunt, the most famous beard in America—none other than the beard of Joseph Palmer? And wherever the beard went there went Joseph Palmer in person—cantankerous, exceedingly muscular, and as gnarled as an old apple tree—to protect it and save it from insult. In all the Massachusetts counties there was no more irascible, no kinder, no more helpful, and no more laughable man than this Joseph Palmer of No Town. Fruitlands had him as soon as he could get out of Worcester Jail; and for many years after Alcott and Lane had gone their several ways he was to have Fruitlands, maintaining it as a sort of asylum for waifs and tramps and men with beards.

We have seen that Lane and Alcott were almost as much opposed to the subjection of the lower animals as they were to human slavery. Accordingly, after the soil had been broken by the plow they turned to "spade culture," with disastrous results to Lane's secretarial hands and temper. Because cotton was derived from the labor of Negro slaves and wool was thought to involve the slavery of sheep, these thoroughgoing emancipators wore linen, at any rate while the sun was riding high. It is significant of their social sympathies that their outer garments were smocked, like those of European peasants. Their hats also were of linen, and so were their trousers. Boots and shoes presented a difficulty, and one fears that in spite of Lane's tentative efforts with canvas the leather-bearing animals must have continued to suffer. By what casuistry they convinced themselves that silkworms may legitimately be condemned to lifelong and unrewarded toil one does not know, but the fact is that Alcott himself planted three mulberry trees in front of the farmhouse, almost certainly with an eye to the somewhat distant usufruct.

It was one of the main proofs of Charles Lane's personal power that not only the Alcott children but Mrs. Alcott and even Miss Anna Page from Providence were soon arrayed in linen garments of the shocking but serviceable style which was to become famous a few years later, under the surname of Amelia Jenks Bloomer. The men bathed in the brook, the water of which attained in November a temperature low enough for the most ascetic taste and purposes. Alcott arranged for the bathing of his daughters by hanging sheets circlewise over clotheslines and then, mounted upon a chair or ladder, pouring water upon their heads from a pitcher and through a sieve. ("I do love cold water!" exclaimed young Louisa to her Journal.) How the ablutions of Mrs. Alcott and Miss Anna Page were managed seems not to have been recorded. The popular view of their lives at Fruitlands would suggest that they were too busy to bathe at all.

So one builds it up, little stroke by stroke, the picture of the strange life that was lived there, over ninety years ago, on that beautiful Massachusetts hillside. If Alcott's Journals of the Fruitlands period had not gone sailing down the Hudson in 184 without their owner's knowledge, one might be more specific. And yet this is not certain. Always too neglectful of the hard and angular fact, Alcott may have been even more vaguely abstract in those Journals than he was elsewhere—may have given no hint, for example, why he set his three mulberry trees so close to the farmhouse that in later years they threatened to overturn the foundations, or why he planted his apple and pear trees in just that part of the farm where they would be least likely ever to justify the farm's new name. One rather regrets, as Alcott did all his life, the loss of those Fruitlands papers—and particularly the manuscript called "Prometheus," in which he seems to have recorded one of his three periods of mystical enlightenment and exaltation; yet those papers, if we had them, could not in any way strengthen one's realization that here had been a complete and uncompromising exemplification of the idealistic way of life.

Forget it not, America! Laugh at it if you will, but do not fail to see what it meant. Refuse to accept the chuckleheaded view that merely because Fruitlands did not conform to the pitiful conventionalisms of the man in the street it must therefore have been in all ways absurd. Remember of course that even while these philosophers were spading the hillside in their smocked tunics, and trying to live like the Pythagoreans of ancient Italy, the mills were beginning their premonitory thunder at Lowell on the Merrimack and armies of Irishmen were going forth with pick and shovel to lay the railways of New England. All of that had its own kind of importance. All of that was thoroughly American. But Fruitlands was American too.

The agricultural record of Fruitlands might have been somewhat better if the philosophers had been able and willing to devote more of their time to agricultural pursuits. Even Isaac Hecker, just from Brook Farm, feared that they were too much given to reading and writing for the prosperity of their enter-

[369]

prise. They were also too much given to conversation on "high themes," and to wandering about the country with no money in their pockets, for men who had a host of weeds among their peas and beans.

Late in July Lane and Alcott walked to Boston—some forty miles—to purchase dishes and supplies. Once there, they thought they might as well go on to West Roxbury, and soon they were having "a pleasant summer evening's conversation" with the people of Brook Farm, whom Lane afterwards described as "playing away their youth and daytime in a miserably joyous, frivolous manner." He was apparently disgusted to find that the children of Brook Farm were "taught languages, etc.," and that the animals occupied a prominent position in the community "there being no less than sixteen cows, besides four oxen, a herd of swine, a horse or two, etc." (Charles Lane could pack a good deal of scorn into "etc.") Worst of all, in his judgment, was the fact that "the milk is sold in Boston, and they buy butter to the extent of five hundred dollars a year."

In September, just when they should have been getting in their grain, these two peripatetic philosophers went again to Boston and to Brook Farm, to conduct public Conversations. From Brook Farm they drifted on across the landscape to the Hopedale and Northampton communities, both of which they found to be completely "unideal," and then to Providence, where Alcott always had a group of friends. Finally they turned up, still dressed in their linen tunics, in the New York parlor of Lydia Maria Child.

"What brings you to New York?" asked she.

"I don't know," Alcott replied, perhaps recollecting for the first time that there had not been a penny in his pocket when he left home. "It seems a miracle that we are here."

And in the meanwhile, back at Fruitlands, Mrs. Alcott and her children were performing quite as remarkable a miracle in harvesting the summer's crop.

[370]

The gradual change in Mrs. Alcott's feeling about the Fruitlands adventure is an interesting thing to watch, especially when
one realizes the nature of the silent struggle that was going on
from the beginning between her and Charles Lane.

At first she seems to have been an enthusiastic member of the
"Consociate Family," and there is the beauty of a deep happiness
in some of her earlier comments. In June she wrote:—

> Walked over our little territory of woodland, vale,
> meadow, and pasture, hill, grove, forest. All beautiful,
> the hills commanding one of the most expansive pros-
> pects in the country. . . . One is transported from his
> littleness, and the soul expands in such a region of
> sights and sounds. Between us and this vast expanse
> we may hold our hand and stand alone, an isolated be-
> ing occupying but a foot of earth and living but for
> ourselves; or we may look again, and a feeling of dif-
> fusive illimitable benevolence possesses us as we take
> in this vast region of hill and plain. I gathered an apron
> of chips while the children collected flowers. Like provi-
> dent Mother Earth, I gathered for use, they for beauty.
> Both gave pleasure. It was very characteristic of me,
> and most natural in them.

In August, however, came Miss Anna Page from the group in
Providence which had for years regarded Alcott as a great man.
To Mrs. Alcott she was "an amiable active woman whose kind
word and gentle care-taking deed" were of utmost service, but
one fears that Charles Lane, and perhaps even Alcott, would
have made a different report if it had been generally known what
was being said in the kitchen. At any rate, there was a new note in
Mrs. Alcott's Journal after Miss Page's advent—a tendency to
set the two sexes off against each other not at all in the way of
the wise wife and mother but in that of the involuntarily celibate
middle-aged female. By the end of August Abigail May Alcott
was airing feminine wrongs in this fashion:—

[371]

Visited the Shakers. I gain but little from their domestic or internal arrangements. There is a servitude somewhere, I have no doubt. There is a fat, sleek, comfortable look about the men, and among the women there is a stiff reserve that belongs to neither sublime resignation nor divine hope. Wherever I turn I see the yoke on women in some form or other. On some it sits easy, for they are but beasts of burden; on others, pride hushes them to silence. . . . On some it galls and chafes. They feel assured by every instinct of their nature that they were designed for a higher, nobler calling than to "drag life's lengthening chain along." A woman may perform the most disinterested duties. She may "die daily" in the cause of truth and righteousness. She lives neglected, and dies forgotten. But a man, who never performed in his whole life one self-denying act, but who has accidental gifts of genius, is celebrated by his contemporaries while his name and his works live on from age to age.

Miss Page made a good remark, and true as good, that a woman may live a whole life of sacrifice, and at her death meekly say "I die a woman." A man passes a few years in experiments in self-denial and simple life, and he says "Behold a God!"

There certainly is more true humility in woman, more substantial greatness in woman, more essential goodness, than in man. Woman lives her thought; man speculates about it. Woman's love is enduring, changeless. Man is fitful in his attachments. His love is convenient, not of necessity. Woman is happy in her plain lawn. Man is better content in the rural purple.

Except for the heat of anger and the sense of a personal justice, these were the sentiments and beliefs of Bronson Al himself, although he probably would not have felt that the I Eden was an appropriate place for bringing them forth. Lou

[372]

n her *Transcendental Wild Oats,* has Miss Page expelled from
he community for surreptitiously eating the tail of a fish; but
here was a good deal going on at Fruitlands of which Louisa, ten
ears old when the adventure began, knew little either at the time
r in later retrospect. One fears that Miss Anna Page played the
art of the serpent in the Garden, and that the apple she offered
ve—if one may be allowed the mixture of mythologies—was the
pple of Discord.

A highly significant jotting in Mrs. Alcott's Journal is that for
nday, the second of July, when the Consociate Family was
st beginning:—

> Mr. Alcott most beautifully and forcibly illustrated
> on the black board the sacrifices and utter subjection
> of the Body to the Soul, showing the ✝ on which the
> lusts of the flesh are to be sacrificed. Renunciation is
> the law; devotion to God's will the Gospel. The latter
> makes the former easy, sometimes delightful.

One would like to know precisely how much and exactly what
s intended to be conveyed by that old worn phrase "the lusts
the flesh." How much and what did the speaker expect it to
an to Anna, aged twelve, to ten-year-old Louisa, to Elizabeth
o had just turned seven, not to mention the infant Abby May?
obably that they must not ask for butter or cheese or milk,
ause such luxuries depended upon the subjection of the lower
mals, or for molasses, which came from the Slave States, or for
fine dresses and toys from the shop that were too expensive for
losophers' children. But what was the all-inclusive phrase in-
ded to mean to the wife of his bosom, who was certainly for
and for the watchful Lane the chief person in the audience?
Across the river from Fruitlands there was a community of
kers, established there in 1781 by Mother Ann Lee herself.
arles Lane was often among these people, learning all that they
to teach except how to run a farm and believing most of what

he was told. Now the central feature of Shaker life was the prais
and practice of celibacy. To Mother Ann Lee in her prison cell a
Manchester, England, it had been "revealed" that "a complet
cross against the lusts of generation, added to a full and explici
confession before witnesses of all the sins committed under its ir
fluence, was the only possible remedy and means of salvation.
Charles Lane undoubtedly heard those words, or the sense c
them, at the Shaker Village, and they chimed exactly with wor
he had long been hearing, perhaps even speaking, at Alcott Hous
Here, then, is a clue to the meaning that Mrs. Alcott was e:
pected to find in that cross on the Fruitlands blackboard.

In belief and practice alike the Shakers were attractive to the
transcendental neighbors. They had conducted a successful cor
munal life at Harvard for more than sixty years before Fruitlan
began. They were a people segregated from the world and y
highly competent in economic matters. Like the Quakers, frc
whom they were descended and to whom Alcott himself ow
much, they had strong mystical inclinations and lived as much
possible by the guidance of the "inner light." They submerged
families in the larger communal group. And then there was tl
curious idea of theirs—at the time a novel one, positively fascin
ing to Alcott in its implications, and most soothing, one wo
surmise, to the feministic antagonisms of Alcott's wife—about
bisexuality of the Creator. The man who had so often asser
that even a human genius must have in him the traits of b
man and woman could not fail to be interested, although one ho
that he was also strongly disgusted, by this crude and debas
notion of the "Father-Mother God," and by the Shaker teacl
that while Jesus, the son of a carpenter, was the male repres
ative of Christ, Ann Lee, daughter of a blacksmith, was the fer
representative of the same Divine Person.

In several ways, then, the Shaker doctrines were of a sor
command attention, and even some respect, at Fruitlands.
tention was paid, no doubt, by all the adult members of the gr

ut respect chiefly by Charles Lane. He shouted across the tlantic in a letter to William Oldham that here was "the only ligion ever founded by a Woman," as though that would certinly mean that it was the only true one. After leaving Fruitnds Lane actually joined the Shaker community for a month or o of probationary life, and did all that he could to convert illiam Oldham and what remained of the Alcott House group Shaker opinions. Indeed he so far succeeded as to make Oldham y it down as a rule for all institutions such as Alcott House hat the reproduction of the species within such associations ist be discontinued until marriage can be established in Divine der." As to whether this rule was ever really posted on the walls Alcott House we are not informed.

There was something in Bronson Alcott—probably not a sense humor but rather a kind of intellectual inoculation—which pt him all his life immune to the pseudo-religions that spawned d pullulated in his time like forms of unclean life. Always he ild see and could give thanks for any modicum of truth they ght contain, and he was even more certain to recognize any od they might do, any grace or strength of character they might duce. Beyond that he never went. Thus he knew several of foremost American "spiritualists" of his day and attended ny of their meetings with interest, but against spiritualism in eral he spoke almost sternly. Yet Alcott was weak and vulner-e on one side, as most Americans are who have been affected n remotely by our centuries of pioneering: women, to him, were ays exceptionally "pure" and "precious" creatures, as we have e than once had occasion to see. He considered that women e more religious and "spiritual" than men, and accordingly vas all his life on the lookout for that prophetess, that "sibyl," ie loved to call her, who should speak forth the things of the it as never man had spoken. And so now there arose the stion: might this Mother Ann be She? Possibly he might have ight so—in which case the later history of Fruitlands would

have been decidedly different—if the doctrine of Mother An[n]
had not been quite so thickly smeared with sexuality. Pure[?]
Well, no. Even Bronson Alcott could see that "nothing resemble[s]
a swelling so much as a hollow."

And yet the Shakers were highly successful, but Fruitlands wa[s]
failing more and more. Could the reason lie in that one article [of]
difference, their practice of celibacy? Charles Lane, then livin[g]
a celibate life himself and never forgetting the doctrine and e[x]-
ample of the bachelor Greaves, lost no opportunity for suggestin[g]
that reason. His definite purpose was, to put the matter blunt[ly]
to separate Alcott from his wife and children. To this end we ma[y]
be sure that he held up that article in the Shaker creed whi[ch]
taught, by no means for the first time in the history of insa[ne]
religions, that the real occasion of Adam's expulsion from Paradi[se]
had been his "fall" from virginity. And Alcott, as it happen[ed]
was trying to found a "Paradise," a "New Eden." In speaking [of]
Fruitlands he had already used the words many times.

The situation, one sees, was extremely difficult, and not the l[ess]
so because it involved matters which Alcott could not or wo[uld]
not discuss in clear terms with any man. In their association w[ith]
Lane and the Shakers the Alcotts came into a magnetic field alm[ost]
too powerful for them to resist. So sensitive they were to just s[uch]
an attraction that it becomes a problem to find how they mana[ged]
to pull free and make their way slowly back toward health [and]
good sense.

Before attempting to answer that question it is necessary to [put]
one obstacle to a clear understanding out of the way. Our o[wn]
time, positively obsessed by sex as the Shakers and all t[heir]
numberless and inveterate kind were negatively obsessed, is li[able]
to misconstrue the struggle altogether. Within a month after [her]
marriage Mrs. Alcott had written to Lucretia Mott: "Love [has]
ever been with us a principle, not a passion." The words may [be a]
little vague, although one feels assured of their truth; and t[hey]
must remain so because Alcott and his wife shared the qu[?]

otion of their time that we do not really loosen the grip of sex
y perpetually thinking, talking, writing, reading, and—as the
hakers did—"confessing" about it. If the dark truth must be
ld, they were definitely reticent upon this topic. All that one
eeds to know is that both husband and wife were certainly
apable of practising a rigid sexual abstinence in the interests of
ay theory of reform to which they had devoted themselves. But
at, as Alcott saw it, was not the issue. The question was whether
e, who had cheerfully renounced nearly every other thing, would
ow abandon his family and live apart from it, as the men of the
aker village lived apart from the women, avoiding throughout
eir lives every possibility of physical contact.

Charles Lane, the cold and logical theorist, argued strongly for
complete surrender. Only that man, he said, who has abandoned
temporal and earthly loves can ever rise to the Love which is
ine. The man could quote Scripture, as Satan also is said to
, and could remind one that Jesus had no wife, no child. Prob-
y he knew that terrible text which in the old days had drawn
usands into the desert and the wilderness: "Every one that
h forsaken . . . wife or children . . . for my name's sake
. shall inherit everlasting life." He had read Plato, and could
ke devastating hints in which Abigail and the children always
od for the "Many" and the desertion of them was always a
essary first step on the quest of the "One." It was indeed an
old struggle, which has been lived through in human history
umerable times. Always Lane was on the side of the abstract,
Alcott himself had so long been. He was like a vice in the
d, a voice in the brain. It was the hardest thing Alcott had
done to distinguish the loud words that Lane said from those
he Still Small Voice.

ut there on the other side were Abigail and the children.
y were indeed the "Many," the "Creatures," standing not for
bstract "Truth" so much as for the simple facts of warm and
thing human life; yet they were not on that account any the

[377]

less dear. To a transcendental and a Christian mind there woul[d] occur the ancient question, whether it is not precisely by our de[-] votion to such frail children of time that we can best ascend to th[e] love of things eternal. "Lovest thou me? . . . Feed my sheep."

Voluble and even vociferous as Mrs. Alcott could be upo[n] occasion, she seems to have said almost nothing on this one. If w[e] may trust the fictional account of her most ardent champio[n] Louisa, she spoke no word, but merely drew her children about h[er] as a living four-fold argument and abode the result. For th[e] struggle had gone beyond words. She was not merely the intend[ed] victim of this agony, like Isaac in the trial of Abraham. She shar[ed] the torment and the temptation. One whole side of her nature, [as] of her husband's, was inclined to this dreadful decision—for w[as] she not also a reformer, knowing well what self-sacrifice mea[nt] and all its seductive charm? Ah, yes; but even stronger in her w[as] the New England woman's hard and factual common sense, uni[ted] to the fierce devotion of the mother to her brood.

Feministic and indeed predominantly female as we are in th[ese] days, we are likely to sympathize with the wife alone; but thi[s is] to ignore the tension that was tearing at her husband's mind [and] heart. One should see that the struggle in him was not betw[een] a higher and a lower nature but between two aspects of ideal[,] two strong and noble elements in one person. Alcott was not b[e] tempted to do evil. Neither was Lane an evil man. He was [a] much more dangerous thing, a perfectly cool and reason[able] fanatic, able to see only one side of a question at a time. Whe[n he] returned to what William Oldham elegantly called "the repro[duc-] tion of the species" he would go about it with just the same s[ame] concentration that he was showing now in the opposite cam[p. At] present he was attacking Bronson Alcott at precisely the [point] at which that idealizing philosopher was least able to defend [him-] self.

Other considerations were of less moment, but could n[ot be] ignored. Lane owned Fruitlands, and the Alcotts were in [

ense his guests. He had recently paid some part of Alcott's Concord debts, so that his name had been added to the ever-lengthening list of persons to whom Alcott owed money. He might have contended, and probably he did hint, that the suggestion he was making now was no more than what had been implied in the mutual agreement he and Alcott had reached at Alcott House.

And so an æon or two of torment was endured in a few weeks. Apparently there was no outward conflict or even debate. Rather, as one makes it out from a hundred fleeting glimpses, there was innuendo, there were darkening looks and lengthening silences, and there was a slow withdrawal of fellowship. What brought it all to an end is uncertain, but one finds no evidence of any final explosion. By late November all of the new recruits had left, ex-cepting only the faithful Joseph Palmer. Charles Lane was "moody and enigmatical." And then Mrs. Alcott played one trump card. Whatever the philosophers might decide to do, she announced, she would soon remove herself and her children to a house which had been provided by her brother in the village of Still River, one mile away. At this point, probably, Lane began to see that he was beaten. Writing to William Oldham he attributed the approaching failure of Fruitlands chiefly to Mrs. Alcott, who, said he, "vows that her own family are all that she lives for, or wishes to live for." Her hubsand's main fault, he declared, was "constancy to his wife and inconstancy to the Spirit, which has blurred over his life forever."

A note or two from the Journals that have survived may suggest atmosphere of the time and place. Louisa wrote on the tenth December:—

I did my lessons and walked in the afternoon. Father read to us in dear *Pilgrim's Progress.* Mr. L. was in Boston, and we were glad. In the eve Father and Mother and Annie and I had a long talk. I was very un-happy, and we all cried. Anna and I cried in bed, and I prayed God to keep us all together.

And on Christmas Day the mother wrote:—

> Weather severe. Constant succession of snowstorms.
> My eyes have become quite troublesome. . . . Play
> with the children, sing, and try to cheer the scene
> within.

At some time in the first week of January, 1844—one recor
indicates the second and another the sixth of that month—Charl
Lane and his son William left Fruitlands and went to live at th
Shaker Village. On the fourteenth of January the Alcotts also le
the house, taking three rooms and a kitchen at the home of
neighbor named Lovejoy in the village of Still River. The a
venture at Fruitlands and Bronson Alcott's career as a reform
had come to an ignominious close.

THE EVERLASTING ARMS

$\Longrightarrow\{$ 1843-1844 $\}\Longleftarrow$

*tragic man—The success of failure—Paradise in retrospect—
he ministries of labor—Gardens and orchards—Henry Thoreau*

THE LOSS of Bronson Alcott's Journals of the Fruitlands period has left in shadow the crucial event of his life. hough that loss was a grief to him, he did not deplore the dow. Much as he loved words, he was willing always that the pest things of life and death should go unexpressed.
And here had really been a struggle of life and death together. en it finally became clear, in December, that the Fruitlands ad- ture must inevitably fail, Alcott, theretofore "ever a hoper," hed to die. Precisely what happened one cannot make sure. s. Alcott's letters to her brother show that her husband was emely ill, that he would not take what she thought the right sures for recovering, and that she had an agonizing fear of nity. F. B. Sanborn, with whom Alcott certainly discussed the nt in later years, says briefly: "the final expulsion from this adise nearly cost Mr. Alcott his life. He retired to his chamber,

refused food, and was on the point of dying from grief and
abstinence, when his wife prevailed on him to continue longer
in this ungrateful world." Finally, there is Louisa's highly romantic and sentimentalized account in *Transcendental Wild
Oats,* which one hesitates to use because the entire tale in which
it appears is a piece of elaborate embroidery upon a scanty cloth
of fact. Yet Louisa, at any rate, was present; and her father, when
he read her story, did not demur against what she had said of
him. Probably, therefore, she may be depended upon to render,
if not the precise facts, at any rate the general truth of a situation
which must have been stamped indelibly upon her mind.

It is now Louisa speaking:—

Then this dreamer, whose dream was the life of his
life, resolved to carry out his idea to the bitter end.
There seemed no place for him here—no work, no
friend. To go begging conditions was as ignoble as to
go begging money. Better perish of want than sell one's
soul for the sustenance of the body. Silently he lay
down upon his bed, turned his face to the wall, and
waited with pathetic patience for death to cut the knot
which he could not untie. Days and nights went by, and
neither food nor water passed his lips. Soul and body
were dumbly struggling together, and no word of complaint betrayed what either suffered.

His wife, when tears and prayers were unavailing,
sat down to wait the end with a mysterious awe and
submission; for in this entire resignation of all things
there was an eloquent significance to her who knew
him as no other being did.

"Leave all to God," was his belief; and in this crisis
the loving soul clung to this faith, sure that the All-
wise Father would not desert this child who tried to
live so near to Him. Gathering her children about her,
she waited the issue of the tragedy that was being en-

acted in that solitary room, while the first snow fell outside, untrodden by the foot-prints of a single friend.

But the strong angels who sustain and teach perplexed and troubled souls came and went, leaving no trace without, but working miracles within. For, when all other sentiments had faded into dimness, all other hopes died utterly; when the bitterness of death was nearly over, when body was past any pang of hunger or thirst, and soul stood ready to depart, the love that outlives all else refused to die. Head had bowed to defeat, hand had grown weary with too heavy tasks, but heart could not grow cold to those who lived in its tender depths, even when death touched it.

"My faithful wife, my little girls,—they have not forsaken me, they are mine by ties that none can break. What right have I to leave them alone? What right to escape from the burden and the sorrow I have helped to bring? This duty remains to me, and I must do it manfully. For their sakes, the world will forgive me in time; for their sakes, God will sustain me now."

Too feeble to rise, Abel groped for the food that always lay within his reach; and in the darkness and solitude of that memorable night ate and drank what was to him the bread and wine of a new communion, a new dedication of heart and life to the duties that were left him when the dreams fled.

In the early dawn, when that sad wife crept fearfully to see what change had come to the patient face on the pillow, she found it smiling at her, saw a wasted hand outstretched to her, and heard a feeble voice cry bravely, "Hope!"

he passage is a masterpiece in a style of writing now no longer ired, but in its main outlines it seems worthy of trust. There certainly several days, in the cold, bare, and solitary little e at Fruitlands, during which Bronson Alcott, worn to the

shadow of himself by physical toil and the struggle with Lane'
suggestions, would have been glad to leave a world that seemed t
have no place for him. One or two veiled allusions to the exper
ence are to be found in the Journals of later years, where it :
clearly hinted that his hope had been to die of starvation, b
that the sense of obligation to his family had brought him back
life. Death itself had been a luxury which he, as a poor ma
heavily loaded with debt, had no right to claim.

Whatever it was that happened to Alcott at Fruitlands in th
December, with no witnesses other than his wife and childre
divided his life in two. For fifteen years he had been an eager a
active soldier of the Lord, fighting the good fight with hand a
heart and brain. For ten years, ever since he had read and thoug
his way into transcendentalism at Germantown and in M
Eaton's attic in Philadelphia, he had been convinced, as t
Hebrew prophets were, that God was speaking to his soldi
telling him what to do. For five years, since the failure of Tem
School and the loss of all hope for a literary career, he had be
more and more swept along in the charge of the reformers; a
in recent months his life and thought had been convulsed
alien influences, all but insane in their violence and thoroug
militaristic in method, of the English reforming group. Then
conflict had entered the man's own thought. His mind itself
become a battleground, swept over and scarred and irrepara
torn by contending ideals and ideas. The world had taken
outer walls and gatehouses; it had stormed into his outer
inner ward. How now? Must not the man die?

But he did not die—or, at any rate, not all of him, and not
better part. There was yet a well of water in the rock fou
tion of his central keep, and this the world never took, n
poisoned. Upon this water he lived even while he longed to die,
by the strength of it he came back into the world of the li
and went onward there for more than forty years, a chast
and quieted man. He was still to work with hand and heart

[384]

ead wherever he found opportunity; but all haste, all heat of strife, all anxiety for the result, had fallen from him. After the ultimate defeat at Fruitlands, that defeat which was also a triumph, Bronson Alcott was a deeper man. He was no longer merely a man who had more or less interesting ideas, and could express them. He was now a tragic character.

For there had been something nobly tragic and grandly normal about the Fruitlands catastrophe. One must not be put off by the paltriness of the setting, but must remember that high tragedy can occur as well in a remote New England farmhouse, with one woman and four frightened little girls for audience, as in a royal palace. The height of Lear's agony was reached in an even poorer place. And neither should one ignore the tragic catastrophe because it passed with hardly a word spoken, or because there are no adequate words to record it. Words have not been made for such uses. It was really a deathbed on which Bronson Alcott lay in that upper room with his face to the wall. His self-will was dying. But it was also a bed of birth. Simple wisdom, or what Wordsworth had called "a wise passiveness," was being born. Alcott lay down a broken and beaten reformer. When he rose he was by way of being a wise man. What had he learned in the silent interim? Not to strive, not to try to force his will and way. He had learned that "underneath are the everlasting arms."

He had been obliged to fall, to sink, and to let himself go for a, before he could touch that elemental wisdom. Only in despair of his own strength could he find the strength that is greater. And there was this further paradox: he had to abandon all thought of commanding the wills of others before his own will could become truly effective. It is a law—a law that few discover, but its truth does not depend upon the number of its adherents. Test it where you will, in the life of every man who has powerfully shaped the will of others there has necessarily been some defeat, some rejection and exile, some wandering in the wilderness during which he has come upon "the Rock" which is greater than he.

[385]

There is a new nobility of quietness in the prayer that Alcott wrote out for himself shortly after the defeat at Fruitlands:—

Light, O source of light! give Thou unto thy servant sitting in the perplexities of this surrounding darkness. Hold Thou him steady to Thee, to truth, and to himself; and in Thine own due time give him clearly to the work for which Thou art slowly preparing him, proving his faith meanwhile in Thyself and in his kind.

And then, having addressed those words to the Presence with which he had first communed on New Connecticut Hill, he went on a little further, talking to himself:—

Shall I say, with Pestalozzi, that I "was not made by this world nor for it,—wherefore am I placed in it if I was found unfit?" And the world that found him thus asked not whether it was his fault or that of another; but it bruised him with an iron hammer, as the bricklayer breaks an old brick to fill up a crevice.

In the mood of these words, and in the words themselves, there is an unmistakable grandeur of simplicity such as only strength suffering and great joy can teach. Alcott can use the simple language, at last, and can bend to his thought the most familiar scenes of every day. It is Emerson's secret, and Thoreau's. Among other more important things, and because of them, he is learning now to write.

Emerson, who had been through his own dark valley, said little of what was happening to his friend. Shortly after failure at Fruitlands had become manifest he wrote, with Alcott almost certainly in mind:—

A few persons in the course of my life have, at certain moments, appeared to me not measured men of five feet five or ten inches, but large, enormous, indefinite. These were not great proprietors or heads of committees, but, on the contrary, nothing could be more private. They were in some want or affliction or other relation that called out the emanation of the Spirit, which dignified and transfigured them to my eyes.

Even Charles Lane had failed sufficiently in his effort to capture the will of another so that he too caught some glimpse of the law. "It is hard work, certainly," he wrote to Alcott from New York City, "to subdue the love of being useful,—it seems so holy and sacred—but I presume even this is selfish enough to demand suppression. I cannot too constantly urge upon you and upon myself to preserve unbroken the pure love for the Highest. Feel assured that all the rest will follow without any special effort of ours."

Alcott never ceased to acknowledge his debt to Fruitlands. As the experience faded into the past he forgot many details of what had happened there and even some of his former hopes and purposes, but the lesson he had learned was never lost. In 1857 he wrote:—

Fruitlands was an adventure mistimed, and in some sense visionary, for planting in good faith a Paradise here in Puritan New England, in hope of enjoying the pastoral life in more than pristine simplicity with a little company of men and women smitten with sentiments of the old heroism and humanity. It was undertaken too soon; the parties were all too unripe to sing and serve finely their song of a purely ideal life—possible for all some time but for none as yet in practice. . . . Ah! the pains, the pleasures of that endeavor! The issue! For so earnestly did he prosecute his enterprise, with an enthusiasm so fervent, an abandonment so entire, that it was not permitted him to discover how vast was the disproportion between his materials and the idea that had drawn those about him, till all had vanished and left him alone in its unclouded brightness.

[387]

Just thirty years after he had closed the door of the little red farmhouse for the last time, Alcott was saying to an audience in St. Louis: "My debt to Fruitlands was vast, for while there I lived an Age, and learned what neither friend nor foe could have taught me by counsel or rebuke." And three years later still he set down this note:—

> Returning from Worcester by way of Ayer Junction, I pass Fruitlands, lying there in that "sequestered dell" and distinguished from the surrounding farms, I alone of the passengers associating with its sloping pastures and dilapidated homestead the real history of that social endeavor—a history that can never be fairly told by any one, and as imperfectly by myself as any.

Neither did Alcott lose interest entirely in the "consociate family life." While at Lovejoy's house in the winter of 1844 and all during the following eleven months in the village of Still River, he received letters from persons in many parts of the country who would have been glad to join in just such an enterprise as the one that had lately failed. Both he and his wife went here and there among the "communities," seeking a home for themselves and their children. In August, 1844, he even visited the Oneida Community in New York State, taking Anna with him and losing his Fruitlands manuscripts on the way. Probably he had heard of the experiments in "complex marriages" that were then going on there, under the leadership of that same John Humphrey Noyes who had formerly urged Garrison to defy the Constitution. At any rate, he said nothing of them on his return, merely reported that Oneida would not do. Nothing would do that did not recognize the family, in its simple and chaste integrity, the basis of all right living. Even so late as October, 1844, he had not abandoned hope of such a community, for in that month he wrote to his brother Junius asking him to join a "consociate family" to be established at the place in Concord which he later called "Hillside."

[388]

Emerson has offered to buy me a few acres and build me a plain house, and Mr. May and others desire to aid in placing us on the soil, free of rents and landlords. I hope to obtain space and dwellings for several families by these means. I cannot consent to live solely for one family. I would stand in neighborly relations to several, and institute a union and communion of families instead of drawing aside within the precincts of one's own acres and kindred by blood.

In this letter it is certainly to be observed that the cure of Alcott's reforming fever is not yet complete, yet the cure is progressing. There is here an even stronger emphasis laid upon "family" than there was at Fruitlands. The same feeling and conviction that finally saved Alcott from Charles Lane is here—the conviction that there is something holy in the family relationship. The Saxon in Alcott, and memories of Spindle Hill, are clearly overcoming a set of abstract ideas emanating ultimately from the Frenchman Fourier. Already Alcott can say, in one of the less awkward of his attempts at verse:—

> I drank delights from every cup;
> Art, institutions I drank up.
> Athirst, I quaffed life's brimming bowls,
> And sipped the flavors of all souls.
> One sparkling cup remained for me—
> The brimming fount of family.

And there was another influence, quite as closely related to Spindle Hill, that was hastening Alcott's cure. He was being sobered by labor, and quieted by the "ministries" of Nature. "I have now abrogated all claims to moral and spiritual teaching" he wrote to Samuel May—"I place myself in peaceful relations to the soil, as a husbandman intent on aiding its increase, and seem no longer hostile to the powers that be. My little cottage lies low and humble in the bosom of nature, under the sky of God, and I

[389]

am to ornament its walls and its acres by honor and independence."

We have seen what pleasure Alcott's contemporaries took in thinking of him as an "Orpheus at the plough." Emerson said that "after all his efforts on that most incorrigible of materials, man," Alcott was finding "a real comfort in working on that most corrigible and docile of all pupils, Nature." This was nearer the truth than his quite contradictory statement that Alcott did not love hard work. Many things go to show that he did love it—among them, the grounds at "Wayside" and at "Orchard House" as one sees them to-day. To be sure he did not find, any more than Emerson, that labor with axe and spade was conducive to the loftiest thinking; but he did find it conducive to lowly thinking and that, he was coming to see, was at least as good. "All moral grandeur," he said, "consists in stooping."

> Descent to the senses is ascent to the Soul. Did not the Son of Man take upon himself the fullness of human infirmities, and stoop to the washing of the Disciples' feet? . . . Ploughed my grounds. Began to set out some beets and turnips.

Nothing more surely than labor on the land persuades a man that not his will is to be done in this world but some other and greater Will. Nothing, therefore, could more swiftly have cured Alcott's brief attack of the reforming sickness, or returned him more promptly to his normal state of health as a teacher and a generator. His laboring of the soil, moreover, was to him a kind of worship. He planted beans and potatoes to the glory of God. His spading was in the nature of prayer, as his mowing in Concord meadows a few years before had been to him little short of a religious ecstasy. The echo of his humbler thoughts and pirations is heard even in his wife's Journal. Writing in April 1844, she says:

Removed to Still River Village, a quiet little nook in God's creation where, with his blessing, we will try to vegetate and bring forth abundantly of spiritual as well as material food. Our home is humble, but we have much comfort and few responsibilities. Mr. Alcott laboring unremittedly in his garden, producing rapid and beautiful changes. What a few days since was stone and stubble, a rude rough chaos, is now squared into neat regular beds and borders, verdure presenting itself and food promising for us. What a holy calling is the husbandman's! How intimately he relates himself to God!

And Alcott himself, slashing at the briars and tugging at the ardhack, made up a grim little philosophic jingle to mutter with hortened breath:

> Soul and muscle
> In mundane tussle—
> I deem sodding
> A sternest godding.

In the autumn of 1844 the Alcott family moved from Still River ick to Concord—for it had the habit now of moving at least ice a year—and occupied a few rooms in the farmhouse of Edund Hosmer on the eastern side of the town. There, on the first January, 1845, Hosmer negotiated the purchase, for thirteen indred and fifty dollars, of the "Cogswell Place," Emerson pay-ז five hundred dollars and Samuel Sewall eight hundred and fif-out of the bequest of Mrs. Alcott's father. On the first of April e family moved into the house, which they called "Hillside," d began extensive repairs within doors and without. They were ely needed, for the house was not then the sound and honest ucture that one sees to-day beside the Lexington Road, made ious as "The Wayside" by Hawthorne's occupancy, and the unds, then almost devoid of trees, were mostly bare gravel and d, except for the additions made by the hogs of Alcott's predecessor. The new landlord toiled through spring and summer and autumn, one day indoors with hammer and saw and the next outdoors with mattock and spade. Nothing could distract him. He read little, talked scarcely at all, and his Journal for that year was a grubby, diminutive, ill-conditioned book written quite evidently by a laborer's hand. He had a way of doing one thing at a time

In August came Charles Lane, greatly daring, to spend six weeks at Hillside. Bronson Alcott was courteous and hospitable but he was also deeply engaged. No sooner had Lane gone away to New York, and so out of Alcott's life forever, than the mos famous reformer then alive, Robert Owen, arrived and stayed two days. This man Owen had been one of Alcott's earliest teachers but Alcott cared little for reformers now. He was bent on gettin in his harvest.

And so Alcott's life proceeded for several years, with strenuot gardening from April to October and with swift and eager reac ing throughout the winter months. The bare record of his activit in 1846, for example, does not suggest that he was an indoler man. It may be given in his own words:—

1846

January: Write to Charles Lane, New York City; Thomas Davis, Providence; teach my children. Readings: Carlyle's Cromwell, Miscellanies, Heroes and Hero Worship, and Sartor Resartus. *February:* Visit the Concord Schools and address the children. Also Normal School at West Newton. Read Swedenborg's Animal Kingdom and Principia and Ritter's History of Philosophy, and teach my children. *March readings:* Richter's Life, Fichte's Destination of Man, Goethe's Faust, Wilhelm Meister, and Essays on Art, Coleridge's Friend and Church and State; also Behmen's Epistles. Children's school continued. *April:* Begin some planting, sodding and laying out of grounds. Also set apple, pear, peach trees. Readings: Goethe's Helena, or Faust second part, and the Fairie Queene to the girls. Conversation with some of my townspeople: Mrs. Barlow, Mrs. N. Brooke, Elizabeth Hoar, Henry Thoreau, Mrs. Emerson, and others. *May and June:* Gardening and improvements. Meet Emerson and my neighbors for Conversation. Readings: Bhagvat Geeta, Goethe's Correspondence with Bettina and Autobiography, also Downing's Landscape Gardening and Cottage Residence. Sunday readings at Emerson's to children. I pass Sunday with Emerson. *July–September:* Gardening and laying out grounds, busily. Harvesting, mowing, etc. Build a summer-house at Hillside, also garden and bathing-house. Meet Emerson and Thoreau often. Charles Lane sails for London. Readings: Landor's Pentameron and Wordsworth's Description of the Lakes. *October–December:* Harvesting and improvements. Purchase three acres of land of A. Moore for $75. Set apple trees.

Bronson Alcott was the only member of what may be called e "Concord Group" who kept a garden, assiduously and successlly, with his own hands. The spring and summer entries in his urnals during many years of his Concord residences are crowded th references to his flowers and vegetables, his trees, paths, ces, and summerhouses. By the time he had been at Hillside ree years his garden there, beginning at rather less than noth-, was recognized as the best in town. And yet, except for heavy ming, he did all of his work alone until old age came on. For imals of any kind he had little liking, and he never learned the mes of even the commoner birds, but one might almost have d that there was a natural consanguinity between him and the mbers of the vegetable kingdom. The pensile grace and lofty ancing of the Concord elms entranced him. Day after sum-r's day he would be up at dawn to see what new curves and

[393]

delicate spirals and unerring geometrical patterns had been impro
vised by some single grapevine spray in the arbor. Apple trees he
loved with the heart and delighted in with every sense. Was this a
renewal of the pleasure he had taken in the great old trees behind
the house at Spindle Hill? One who sees how all his days were
"bound each to each by natural piety" is inclined to think so. His
delight in country things was probably no more than the re
emergence of a taste and need which had been thwarted durin
most of the years since he had left his father's house. New trait
and interests, even new ideas, were seldom developed in him afte
he reached maturity. He grew from within, by a natural unfolc
ing.

When Emerson said that Alcott had "no senses" he had not ye
read that never-published manuscript, sometimes called "Th
Husbandman" and at other times "The Orchard," in which h
friend had written, like John Keats, for all the five senses at onc
There is certainly too much quotation of ancient authors in th
essay, and by far too much of banal platitude, but nevertheless
renders as only a strong affection could do the taste and textur
the shape and hue and odor of New England apples, togeth
with the lisping sound of apple leaves in the wind and the inte
lacing of sun and shade.

This interest in gardening and husbandry was never, of cours
utilitarian. It was æsthetic, intellectual, and, as we have seen,
most religious. To some extent it was even scholarly. Alcott re
the Latin agricultural writers—Cato, Varro, Columella—in
English translation from his own library, and he could lend th
writers to Thoreau in the original Latin. He read Abraham Co
ley's Essays almost every year, with a special lingering over
essay on Gardens. Bacon's essay on the same topic was famil
to him. He knew Gerard's *Herbalist*, Culpeper's *Herbal*, Co
Paradise of Plants, and Phillip Miller's *Gardener's Calendar*. F
Sir John Evelyn *Sylva* and *Acetaria* and *Gardener's Manual*
had a strong liking, and it is pleasant to think of him as trying

[394]

grow in the Concord meadows some of the same plants that
Charles the Second's courtier had tried so long before at Wotton
in Surrey—that is, in George Meredith's "Woods of Westermain."
Tusser's *Five Hundred Points of Good Husbandry* was the oldest
book of the kind that he knew in English, but he fed his love of
country life also upon the letters of Pliny, the pastoral poems of
Virgil and Theocritus, and even Hesiod's *Works and Days*.

Alcott's feeling for nature, however, is always that of the gardener, the husbandman, and the conscious artist; it is never that
of the naturalist, the hunter, or the frontiersman. He feels that

it is a pleasure to add something to the landscape, completing in some sort the design of nature. . . . The
hands were meant to be mates and servants of the eyes,
both conspiring to build beauty into the shows of
things. . . . A good man impresses his image on the
landscape he views daily, and imparts to it qualities
that remind him of himself. . . .

Gardens and orchards distinguish man properly from
the forester and hunter, who are such by ascendency
of the savage and animal life. The country, indeed,
as discriminated from the wilderness, is purely of man's
creation. His improvements are the country. The savage
has none. . . . Gardening, properly considered, is the
blending of man's genius with natural substance. It is
the intermingling of mind with matter, and a conversion
of the earth into man through the mind, the hands
assisting. . . . The woods do not belong to art nor
civility till they are brought into keeping with man's
thoughts, nor may they encroach upon us by nearness.
Graceful in the distance and stately as they are, they
appear melancholy and morose when crowded around
our dwellings. Like unkempt savages nodding saucily
at us, they need to be cropped and combed before they
are fairly taken into our good graces as ornaments of
our estates.

[395]

One must call it a remarkable thing that any American should have written such words as these in what was still the heyday of the American Romantic Movement. More closely related to the classical than to the romantic tradition, rather European than of the western hemisphere, and suggesting not so much the nineteenth century as the earlier half of the century preceding, they show an extraordinary independence of taste and judgment. Most American painters, poets, and fabricators of *belles lettres*, when they were written, were still celebrating the forest primeval—and not at all because America was really fond of that forest. If she had been, there might now be some of it left. No; the forest was still our obstacle, our enemy, and American art was glorifying it chiefly for the reason that Europe and England, tired of cities had made it a fashionable thing to do. Henry Thoreau himself, in so far as he was really a panegyrist of the wild and of the "noble savage," was by no means the bold way-breaker that some have thought him and praised him for being, but a quite conventional follower along old and beaten paths. The fresh and original thing and also the sound, right thing for an American to be saying in 1850 about our landscape was not that it should be left to sprawl in its own wild way but that it should be mastered, controlled humanized. And that is what Bronson Alcott did say—not only with his pen, as in the words just quoted, and not only by word of mouth in many a talk at Emerson's house and in the hut Walden Pond, but with spade and axe and hoe. If there had been ten thousand men saying the same thing in his time America would now be a fairer place. For Alcott's humanistic attitude toward Nature, though never utilitarian in itself, was such as utilitarians could have understood. On the other hand, it is precisely the opposite attitude, the sentimental and romantic feeling for "the wild," that has laid the American wilderness open for game slaughterers, stream-stiflers, converters of forest into match-sticks and the common horde of vulgarians generally, to trample and crush and almost destroy.

[396]

On a winter's evening of 1860 Thomas Wentworth Higginson lectured before the Concord Lyceum on "Barbarism and Civilization." Alcott tells us that the speaker "defended civilization against Thoreau's prejudice for Adamhood," and that after the lecture all three men went down to Emerson's house for further discussion of the topic. Of their talk Alcott reports:—

> I ask if civilization is not the ascendency of sentiment over brute force, the sway of ideas over animalism, of mind over matter. The more animated the brain, the higher is the man or creature in the scale of intelligence. The barbarian has no society; this begins in sympathy, the perception of personality binding generations in one. Thoreau defends the Indian . . . and thinks he holds a place between civilized man and nature, and must hold it. I say that he goes along with the woods and the beasts, who retreat before and are superseded by man and the planting of orchards and gardens. . . . Man's victory over nature and himself is to overcome the brute beast in him.

In this last remarkably compact and thoroughly "humanistic" sentence Alcott sums up a large part of his thought concerning not only the outer and "sub-human" world but also the inner world of thought and will and moral being. One sees that he regards these two worlds as by no means independent of each other. Most striking is the clear implication that the conquest of external nature should follow and not precede the inward victory. He would go farther, and assert that it cannot possibly precede. But once the brute beast within man has been overcome, then, Alcott means us to understand, every savage wilderness of the outer world is at once and automatically pacified, as though by mere reflection of man's now peaceful and ordered thought. The conception is almost inexhaustibly pregnant and profound, lying close as it does to the central core of Alcott's idealistic thinking. It would be interesting to show that Milton suggests much the same idea, although as it were in the reverse order, in making external Nature go "wild" after the fall of Adam; but our present concern is to relate this thought to Alcott's gardening and to indicate some of the ways in which it set him off from his associates in Concord.

Emerson's sympathies in this regard were, upon the whole, on the side of Thoreau. He did indeed keep a garden, but chiefly by the hired labor of other men; and he did grow pears—concerning which the Horticultural Society wished to be informed how he managed to produce "such poor specimens of such fine varieties." The garden of his choice, however, was the wild one at Walden Pond, where he grew mainly thoughts and moods and tenuous intimations. Subtle-brained, hypersensitive, over-refined, a product of all the learned centuries, he touched earth like Antæus in those untamed acres, and doubled his strength at each return. How characteristic of both men was his complaint that when he took Alcott with him on his daily walk—and that would be nearly always in the direction of the Pond—his friend would stop for a talk at the first fence-rail and would soon propose that they turn back! For indeed the miscellaneous, if not quite aimless, wandering-about among Concord fields and woodlots in which Emerson and Thoreau and Ellery Channing indulged themselves for the better part of every afternoon was not at all to Alcott's taste When it was a matter of going somewhere he could take step for step with any man, but he did prefer to have a definite goal. Tha goal was usually a Mind, or, better still, a group of Minds, an not some undiscovered country in the woodland which was value by Channing and Thoreau precisely because mankind had neve been there. If he went to the wildwood it was to bring back som curiously curved or twisted bough for his summerhouse or h fence, or else to get a young tree for the plantation with whic he gradually transformed the long sandy hill behind his two hous on the Lexington Road. Aside from a few social merrymakin and picnics, in which he always gaily joined when he had not be their instigator, one does not hear of his having anything to with the Concord River, that broad curving band of liquid topaz and sardonyx charged with somnolent mystery which meant almost unutterable things in the imaginations of his associates. Take the Concord River out of the poetry and prose of Thoreau, Emerson, Channing,—even of Hawthorne in his earlier Concord days,—and a yawning gap would be left; but in the writing of Alcott its total absence would not be observed. And the simple reason is that through nearly all their thirty miles between Framingham and Lowell the river-meadows, assisted by the wide spring freshets, have always held mankind aloof, providing asylum chiefly for the turtle and muskrat, for the redwing and coot and wading heron. Alcott never called the river, as its lovers liked to do, by its beautiful Indian names, Musketaquid and Assabet. The aboriginal names of Concord hills—Annursnack, Ponkawtasset, Nawshawtuckt, and the rest—almost never occur in his pages. To his feeling, Concord was not an intrusion of civilized men upon a savage settlement. Rather it was and had always been an American village founded by Englishmen; and he loved the English names of its streets and districts—Old Virginia Road, Kibbe's Place, Nine Acre Corner, Seven Star Lane. In short, he took his stand on the side of civilization.

That was because he had a clearer notion than any of the men about him as to what civilization has cost. Among the transcendentalists—unless one wishes to include Theodore Parker—he was the only husbandman, the only mind that could take its view of things natural, human, and divine, from the steady and central point of view of the man who works on the land. Emerson, born in Boston and Harvard-bred, had "gone back" a good way toward that wild nature which Thoreau had scarcely ever left; yet it always remained to him largely a spectacle rather than a stern antagonist, and he never allowed enough in his praise of the spectacle itself for the two centuries of human toil that had been spent upon it. But Alcott had been taught by the boulders and brush of Spindle Hill that man's task is to tame Nature, to put it under his feet and keep it there. With his memories of briar-thickets and stony fields, of storm in the Great Dismal Swamp and of his unending strife with the gravel at Hillside and Orchard House, there was small danger of his ever wandering off into the simply inexperienced notion that "Nature is ancillary to man." And the pantheistic deification of Nature toward which his daily companions were always drifting was equally remote from him.

Bronson Alcott was neither a naturalist nor a "primitivistic dreamer." In his attitude toward Nature, at any rate—and what attitude is more revealing?—he was the reverse of romantic. Hardly any famous passage in the world's literature would have been less comprehensible to him than Cowper's world-sick cry:—

> O for a lodge in some vast wilderness,
> Some boundless contiguity of shade!

Although he spent his life near the Atlantic seaboard and in a society which had forgotten what the forest had once been, his feeling for the wilderness was still that it must be subdued. Thus he looked forward in imagination, as Thoreau looked backward to the time before the white man came. But Alcott's thought was in keeping also with the greater human past. Allowing always for the mystic in him, ever ready for an "impulse from the vernal wood," he could have sympathized with the remark that Socrates made to young Phædrus as they two lay beside the Ilissus outside of Athens: "Trees and country places cannot teach me anything, but men in cities can."

Clearly, one does not soon exhaust the implications and consequences of this idea, originally acquired in hard labor on the land, that man's duty is to impose a human stamp, leave the mark of mind, upon a raw and recalcitrant Nature. At times one is almost tempted to attribute Alcott's transcendental thought as a whole not to any book—even Plato or Coleridge—that he ever read but to the fact that from boyhood to old age he was accustomed to toil in the open air with his hands, and to think while toiling.

Certainly we come closer to his mystery when we regard him as a reflective laborer than we do in trying to explain him as a mere intellectual living for thought alone. It may have been brush-clearing, wood-chopping, sodding, which suggested to him that Nature is lower than we are. Thence may have come his early dualism, and perhaps even that strange doctrine of "Genesis," according to which all the forms and matter of the world are only figments of mind. His building of stone walls may well have suggested what some other American—was it not Henry Ward Beecher, that other country boy from the hills of western Connecticut?—was to call the essential and inherent "cussedness of things." Would it be entirely fanciful to derive from this Alcott's doctrine of the "Adversary," and his theory of evil, far outreaching that of Emerson?

At any rate, it was Alcott who said: "Man's victory over Nature and himself is to overcome the brute beast in him." This was one of the profoundest and also one of the most civilized remarks ever made in Concord.

One sees the radical difference between all this and Whitman's warm luxurious wallowing in the landscape, so suggestive of the habits of the dinosaur, and also the distinction between it and Thoreau's cherished fancy of spending a whole day sunk up to the chin in a sphagnum swamp, conversing with the frogs. Therefore it is the more interesting to know and remember that Alcott was one of the first and most discerning of Walt Whitman's admirers, and also that he was one of the warmest friends Henry Thoreau ever had. He could hold a theory with absolute conviction, could urge an idea with the intensity of passion, and yet love the man who disagreed with him entirely. Nay, more; he could enter into such a man's disagreement, see it from the inside, express it with perfect fairness, and hold it up for admiration. In all the annals of letters one does not know where to find a more beautiful magnanimity than was shown on those many winter evenings of 1847 when Alcott walked out to Walden Pond through

[401]

the snow or rain to hear Thoreau read his long manuscript of *The Week*, based upon thoughts and feelings in many of which the listener did not believe at all.

The genius of Thoreau was recognized by Alcott before there were any clear signs of it to show the world. Alcott recognized and described the peculiar kind of Thoreau's genius long before even Emerson had addressed himself to the task. When living in Boston in 1851 he wrote, one November day:

> Henry Thoreau comes and passes the afternoon and evening; also sleeps under my roof. A very welcome guest, this countryman. I meet nobody whose thoughts are so envigorating as his, and who comes so scented of mountain breezes and springs, so like a luxuriant clod from under forest leaves, moist and mossy with earth-spirits. His company is tonic, never insipid, like ice-water in the dog-days to the parched citizen. . . . Here is a solid man and valid, sane and salt, and will keep forever—a friend who comes never too often nor stays too long—comes, it may be, a little unwillingly, as streams descend into the urban valleys below, yet sighing as they descend as leaving their mountain springs behind.

There was something paternal in Alcott's feeling for this strange and crotchety young man, eighteen years his junior. Everything that Thoreau wrote or did, every surprising thing he said, was promptly recorded with appropriate comment in Alcott's Journal. Indeed if the record in those Journals is to be trusted as an index one must say that the growth of Thoreau's literary reputation meant more to Alcott than that of his daughter Louisa, although that too meant much. Henry Thoreau was the first of a rather long succession of young men—Ellery Channing, William T. Harris and Frank Gunsaulus among them—to whom this man who never had a son felt somewhat as a father feels. In everything that Alcott said of Emerson veneration is mingled with a love that never quite found a voice, but in all his remarks about Thoreau affection is mingled with a fatherly pride.

And there is evidence enough that this affection was returned. Alcott was a welcome visitor by night or day at the Walden hut, for the construction of which he had lent his axe and which he had helped to raise. Thoreau's account of him—as given in the original manuscript of *Walden*, which differs considerably from the printed version—is a remarkable panegyric:—

> I think that he should keep an inn, a caravansery, on the world's highway, where the thinkers of all nations might put up, and on his sign should be written: "Entertainment for Man, and not for his beast. Enter all ye that have leisure and a quiet mind, who earnestly and without anxiety seek the right road." A thought floats as serenely and as much at home in his mind as a duck pluming herself on a far inland lake. He is perhaps the sanest man, and has the fewest crotchets, of any I chance to know—the same yesterday and to-morrow. Of yore we had sauntered and talked and effectually put the world behind us; for he was pledged to no institution in it—free-born, *ingenuus*. There we worked, revising mythology, rounding a fable here and there, and building castles in the air for which earth offered us no worthy foundation. Whichever way we turned, it seemed that the heavens and the earth had met together, since he enhanced the beauty of the landscape. A blue-robed man, whose fittest roof is the overarching sky, which reflects his serenity. I do not see how he can ever die. Nature cannot spare him.
>
> Great Thinker! Great Expecter! to converse with whom was a New England Night's Entertainment. Ah, such discourse as we had—hermit and philosopher and the Old Settler I have spoken of—we three! It expanded and cracked my little house.

[403]

THE TOWN OF AGREEINC
MEN

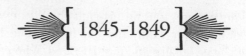

{ 1845-1849 }

A lover of little towns—The coldness of Concord—The Conco
group—A new kind of New Englander—Emerson's summ.
house—Hillside—Kindness to insects—Father and daught

CONCORD was dear to Bronson Alcott. He had gone th
to be near Emerson, but he had learned to love the town
its own account. Always it seemed just on the point of satisfy
that taste for the "villageous," as Thoreau called it, which persis
in him through all his life. Boston fascinated him, but he co
never love it. Forces of attraction and repulsion kept him fore
going up to Boston with high hopes and coming away again v
a mild disgust; and if Boston had been New York or Paris or L
don the result would have been the same. Disliking both the
and the wilderness, he longed for a third thing—not a mere c
promise between them but a vital union of neighborly men
women with a humanized Nature.

Whether because of the Saxon in him or on account of m

:ies of Spindle Hill, Alcott was one of the few Americans who
ive clearly and steadily imagined the ideal of the little town;
id he was always hoping, even expecting, that Concord would
me day fulfill his dream. He loved its old houses and trees and
e long lovely hill extending all the way from the center to Mer-
im's Corner. How beautifully the slopes of that hill had been
olded by the centuries of human use! What a gray antiquity the
wn had! How the dust of the earth and of man had been inter-
ingled there! On the hoary old burial hill, where the fathers
pt under their moss-grown monuments among the quivering
:ust shadows, imagination plunged back and backward into
ie and found no end.

Alcott would have been glad to serve this beautiful old town.
every way open to a man who, in his more active years, did not
nmand the full respect of the townspeople, he did serve it.
tried to draw Concord together, as the people of Spindle Hill
d been drawn. His Conversations in the village parlors, his
ekly meetings with "poor children," and, most of all, his work
Superintendent of Schools, gave him a deep, scarcely definable
asure. They gave him a hope that he might some day really
elong."

But Concord finally disappointed Alcott. It did not take him in.
ncord people were not "proud"; they did not give the impres-
n, like a certain class in Boston, that they had a sacred citadel
defend; and, as individuals, they were hospitable and kind
ugh. But what and where *was* Concord? Could one find it
hered in church or club or friendly circle anywhere, at the Ly-
m, or even at Town Meeting—or was it merely so many small
te houses scattered along the river-meadows under their sep-
te trees? Simon Willard, the founder, had said that the name
he place should signify "the town of agreeing men," but now,
centuries later, where was the agreement? Great individuals,
ainly, the town still had, and Alcott could never quite express
gratitude for them.

[405]

I am not unmindful [said he] of this best gift of the gods, seldom granted to one mortal—the enjoyment of such contemporaries as these: having a Thoreau if I will betake me to Walden; at the Road Forks I may have Saadi, Confucius, and Zoroaster; and without stirring abroad I have Belus, Minos, Memnon, and the Sphinx.

Yet these wonderful individuals would never cohere even und the magic of such an impresario as himself. If one could spe of the Concord thinkers as a "group" at all, then they were group of infinitely and mutually repellent particles. What shou have been, in Alcott's opinion, a community of minds fired by common purpose, fused by common ideas and enthusiasms, ar surely, warmed by some sense of affection, fell apart and was d membered into Henry Thoreau, Ralph Waldo Emerson, Nathan Hawthorne, Ellery Channing, Bronson Alcott, and the rest. was deeply perplexing. Was not the whole of America and all i wild, matter-worshipping, dollar-collecting age against the Why, then, should they not stand together?

Thoreau was showing the warmth of his human affections, v doing his part in the shaping of a Concord Mind, by living al at Walden Pond and pursuing his amours with a scrub-oak. it Elizabeth Hoar who had said of Henry that "one would as s take the arm of an elm tree"? The implication was not quite t for there were depths in Henry of which the world knew little, : he himself had said that "the flowing of the sap under the rind of trees is a tide which few suspect." But why should a r pretend that he was really a tree? Why this elaborate conc ment of the fact that a fully equipped human being has a hea

Then there was Ellery Channing, capricious and evanes and cold as a will-o'-the-wisp. One day he would come and sit talk by the hour—talk brilliantly, learnedly, and almost li person of this world. On the morrow he would pass you by in

[406]

reet without a nod or a glance. Ellery's wild gray eye seldom met
᷉e eye of another man, and if for an instant it did so then it
᷉uld go darting off into unimaginable fastnesses of retreat. No
᷉e had ever seen him in any assembly. Like the shadowy uni-
rn, he stalked alone. Such a votary of solitude he was that one
᷉ight almost think the two lobes of his brain held no intercom-
᷉nication. At any rate, he would never think or talk on more
᷉an one side of any question at a time. On Monday he would
᷉rse Carlyle and all his works until one began to regard that
᷉rmudgeonly Scot as the worst writer who had ever spoiled good
᷉per, but on Tuesday morning Ellery would come round to ex-
᷉in the many ways in which Carlyle was really superior to
᷉akespeare.

᷉And yet if one decided that Ellery Channing was the hardest
᷉n to draw into human association, that would be only because
᷉ had forgotten Hawthorne—the "boned pirate," as Ellery
᷉ed him—who always looked, in any assembly of men, as Henry
᷉es kindly remarked, like a criminal at a convention of de-
᷉ives. Living next door to Hawthorne for year after year, Al-
᷉ saw him perhaps once a month as he glimmered up and
᷉n on the hilltop, making one think of a wild Indian's way of
᷉ting from tree to tree. Once or twice he ventured down the
᷉d-paths to sit on the edge of a chair in Alcott's study; but
᷉er he perched there, like a great black bird crouching and
᷉ly for flight. How did he know at what moment Mrs. Alcott
᷉ht appear at the door? And once, only once, he had appeared
᷉merson's house during a Conversation—had sat there, dressed
᷉lack, among the shadows under the bust of Dante, uttering
᷉even so much of a word as Poe's raven, but warily peering out
᷉he assembled company from behind the impenetrable *che-
᷉:-de-frise* of his mustache. One could see that he was taking
᷉tal notes of this odd stiff company of men, each of whom was
᷉g perfectly silent with one question in mind: "Who will now
᷉eed to utter the profoundest thing that ever was said?"

[407]

Was it that they gave each other stage fright? Or was it no
rather, that each man regarded himself as an audience and all tl
others as his spectacle? At any rate they stood off and watched ai
listened, with results not highly conducive to good fellowshi
Every one of them knew that every one was keeping a priva
Journal and was making his daily observations upon all the re:
Self-consciousness was hard to avoid. Each man pretended,
least, to be a devotee of solitude, but what he actually found
Concord was more like the fierce and unremitting publicity
monastic life.

Of course there was always Emerson. Indeed, if there had i
been Emerson there would scarcely have been any others. A
yet—how was one to make quite clear, without any derogati
from one's deep sense of gratitude, that other dull and achi
sense, increasing from year to year, of disappointment? Oh, it v
not that Emerson's thought disappointed expectation; or at ε
rate that was not the main thing. Neither was it that Emer:
fell below his early promise as a rhetorician, as a past master
the delicate art of saying whatever could come into his mind
be said. And certainly Emerson's reputation, even his influe
both at home and abroad, was all that one had foreseen far b
there in the days of early acquaintance. But there was sometl
else—something that Henry and Ellery felt too, in their diffei
ways. It was that Emerson held one off. He seemed to fear s
invasion of his sacred places. As though that could ever be
sible!

Emerson had been most kind. He had been generous past
lieving. With a family of his own to support and with no I
means to support it, he had quietly taken his stand, ah, n
a time, between the Alcott family and sheer destitution. He
given much money, some encouragement, good counsel accor
to his lights, a little criticism, mostly adverse, and many pag
sufficiently laudatory comment, or so he said, in his private
nals. Alcott had never seen those pages, nor did he care t

[408]

hem. Emerson said that he was making a separate book of notes
or the essay or biography that he would write about his friend
fter that friend was gone. That is, Emerson would do for Alcott
hat he had already done for Margaret, now that she had returned
> the dream-people who loved her. And that, of course, would be
kind and generous deed; but in the meanwhile one felt more and
ore as one walked past the house at the road-forks that it was
tter not to intrude upon the great and famous scholar's privacy.
ow and then Alcott would meet Emerson on the daily excursion
the post office, and then might walk the half-mile homeward
th him and hear what he was doing, writing, and thinking now.
every such occasion there would be a note written down that
ening in the Journal at Hillside or at Orchard House. Once
en it was raining Emerson had suggested that Alcott take his
m so that they might walk together under the same umbrella!
ly with difficulty, one fancies, did Alcott restrain himself from
tering in red ink the record of that event.

It was clear that Emerson gave all he could—even, in some
se, all that he had to give. And Alcott knew that this was much.
ain and again he broke forth in hosannas of thanksgiving for
boon of association with the greatest mind, or certainly with
greatest and most beautiful person, that his world contained.
nobly the mind and the spirit were served in those hundreds of
g deep talks by Emerson's fireside, under the organ-toned pines
Walden, or else at Hillside and Orchard House! And yet in spite
ll that Yankee reticence and manly pride could do to stifle the
lization, it came to this, that Emerson admired Alcott and Al-
loved Emerson. He loved him much as Margaret had done,
as Henry and perhaps even Ellery still did. All four of these
ld have loved Emerson, one feels confident, if he had never
ten a line and if his name had never been heard beyond the
ndaries of the town. For, quite independent of the marvelous
d and beautiful voice and the arch-angelic glory-snatching elo-
nce that all the world could honor, there was something name-

[409]

less in Emerson that made the heart bow down in a simple, hum
ble, and half-adoring love which asked and expected no return
And no return did it get.

Emerson almost knew this himself. He half-suspected tha
there was frost in his blood. What else can he have meant by h
sorrowfully noble poem "Rubies"? Perhaps it was around tha
inward chill that a large part of his "philosophy" was gathere
unconsciously, as a concealment and a protection. Did he find
almost impossible to meet the friendliest advances with a warr
frank welcome? Why then, "We descend to meet." Did he feel
scholar's shrinking from the raucous multitude? "Society ever
where is in conspiracy against the manhood of every one of i
members." Did even the gatherings of the faithful assembled f
divine worship irk him? "God is here within." Was he troubl
and inept in every effort to work with others? "Dear heart, ta
it sadly home to thee that there will be and can be no coöper
tion."

Even to-day it is hard to set down these phrases in such a cc
nection without seeming to imply a blame one does not inter
Alcott never set them down or thought of them in connection.
implied no blame and made no complaint.

Yet Alcott did feel cold in Concord. Nearly everyone was p
tending that several degrees of social frost was good for thinki
as though ideas were Baldwin apples on a New England hillsi
Emerson was saying that "to hardy natures cold is genial a
dear." Thoreau was writing an essay on "Friendship" that bur
like ice. Everyone was trying to show how fond he was of
neighbor by remaining far away from him. But perhaps t
were carrying the thing a little too far when even Hawtho
came down from his retreat among the pines and complaine
Alcott that he "did not see anyone nowadays." It had gone
yond reason when Emerson himself wrote concerning a long
with Thoreau:—

[410]

We stated over again, to sadness almost, the eternal loneliness. . . . How insular and pathetically solitary were all the people we knew.

But the clearest statement comes from Alcott, the one man of the group who really knew what a group might be. Writing one night in March 1848, he said:—

I asked Thoreau if it were not a proof of our ineffi-ciency that we had not as yet attracted some fine soul, some maid from the farmer's hearth or youth from farm or workshop to our houses, and there found a proof undeniable of having a positive and real existence here in this world. . . . Neither by Lyceum or other manner has anything like a real intercourse been had between ourselves and our townspeople. . . . It is the office of a great life that it shine abroad and educate all within its neighborhood, and instruct if not the adult, the youthful population who are nearest to it. But between us and our townspeople only relations the vaguest, and in most instances of a character wholly fabulous, exist. We are ghosts and spectres, chimeras, rumors, holding no known relation to the fields and houses where we are supposed or seen to abide; and our deal-ings with men have an aspect ridiculous and to be made game of at the bank and bar-room. Our very virtues are mythological.

How sensible and sound, after all, this is! Hitherto the admirers Henry Thoreau and his companions have assumed that if Con-l did not also admire their hero the fault must have been Con-l's alone. But is it not always part of a man's duty to make self as much as possible understood?

lcott, one sees, was a new kind of New England man. To put riefly, he belonged to the social kind. Independence and indi-uality were quite as dear and sacred to him as to any Yankee

one might name, but he saw no need of keeping them in a glas
case. To him they were not private possessions, curios to be take
out and fingered, admired, exhibited to one's friends, and then re
turned to the cotton batting. Their value, he thought, lay in the
currency.

But what success did Alcott have with these views in the Co
cord of his time, and how "current" did he actually become there
His acquaintance among the townspeople was remarkably limite
Mrs. Sarah Ripley, the learned lady of the Old Manse, certain
one of the most remarkable persons the town contained and
good transcendentalist into the bargain, figures hardly at all
his Journals. Perez Blood, the local astronomer, and Cyrus Stov
the retired butcher, he never mentions. There is no evidence th
he had anything to match Thoreau's acquaintance with to
drunkards, human derelicts, and poor Irish; and by persons at
other end of the social scale he was hardly accepted at all. I
standing in the town during his lifetime is vaguely indicated
the fact that the excellent bust of Alcott which the Concord F
Public Library has long possessed does not stand in that dignif
semicircle of local worthies which greets the visitor at his entrar
but is to be found only by the curious and persistent in a m
less conspicuous place. At Orchard House—the house that Br
son Alcott made and loved and lived in delightedly for more t
twenty years, the house that Louisa inhabited rather relucta
when she could not, for one reason and another, live in Bosto
one reads on the sign at the gate that this was "the home
Louisa M. Alcott."

Although such matters have a certain significance, prima
humorous, they are of little moment in comparison with Alc
failure to make a coherent company of his own peers. And
after all, what was to be expected? Here were half a dozen t
scendentalists, each of them bristling with sensitive peculia
and each waiting like a stiffly separate lightning-rod for a sep
flash to fall. Here were five or six isolated particles of a Protes

[412]

m that had gone on protesting until there was no human asso-
ation left, and one was likely to meet even with God only "in
ie bush." Here was a handful of brilliant and even intelligent
en each of whom insisted upon standing like a solitary sentinel
i his own individual iceberg; and the icebergs were steadily
ifting apart. They were not the sort of men of whom social
oups are made, any more than joint-stock companies can be
mposed exclusively of bankrupts. Bronson Alcott pored over
e mystery and mourned over it. He did everything he could
out it except despair. Near the end of his life, for a few hal-
on summers, he did raise the local temperature considerably by
ransfusion of Western warmth. Once and again he turned the
issippi, so to speak, into the Concord River, so that it was
t so hard to make sure which way that placid stream was flow-
;. But by that time all the other lonely men whom he would so
dly have brought together were gone.

During the summer of 1847, in spite of his loneliness, Alcott was
ipy. Emerson, who was soon to go abroad, had asked him to
ld a summerhouse in his garden—not so much because Emer-
stood in need of a summerhouse, probably, as because he
ught his friend Alcott needed a congenial task. But that it cer-
ily was. Never in his life did Alcott work more *con amore* or
le down upon the common sense of his critics with a more
plete cheerfulness than he did when astride of Emerson's rustic
epole with a hammer in hand and nails in his mouth. For
e months and more, from the twelfth of August until Thanks-
ng Day, he could think of nothing but the "arbor." Like his
hing, like his reforming, like his observation of his own chil-
i, this new work absorbed every other interest and grew every
more grandiose. Soon it ceased to be an ordinary summer-
ie on which he was working, for the manufacture of which
rson had paid him fifty dollars. It became a "Bower" in which
'Bard" was to "entertain the Muses." There had to be nine

[413]

upright joists because the Muses were of that number. It was
work of love, and also a work of creative art carried out in a ne
manner—the manner of Bronson Alcott. "I call this my style
building the 'Sylvan' " said he—

> One merit is its simplicity. The curved rafters to
> the gables and the depending brackets under the cor-
> nice are original with me. . . . It occurred to me to-
> day, as I set my sweeping brackets, that I had seen
> the same style in pictures of the Egyptian architec-
> tures. Such things must originate in the One Idea of
> the Infinite Beauty and fitness of the curve over
> the straight line in building. The highest art will em-
> ploy the curve always. The serpentine is ever mystic.

Henry Thoreau, a geometrically-minded person and a survey
helped Alcott with some of the carpentry for a day or two.
liked straight lines. He said that he felt as though he were "
where, doing nothing." His views of architecture were eviden
unaspiring and utilitarian. So were those, apparently, of all
other citizens of Concord, most of whom turned up in the cou
of the summer and autumn to wonder and condemn. "My tow
people come every day to examine my work," wrote the wo
man.

> It would be quite amusing to report the remarks
> they make upon it, applying many strange epithets to
> this strange production of art. "It is odd," "the strang-
> est thing I ever saw," "a log cabin," "a whirligig,"
> etc. etc., are a few. It impresses all as something very
> curious, and belongs to a department of handicraft with
> which they are but vaguely familiar. The finest work
> of M. Angelo set in the market place would doubtless
> provoke as many and as alien remarks. It needs ac-
> quaintance with the state of mind from which a work of
> art is produced, on the part of the observer, in order
> to appreciate it and criticise it.

[414]

EMERSON'S SUMMERHOUSE

CONSTRUCTED IN EMERSON'S GARDEN
CONCORD, IN 1847–1848, BY BRONSON ALCOTT

After an original pencil sketch by Abby May Alcott

But the main thing, doubtless, was that Alcott was a happy
an. He wrote:—

> I seldom reach home from my work at Emerson's till
> quite dark; and, after a supper of cream, honey, and
> wheaten cakes, with apples and peaches, find myself
> pursuing my charming occupation to bed and all
> through the night long, in happy dreams; and when
> the morning comes it is with an urgency to resume my
> toil again as soon as the needful family chores are done,
> and I am at E's field with my hammer and saw again.

The summerhouse was not finally completed until the follow-
; year and, as soon as it was finished and stood forth in all its
ricate glory of "aspiring rafters" and "handsome curves," Mrs.
1erson dubbed it "The Ruin." This was disheartening—and, bees, the epithet may have been unfair, for it is certain that Emer-
. was asking Alcott to make a few repairs upon the building
y fifteen years later. He had found two serious impediments
.he entertainment of the Muses in his Bower: first that it did
exclude the rain, and then the fact that it admitted a vast num-
of mosquitoes. Otherwise, it had been entirely satisfactory.
his may be the best place in which to say, if the subject is not
trivial, that Bronson Alcott was always gentle with mosquitoes.
1 vegetarian he probably deplored their carnivorous, or rather
r "sanguinary" habits, but, on the other hand, as a Pythago-
. he disliked to destroy life. Self-defense might extend to wav-
1 mosquito aside, but never to slaughter. And the same forbear-
· was shown toward other insects. The legend still lives in
:ord that when Alcott was residing at Hillside and was keep-
1 vegetable garden in the meadow across the road he used
ys to collect his potato bugs in a can, being careful not to in-
them in any way, and then to dump them tenderly over the
: into Sam Staples' garden—Sam Staples being the famous
ty-sheriff who had an annual argument with Alcott about

[415]

the propriety of his paying his poll tax, and who could never se
any connection between the paying of such taxes and what th
Federal Government was doing to Mexico, or was refusing to d
for the slaves. He and Bronson Alcott remained always on the be
of terms.

Hillside was a pleasant home, far down there between the h
and the meadow, where the four Little Women played in a sort
merry desperation as though they knew their playtime would n
be long. They played by themselves in the great old barn, maki
up their own games, shaping their own toys, thinking out and c
ting and sewing their costumes for the little dramas that th
wrote and rehearsed and acted for themselves as audience. Su
childish paraphernalia as they had they made for themselv
mostly, out of the nearest and cheapest materials—exactly a:
certain boy had been doing forty years before on Spindle Hill
Connecticut. That same boy, although his hair was nearly wh
now, would often play with them in the barn or on the floor
up the hill. He was their teacher, too. He planned their dres:
tended them when they were ill, and got their meals. He told th
numberless stories about the time when he had gone pedd
and about his boyhood home. He read to them, every year, q
through the *Pilgrim's Progress*—until even the baby knew it
most by heart. He read the *Faërie Queene* to them and explai
its inward meanings so clearly that the youngest could underst
and the oldest would always know that there was more of mea
beyond. Sometimes he was stern. When one of them had spo
harshly to a sister, she was told that for that day she should
mind the baby. For some other childish error the penalty w
be exclusion from lessons or from housework in helping Mo
Louisa, with eyes and hair so strangely dark, and with the
sionate "demonic" disposition that Jakob Boehme had said i
always go therewith, was oftenest the sinner and the bitterly v
ing penitent. In February, 1847, the father wrote:—

[416]

I had a possessed one sitting by my side all winter; and it was remarkable to see what sway was exerted by the eye, the dialect of the moral sense, over the fancy of the damsel. . . . It was pathetic to see how inexorably her will was bound in chains, and that never . . . by her passions but only by the service of others could she put forth a hand or a foot or a faculty to serve herself.

But if the father was sometimes stern, he was always perfectly kind and gentle. Whenever one of them went to Boston to visit the Sewall cousins, there would come a letter from father, simple in thought and words but somehow beautiful. He had written to them all when he was away in England, years before:—

My dear Girls:

I think of you all every day and desire to see you all again: Anna with her beauty-loving eyes and sweet visions of graceful motions, of golden hues and all fair and mystic shows and shapes—Louisa with her quick and ready services, her agile limbs and boundless curiosity, her penetrating mind and tear-shedding heart, alive to all moving, breathing things—Elizabeth with her quiet-loving disposition and serene thoughts, her happy gentleness, deep sentiment, self-centered in the depths of her affections—and last, but yet dearest too in her joys and impetuous griefs, the little Abba with her fast falling footsteps, her sagacious eye and auburn locks. . . .

It was a characterization that would hold for the four Little women through all their lives.

Bronson Alcott failed in many things, but he did not fail as a father. With a wisdom never heavy or prosaic and with a gentleness that was always strong, he made for his children a home that was in itself an education. He had not come back from the gate of death for nothing. "My children," he wrote, in a letter addressed "to the Young Inmates of the Cottage" while supping around the hearth—

> I will show you what is beautiful, beautiful indeed: It is a pure and happy, a kind and loving family, a home where peace and gentle quiet abide . . . around whose hearth gather serene and loveful countenances, where every hand is quick to help, every foot swift to save, every eye agile to catch the wishes and every ear the wants of others; where every day is a long and well-gotten lesson of love and wisdom and patient resignation and steady trust in that Good and Generous Power that sends Health and Hope and Peace.

And he *did* show them, and it *was* "beautiful indeed." Neithe sentimentality nor the fear of it, which is a much more grievou thing, should prevent one from seeing that the home Bronsc and Abigail Alcott made for their children, in spite of povert and social disapprobation, was triumphantly beautiful. It is l this perhaps, chiefly, and not by his schools, his Conversatior his writings, or his reforms, that the friends of Alcott should wi him to be tried. It is when one thinks of him as a father—and n only of his children in the flesh but of the many young men a: women to whom his relation was warmly paternal—that he stan forth most clearly. Then it is, and perhaps then only, that o sees him "in focus," with every feature sharp and fine.

Alcott's love for his four daughters was certainly one of t deepest and highest things in his life. He would have said that loved them equally, though perhaps for different reasons. To th all—or to all but one—the mother had given a force and ene greater than his, but in each of them there was something of h self: in Anna his patience and shyness; in Louisa his power completely concentrated devotion; in Elizabeth his serenity; Abby May his æsthetic sensitiveness and manual skill. Yet Lo and Abby May were more like their mother, and the strong

[418]

Anna—though she was always very close to her father—did not seem so much to need him. But Elizabeth?—Bronson Alcott had a secret which probably no one ever suspected. He loved Elizabeth best of all.

Few families of children have grown up in America, or for that matter in the English-speaking world, that can be brought so vividly before the mind's eye as this little quartette that lived and worked and played at Hillside ninety years ago. The house itself and the meadow and the wooded hill that made their world are but little changed to-day, except that they are now more beautiful. In the Orchard House next door, into which three of them moved—but not, ah, not Elizabeth!—when they were young ladies, one may still see their dresses and shoes and toys, their childish diaries, the letters from their father and mother, and the letters they wrote in reply. And the whole makes a most delicate picture. As compared with the Brontë children, upon whom so much attention has recently been lavished, these children were less brilliant; they were also more normal and healthy. Indeed, no small part of the charm that one feels increasingly in studying this household is the charm of its normality and simple health. Hear Elizabeth, aged nine, talking to her Diary: "It was a sunny morning. I carried my dollies to the hill, then went to the village. I sat in a cherry tree and wrote my Journal. I read to Abba about Oliver Twist, and she cried because he was so poor." (The Alcott children were always very thoughtful about "the poor.") On the first of May in 1845 the child wrote her account of the merrymaking her father had devised, out of which Emerson, many years later, wove a famous poem:

Father took us to Mr. Emerson's in Mr. Watt's hay cart. We danced around the May pole, and I had a very pleasant time. Mr. Emerson said he would take us to ride in the woods. But it rained so we came home. After the shower Abba and I played in the barn. We made dirt cakes and a little wagon to draw our dollies in.

[419]

On the fourth of May the little girl wrote again:—

> After lessons I sat in my chamber and read "Un-
> dine." Mr. Emerson took us to ride. We went to the
> place where he is going to build a Lodge to study in.
> He drove us to Waldron Pond and took Gary Pratt,
> Ellen Emerson, and me in a boat. It was very pleasant
> on the water.—At breakfast father read about Jesus
> riding the colt in Jerusalem.

And so one leaves the four sisters who were one day to become
under a faint disguise of names but not of character, the most fa
mous children in America. So far as they knew they were ver
rich—or else how could their father and mother be always givin
things away to the "poor people," and why should the black sla
from Maryland have come to stay at their house for a month ar
to eat at the table with them and then be sent on to Canada wi
Father's money in his pocket? Ah, yes; they must be rich. And ce
tainly they were happy. Mr. Lane had gone back to England, ar
home would last forever.

[420]

THE FOUNTAIN OF
YOUTH

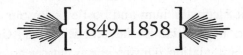

{ 1849-1858 }

*oston again–Conversations–The uses of adversity–Mr.
;eudo Pistos–"Pythagorean diets"–Boston Vigilance Com-
ittee–The fountain in Boston Common–Genealogy–Central
eas–"The Great Good Walt"–The Death of Elizabeth*

HE three years and a half at Hillside had been a longer stay
in one house than Bronson Alcott and his wife had ever be-
'e made during their married life. On the seventeenth of No-
nber, 1849, they moved to Dedham Street, Boston, and Alcott
ed a room for Conversations in West Street, next door to Eliza-
h Peabody's famous "atom of a bookshop."

The reasons for this change were partly financial. It was
ught that Alcott would be able to make more money in Boston
n he had in Concord—and that was certainly a moderate ex-
tation. Mrs. Alcott, moreover, who had never been fond of
1cord and who wished to be near her Boston friends and rela-
1s, hoped to be able to do something toward the family's sup-

[421]

port. But probably a more persuasive reason was the wish of both
husband and wife for a warmer social environment and a greater
stir of life. This they found. Mrs. Alcott was engaged by a
philanthropic society in the distribution of charity and she con
ducted for several years an agency for domestic servants. The
irony of these occupations, for a woman who was herself living in
no small degree upon the bounty of others and who seldom had
servant of her own, was not lost upon her. Often querulous but
always essentially brave and kind, she did her work well, and wo
the respect of all the many who knew her.

To Bronson Alcott the hum and bustle of Boston, coming afte
the quiet years at Fruitlands and Still River and Concord, wer
an immediate stimulation. During the twenty years since he firs
came to it by stagecoach from western Connecticut, the city ha
changed, developed, and ripened. For one writing or thinking ma
that it had formerly contained there were now ten, and most o
those ten could talk. However it might be in Concord, here in Bos
ton enough sticks had been brought together to make a fire. Mis
Peabody's shop, furthermore, was a rendezvous at which in th
course of a week one could see most of the persons of light an
leading within a circuit of twenty miles. It might almost have be
called a Transcendental Exchange—for although the Symposiu
was no longer meeting, transcendental thought was pushing o
into the world in wider and wider circles. Miss Peabody herse
who knew nearly everyone and everything, was the chief attra
tion there, although she carried the best stock of foreign boo
to be found in the city. Her enthusiasm for Alcott as a teach
had been transferred by this time to Friedrich Froebel, but
spite of that old unpleasantness about the Temple School s
was still Alcott's good and faithful friend. Her impression was,
doubt, that she had forgiven him.

Before Alcott had been in Boston a week he had posted a hu
dred or more printed cards with the following announcement:

Mr. Alcott proposes to open, on Saturday Evening, Dec. 9th., at his rooms in West Street, a Course of Conversations on Man—his History, Resources, and Expectations,—illustrated from the Experiences of the Company, and from the Text of the eminent Teachers of Mankind, ancient and modern. The course will comprise Seven Conversations, to be held on Saturday Evenings, weekly, beginning at 7 o'clock.

Tickets admitting a lady and gentleman at $5.00, and single tickets at $3.00, may be obtained at Miss E. Peabody's Bookroom, No. 13, West Street, and at the Bookstore of James Munroe & Co., 134 Washington Street.

The series of Conversations that thundered thus in the index included these remarkable topics: Man Monadic, Man Embrynic, Man Natural, Man Demonic, Man Humane, Man Intellectual, and Man Divine. What is more remarkable still, not a few of the more intelligent persons of Boston actually attended and took part in these Conversations. But the thing really difficult to believe is that many of the same persons were to be found in attendance upon Mr. Alcott's Conversations in following years. Such, however, are the facts, whatever may be their meaning. One must agree with Emerson's remark upon the phenomenon: "It is not the least characteristic sign of the times that Alcott should have been able to collect such a good company of the best heads . . . What was never done by human beings in another age is done now. There they met to discuss their own breath, to speculate on their own navels with eyeglass and solar microscope, and no man wondered at them." The only explanation that one can offer for this phenomenon is to point out that it occurred in Boston. These were stirring times for Bronson Alcott. While he was discoursing on "Man" in West Street, Emerson, on different days

[423]

of the week, was lecturing at the Tremont Temple on "London,"
"The Intellect," "The Superlative," and other topics almost a
vague as Alcott's own. After the lectures a considerable part o
the company, always including the lecturer himself, would repai
to Alcott's rooms for discussion of what had been said; and a lis
of those who were thus gathered at various times would includ
most of the better heads in the city. Forty years later Mrs. Edna
Dow Cheney was to recall those occasions with delight: "M
Emerson would offer his escort to one of his friends to walk t
these rooms, and Theodore Parker, Mr. Alcott, and other favore
guests followed. . . . The tones of his voice filled the night air wit
music, as if the winds of heaven were playing over an æolian harp

However it might have been in Concord, there was little chan
here for mental stagnation. On a Saturday night in February A
cott gave one of his Conversations on Man; on the next day
read the New Testament, heard Emerson lecture, and entertaine
twenty persons at his rooms; on Monday he rode to Cambrid
in the morning and spent several hours with James Russell Lo
ell, from whom he borrowed Cattermole's *Sacred History of t
Seventeenth Century,* Cottle's *Early Recollections of Colerid*
the Poems of Wither and those of John Donne. That same e
ning, back in Boston, Thoreau called.

A hearty friendship which did honor to both men sprang up
tween Alcott and Lowell. They were so far apart in almost eve
essential respect that each could like the other with a faint se
of amusement and could also find in him much to be admir
Lowell, in those days something of a transcendentalist, was lo
ing at Alcott as a painter does at his model—and with these lir
in part, as the result:—

> Hear him but speak and you will feel
> The shadow of the Portico
> Over your tranquil spirit steal
> And modulate all joy and woe
> To one subdued subduing glow.
> Above our squabbling business-hours

[424]

Like Phidian Jove's his beauty lowers;
His nature satirizes ours:
A form and front of Attic grace,
He shames the higgling market-place,
And dwarfs our more mechanic powers.

What throbbing verse can fitly render
That face, so pure, so trembling-tender?
Sensation glimmers through its rest,
It speaks unmanacled by words,
As full of motion as a nest
That palpitates with unfledged birds;
'Tis likest to Bethesda's stream,
Forewarned through all its thrilling springs,
White with the angel's coming gleam,
And rippled with his fanning wings.[1]

This was much for a man of Lowell's nature to have seen, and
the description of Alcott's mobile face with its occasional look of
almost ecstatic expectation is particularly valuable. But Lowell
saw the other side of the tapestry as well:—

So great in speech; but ah, in act
So over-run with vermin troubles!
The coarse, sharp-cornered, ugly Fact
Of life collapses all his bubbles.
Had he but lived in Plato's day,
He might, unless my fancy errs,
Have shared that golden voice's sway
O'er bare-footed philosophers.
Our nipping climate hardly suits
The ripening of ideal fruits.
To see him 'mid life's needful things
Is something painfully bewildering.
He seems an angel with clipped wings
Tied to a mortal wife and children,
And by a brother seraph taken
In the act of eating eggs and bacon.

[1] From "Studies for Two Heads."

The "ugly Fact," very coarse and sharp-cornered indeed, was, simply, that Alcott was desperately poor, and had by this time given up all hope, even he, of ever freeing himself from debt.

His poverty, to be sure, had never been mean. On the contrary, there had always been about it something grand and majestic, as there was in the "holy poverty" of the Ages of Faith. It had been a deprivation of the body alone, and had never corroded inward to the mind and the very soul. He had endured penury without ever becoming penurious, so that always in the extremes of his destitution he could be bountiful to those who were poorer than he. The story is told that after he had prepared the supper one evening at Dove Cottage he suddenly remembered a neighbor who, he feared, would have nothing whatever that night to eat. Making a rapid calculation, he divided what he had prepared into eight portions and sent one of them to his neighbor. As there were at that time just eight persons at his own board the probability is that he himself ate nothing on that evening. Rather well known is the tale of his giving the last of his winter's wood to a poor neighbor on a bitterly cold March day, and then bearing the reproaches of his wife with the cheerful assurance that "God would provide." When the last sticks were turning to gray ash on the hearth a woodsman turned in at the gate with a wagonload of billets which he asked permission to leave, as a storm was coming on and he would be unable to get to Boston. Still more familiar is the story of Alcott's giving a ten-dollar bill to a confidence man who had asked him for only five, and of his getting it back some months afterward, the "Jeremy Diddler" having been unable to endure the pangs of his conscience.

Instances of this kind were many. From the point of view of a society almost exclusively mercantile—and of a society, too, entirely Protestant, and therefore untouched by the beautiful Catholic legends of poor men's munificence—some of Alcott's benefactions looked ludicrous in the extreme. At the least, however, they showed that he had kept the innocence of the heart

Poverty had not conquered a man who could do such things. There is a possibility that wealth would have been a more dangerous foe.

But it was a small matter that Alcott himself had to do without all of the luxuries and most of the comforts of life. It was a far harder thing for him to bear, of course, that his family should be obliged to do without them—that Louisa, for example, who in her lithe and active youth loved country rambles, could seldom indulge in them because those of her stockings that had whole toes were so likely to be deficient in heels. But we begin to take the measure of Alcott's serenity only when we realize that during most of his middle years he lived on the bounty of friends and, worst of all, on that of his wife's relations. At various times and for various immediate needs he was given many sums, large and small, by Emerson, Lane, Sewall, Jonathan Phillips, Thomas Davis, Colonel May, Samuel May, James Eddy, and George Luther Stearns, to mention only those benefactors of whom one is sure. He usually called such gifts "loans," by a euphemism mutually understood. Yet there is no evidence that he ever lost the friendship or confidence of any man who had given or lent him money; and there is evidence in plenty that he walked the streets of Boston and Concord for many years owing money to tradespeople and citizens on every hand, but always holding his head high and looking as though he owned the town and the city. He was like Robinson's "man Flammonde" in this respect at least, that

> . . . what he needed for his fee
> To live, he borrowed, graciously.

And he could just as graciously decline to pay it back. There is gaiety, not to say an insouciance, in some of his references to his creditors which cannot fail to be positively shocking to certain classes of opinion. He lived and talked and wrote as though he thought the world owed him a living. And his friend Emerson evidently thought that it really did so when he said, recalling

Socrates' reply to the judges who had just condemned him to death, that Alcott was a man "who should be maintained at the public cost in the Prytaneum." And the mention of Socrates reminds one again of the distressing way Alcott had of accepting at face value the teachings of persons who are to practical men of the world no more than hallowed names. Socrates had apparently not spent much time, he reflected, upon his stone-carving. It was not recorded of Pythagoras that he worried about his grocer's bill. And as for Jesus, who had not where to lay his head, did he not distinctly say "Take no thought for the morrow"?

"Things seem strange to me out there in Time and Space," Alcott once wrote in a season of "family straits."

> I am not familiar with the order and usages of that realm. I am at home in the Kingdom of the Soul alone. This day I passed along our great thoroughfare, gliding with Emerson's check in my pocket into State Street, and stepped into one of Mammon's Temples for some of the world's coin. . . . It was the hour for business on 'Change, which was swarming with worshippers. Bevies of devotees were consulting on appropriate rites wherewith to honor their divinity. One of these devotees (cousin german of my wife) accosted me as I was returning and asked me to bring an oblation with the others. Now I owed the publican a round thousand which he had proffered me in days when his God had prospered his wits; but I had nothing for him. That small pittance which I had just got snugly into my fob (thanks to my friend E——) was not for him but for my wife's purse, and came just in time to save her from dismissing utterly the succours of Providence.

There is an almost startling suggestion of Mr. Micawber in these last words which makes it appropriate to say that Dicken and Bronson Alcott never met; but there is also an undertone of complete self-respect in the whole passage which the bourgeo world of to-day must find difficult to understand. Alcott's own time found no less difficulty, for it was not a time remarkably gentle with the insolvent. If he had contracted his debts only a generation earlier he might have spent a good part of his life in jail. Even in 1830, when his indebtedness was already considerable, there were some fourteen hundred persons in the jails of Boston who had been imprisoned for debt alone, and in the preceding year there were seventy-five thousand debtors in the jails of the United States, more than half of whom were being held for sums less than twenty dollars.

So good a friend as Samuel May found it impossible to understand Alcott's attitude toward money—or rather toward the lack of it; and even Mrs. Alcott admitted that it was "very difficult to explain." Where they failed, in spite of their intimate knowledge and their strong pride and affection, there would seem to be little chance of success for a much more distant commentator. Yet the problem cannot be avoided, lying so close as it does to Alcott's "idealism" and connected so obviously with the effect that he made upon his world. It is not wholly unconnected with his effect upon us, for there are still a few people alive who feel that it does not much matter what a man thinks and does unless he can pay his bills, and that no man is entitled to self-respect unless he is respected by his butcher.

One may say to begin with that few or none of Alcott's contemporaries whose opinions are worth recording ever seriously entertained the notion that he was either lazy or a "dead beat." All who knew him were convinced that he had some reason, hardly statable even to himself and yet somehow sufficient to his conscience, for an almost complete abstention from money-making activity. They only asked what this good reason might be.

There are definite advantages in a distant point of view, and one that it enables us to see environing circumstance. Now the environment of Alcott's life was almost exclusively bourgeois, but he never accepted the central bourgeois doctrines and dogmas. He missed them on both sides, being by birth not far removed from what in Europe is still called the peasant class and being by taste and intellect intensely an aristocrat. Like most deeply thinking men and most artists, he belonged, really, to no class; but least of all did he belong to the lower middle, of which the America of his time was chiefly composed. The proper allowances should be made.

But it was not merely that Alcott refused to accept the bourgeois standards of his time and place. He was convinced that they were hostile to that higher life of the Mind and Spirit which he thought it his main business in life to exemplify. Having seen him turn away from the factories on the Naugatuck, from the new West, from peddling, and from a proposal which would have doubled his salary in return for a slight change in his emphasis as a teacher, we must admit that, whether he was right or wrong in this conviction, he was at least consistent. In a land, furthermore, in which nearly every able-bodied male was living as though the collection of dollars was the chief end of existence, it may well have seemed his duty to make his abstention from such collecting as conspicuous as he could.

We should remember, too, that during Alcott's boyhood and youth on Spindle Hill he saw and handled little money. Every household in that closely knit community strove to be economically independent by raising and manufacturing most of the necessities of life, and the community as a whole did not fall far short of such independence. The immemorial custom of barter was by no means forgotten there. Alcott had seen his own father exchange ox-collars and whiffletrees and baskets for such needments as his own shop and farm did not produce. May not this have suggested that ideas too ought to be exchangeable for the world's more ponderable goods? And his rather superficial observations among the Southern planters did nothing to correct that suggestion. So far as he could see, those elegant gentlemen toiled not at all. Their wives did not even spin. And yet Solomon in all his glory—we the coat from Broadway with which Bronson had dazzled the maidens of Spindle Hill and saddened his father's heart revealed what he had thought of how those gentlemen had been arrayed.

One sees that Alcott was simply unfortunate with regard to the whole profoundly serious morality of money. As others are smitten with inherited kleptomania, so he was marked in his innocent youth with an indifference to personal possessions which almost passes belief. And it is clear that a man with such deficiencies, amounting almost to a taint in the blood, would fall an easy prey to the "no-money" theories of Alcott House and of enthusiasts like his friend Edward Palmer. Yet he never quite went their distance. He was always serenely content that others should own many things, many dollars, if only he might "borrow" and enjoy them.

Perhaps the main question is whether, in any sense and in any kind of goods that the world stood in need of and could be induced to consume, Alcott "paid his way." By way of answer to that question, there is a perfect "emblem" of his entire life in the pleasure trip he once took on the Nantasket boat. During the first half-hour out from Boston he delighted his fellow-passengers by a continuous flow of gay and yet thoughtful talk; but when the purser asked for his ticket there came into his eyes a vague and dreamy expression, as of one who had never yet despaired of the "succours of Providence." The trip, he said, had attracted him and he had been enjoying it, and he doubted not even yet that "some provision would be made." It *was* made, and the stream of talk went purling on.

Well, is it possible that seventy years of talk from Bronson Alcott may really have been as valuable, even to the pursers of America, as a few passenger-tickets more or less? Many were the fellow-passengers, we may be sure, who enjoyed their life's voyage a good deal more because Bronson Alcott went along.

For we must not ignore the fact that Alcott had a calling, a profession, at which he worked hard all his days. He was a thinker, a teacher, a "Dedicated Mind"—and if America had not yet provided for the support of such a person he must not turn aside on that account from his divine mission but must make what arrangements he could. He stood ready, and eager, to give his life; and all that he asked in return was a bare livelihood.

Just here we come closest to the solution of our problem. Alcott was a teacher who had been thrust forth from his holy vocation for reasons which he never accepted as any fault of his own. During the last forty years of his active life he was always striving to get back into the work of that high calling, or was keeping as near to it as he could; and to that end he held himself as far as possible above the mire and squalor of the economic struggle. There were certain things that a teacher, a thinker, a "Dedicated Mind," ought not to do, and these were the things that men do merely for financial reward. Such things he would not, and perhaps could not, do. To him, as to Thoreau and Emerson, it was a matter of first-rate importance, a matter of the soul's honor, that a man should earn his livelihood by those activities only which sprang from his deepest nature. Anything else was prostitution. One might illustrate this feeling and belief from many a page of *Walden,* but Emerson's words go straight to the mark: "Alcott holds the school in so high regard that he would scorn to exchange it for the Presidency of the United States. The school is his Europe; and this is a just example of the true rule of Choice of Pursuit: you may do nothing to get money which is not worth your doing on its own account."

There is no evidence that Alcott ever stipulated a fee for his services in conducting Conversations arranged by others. Always he took what he was offered, without a word other than simple thanks; and when he was offered nothing, as frequently happened, his thanks for the pleasure of talking with such interesting people were always forthcoming just the same. In October, 1853, he started on his first "Tour at the West"—"so poor," as Louisa said, but "so hopeful, so serene." About four months later he turned

[432]

up at 20 Pinckney Street on a cold and rainy night. Louisa's Journal tells the story unforgettably:—

> We were waked up hearing the bell. Mother flew down crying "My husband." We rushed after, and five white figures embraced the half-frozen wanderer who came in hungry, tired, cold, and disappointed, but smiling bravely and as serene as ever. We fed and warmed and brooded over him, longing to ask if he had made any money; but no one did till little May said, after he had told all the pleasant things, "Well, did people pay you?" Then, with a queer look, he opened his pocket-book and showed one dollar, saying with a smile that made our eyes fill, "Only that. My overcoat was stolen and I had to buy a shawl. Many promises were not kept, and travelling is costly; but I have opened a way, and another year shall do better." I shall never forget how beautifully Mother answered him, though the dear hopeful soul had built much on his success; but with a beaming face she kissed him, saying "I call that doing *very well.*"

In Alcott's own life the uses of adversity were almost always sweet. He reminds one of a sentence written by his wife in one of her darkest hours: "There are some plants that must be bruised to give forth their sweetest odors." To him, furthermore, poverty was a sort of automatic good taste. It framed his life. It kept the nomad in him from mere aimless gadding. In almost everything except the small matters of prose style and penmanship and the construction of summerhouses it prevented the full efflorescence in him of a certain tendency to the flamboyant. On the whole, then, he was a better man because he was always poor. "Blessed poverty," he once wrote, "if it makes me rich in gratitude and a temper that rails at none." We may say with assurance that it did

[433]

do so. Furthermore, it gave him long and arduous discipline in wha[t]
may be called the higher generosity. We have heard that "it is mor[e]
blessed to give than to receive," and the words are scarcely mor[e]
than a platitude. What needs to be urged, and without the slightes[t]
tinge of irony, is the fact that it is far more difficult and more mag[-]
nanimous to receive than it is to give. Bronson Alcott's life wa[s]
one long exemplification of that serene magnanimity.

But what of his wife and children? Had he been alone in th[e]
world, like Thoreau, he might never have known that he was poo[r]
and certainly he would never have cared; but to think of h[is]
patient Anna, and also of his highly impatient Louisa, serving [as]
housemaids at two dollars a week for ignorant and insolent mi[s]
tresses—there was something to perplex and sadden the cheerful
est philosopher. To be told by his weary and all but heart-brok[en]
wife that there was no food in the house and that the trade
people declined to extend further credit—there was a freque[nt]
cause of "family straits" sufficient to drive a man into reading t[he]
Rig-Veda, the Confucian Analects, and the incomprehensib[le]
writings attributed to Hermes Trismegistus. Such were his su[b]
stitutes for strong drink, and one can only hope that they we[re]
sufficient.

Of course it may be said that Alcott might have earned the b[are]
necessities of life by some kind of labor. For several years he [did]
this. He thought more than once of returning to Spindle Hill a[nd]
working in the factories at Waterbury, and he once offered [his]
services to a turning-mill in Boston. His wife, however, was [un]
willing that he should earn money in these ways. Book-keep[ing]
was not open to him because he had not learned it. As a teac[her]
he had failed, at least in the world's opinion, a sufficient num[ber]
of times. Emerson had made him feel that as a writer he co[uld]
never hope to succeed—and, besides, not even Emerson m[ade]
money by writing. What was there left? By means of his C[on]
versations Alcott earned, during his second long residence [in]
Boston, some two hundred dollars a year.

About the year 1855 Ellery Channing produced a ninety-page manuscript, still unpublished, in which he outrageously caricatured his friends Alcott and Thoreau under the sobriquets of "Mr. Pseudo-Pistos" and "Moses Bucolics." For himself he took the name of "Major Leviticus," and the thread of the slight narrative is concerned with this Major's visit to town, obviously Boston, from the village of "Seedhelm," or Concord. The value of the manuscript for the present purpose lies in its grossly exaggerated picture of Alcott's poverty, of the cheerfulness with which he bore it, and of certain peculiarities in his speech, manner, and habits of thought.

Somewhere near the middle of this manuscript the Major, who has just paid a fruitless visit to his own publishers, inquires: "And how do you publish your works, Mr. Pistos?"

> "Br," answered the sage. "Br"—this "Br" being the natural note of the much food-lacking man. "I have thought about that a good deal. . . . After his death a philosopher may publish his works with more advantage than during his life. Thus mine, which have now reached the 36th volume, corresponding to the 36th annual publication of my married life, I mean to have got out by my executors. The first volume opens with this significant passage:

> | To 4 gall. molasses | 1.00 |
> | To 3 doz. ivory shirt buttons | .18 |

> And when we consider that only the skeleton of a philosopher belongs to him while living, and that even this may probably find its way to the College of Surgeons, I see no need for the immediate publication of his works. . . . But come home and dine with me, and we will confabulate on these things. . . . Come to my cave, my Eskimo snow-house in the tropics of the blazing metropolis. Come, to unbuttered bread and steaks of frosty curd.

[435]

The Major and Mr. Pistos then make their way into the slums of the city, through the Irish quarter, and "into the mixed world of drays, dry-goods boxes, hides, wool, and blue-breeched wagons," until they reach a gate surmounted by a cake of ice, upon which is cut in small letters the "reverend and symbolic name of 'Pistos.' " In the passage they are met by "the great Mrs. Pistos herself who gently waved them aloft, as she was busy in the duties of her profession—the coddling of valetudinarian dress-pieces and the resurrection of the Pistos linen":—

On the panel of the door at which stood the great philosopher . . . the Major saw written in a fine hand, with many flourishes: "Mr. Pseudo-Pistos is in the country." They then entered the cave, fitted up in the Eskimo manner with Mr. Pistos and thirty-six volumes of due-bills. "Take a volume," said Mr. Pistos. "The usual saloon-furniture was lost in the great gale of the preceding winter, when, the last stocks of dwarf andromeda being consumed, the luxuries of life yielded to the necessities of Fate, to which even the unthinking bow."

Leviticus extracted the 14th volume and sat down upon it, while the great philosopher hung up his hat and coat, smoothed his long usnea-hair, and, drawing out the 8th bound volume of his works, himself sat gracefully down. . . .

"Life," said Mr. Pistos, "life may be appropriated to ourselves in defiance of Society and its inherited formulæ—Br—which I have long been accustomed to disregard, myself, when called upon by higher arguments. . . . I see on every side so vast a disproportion between the different races of men, both in their talent, education, and employments, that I am accustomed to believe that men belong to different races, as it were, in the same race. No theory of social compensation can sufficiently explain the vast, the incalculable diversities of the human condition."

[436]

The philosopher had fairly prepared his cudgel or thought-lash, and was about to belabor the prominent ribs of his somnolent thought-eclipse, when a shrill voice was heard crying in the desert of the Eskimo-entry: "Mr. Pistos! Mr. Pistos!" Whereupon that good man opened a crack of the door.

"Are you in the country, Mr. Pistos?"

"I am," replied the great man softly, looking over the bannisters. "I am, my dear."

"I thought as much," cried the excoriating tongue. "It's only a baker's bill."

At the same time a strip of paper pelted against the door. Mr. Pistos brought in the document, opened the 37th volume of his Philosophical Works, and put in the unreceipted bill. He then continued his flight upon Pegasus.

That was one aspect of the truth, gaily and irresponsibly aggerated by one who, in a different mood, could write about e same man with veneration. Another aspect is suggested the fact that Bronson Alcott did not often get enough eat. Since 1835 he had been a vegetarian. What was more portant, he usually ate only two meals a day, and those re likely to be both monotonous and extremely abstemi- s.

Alcott's poverty was not the only reason for his spare diet. had discovered, as many had done before him, that a re- rkable clairvoyance sometimes follows long abstinence from d. Thus, after his period of voluntary starvation at Fruitlands had been able, or so he thought, to look directly into the full ze of Truth; and during the years that followed he tried re- tedly to reproduce the conditions out of which that experience come. In the summer of 1849 he had another period of il- ination or of what he called "introversion," unlike any former erience and too remarkable to be forgotten, but most difficult

to describe. While still held in this rapture he was able to se
down the following words about it in his Journal:—

> And this seems to be our Apotheosis. Shall we name
> fitlier by another name what we see and feel as Our-
> selves? For now the mysterious meters and scales and
> planes are opened to us, and we view wonderingly the
> Crimson Tablets and report of them all the day long.
> It is no longer Many but One with us; and all things
> and we live recluse, yet smoothly and sagely, as hav-
> ing made acquaintance suddenly as of some mighty
> and majestic friend, omniscient and benign, who keeps
> modestly aloof as if it were beneath some intervening
> umbrage, and yet draws me toward him as by some
> secret force, some cerebral magnetism, while he en-
> joins the writing of things he extends to me from be-
> hind the mystic leaves. I am drawn on by enchant-
> ment, and seem taking the leaves of the tree of life there
> plucked for me, and to sojourn I know not whither
> through regions of spirit—some Atlantides, perhaps, of
> the Mind and Seats of the Blessed. And now come the
> old memories into me; and I fear, almost, that this blaze
> of being, this survival of the foregone periods in me,
> shall blot from the memory forever the spots and forms
> and names I so lately knew. . . . Far too slender is the
> thread that holds me to this, now that I forebode its
> snapping asunder with every inspiration.

A remarkable passage, certainly, and one that by the very sp
and breathlessness of the expression does suggest a mind bc
darkly and fearfully afar. Though phrased in the present te
perhaps it is a little too literary and self-conscious to be accep
as an immediate record of mystic vision, of what Emerson ca
the "ecstatic moment" and Plotinus the "flight of the alon
the Alone." At the least, however, it is a vivid recollection of s
a vision, and one not easy to match in American writing.

Yet the experience as a whole was not on quite such a l

[438]

lane. Toward the end of it, Alcott said, he "saw a goblin or two." Having read Swedenborg and the German naturalist Oken just before the vision came upon him, he found himself imagining the entire universe as one vast spinal column. This, he sensibly deded, was going too far. Urged thereto by his wife—who again thought that he must be losing his reason and that he was going to die—he went to Concord for a fortnight's rest, and there had many long sessions with Emerson and Thoreau, walking ten miles a day and sleeping ten hours. He came to realize that there is such a thing as intellectual, even spiritual, as well as physical, deauch. Thereafter he was more temperate.

Alcott's temperance, however, never involved the abandonment of his "Pythagorean diet." During the last fifty-three years of his life he ate not only no meat but no butter, no cheese, no eggs. It true that for a few brief periods, and particularly during the regency of Charles Lane, he asked his family to observe similar restrictions, but for the most part they did not do so—as the following note from his Journal of 1839 will indicate:—

> The butcher again took advantage of my simplicity this morning at market. I asked for what I did not want, not knowing the dialect nor having the air of the market. He, well knowing what I wanted, took me literally, saying "You see what it is; this must be the piece you want, and here I will cut for you." So he cut me my flesh. Instinctively I felt that he was cheating me. But who can chaffer with Blood? . . . Any revision of the carnal code of practice was above his morality.
> The piece was sent home, and forthwith I was sent for, from the school-room, to survey the strange flitch as it lay on the kitchen table. I knew this marketing to be a fool's errand for me, and I could only plead guilty to not knowing one piece of flesh from another. And so I might not be used in this service more.

[439]

But what have I to do with butchers? Am I to go sweating about markets? Both are an offence to me. Death yawns at me as I walk up and down in this abode of skulls. Murder and blood are written on its stalls. Cruelty stares at me from the butcher's face. I tread amongst carcasses. I am in the presence of the slain. The death-set eyes of beasts peer at me and accuse me of belonging to the race of murderers. Quartered, disembowelled creatures suspended on hooks plead with me. I feel myself dispossessed of the divinity. I am a replenisher of graveyards. I prowl, amidst other unclean spirits and voracious demons, for my prey.

Alcott's ideas of diet had come to him directly, it seems prob able, from his cousin William, who in 1835 started in Boston th monthly magazine called the *Moral Reformer* and followed it two years later with the *Library of Health,* both strongly veg tarian. William Alcott, in his turn, had been influenced by t writings and lectures of Dr. Sylvester Graham, who, in 182 had met at Philadelphia a group of "Fundamentalists" calli themselves "Bible Christians." These people, recent immigra from England, held as an article of religious belief that "eat the flesh of animals is a violation of the first dietetic law given mankind by the Creator." But Bronson Alcott might well ha become a vegetarian without any modern suggestions. His vene tion for Pythagoras would probably have been sufficient by it. to make him abandon animal diet without reference to the reasc such as belief in transmigration of souls, which the ancient s had in mind. In addition to Jamblichus' *Life of Pythago* always one of his favorite books, he owned and read the powe and disgusting little treatise *On Abstinence* by the Neo-Plato Porphyry, the same treatise that had made a vegetarian of poet Petrarch. And besides all this he was a vegetarian, as he l self said, "by instinct."

[440]

There was not the slightest suggestion of bigotry, however, in Alcott's abstention from animal food, although it kept him from many banquets and club dinners which he might otherwise have liked to attend. At the monthly meetings of the Saturday Club in Boston he was known as the "after-dinner member" because he usually came in "for the best of the feast—the nuts and apples, the wit and philosophy abounding—after the abominations were removed." Henry Thoreau could scarcely have endured those meetings, partly because he hated clubs in general and also because he loathed tobacco smoke—except, perhaps, when it came from Ellery Channing's pipe. Alcott loved clubs to such an extent that he could ignore tobacco completely, and never even mention its name from end to end of his Journals. What he made of Emerson's moderate indulgence in tobacco and wine is not recorded, although he probably referred it back to his general conviction that Emerson could do no wrong. It is certain, however, that he took no great pleasure in the dinners Emerson often gave for persons of distinction who visited Concord. On one of these occasions the host is said to have dilated at considerable length, while carving a roast, upon the horrors of cannibalism. Bronson Alcott's face was working with amusement and barely suppressed glee until he suddenly burst forth with "But Mr. Emerson, if we are to eat meat at all why should we *not* eat the *best?*"

Considered as a whole, Alcott's seven-year residence in Boston at the middle of the century was not a successful period, nor was it entirely a happy one. The family seemed to grow poorer year by year, if that was still possible, even though Anna and Louisa went out to service and began to teach a little school of their own before they had quite attained maturity. During those seven years the Alcotts moved six times. Mrs. Alcott worked hard and well as the agent of charitable societies and made for herself an independent place in the city's life. Alcott conducted Conversations wherever he could. Using the ticket of admission secured

for him by young Henry T. Tuckerman, he read enormously a
the Boston Athenæum. He read and browsed and turned over ne
books and old at the Old Corner Bookstore, at Munroe's, at Mis
Peabody's, and at Little and Brown's. His Journal-entries ir
creased in depth and length. He spent more and more time o
Boston Common.

One could not have called him idle, and yet there was somethir
of the effect of sauntering in his life during these years, i
which one might have expected him to be approaching his summi
Perhaps he had a vague fear that life was passing him by witho
the fulfillment of any fundamental hope or purpose. His fiftie
year came and went, and he began to think of himself as an o
man.

But at the first faint premonition of the coming frost Alco
reached out, as never before, toward youth. He took every char
that offered to talk with the children in the little school kept by l
own daughters. He thought back to his own boyhood, pierci
down and down to his earliest recollections. More and more f
quently the names of the people and the places he had first kno
appeared in his Journals. And it was at this time, too, that he ma
the first of his several friendships, all of them delightfully na
and charmingly innocent, with young women. Ednah Dow Lit
hale, one day to be almost famous as the wife of the artist S
Cheney and as the biographer of Louisa, was for several ye
his devoted and beloved companion.

Looking back upon these years in later life, the event of 1
that Alcott most clearly remembered was the "apotheosis"
mystic vision which had nearly snatched him out of life as
world knows it. But he recalled too, and with great vividness,
twenty-sixth of May when Henry Thoreau had called at Ded'
Street to leave a copy of his *Week on the Concord and Merrin
Rivers,* just published by James Munroe at the author's expe
Alcott knew most of the contents already, but now he sat d
and read the book right through, "admiringly." He called it

[442]

merican book, worthy to stand beside Emerson's Essays on my
helves." He was in fact not only the first reader of Thoreau's first
ook but also one of the most discerning and sympathetic readers
at Thoreau has ever had—and this in spite of a fundamental
sagreement, both of mood and of mind, with his friend's treat-
ent of his main theme.

In that same year of 1849 Alcott had founded and organized
e "Town and Country Club," composed of one hundred men
iefly of his choosing. Much against his own wish, but at
merson's earnest request, women had been excluded. That was
strange thing. In Emerson himself there was the mingling of
an and woman to be found, of course, in every person of genius;
d yet Emerson would not have women in the Club. Perhaps
r that reason, the Club had not lasted long.

The year 1850 Alcott remembered as a bleak and lonely time.
verty had increased. In the early summer Mrs. Alcott had fed
ne poor immigrants, just come from the boat, in the back yard;
d from these poor people the Alcott girls, all four of them, had
tracted smallpox. Their parents brought them through, and
n the parents themselves had been taken down by the disease
l had been desperately ill. The girls nursed them. For a month
human being had crossed their threshold—no neighbor, no
se, no doctor. The Alcotts had little faith in doctors and none
all in medicine, unless it were the little harmless homeopathic
es of Hahnemann, which were, in their opinion, "the next best
g to nothing."

t was in June of 1850 that the terrible news had come of
rgaret Fuller's death in shipwreck off Fire Island. One had
ays known that she, the Priestess, was somehow tragic, and
the veil of the ultimate mystery had fallen round her. There
e things that people whispered about her son, her husband.
at of that? All three of them were now transfigured "into some-
g rich and strange." She had been a great and a most noble
.

[443]

So began for Alcott the long series of farewells to which every man who has reached the age of fifty may look forward.

Bronson Alcott had supposed that his reforming days were over: but when, in April of 1851, Boston arrested and tried and re manded the fugitive slave Thomas Simms, he felt his share of the huge public excitement and worked eagerly on the Boston Vigilance Committee, striving to save Negroes from the clutch of the law. Again, in May of 1854, when the whole city was convulsed by the arrest of the fugitive Anthony Burns, he served with skill and energy, calmly putting his own life in peril—for he would have been entirely glad to die in such a cause—in a way which some of his contemporaries never forgot. He saw much of Theodore Parker, one of the bravest and most powerful friends that black men had in Boston. As Alcott had prophesied long before, Parker was indeed giving a good account of himself these days that tried men's souls.

Looking back into 1852 Alcott remembered one thing above all: the death, in April, of his favorite brother, Junius. There had been some things about that young brother that were not pleasant to recall, though there was nothing that suggested blame. High strung, sensitive exceedingly, deeply thoughtful and utterly good he had not been granted the strength of nerve and brain that would have enabled him to bear life's burdens. In 1844 he had been for a time deranged, and the manner of his death suggested insanity. In the diary of Alcott's uneducated but bright and brave-hearted mother one finds these words:—

> *April 26, 1852*—Munday—Junius came in and to see me Shook hands with me and Saying that he was go-ing to Boston and the Left and went directly to the factory with Embrose and went Streat into the wheel and was gon the nuse came that he was dead which was Supprising to me but I bore it with reconcelation he was Laid in the Earth that day where we all must as-send to god that gave us Life and may his death be

[444]

the meands of preparring me to following his example in Life and Leave the world as good as he Left it
in as great faith.

Alcott's own quiet words about the shocking event were written
n the eighth of May:—

Receive letter from my mother today, giving intelligence of my brother Junius's death on the 24th April
last, AE. 32.—A man of tenderest sensibilities and the
mystic mind, ingenious, eminently practical, friendly,
much respected by his friends, who leaves this world
to his great gain. A wife and four small children survive
him.

In his writing, at any rate, Alcott never mentioned his brother
nius again.

And yet the death of Junius set the elder brother to thinking
en more than he had recently done about his family, his boy-
od, and Spindle Hill. Ellery Channing and James Russell Lowell
re both urging him to write the story of his life, and although
was never to feel equipped for this larger undertaking he did
ept as an obligation the laying-out of all the materials that a
sible future biographer might need. No sooner did he face that
than there came to mind the strong emphasis laid upon
rth" by the English friend and teacher whom he had never
. If it was true, as James Pierrepont Greaves had so often
, that birth or heredity was more important than education and
ronment in determining the set of character, then it behooved
to find out all that could now be discovered about those for-
en lives in which his own had begun. His Journals and other
rs would serve sufficiently to show his individual experience
fe, but for all that lay before that experience he must now
r himself.

From early May of 1852, therefore, until the end of October cu
short his researches, Alcott labored hard and continuously i
tracing back the lines of his father's and his mother's ancestry a
far as American records enabled him to go. Working without th
help of professional genealogists and without any of the innume·
able printed authorities which have made such researches con
paratively easy in our time, he plunged into town histories and tl
records of town clerks, he visited graveyards and copied epitapl
by the score, he spent several weeks on Spindle Hill consultii
the uncles and aunts and cousins that he could still find thei
establishing a habit of annual return to those familiar scenes whi
endured throughout his life. The records of his findings fill sevei
large bound volumes of manuscript. Like every other task
which he seriously set himself—like the construction of Emerso
summerhouse or the founding of Fruitlands—these researcl
became an obsession, crowding out of his mind for the time nea
every other interest. Even Emerson and Thoreau laughed at ·
democrat, the reflective laborer, the philosophic peasant, v
seemed to be trying to prove that he was really an aristocrat
descent. To them the whole effect was grotesquely un-Americ
But they missed the point entirely. They did not understand t
Alcott was merely carrying out the injunction of all the anci
sages: "Know Thyself."

What Alcott discovered in these studies was not remarka
As almost any other man born in Connecticut toward the eni
the eighteenth century might have done, he found that his
cestors had been in New England from the beginning, that ·
had ranged all up and down the ladder of social distinctions,
that they had intermarried in the course of two centuries
sixty-two different families, many of them the most promi
and influential that New England contained. He found, of coi
that he was a "son of the American Revolution" several t
over, and he was not impressed by the finding. Thomas Alcc
the first of the name in America, had come over with Gove

[446]

Winthrop in 1630 and had been the town's cowkeeper on Boston
Common. His son Phillipp, born in 1657, had lived most of his life
in New Haven Colony as a man of some slight distinction. Then
had come three Johns in succession, the last of whom had been
the first settler at Spindle Hill. His grandson Joseph had married
Anna Bronson in 1796, and to them ten children had been born,
of whom only four were still living when Bronson Alcott began
his researches.

But if these studies were not remarkable in their factual results,
they were at any rate deeply characteristic of Alcott in their
origin, method, and final effect. They involved the whole man.
Nowhere can one find a better illustration of his intellectual habit
and native power of bringing all he had and was to bear upon
each task that he undertook. Like the cloud in Wordsworth's
poem, his mind moved all together when it moved at all. His mind
was neither subtle nor profound, but it was a unit, and every
major idea it contained was related to every other like a body in
a planetary system.

Such an assertion need not imply that Alcott's thought was
always logical or even self-consistent. It was not. But there was
always a process of integration going on in his thinking which, in
spite of manifest flaws in logic and consistency, held his mind together as one harmonious whole. Emerson observed in Alcott, as
we have seen, that he would frequently unsay in the morning what
he had said the night before; but it was also Emerson who observed, with great acumen, that—

> The comfort of Alcott's mind is the connection in
> which he sees whatever he sees. . . . For every opinion
> or sentence of Alcott a reason may be sought and
> found, not in his will or fancy but in the necessity of
> Nature itself, which has daguerred that fatal impres-
> sion on his susceptible soul. He is as good as a lens or
> mirror, a beautiful susceptibility, every impression on

which is not to be reasoned against or derided, but to be accounted for—and, until accounted for, registered as an indisputable addition to our catalogue of natural facts. There are defects in the lens, and errors of refraction and position, etc., to be allowed for, and it needs one acquainted with the lens by frequent use to make these allowances; but 'tis the best instrument I have ever met with.

The criticism is searching and sound. It winds unerring: through all the outward chambers of Alcott's speech and condu and ideas to the innermost center of his thought. Emerson great valued in his friend that strange fecundity of mind which enabl him at times to scatter ideas up and down his talk like a you god in a frenzy of improvisation; but he saw in Alcott somethi more than this sheer procreative vigor—a rarer thing, and mc beautiful. Again and again he came back to what he sometin called the "astronomical" quality of Alcott's mind, and called other places its "constitutionality." There was no simple wo seeing that "consistency" would not serve.

I told Alcott [he wrote in 1853] that I should describe him as a man with a divination or good instinct for the quality and character of wholes; as a man who looked at things in a little larger angle than most other persons; and as one who had a certain power of transition from thought to thought, as by secret passages, which it would tax the celerity and subtlety of good metaphysicians to follow.

This was something that Alcott probably did not know a' himself, until his friend had told him. His transitions from tho to thought were often, indeed, unerring; but they seem to been instinctive and unconscious. When he thought well, it not on account of any external discipline to which he had b

[448]

himself. If only for want of any other explanation, we must attribute his intellectual successes to the mystery he called "Birth." And when he thought absurdly, as he often did, his thinking was equally the movement of a whole and unified mind—in the wrong direction.

Expert opinions would differ even to-day as to whether Alcott was on the right or the wrong road in his genealogical researches and meditations. However that may have been, he followed the road before him with complete forgetfulness of every other. Once more his head was down, his blinkers were adjusted. And it was strange how many of the paths of thought he had traveled in earlier life fed into this one. For was not his present study a continuation of those obstinate questionings beside Anna's cradle? Was it not in complete accord with that king-thought of his, that all things are to be explained by descent or lapse or devolution rather than by evolutionary process, by ascent, and ultimate culmination? From the ordinary point of view, he saw everything upside down. Thus a man, to him, was an organism carrying its root in the air—a system of branches depending from a brain. Just so the entire universe, to him in Boston as to Plotinus in ancient Alexandria, was an inconceivable Many emanating and descending from the One. And why should the family be an exception? There were no exceptions to these divine laws. Bronson Alcott had made God, as we all do, in his own image. He assumed that the Creator's thinking, like his own, was single, harmonious, and whole.

It should be clear that Alcott was not trying to establish a claim to "blue blood" as he went about searching for ancestors in Roxbury, Plymouth, Charlestown, Marlboro, Sudbury, Hartford, Wethersfield, New Haven, Farmington, and Spindle Hill. There was little to flatter the "pride of birth" in the records of the first American ancestor which he found in the Boston Towne Book. They read thus:—

1651, Apl. 28.—Thomas Alcocke appointed cow-keeper, at 2s. a head.

1652, Mar. 29.—Thomas Alkok to keep the cows, wch goe one the Common one this Neck, and to have 2s. and 6d. each, and to pay for wintering of the Town bull.

1654, April 24.—Thomas Olcott shall kepe the cows, and to have 2s. for every cow that goes upon the common, and 6d. a head for the hire of 2 bulls wch he hath hereby power to gather upon every cow.

That had been good enough for an American beginning—an as for the English backgrounds of this Thomas or any oth Olcott-Alkok-Alcocke, they were too remote in sea-miles and time to matter. Yet even for Bronson Alcott there was a modicu of truth in the remark that Harriet Martineau had recently mad "It is not to be supposed that the mere circumstance of living a republic will ever eradicate that kind of self-love which tal the form of family pride." He did take a definite pleasure in lieving, where he could not prove, that he was descended fr that once-famous John Alcock who had been successively Bisl of Rochester, Worcester, and Ely, and had served under He the Seventh as Lord High Chancellor of England. He copied ov passage from Barclay's Eclogues about this Bishop John:—

> Yes, since his days a Cock was in the pen;
> I knew his voice among a thousand men . . .
> He All was a Cocke; he wakened us from slepe,
> And while we slumbered he our foldes did kepe.

The mere fact that this good Bishop had been a cleric in Ro Catholic times and that Barclay himself dared to swear "tha trode never hen," troubled Alcott's faith in this ancestry n all. Somehow it must have happened, and without any intr of bars sinister, that he, the Cock of modern Boston, ha

[450]

scended from that man who had kept all England awake nearly four hundred years before.

It was definitely pleasing, furthermore, to discover in Guilliam's Heraldry the old punning coat-of-arms, with its description:—

> He bears gules, a fess between three cocks, argent, barbed and crested, or: by the name of Alcocke. This coat was assigned by Sir William Segar, Garter, and Richard St. George, Clarencieux, by patent, dated the 8th of June, 1717, to Thomas Alcocke of Silvertoft in the County of Leicester.

And the family's motto, not mentioned by Guilliam, was *Semper igilans*. To Bronson Alcott, more and more convinced that basic aits never died out of a family, all these things were deeply sigificant. They seemed to tell him much about himself. Underneath e Alcock coat-of-arms he copied a charming poem by Henry aughan which suggested a perfect "emblem" of his own mind d spirit:—

THE COCKE

Father of lights! What sunny seed,
What glance of day, hast thou confined
Into this bird? To all the breed
This busy ray thou hast assigned;
Their magnetism works all night
And dreams of Paradise and Light.
Their eyes watch for the morning hue;
Their little grain, expelling night,
So shines and sings as if it knew
The path into the house of light.
It seems their candle, howe're done,
Was tinn'd and lighted at the sunne.

hese were delightful fantasies; but ideas too were involved— s that reached far and wide through all the ranges of Alcott's thought. When he accepted the basic teaching of Greaves that the course of life is determined by birth and not by education, did he see that this would logically involve an abandonment of teaching, of reform, and ultimately of the whole democratic faith? Carried to an extreme, as Alcott was so likely to carry it, would it not mean even the loss of his optimism and a final settling down into fatalistic despair? How could one go on hoping if everything had been already decided?

Emerson saw quite clearly to what end this new doctrine would lead, and he saw it as "a system of despair." Intuitively he realized, if Alcott did not, how it would poison the very roots of America. In his thoughtful address on "The New England Reformers," delivered shortly after Alcott had returned with his dangerous cargo of English ideas, Emerson pointed out that a rift was growing in the sea-wall of the American faith, and that there was no foretelling what inundation by alien notions and what destruction of home-bred hopes it might cause. The fatalistic view was already common, and clearly it had entered his own mind. He said, in tones of grave warning:—

> We do not believe that any education . . . will give depth to a superficial mind. Having settled ourselves into this new infidelity, our skill is expended to procure alleviations, diversions, opiates. We adorn the victim with manual skill, his tongue with languages, his body with inoffensive and comely manners . . . Is it strange that society should be devoured by a secret melancholy?

But Bronson Alcott was not devoured. He was not even bitter. Probably he never guessed how destructive the notion of "Birth" would become in its new and alien environment. He was as innocent and unforeboding as a man who introduces an almost microscopic parasite, from a land where it has long been held in check, into a country where it is to work havoc and ruin.

[452]

Shall we blame him? Shall we be severe with him for his manifest and egregious blunder of thought? Shall we ridicule him for retaining most, if not all, of his New England faith in education, reform, and democracy, while holding fast to another faith or belief that harmonized with this one as vinegar does with milk? Probably we had better postpone all that until we ourselves have decided which of these two contradictory things we ourselves are going to believe: first, that as all good Americans are born "free and equal" therefore they are all equally "perfectible" by the processes of school and college; or, second, that the potentialities of every individual are unalterably decided at birth, as the results of our "scientific intelligence tests" seem abundantly to show. At present, we believe them both, as Alcott did. Why, after all, did Providence supply two lobes, instead of only one, for the human brain?

Involved and entwined with Alcott's doctrine of "Birth" was the much more basic and pervasive doctrine to which he gave the unfortunate name "Genesis." In this doctrine he addresses himself to the two fundamental problems of abstract thought: How have the matter and the forms of the universe come into being? And How can the mind apprehend them? To these questions, respectively ontological and epistemological, he gives the idealistic answer to be expected of a mind with a definitely Platonic, or rather Neo-Platonic, slant. That is to say, he finds reality not in matter and its forms but in Mind and its Ideas. Mind and Ideas he regards as prior to matter and forms, both in the order of time and in that of causation. The objective world of the senses he subsumes under the subjective world of thought and spirit. "I set out," he wrote in 1835, in words that Emerson had before him while writing *Nature,* "from the wide ground of Spirit. That *is.* All else is its manifestation."

The startling thing about these words is certainly not their novelty. They merely express what may be called the normal

[453]

point of view of deeply reflective minds in all ages—of minds,
that is, with sufficient force and tenacity of purpose to pass beyond
superficial appearances. The sages of India had been saying
precisely the same thing as this for thousands of years, and so had
the numberless intellectual children of Plato and Plotinus. The
surprising thing is to come upon such a purely idealistic utterance at the beginning of an almost purely materialistic time, to
encounter this glorification of the Spirit in a land which is generally thought to be interested in matter alone. The interesting
thing is the sharp uncompromising contrast between this idea
of a universal descent or devolution, and that other idea of universal evolution and struggling-upward which the nineteenth
century was soon to choose as the master-key to every problem

If Bronson Alcott's thought was sometimes illogical, it was
usually thorough. He seldom stopped short of a conclusion
merely because it seemed absurd, or because it flew in the face
of common sense; and he carried his doctrine of "Genesis" to
extremes which sometimes raised a smile even among his fellow
transcendentalists. Man, he held, was an emanation from the
divine and original Mind, although it was only in such moments
or brief periods as that which Alcott himself had lived through
during his "apotheosis" in 1849 that he was fully aware of the
origin. And just as Man had lapsed from Mind, so all Nature,
held, had lapsed from Man. The lower animals he took to be the
incarnations of Man's lower self—and that was one reason why
he "declined" to eat them. Nature was "Man in ruins," he said
Nature in all its parts and forms and in every atom of its matter
was the creation not of the Original Mind but of Man—and
Man, too, in his lower and downward-looking moments. Alcott
did not, with the Oriental seers, deny all reality to Nature and
call it mere "Maya" or illusion. In fact he attributed more
reality to natural forms and phenomena than even Thoreau,
his deeper musings, was likely to do; yet he thought that such
reality as they had was at the second remove from the true

[454]

source of Being. Unlike the Deists of the eighteenth century, he hoped to penetrate not "through Nature to Nature's God" but through Nature to Man, being certain that Man had made Nature in his own likeness.

All this led to certain deductions which one calls audacious, naïve, or merely insane, according to one's intellectual point of view. Alcott believed, for example, that the envelope of air surrounding the earth is nothing but the accumulated breath of earth's human inhabitants. When he found this atmosphere upon the whole salubrious he gratefully attributed the fact to the predominance, for the time being, of just and right-minded breathers; but when it grew noisome he had to conclude that unjust and unidealistic persons were temporarily in control. On brilliant and beautiful days he often asked himself what mankind had been doing to produce such halcyon weather.

Here it is that one who wishes to think well of Alcott should take firm hold of whatever metaphysical idealism there may be him.

> I bestow a benison on Nature [he says] whenever
> I walk forth in hope and joy and breathe forth my
> Soul into her atmosphere. I give more than I take. . . .
> Let all men see to it that they sweeten the airs of God.
> . . . A sweet soul circulates around the globe and
> sends health to panting, yawning, languishing invalids
> on every breath that it launches into the common cur-
> rent. Like ocean, it tumbles round the world, and stirs
> the whole mass of fluid air, giving it vitality.

From one point of view—the one which we nowadays call "scientific"—that passage is simply absurd. But there are a few other things to be said about it. In the first place, it is not one bit more absurd than the materialistic preconceptions upon which the greater part of our scientific thinking still uneasily rests. For another thing, it is in perfect logical keeping, at any rate, with the bases of Alcott's metaphysical thought. And

[455]

finally, one should observe that however wild it may be in its treatment of external things it is not blind to the moral facts of the universe. By implication, at least, it admits the reality of sin suffering, and evil. Alcott's optimism was innate, and he lived in an optimistic time and place, but with all his courteous desire to speak well of God's creation he never denied the terrible actuality of wickedness, cruelty, pain, and absolute wrong. Evil to him, was a positive ingredient of the world. All those, therefore, who would like to claim him as a member of the sweetl smiling school, all who think that he too expected to annul life' pain and failure by the bland expedient of mere silence, will d well to look elsewhere.

> What fact in the Soul [he asked] do vultures, hawks, herons, eagles, kites, etc., cover? The same of beasts of prey? Is man by nature a beast of prey?— Read Aububon's "Biographical History of Birds" and Cuvier's "Natural History." Also "History of Man." But this last is not written.

Audacious, absurd, or insane as such passages may seem us, is there not a definite advantage, at least to the devout, attributing the horrible ways in which life everywhere pre upon life not to a God whom we should like to think loving ' His very nature but to some flaw of essential cruelty in or selves? Whoever has seen a shrike impaling a sparrow on a tho has watched a hawk engorging a goldfinch, or has witnessed fascination of a flock of screaming birds by a blacksnake, m have wished that he could exonerate the President of the mortals from all such degraded conceptions. And here is Alc telling us how that may be done. We may take the crimes Nature upon our human consciences. The suggestion has charm of magnanimity, and is far more self-consistent than orthodox Christian view. Henry Thoreau said a similar th possibly echoing Alcott, when he remarked "I am guilty muskrats."

[456]

Alcott said that "Man is older than Nature," with a faint suggestion that, in such a case, he ought to set it a better example. Nature, he thought, was Man's cast-off clothing, which still kept the shape of Man's body. He regarded the starry universe as one enormous web that Man has spun, like a huge omnific spider, out of his own vitals.

A man with such ideas, living in Boston through the middle decades of the nineteenth century, was likely to have some interesting encounters. For Boston had read Sir Charles Lyell's *Principles of Geology* and Hugh Miller's *The Old Red Sandstone*—so, indeed, had Alcott—and had begun to get some conceptions of geological time. Boston knew the palæontology of Cuvier and Lamarck, and had some idea of man's relative position in time with reference to the lower forms of life. Boston was so well prepared for Darwin's *Origin of Species* that when the book appeared in 1859 there seems to have been a general feeling, in well-informed circles, of having known all that before.

It is a matter of some curiosity, therefore, to see how a thought like Bronson Alcott's theory of "Genesis" would prosper in so extremely sophisticated an environment.

Its diverse fortunes there are clearly indicated by Alcott's record of an afternoon at the Saturday Club. For the twenty-fourth of April, 1857, he writes:—

I find today, and seated, all but Longfellow, who comes in just after me. Agassiz, Emerson, Prof. Pierce, Lowell, Sam. Ward, E. P. Whipple, Tom Motley, John Dwight, Ed. Quincy, Woodman. Prescott and Richard Dana, Jr., are sometimes of the party, and Quincy is Lowell's guest for today. The conversation is for the most part colloquial. Only one passage—on the Generative Ideas, suggested by some assertion of mine on the necessary priority of Man and the animals to the earth, afterwards put by Agassiz for votes—gives it a philo-

[457]

sophical and general turn, and tried the strength of the heads present unmistakably. Ward, Whipple, Dwight, Lowell, Pierce, Emerson for the ideas clearly; the rest for Agassiz and his facts in preceding or contemporaneous order of out-working to the senses.—Of the persons present whom I had not met before, Prof. Pierce interested me for depth and comprehensiveness, interpretation and scope of his logic upon this nut of the Genesis. But, 'tis plain, with Agassiz I shall neither make heads nor mend, he the analyst, the observer— ideas, as he views them, being inferences from observed facts and generalized therefrom, not his patterns and models in the creative order. Purely Aristotelian, his Genius plays the naturalist habitually, never the spiritualist; nor can. Such breadth of brain and horizontal over-capping of the ears, globe-shaped, yet not ensphered nor astral, takes temperamentally to anatomic and mundane studies, to the forces and forms following, not leading the sun.

On several other occasions, and once in particular at Emson's house in Concord, Bronson Alcott, perhaps the most treme idealist in America, met Louis Agassiz, the foremost server and recorder of Nature's ways that America then he in head-on encounter. Alcott respected this antagonist. He s and said that Agassiz was a great teacher, a great observer, a on his level, even a great thinker; but that level, he believed, comparatively low. He was grateful for everything that Aga discovered, feeling sure that he could use it in his own ideali thinking. (It is not recorded, apparently, that Agassiz thought of using any of the ideas of Alcott.) He had not slightest touch of that fear of science which is sometimes tributed to the more orthodox Christians of his time. On contrary, his complaint was that science halted and lingered o way, and was by far too cautious and careful. Without a mom

[458]

doubt he would have underwritten Emerson's brave remark: "Fear not the new generalization. Does the fact look crass and material, threatening to degrade thy theory of spirit? Resist it not; it goes to refine and raise thy theory of matter just as much." But the trouble with Agassiz was, in Alcott's opinion, that after he had most accurately observed and codified the facts, he had not the energy, the curiosity, or perhaps the intelligence, even to inquire what those facts might mean. For Alcott subscribed also to that other Emersonian declaration, as true in our day as it was when first put forth exactly one hundred years ago: "At present, man applies to Nature but half his force. He works on the world with his understanding alone."

And what did Emerson think about the theory of "Genesis"? At some times one thing, and at other times another. Emerson is called, with reason, a Neo-Platonist; but when we bring him into comparison with Bronson Alcott we see with what large reservations the term must be applied to him. There is a page in Alcott's Journals which illustrates some of the basic differences between the two men with startling vividness. Early in August, 1849, when Alcott's mind was seething with his "apotheosis," he went to Concord to find out what Emerson might think about his notion that Nature is the creation of human mind. His own note for Sunday, the fifth, is no more than a memorandum for his own convenience: "All day discussing the endless and infinite theme in the study and while walking—the late revelation leading all the rest." But on the same page with these words there and written in pencil, in Emerson's own handwriting, the following now familiar lines:—

> A subtle chain of countless rings
> The next unto the farthest brings;
> The eye reads omens where it goes,
> And speaks all languages the rose;
> And, striving to be man, the worm
> Mounts through all the spires of form.

[459]

The full significance of this is discernible only to one who has before him Alcott's Journal for 1849, in which there are several diagrams, consisting of "chains" and "rings," intended to illustrate his conception—based, as he thought, upon revelation or "apotheosis"—of the way in which all Nature *descends* from Man. But Emerson, clearly, did not at the time agree with this conception. On the face of the evidence it seems likely that he glanced at Alcott's diagrams, saw that they could be read and understood as easily in an ascending as in a descending order, and so wrote the six lines which have ever since been taken as an early adumbration of the theory of evolution. The word "mounts," and the phrase "striving to be man," leave no doubt that when he wrote the lines Emerson was thinking of Nature's course as an upward effort rather than as a gradual "lapse."

Emerson used these six lines as the motto for the second edition, appearing in 1849, of his first book, *Nature*. But it is interesting and significant to observe that in their clear suggestion of an upward instead of a downward movement in natural history they are definitely out of keeping with the Neo-Platonism of which that book is full. Glancing down the pages of *Nature*, written shortly after Emerson had become acquainted with Alcott and while he had actually before him Alcott's Journals for 1834 and 1835, one comes upon such a purely Neo-Platonic or Alcottian sentence as this: "Nature is so pervaded with human life that there is something of humanity in all, and in every particular." On the same page one reads "The Supreme Being does not build up Nature around us but puts it forth through us." And again, this: "Once inhale the upper air . . . and we learn that man . . . is himself the creator of the finite." These statements cannot be made to harmonize with the evolutionary view that

> . . . striving to be man, the worm
> Mounts through all the spires of form.

The conclusion seems to be that when Emerson wrote *Nature* he agreed with the doctrine of "Genesis," which Alcott had first thought out, perhaps with the help of William Russell, in his years at Germantown. Thirteen years later, Emerson found that he had adopted the opposite view. By so doing he had placed himself in the stream of intellectual tendency which ran with increasing volume throughout his time and on into our own day. Bronson Alcott, on the other hand, had, and has, hardly any but the thinkers of the great past and of the Orient to lend him any substantial support for his theory of "Genesis." Only in the most advanced and daring speculations of our time has anything been recently said in the West on his side of this question.

But "Genesis" was Alcott's central idea. He maintained it for fifty years, not against Emerson and Agassiz alone but against the whole contemporary current of thought. What this cost him in the way of intellectual solitude, and also what intellectual courage and persistence it represented, one can only imagine. As the flood of materialism increased, the idea that Mind or Spirit could be the source and cause of reality was simply tossed aside. It became merely the sort of thing that men said in church on Sundays.

Alcott's statement of his king-idea was unfortunately vague and ill-defined. Necessarily addressed to those few persons capable of taking an interest in abstruse themes, it was not laid before them in the precise and clarified language to which they were accustomed and entitled. There was a tone of vaticination and of "thus saith the Lord" in Alcott's statement, when a plausible and moderate tone was clearly called for. Thus, for once, he antagonized his audience. He might have gained almost a favorable hearing if he had been content to point out that Nature *as man perceives it,* whether in his scientific and metaphysical or in his common-sense formulas, is certainly—one would say "obviously" if the fact were not everywhere ignored—the efflux of his own mind. With a little more care for expression, Alcott might have brought a few persons to realize that man's interpretations of Nature must always carry with them the mental habits of man the interpreter, so that the long-vaunted "objectivity" of scientific thought and research has always been, and must always remain, mere illusion. And thus he might have hastened the day when science and philosophy alike will recognize that Nature tends to "be" what the human mind can think it.

The thing that Alcott remembered longest and with most delight in looking back upon those years in Boston was the majestic fountain in the Common. For hours at a time, and often, during the sound summer weather, on every day of the week, he would sit under the great elms that Governor Hancock had imported from England and watch that leaping and falling jet with the changing lights of morning and noon and afternoon upon it, wondering at its mystery, thinking of what it meant. For unquestionably it was an emblem, a symbol, with significance deeper than the eye could ever probe. He would think of the high still lake where these waters had recently lain in sleep beneath the open sky, and then of their long journey under the ground, racing and crowding downward and ever down through the dark in their haste to leap up in the light. So it was, just so, that as man went onward through the echoing dimness of these earthly years the longing grew upon him more and more for the last release, for the return to the light whence he had come. And the fountain itself—how it surged up and forever up! Perhaps the best motto that a man could choose for his life, and for his death as well, would be the one word "Up."

Emerson came one day and saw the fountain. He admired the long lines of motion, the sweeping parabolas. Yes, there they were —but could it be that Emerson did not see the emblem? Emerson said sometimes that he, Bronson Alcott, was a man without senses; but that was hardly true. The truth was that the sight, the sound, the odor, was so rapidly hurried away and merged

[462]

and lost in its meanings. . . . This fountain, now. One saw its sweeping lines, its shape like a tree, its colors; and yet all these became very soon a picture in the mind, a parable. The beauty was all within. One could go away now, and never lose what the fountain had meant.

Whether it was the fountain that changed him or some other influence, Bronson Alcott gave up, about the year 1855, all thought of being an old man. He was never to return to that thought. He began to consider, much as young men do at the very entrance upon life, what work he should undertake for a livelihood. Once more, as he had done twelve years earlier in Concord, he asked advice of all his friends, and he himself made several suggestions. Gardening at Concord occurred to him, but his wife and daughters were not fond of Concord. He thought of the clock factories in which he had worked as a boy, but he was not fond of factories. He thought of farming on Spindle Hill, of going to England as a purchaser of books for the Boston trade, and also —for that good plan had never been forgotten—of taking to the road once more as a conversing pedlar. But Mrs. Alcott had a plan of her own. At Walpole, New Hampshire, in the beautiful valley of the Connecticut, her brother-in-law had a house which he offered to her rent-free. In June, 1855, the family moved to Walpole.

Alcott was not unhappy during his two years of exile from Emerson and Concord and Boston. Once more he gardened nightily and read the few books he had with him. His girls were leaving him. In October Anna went to Syracuse to teach in a lunatic asylum and one month later Louisa set off to seek her fortune in Boston, with twenty dollars of her own earnings in her pocket and a large bundle of manuscript. During the winter Alcott somehow secured a copy of Walt Whitman's *Leaves of Grass*, just published in its first edition, and admired it so intensely that his own prose style was for a time affected. Late in

September he went to New York City, where in the course of a three-month stay he saw much not only of Whitman but of Fanny Kemble, of Henry Ward Beecher, of Samuel Longfellow and, as it happened, of Henry Thoreau.

The record of these three months, if it were not by far too long and too intricate to set down here, would prove conclusively tha Alcott had somewhere and somehow taken "a new lease of life." Not only the variety and number of his social engagements and public appearances but a pervading tone of exhilaration, almos of gaiety, in what he says of them, give the effect of abounding an youthful strength. There was some quality in the air and societ of New York that was highly stimulating, perhaps slightly ir toxicating, to a man who, after fifteen months in the upper Cor necticut Valley, was thirsting for intelligent society and burstin with accumulated talk.

Walt Whitman was a study to Alcott. He was a revelation an a huge delight. Alcott saw at first glance that here was a man a new sort—a sort quite unrepresented in Boston, but one whic was somehow important, or was going to be; and he set himse to draw the man out, to sound his depths, and to test the ran of his interests. He was amused by Whitman's egotism and what he took to be his affectation of manners somewhat too fr and easy, but he made no mistake about the power of the man, even about its nature. Probably the best and most enthusias writing in Alcott's Journals is that concerning Thoreau, next to it in value is his long description and discussion of t astonishing man whom, from the start, he called "Walt."

With perfect ease, and with hardly a sense of transition, Alc let himself down from the mood of Boston and of its many earn reticent, hard-reading men and women, all so intent upon hig laws and over-souls, and moved out easily and at once on the l level reaches of this new man's mind as though he had alw lived upon them and was perfectly at home among their bo acres soaking in the sun. It was like going down a mountain.

[464]

again, it was very like a re-discovery of America—a part of America, at any rate, which had been too long ignored. Bronson Alcott had always known that it was there. Ever since his wanderings among the Southern swamps and plantations he had known that America was not everywhere a country of steep and stony hills going up to meet the sky. Somewhere it sprawled and loafed and merely took what came. Not everywhere in it were lips and hearts locked tightly, nor was there everywhere, as in Boston, quite such a sparkle of intellectual frost along the knife-edge of the mind. It was the comfort of the "great good Walt" that he reminded one of those extensive and really quite important portions of America which lay outside of Boston. The excellent people of that city, of course, regarded all such outlying portions as mere provinces, but Walt made one ask whether Boston itself might not be a province—a most audacious conjecture! For all that Walt seemed to care, Boston might as well have not been there at all.—Well, yes, it was true that Emerson had been born there. Perhaps one had better let Boston off on account of Emerson, that one wholly righteous man.

Walt somehow reminded one of the Mississippi, so hulking he was and hirsute, so coarsely clean, so full of power at rest. Walt's "pomes," as he called them, were like that river. They made the neat little effusions of Dr. Holmes and the learned frivolities of Mr. James Russell Lowell look like rivulets. You little New England streams, born of the granite and eastward-running, singing the Old World tunes, can you hear this vast low voice of the Father of Waters—singing perhaps not at all, but rumbling forever on in its broad strong bass while the river fumbles blindly at the prairie-mud, bearing onward the blood of the land? Bronson Alcott heard it. To him it seemed to be saying "Come West, young man! Come West!"

Alcott liked New York far better than he did Walpole. After his three months there he was back again in another month for another round of Conversations, lectures, dinners, calls upon Horace Greeley and Walt Whitman, and evenings at Mrs. Botta's salon. The people of New York had heard of him, yet liked him well. He was beginning to accumulate a modest fame. His acquaintance was phenomenally wide; he had been for many years a leader in movements that were acquiring the dignity of distance; and the heresies of his younger manhood were remembered, if at all, with an indulgent smile. Already venerable in appearance, with a mobile face written full of patient and hopeful meanings, with a beautiful voice and an utterance strange yet delightful, he commanded respect wherever he went. He was more and more regarded as a thoroughly American exhibit, with the kind of mental thews we could make here in this land out of our own materials. The newspapers of New England began to make a large amends for the earlier ferocities of the Boston press. They were calling him "Emerson's master" now. It was absurd, of course, and yet. . . . But how could they have found out a thing like that, which he himself had never said, never thought, never even felt? Emerson was a very great man. He, Alcott, was simply a man to whom ideas occasionally occurred—ideas which he liked to talk over among his friends. And besides, what did it matter who Emerson's master might be? A good teacher must die into the life of his pupil, and must be glad to die.

At Yale College, whither Alcott ventured with some hesitation in March of 1857, all this connection with Emerson and this leadership in transcendental reform was less than no recommendation. Yale College was still carrying on in the traditions of orthodoxy which Cotton Mather had hoped she might maintain, so that Alcott was not greatly surprised to find himself publicly preached against in the College Chapel after he had been in New Haven less than two weeks—not by name, to be sure, but as representative of "the new philosophical infidelity." "New"? Well, perhaps. It had been only twenty years since Andrews Norton had

[466]

been flying the same storm signals to warn the youth of Cambridge.

And so the days at Yale, all his earnest talks with a handful of earnest undergraduates, seemed to go for nothing. Alcott did not then know that a certain junior named William T. Harris was finding in those Conversations on Plato and Plotinus the turning-point of his intellectual career. Not for ten years more would Alcott discover that in his talks at Yale, which had seemed a complete failure, he had raised up for himself the most ardent, perhaps the most able, of all his interpreters and defenders.

During his two visits to New York and his stay at New Haven Alcott had been keeping in the dark of his mind, in those hidden recesses where he habitually left the troubles that could not be helped, a dull anxiety. His daughter Elizabeth was not well. In the preceding summer his wife, with her somewhat impetuous charity, had done what she could to help a neighbor at Walpole whose children were ill with scarlet fever, and the result had been that Elizabeth had come down with the same disease. After a serious illness she had seemed to recover in part, but her strength had never returned. Week by week, day by day, she was fading from them. In August her mother took her to the seashore. In September, when the family moved back to Concord and bought Orchard House, it was clear, in spite of the doctor's repeated assurances, that she had not long to live. She had "consumption." In January she began to say her quiet farewells. She gave away all of her few possessions—her piano, her writing-desk, her copy of "Undine," and the letters from her father and mother. She was not in the least unhappy, nor did she wish others to be so. Bronson Alcott watched through many nights and days beside his dying girl, reading to her, talking with her about the incoming springtime, or only sitting silent and feeling that no springtime could ever blossom for him again. It was on the fourteenth of March, 1858, that he finally knew the sharp swift

[467]

pang which had come to his brother, Emerson, sixteen years before.

Louisa had gone to Emerson's door to ask about little Waldo. "Child, he is dead," had been the father's only answer. And now, within an hour of Elizabeth's passing, there was Emerson at the door.

Soon after came Thoreau, her friend.

GO WEST, YOUNG MAN

)rchard house—The pedlar takes the road again—First view
f the West—The St. Louis Hegelians—"Slovenly greatness"
Concord's ambassador at large—Weaving the land together

IFE might falter and stumble and stop, yet somehow life went
on. For the day on which Elizabeth died her father recorded,
a part of the work going on at Orchard House: "Bricklayer
uilds the west-parlor fireplace, fashioning it after my design,
e bricks projecting from the jambs and forming an arch." Two
ys after her death came Anna's birthday, and to Bronson Alcott
ere came "pleasing memories of the dear one and a night of
od and refreshing rest." One day more and we read in the
urnal:—

> Today comes McKee and his man, and begins re-
> pairs on the house. They look first at the foundations
> and work on the sills of the buildings. Benjamin car-
> ried the chimneys together in the garret, Garfield
> helping, and I overseeing and planning as the work pro-
> ceeds.

So, for more than a hundred pages of the Journal for 1858, and throughout the spring and summer, the record of alterations and renovations at Orchard House runs on and on. Elizabeth had her new house at Sleepy Hollow, and her father was building his. A house for time and a house for eternity—what was the difference? "Wherever we may lodge," he said once, "there is but a thin casement between us and immensity." During all the rest of his life there would be an unassuageable ache of longing at his heart for this dead girl who had been more dear to him than any other creature. But he was like a hale old apple tree: let the wind tear off its central bough—it goes on growing.

Alcott made Orchard House what it is to-day—a sound, substantial, dignified, and in some ways even beautiful building. In spite of the "unconquerable stupidity" of joiners and carpenters, he made it to suit himself, although he had constantly to remember the truth of the words he quoted from Thomas Fuller: "He who alters an old house is tied as a translator to the original." The old house upon which he was working had been so decrepit that it was thrown into the bargain as of no value when the land was purchased; but he kept every original beam and rafter in its place and converted the old ash-holes and ovens into arched alcoves. Taking example from his father's building on Spindle Hill, he added a washwoman's shanty to the rear. Thus he built the house of his body as he had the house of his mind and spirit out of materials which had been discarded as of no further use. Once more he showed himself to be that good kind of antiquarian who values the past solely for what it can give to the present and future.

Orchard House is beautiful not so much in architectural symmetry, for indeed in that respect it leaves something to be wished, as in the clear mark it bears of a mind and a character. One might say that it was made as a bird's nest is shaped by the pressure of the bird's own warm breast. Concord people were amused when they saw that Alcott was painting his house

ORCHARD HOUSE

CONCORD, MASSACHUSETTS

earthen color; but they did not know what good reasons he had for loving the color of earth—and especially now, when he thought where Elizabeth was lying. That dark reddish brown was a symbol to him, and he was to choose it for the binding of one of his later books. So in every detail of structure and hue he found out and obeyed his deepest impulse, as a poet does, or a composer. Having lived in a hundred houses, he was at last building a home, or at least the outward shell of that holy thing. What he built is the house of a self-made man, but it is also the house of a man who made things in his own way and made them like himself. Of a dignified amplitude, simple without bareness, slightly odd and with just a touch of the Victorian Romantic, there it stands to-day under its one vast surviving elm tree, unmistakably the house of Bronson Alcott, and one of the most successful of his undertakings.

And the decorations of the interior by Alcott's three daughters, especially the mural paintings of birds and flowers and faces done by the youngest daughter, May, are quite as much an expression of the father's mind as they could have been if done by his own hand. They perfectly represent his sole and life-long dependence upon an inward and personal wealth, and also his determination to bring that wealth totally to bear upon the sanctuary of the home. With his daughters, at any rate, he had not failed as a teacher, for he had taught them to depend upon themselves. It is no derogation from the service of a faithful wife and mother to say that whatever these daughters ever did, most certainly including the famous and widely beloved books that Louisa was to write at Orchard House, was only a free extension of what had been in the heart of that boy who had carved a violin for himself out of a maple stump and had begun his artistic career by decorating his father's barn floor.

Alcott loved the place as he never loved any other. He hoped to live out his days there. At the age of fifty-eight the pedlar seemed to be settling down. The mere age of the house, and the magnificent antiquity of its two great elms, was a constant delight to his imagination. It bound his life to lives far back. Who should say now that he, Bronson Alcott of Connecticut, did not belong to Concord?

And as Alcott rebuilt Orchard House, the house had its subtly reciprocal effect upon him. Henceforth he was to be no longer a lackland, who could think and advocate almost anything. He was to be a landowner, a householder, a man with a stake in things as they are—that is to say, a man on the inside looking out. Ah, and what a difference it made, that simple shift in the point of view. Society, propriety, even private ownership of this world's goods were no longer things to contend against from an ignorant distance, but things dear and near and necessary. If in his last decades Bronson Alcott gradually let fall one long-cherished heresy after another, until it was hard to distinguish him from almost any orthodox person, the reason was not so much that he was growing old but, partly, that he had a fine old house of his own in a fine old town, and that he needed a set of opinions—theological, social, political—to harmonize therewith.

The pedlar was indeed settling down, but that was no reason for giving up peddling. The wanderer had at last a home, but a main advantage in such a possession is in having a place to leave and return to. Early in December, therefore, as soon as he had begun to feel well established at Orchard House, Alcott set out for St. Louis. He had been urgently invited thither by William T. Harris, that same brand which he had snatched from the orthodox burning down at Yale hardly more than a year before. Ordinarily it took a pupil at least ten years to find out that he had been taught at all, but this energetic man, twenty-three years old, was already the ring-leader in a group of philosophers banded together out there to think the oldest thoughts in the youngest way. They wanted Bronson Alcott to come and "show views."

[472]

Alcott had conversed twice before "at the West," but never beyond those parts of Ohio which seemed a mere extension of Connecticut. Now, at Christmas time in 1858, he got his first glimpse of what was then the real West—and did not like it. The farmer, the villager, the gardener in him, the lover of civility and decorous human association, found nothing in the featureless landscape of southern Illinois that the eye could pause upon with pleasure, nothing that an American from New England could recognize as his own. While the train puffed and lumbered and lurched across the prairie lands, the man who had been accustomed from boyhood to walking out of one town and immediately into another began to ask himself where were the towns. He did not know that the talent for town-building, or rather the art of the village, which had been brought up out of the Punjab many thousands of years ago and had spread its beautiful works over Europe and all over Old and New England, had been lost irretrievably in the crossing of the Appalachians. It had tumbled out at the tailboards of the West-bound wagons. It had not got even so far as the highboys and the old four-poster beds. For these pioneers had wanted land above all things; they had left nearly all other good things behind for the land; and they had built their Western houses not in the warmly sociable New England way but in the midst of interminable acres of corn. Even at midwinter the man from Spindle Hill could see that they certainly had found the land they sought—but at what a price of all that made life worth living! This must be the loneliest country on earth.

"We pass several places . . . called cities," the traveler wrote the twenty-eighth of December.

They consist of a few rude dwellings, embedded in mud at this season, standing in the open prairie country. Here and there a pretty coppice of timber is seen, a clump of trees along some straggling stream of turbid water, sparse cornfields and log-hovels—the general

[473]

landscape looking slovenly and dismal enough. Wild, and spreading indefinitely into the distance, the prairie is yet tame and monotonous, and the eye takes flight into the over-spreading sky to get relief from the sameness, and fancy prospects above and beyond the horizon of sedge and sward extending far into immensity. It is an ocean of gray grass, yet without the grandeur of waves and mountain crests to awaken the picturesque and delight the imagination.

At the end of his first day in St. Louis Alcott wrote in similar strain:—

I return by the levee along the Mississippi, seeing the steamers, the mound, the people—all novel and strange to a New Englander, showing me how purely Eastern I am, how little I have in common with the wild life of the West. I seem to be older than this wilderness, its trades, its rough ways, and look about me for the mankind, the landscape, of which I am part and parcel as if I had been thrown upon the banks by some mishap, and some centuries too soon.

Thus Alcott felt himself almost a foreigner in the very mid of his own country. He was not really "older" than anything, b flexible though his mind was, he could not immediately adjt himself to the sudden and violent change from New England, w its neighborly little towns, to this shambling and shapeless cou try in which there were no real towns whatever, or apparen even the seeds of them. As he had done in England, he looked what was not there, and so did not see what was really prese All about him, if he had but known it, there was a country t would have delighted his mystical space-loving eyes; and round him, as he was to discover in later Western journeys, w hearts at least as warm and minds at least as keen as those t he knew at home.

[474]

On this trip, however, even the St. Louis philosophers were
somewhat disappointing. They were a contentious lot, and, with the
exception of Harris, not in the least admiring. It was little to them
that a man came from Concord and knew Emerson. They lived in
St. Louis, the "Athens of the West," and knew their Hegel. Most
embarrassingly well they knew their Hegel, and Alcott knew him
hardly at all. They were planning to translate all of Hegel's works,
and in the meantime they were living as they thought good Hege-
lans ought to live—not as thinkers only, and not as mere "Dedicated Minds," whatever that vague phrase might be supposed to
mean, but as businessmen, lawyers, politicians, scholars, and, above
all, citizens. They were deeply and most respectfully, almost reli-
giously, interested in "the State," which they appeared to consider
a vastly more important thing than any individual or combination
of individuals could ever be. One even heard them say that the State
or Nation was not a means to better living but somehow an end in itself. Bronson Alcott, who had never yet voted in any national election, had difficulty in believing that a group of men who took politics so seriously could be philosophers at all. What would Henry
Thoreau have said of them—he who so often remarked that he
failed to see how politics concerned him in any way? What would
Emerson think of this doctrine that Man in the aggregate is
somehow greater than the sum of his individual parts? And then
they were so learned, so logical, so determined to see everything
in its historical relations. They told Alcott that nothing was to be
understood, and least of all an idea, except in terms of its history;
and this, to him, a good transcendentalist who knew scarcely any
history whatever, was a most perplexing assertion.

Alcott read the philosophers some of his "Orphic Sayings."
Their response was not the respectful silence to which he had been
accustomed. They were aggressive. They wished to be told precisely what he meant by this and that vague term, and often he
could not tell them. Oh, in a way they were respectful enough.
They did not try to howl down the "Sayings," like those ex-

[475]

tremely merry young gentlemen of the Boston newspapers. They
saw that there might be something in them; but they wanted to
question it, turn it this way and that, classify it, rather than
merely accept it gratefully as an inspired and prophetic utterance
Inspiration meant far less to them than it had long meant in
Boston. They had more to say about "dialectic" and "method"—
terms by which they seemed to suggest something like hard, close
logical thinking. In other words, they depended rather upon
what Coleridge had taught Alcott to call the "lower understanding" than upon the "Higher Reason." Philosophizing to them
was not at all the sort of thing that Alcott had done when he
wrote his "Orphic Sayings"—that is, a rapid jotting-down of
such ideas as happened to come. Rather, it appeared to be a
decidedly laborious kind of intellectual work. In a word, these
men were Hegelians, and, more remotely, Aristotelians. Alcott, on
the other hand, belonged to the great Platonic race.

On his first visit to St. Louis, therefore, Alcott did not have
pleasant time. One infers from several minor indications, indeed
that he experienced some definitely bad quarters of an hour in t
terrific mental grip of a certain Western philosopher named Henr
C. Brockmeyer, who was far more like an anaconda than Theodo
Parker had ever been when it came to the crunching of tra
scendental bones. Alcott appears to have been simply dazed
these attacks. His health was seriously shaken by the hard wo
of the winter and by the effort, which seemed at first nea
hopeless, to comprehend and to share views with this aggressi
energetic, rough-and-ready West. As soon as he returned to C
cord he secured two or three simplified expositions of the philo
phy of Hegel, but they meant almost nothing to him. Neit
could Emerson make much of them.

Alcott decided that a man should not start in at sixty ye
of age to learn a new philosophy, a totally new habit of thou
Gardening was more in his line than Hegel. And the Supe
tendency of the Concord Schools, to which he was elected in 1

[476]

of 1859, was of course entirely in his line. For six years he did the
work of that office, walking from school to school,—and it was a
long distance from the school at Bateman's Pond to that at Nine
Acre Corner,—interviewing teachers, holding classes, managing
school festivals, and writing enormous annual reports. His
salary was one hundred dollars a year.

John Brown of Kansas, who came to Concord on the eighth of
May, was a man far more easily understood than Hegel, for he
too was one to whom God had spoken. Alcott heard Brown speak,
took his hand, talked with him for half a minute, and then
went home to write in his Journal: "This is the man to do the
deed." It was one of his most clearly prophetic utterances, although he can have had no notion, when he made it, what particular Deed was to be done. In October he was told, by the
news from Harper's Ferry; and in December he took his part
in Concord's public funeral, managed by Henry Thoreau, for Captain John Brown.

What would those defenders of the State against the Individual
be saying, out in St. Louis, to a Deed like this?

Alcott was to have three more opportunities to find out what
men were saying in the Athens of the West. The Civil War postponed all his Western journeying, but in 1866 he set forth again
toward the Mississippi and the group of thinkers which was now
beginning to be called "the St. Louis Philosophical Society." It is
a months after the assassination of Lincoln when we see him
once more Westward-bound in "the cars." Looking out of the
window on the dead waste and middle of Illinois, he writes in his
Journal: "One mile is like every other. Nothing breaks the prospect, and the faces seen at the stations seem transcripts of the
final landscape." This is what he said in the same place seven
years ago, and one is not surprised. Few men at his age lay aside
a rooted prejudice or take up a novel thought, see a new
horizon. The eyes that first looked out at little rocky up-and-down

[477]

Spindle Hill sixty-seven years ago can hardly be expected to find their prey of beauty in the sprawl of these level miles.

But then, of a sudden, there comes the thought of Lincoln. It is precisely as though the spirit of the dead President, the "Martyr," were whispering in his ears below the thunder of the cars: "This is the land that bred me." Ah, that makes a difference! Bronson Alcott has long been accustomed to testing the worth of a country by the men that it can make; and if this dull unpromising prairie-land has produced "the first great American," as all the North is calling Lincoln now that he lies asleep in Springfield, then it must indeed be a good and great country. At last the ideal American, "the Man" of whom so many hopeful and bewildered voices have been prophesying for fifty years, has been found—has been unmistakably and unforgettably pointed out by the assassin's bullet. This is the Man of that quintessential Americanism which Thoreau could only suggest and Whitman could only describe. And the place he came from must be "America."

We can seldom make sure about any conversion whether it really so sudden or instantaneous as it may seem; but there can be no doubt that Alcott's thought did take a long leap as he sat there in the smoky train on the eighth of February, 1866. How long a leap it was we can only estimate by comparing him with men like Holmes and Lowell whose thoughts about their country remained, for better or worse, Boston-bound. But Alcott was ready for that leap. If forty years in Boston did not bind him the reason is to be sought partly in the fact that he was born and bred on New England's frontier, and partly in those peddling journeys "at the South" which enabled him to draw a long base line for a later triangulation. His return along the ancestral path to Boston, at a time when many of his contemporaries were going West, had not made him really a "back-trailer" because in the return he had sought and found an intellectual frontier. Through all the years in Boston he had been living in the West of

[478]

Mind. His thoughts, if not his body, had gone out pioneering. And so now he is ready for the whispering ghost whose message is to make him out of a New Englander into an American.

How strange that it should be the ghost of Lincoln! Alcott's first ballot in a national election had indeed been cast, in 1860, for the "Rail Splitter," but it was cast with no enthusiasm. Emancipation had made a huge difference in his feelings, as it had in Emerson's also, but more important by far had been the dire event at Ford's Theater. Before the death of Lincoln there was not one completely favorable reference to him in Alcott's journals; yet now, ten months later, Alcott accepts the already full-blown "Lincoln Myth" without hesitation.

> I reflect [he says] that here was the home of the Great American President. Here grew the honest, upright Chief Magistrate, continuing to catch from these dead levels, the plain poor images about him, a speech eloquent with native sense and humanity that universities could not have given. 'Tis true, there were skies above, the great river flowing seaward, the wild adventures of the pioneer, the excitements of river and road, to fashion him into the Man he was—the anecdote, the epigram, the argument, the sentiment that went home to the heart and head of a native and made him the first real ruler of a Republic. It seems a victory won from circumstances least favorable to the growth of a character like his; and yet how much of him seems indigenous, and could not have sprung into life elsewhere—a large-hearted, loyal soul with the plainness and slovenly greatness that the West favors.

Slovenly greatness"—when he wrote those words Bronson Alcott was at last beginning to comprehend his America. The es of a merely negative gentility and the blinders of Yankee vincialism were falling from his eyes. As he looked out of the window at the wide mystical land, beautiful exceedingly, but not as he had hitherto known beauty, he was making one of those numberless discoveries of America that may have begun with Leif Ericsson and are certainly still going on. It had been necessary that the greater and the essential America should come to him first in a human manifestation, for he was always able to read from a man back to landscape, though not in the opposite direction. Lincoln had to die and had to pass into popular myth and legend before Alcott could see the West with open eyes. But then—"slovenly greatness"! Was not that the very thing Walt Whitman had, and the thing that the men of Boston certainly had not? Yes, and "the great good Walt" may have had his share in the revelation of America to Alcott. Under the rumble of the cars there may have been some echo too of "Captain! My Captain!" and of "When Lilacs Last in the Dooryard Bloomed." What other land had ever made such magnificent roughhewn forthright songs for a national mourning—songs that needed nothing less than this interminable prairie-sky for the church of their sacred sorrow? "Slovenly greatness." Alcott saw it again, perhaps consciously saw it in American landscape for the first time, as he crossed the broadly rolling Mississippi.

Therefore the second visit to St. Louis was profoundly different from the first. Alcott was ready now to meet and to understand that amazing Westerner, Henry C. Brockmeyer. The man's life read like a quite incredible romance. What had he not done, been, seen, and known? He had been a German immigrant, a deserter, gigolo, a bootblack, a bootmaker, a hermit, a student at Brown University, a crack-shot hunter, a leader in the Missouri conflicts, a lawyer, a spellbinder, a politician, a philosopher, and an officer in the Union Army. He was yet to be Mayor of the City, Lieutenant Governor, and Governor of the State. And all the while he was an impassioned student of Hegel and an inspired interpreter of Goethe. He was translating Hegel's *Logic* with a gigantic power of thought, and also with a perfectly tyrannical

[480]

difference to the niceties of English idiom. Boston's paltry and Puritanical doubts as to whether Goethe had not encouraged the amatory enthusiasms of rather too many women awoke in him nothing but a scornful and tempestuous laughter.

Alcott had retired from his first encounters with this man considerably dazed, perhaps with a suspicion that he had been insulted, and undoubtedly with a sense of having been bruised in various sensitive places. And yet now—but let us listen to him:—

> Brockmeyer comes and talks all day, telling us of his Prussian life and his adventures since coming to this country. It seems he graduated at Brown University, was offered a Professorship—as a bribe, he thinks, to silence his wild free-thinking. But he went West and South, fell into various straits of love and want, redeemed himself by labor at an iron-foundry, then purchased a farm in the wilderness some sixty miles from St. Louis, built his cabin and hunted game, and now comes from his solitudes to interpret the Kantian philosophy to this little Yankee Club—for which he is very competent, being well read in it and having an original genius for metaphysic and the hard logic of his master.—A rough sample of intelligence and fire; yet affectionate, very entertaining, and with a jealous sensitiveness to freedom and the rights of genius that might sometimes pass for audacity and impudence, regardless of consequences and the due respect proper to well-bred companions. He stays late, talking all the time with an abandonment very rare to see.

Except for the fact that the "Club" was not "Yankee"—hough Harris, to be sure, hailed from Connecticut—and that ockmeyer did not "interpret the Kantian philosophy" unless th shouts of derision, this account was as accurate as the tales cott heard enabled it to be. Alcott did not know that Henry ockmeyer was already a titan in the eyes of many young men,

[481]

or that he was himself actively contributing to his own mythos. Alcott believed what he was told—as Yankee visitors in the West have usually found it convenient to do.

He remained four weeks with this little group of Hegelians, amazed to find such a company encamped there on the edge of the wilderness and burrowing deeper into the thought of Germany than the academicians of Boston and Cambridge cared to go. Brockmeyer—at any rate when he was not idly whittling sticks or spinning tall tales—was a perfect tornado of intellectual force and speed. Harris had a precision and delicacy of metaphysical thought to which Alcott had never pretended and the like of which he had never before seen. Dr. Watters, a physician, had been thinking out for years, it seemed, precisely Alcott's own favorite doctrine of "Genesis." He had perfected it by the camp-fires of the Union Army, and meant to publish his results as soon as he could get free from political work. Kroeger, primarily a student of Fichte rather than of Hegel, was Treasurer of the City and a man of many affairs. Howison had a surprising erudition in many fields. Young Denton Snider, although not a man of any deep thoughtfulness, had an audacious and irreverent wit that sometimes made one uncomfortable. Snider was an adorer of Brockmeyer, and also a student of Shakespeare—whom Alcott could never understand.

Bronson Alcott was not sure that he had met the expectation of this exacting group. In some ways he found them bewildering even on his second visit. Yet their eagerness of thought, the manly warmth of heart which no bluntness of Western manner or tough contentiousness of debate could hide, pleased him. And, upon the whole, they seemed inclined to take him in. They thought that they saw some hopeful hints and gleams of Hegelianism in him, although he could not imagine how such things had ever got there.

One can see, to-day, that there were other grounds for sympathetic understanding. The training of all these Western

[482]

philosophers, with the exception of Harris and possibly of Brock-meyer, had been as irregular as Alcott's own. From the official and academic point of view they had as little right as he to be meddling at all with the deep matters they discussed. Like the railroad that had brought Alcott Westward, fumbling and groping its way toward the Western sea, or like the mighty river flowing near the houses where they met, their thought was audacious and energetic but also tentative, exploratory, and utterly unsure. Scholarship of a sort some of them had, but only one or two had intellectual discipline. Their thought was like the sprawling fenceless prairie-lands where the buffalo still ranged and roamed and stampeded under a traveling canopy of dust. Intellectually, they too were self-made men—and Alcott liked them none the less for that. He thought that there was something gallant, something wholly American, in the way they had set themselves down there, on the last tremulous frontier of time, to ask and answer the eternal questions.

Indeed it is little wonder that Alcott soon came to feel at home in St. Louis, as later at Dubuque and Jacksonville and Rockford, and finally wherever he went in the West. In every town that he took on the routes of his thought-pedlary there would be a group, small or large but always enthusiastic, of persons as untrained as he was and quite as undaunted as he by their lack of formal education. They were people of his own kind. Many of them had gone West about the time when he went to Boston. It was not strange that he had failed to find them in Boston during his search of forty years. He found them now.

"These western minds," Alcott wrote while still in St. Louis on his second visit, "drive home the argument at a fearful rate." Argument was just the thing he had never before been able to stand; but now he endured and liked it. "Custom, tradition, and what we call deference to authorities," he went on, "they hold embarrassing and set them rudely aside. They ignore them altogether. 'Tis refreshing to see, and worth the journey. Nothing better for dissolving superstitions." He suggests that every divinity student "should take three months of his course out here with these loaded brains," so that he may return to the East "with some prospect of touching men and times instead of speaking to ante-diluvians and Hebrews." He sees no chance of a hearing for a mere scholar and bigot in these free wild parts. "And though I value the reserves more than most," says he, "loving the sacred names and persons as I find few of my contemporaries do, yet this free, frolicsome, slovenly sense of able, earnest men has a formidable attraction." Once more, no doubt, it was the delight in companionship and the need of association that was drawing him on, but also he was gaining a new comprehension of America's width and range.

We have seen that the Hegelianism of the St. Louis group remained almost a complete mystery to their visitor. Yet there is this curious fact to be remembered by future historians of American thought, that Alcott the transcendentalist was a main influence in the intellectual awakening of William T. Harris, who in his turn—as Editor of the *Journal of Speculative Philosophy* and, later, as United States Commissioner of Education—spread Hegelian thought throughout the country. Alcott was partly responsible for the fact that by the year 1900 there was a philosophy dominating the American universities and colleges which he himself had been quite unable to understand.

Upon his return to New England from his second visit in St. Louis Alcott felt like one of the scouts whom Moses sent forth to spy out the Promised Land, and who came back bearing the fruits of that country. First of all, of course, he must tell Emerson of what he had discovered. But Emerson, though always eager enough to believe any good thing about Alcott or America, could scarcely, as Alcott says, "credit this report." He had been West many times himself, and had met all sorts and conditions of people, but he had never had such talk with any of them as the

[484]

that Alcott related. How should he? For Emerson carried an envelope of silence about with him wherever he went, like the water spider's bubble of air. People told Emerson, as a rule, what they thought Emerson expected to hear from them; and in his lectures Emerson told the people what conclusions he had arrived at in the quiet of his study at Concord. The whole thing was highly beneficial, no doubt, to both parties, and certainly Emerson gained much from his half-admiring and half-humorous observations of Western life and manners. His attitude, however, remained that of a spectator, and there was little of co-operation in it. Alcott, in his Conversations, "shared views," and it was therefore natural that he should get closer to the mind and heart of America and should bring back a different account of his travels. He returned with a conviction that the future, the hope of the country, the true center of America, was Western, and that Boston's assurance of its own intellectual and cultural superiority would soon be out of date. Toward the end of his active life he was to introduce to New England a number of the best Minds he had found in the Western States. There, he seemed to say, was his cluster of grapes from the Promised Land.

Between 1853 and 1882 Alcott made ten "conversational tours" of the West—using that word as he did for the entire country beyond the Hudson River. From first to last he spoke in about one hundred towns and cities, in the States of New York, Ohio, Indiana, Illinois, Wisconsin, Kansas, Iowa, and Missouri. His farthest reach into the West took him only to Fort Dodge, Iowa, although when he was almost eighty he toyed with the notion of going all the way to the Pacific Coast and so "belting the Continent with talk." In some towns he appeared again and again, as at Bloomington, Peoria, Dubuque, St. Louis, Chicago, Rockford, and Evanston. In others, such as Cleveland and Jacksonville, he must have been for a time almost a familiar figure, with his erect carriage, his white hair falling to his shoulders, his black "cut-away" coat, black cape, silk hat, and the gold-headed ebony cane given him by Western admirers. He succeeded in the West as he had never done in New England. He succeeded in a way and to a degree suggesting how different many things might have been with him if he had gone Westward with the young men of his generation. From the first of his tours he returned, in 1854, as we have seen, with net earnings of precisely one dollar. From the last of them he came back at the age of eighty-two with twelve hundred dollars, having spoken—more than half of the time for nothing—in thirty-seven towns and cities during a tour lasting for seven months which covered nearly five thousand miles.

The West, so strange and featureless to Alcott on his first journey, filled up with friends as the years went by. In Dubuque there was Mrs. Mary Adams, undoubtedly a "Sibyl," who made that bright and stirring little city like a home to him, and who also began the cairn at Walden Pond on the site of Thoreau's hut. At Jacksonville there was that redoubtable doctor Hiram K. Jones, whom even Alcott came to think "too Platonic." At Cleveland there was the brilliant preacher Frank Gunsaulus, twenty-five years old and already famous, in whose house Alcott stayed for weeks as an honored guest and in whose pulpit he preached. But the list of such names would be endless. Every tour became a series of visits, a succession of reunions, a clasping of friendly hands and a greeting of well-remembered faces. Going West became like going home. It satisfied the traveler's three chief needs, for wandering, for association, and for return. And it was always a happy voyage over oceans of talk.

Clearly, moreover, this Western touring was just the work for a gentlemanly pedlar, going from door to door and—by his smile, his modesty, and some other nameless charm—making friends instead of finding customers, gaining happiness and little money. At eighty and beyond he was still trudging the road with his Yankee notions, dearly bought and for the most part given away. In six years, no change.

[486]

In sixty years no gain—unless, to be sure, we might care to count simple happiness as a gain, and quietly spreading beneficence, and the keeping of the honor of one's soul. Friends seemed to him always a great gain, and so was the warm and growing sense that verily he did belong in this America. Boston had thrust him forth and Concord had been sometimes a little cold, but the greathearted West had taken him in. No little infant town lay so deeply hidden in the country of the corn as not to have heard of the "Sage of Concord." No mushroom city of the plain was so absorbed in its moneymaking as not to wish to hear this man for whom money hardly existed. In new communities thirsting for antiquity he spoke of Concord, and helped to make his home town classic ground. In places newly won by the plow he spoke of Pythagoras, the Upanishads, and the laws of Manu, thus linking Beloit, Onarga, Rockford, Evanston, Peoria, Greencastle, and many another settlement of yesterday, with the misty ages out of which they had come. To regions chiefly concerned with the price of corn and the fattening of hogs he brought the names of Hawthorne, Thoreau, Emerson, and Louisa. When he stood up to speak in a country church or schoolroom, there was the father of Louisa, the friend of Emerson, the citizen of Concord and Boston. He was an unofficial Ambassador at Large from the East to the West, and then from West to East. His audiences were usually small, but they included in every town he visited those who were most likely to determine the thought and feeling of that place. He could not live with Frank Gunsaulus for three weeks without setting up reverberations that would roll on wherever that silver-tongued orator went in the following forty years. At Janesville, Wisconsin, he spent a few days with Jenkin Lloyd Jones. Four decades later Jones was preaching the Gospel according to Bronson Alcott to thousands of uprooted and bewildered Americans in Chicago.

Thus Alcott was like a bee, bearing the pollen of thought from the ancient times to the most modern and from the little mowings

[487]

beside the Musketaquid to the vast plains of the West. He was a shuttle, weaving past and present together, and helping to weave his country, too, into one seamless robe. But always he was most of all a pedlar—a gentlemanly pedlar, at whom the dogs barked less and less, with amulets and garnets and pearls in his pack.

HARVEST HOME

{ 1870-1882 }

"The Sage of Concord"–The failure of success–Society and Soli-
tude–Controversy–Personalism–Louisa's fame–Alcott's books
–The Concord School of Philosophy–Farewell–Ne plus ultra

BRONSON ALCOTT is a fascinating spectacle while one
watches him sowing his seed by the wayside and on stony
places among thorns; but he comes before us almost as a different
man when he begins to bring in his harvest from that good ground
which has yielded him, entirely to his own amazement, an hun-
dredfold. He has been glorious in his failures and heroic in his
defeats; but now during his last years, at any rate in their superficial aspect, he may seem to decline toward the level of that comparatively dull and insignificant person, the successful man. The
last twenty years of his active life were mostly years of success.

One does not at all mean that Alcott was coarsened by good
fortune, as most men are, or that he came to think of himself
more highly than he had reason to think. Beneath that preoccupation with his own thoughts which was the inevitable result

of his solitude there was in him a deep and enduring humility. He took the sunshine as he had the shadow, with a free, grateful, and unsullied heart. He could write signatures by the yard for admiring young ladies, could read the encomiums of the press upon his four or five unremarkable books, could be elected to honorary membership in the Harvard Chapter of Phi Beta Kappa, and could sit on hundreds of platforms, hearing himself called "The Sage of Concord," "The American Plato," and "Emerson's Master," without ever forgetting that he was really, after all, only a somewhat exceptional son of Spindle Hill. He had never sought for fame, and when a modest fame did come to him he received it with perfect sweetness, as he did the new creature-comforts secured by Louisa's far greater worldly success. Through fair days as through foul he kept the innocence of his heart. The child in him never died.

But what of the "Dedicated Mind," now stored with old experience, rich reading, and the gains of various men? Having been set aside for thinking, why should it not think on now, more eagerly and earnestly than ever, in these decades that ought to be the prime of intellectual life? For it was not an old mind. The upward thrust of the fountain had not yet spent its force. Even at eighty years of age Alcott was in several important ways a younger man than he had been at fifty. The final entries in his Journals show at least as much fire and verve as those he had written more than half a century before, and they cover, besides an enormously greater range of interest. There is no such heart breaking disintegration and slow mental deliquescence to watch in him as he was condemned to witness in Emerson. And yet his intellectual march—or, if it seems a better word, his wandering —did pause and come to a stop shortly after the Civil War, when he was about sixty-five. Thereafter he took up no new territory on the frontiers of the mind.

If anything, the elderly Alcott doubled backward on his own trail. In religious belief he rambled vaguely toward the Trintarian position. There came a time when he could charge one of his philosophic friends with being "too Platonic," and when he complained of certain old comrades in reform that they were carrying "individualism" too far. Are not these the familiar symptoms of a merely prosperous old age? In Alcott's tendency to smile down upon the enthusiasms of his younger years can we find anything but the injustice of a senescent man toward his own earlier self? While greed and ambition tightened their grip on the land after the Civil War they aroused in this man, once an idealist, no righteous wrath. About the shameful atrocities of carpetbagging days he spoke no word of denunciation. His silence about the conditions of labor in the factories of his later years was due, no doubt, to the complete ignorance of such matters which he shared with other literary persons, but this was an ignorance to which he, once a poor man, was not entitled. White slavery in the slums of Boston never awoke such anger in him as black slavery in the South had once awakened.

We shall see that most of these withdrawals and tergiversations had a deeply underlying cause, but there may have been certain superficial causes working as well. Perhaps the chief of these was the Civil War itself, which seemed to bring to a victorious end that long struggle in which Alcott's sympathies had been engaged for thirty years. When once the dark stigma of Southern slavery had been removed, might not so optimistic and so badly informed a man as Alcott have felt that every minor ill which American flesh could be heir to would soon be smiled out of existence? He would not have been alone in such a conclusion, for he was living in a time of shallow, unreflective cheerfulness and "expansion" which could not see that the War had made at least as many problems as it had solved. In the very fact, indeed, that the North had lost its passion, its sense of a divine errand, and had not gained in recompense anything like the South's ennobling experience of tragedy, there was cause enough for Alcott's apparent retrogression. More important still, however, was the gradual loss of his peers. First went Dr. Channing, then Thoreau, then William Russell, and finally, little by little, Emerson. Their places were taken by William T. Harris, Joseph Cook, Frank Gunsaulus, and F. B. Sanborn—all good and faithful friends, but men of lighter weight and slighter mold. It was not to be expected that Alcott would think so adventurously for such listeners as he had for the friends of his earlier years.

But he did continue to think—if not so adventurously as before yet with all the vigor he had ever shown. If he did not advance it was because he was solidifying his gains. In order to understand the final phase of Alcott's active career one must look not so much at its outward circumstance as at the permanent shape and habit of his mind, remembering that his intellectual life had never been primarily accumulative. In his age as in his youth he was the very antithesis of Browning's absurd old grammarian, forever piling up crude information without once asking how it might be put to a human use. That pitiful figure stands for the modern and the Western mind, always bursting with a random and explosive energy and asking never "How good?" but always "How much?" By comparison with its romantic vagabondage Alcott suggests the Oriental quest of a central unity and the ancient classic ideal of return. He is far more like the true Homeric Odysseus in his continual striving backward toward the simplicities of home than he is like Tennyson's Ulysses with his tireless pursuit of the horizon. Alcott's entire journey of thought led him backward through the bewildering Many toward the original One. We cannot too much insist, furthermore, that Alcott was a higher utilitarian, asking always what might be the value for actual living of this and that idea. A thought that could not be set to work in the contemporary American scene had little interest for him, and he saw, moreover, that America did not so much need new ideas as true ones, sifted, clarified, and worked into coherent scheme. Therefore the mere amount of his knowledge and the number of his ideas had never been to him a matter of any more concern than the quantity of his worldly goods. Margaret Fuller missed this point entirely when she complained to Emerson that Alcott's thoughts were few. Alcott himself would have preferred to have not few thoughts but only one.

Emerson's extensive comment upon the man who interested him more than any other contemporary is not entirely self-consistent, but it never deviates from the recognition that Alcott's thought was beautifully single and whole. His testimony on this matter will bear repetition. "The comfort of Alcott's mind," says he, "is the connection in which he sees whatever he sees. He is never dazzled by a spot of color or a gleam of light to value that thing for itself, but forever and ever is prepossessed by the undivided One behind it and all." Again he writes of his friend: "All that he sees and says is like astronomy, lying there real and vast, and every fact in eternal connection with the whole." After he had known Alcott for thirty-one years he wrote these words: "Last night's discourse only brought out with new conviction the old fundamental thoughts which he had when I first knew him." Emerson might sometimes complain that his friend's thought was monotonous, but his usual feeling was that of admiring gratitude toward a mind which seemed to him a single cosmos governed from within. This was his mood when he said of Alcott: "As pure intellect, I have never seen his equal."

Clearly, therefore, it is not of such a mind as Bronson Alcott's that we ought to expect a never-ending pursuit of an ever-receding goal. True "progress," in his belief, involves not an interminable pioneering like that of Cooper's Natty Bumpo but a thoughtful return upon a course once traversed. Living in a centrifugal age and country, his mind was unconquerably centripetal. The word that best sums up the habit of his thought is the word "integration."

This being so, one is led to ask in what single idea it was, if

[493]

any, that Alcott finally summed up his thought. He called that idea "Personalism," using a term which he may have borrowed from the St. Louis group. To him as to George Howison and, later, to Borden P. Bowne, Personalism was the doctrine that the ultimate reality of the world is a Divine Person who sustains the universe by a continuous act of creative will. A main advantage of this doctrine is the mediation that it provides between the extreme idealistic and materialistic positions, and this alone would have commended it to a thinker who had always been fascinated by the duplex aspect of the world. Even more important to a man of Alcott's intense sociality, however, was the clear implication that all apparently separate minds are bound together, like the planets of a solar system, by their common relation to a central Mind. In the philosophic vocabulary of his later years the antonym of "Personalism" was "Individualism"—a term into which he crowded all human ignorance, strife, misunderstanding, and even reform. All sin and error were due, he came to think, to the effort of individual wills to act as though they were independent of all other wills human and divine. Writing in 1868 to an inquirer about these matters, he said:

> I can only ask you to distinguish finely that in yourself which differences you from other persons essentially and that which unites and makes them one with yourself, also makes you one with them, indissolubly and forever. The unity is the Personality; the difference is the Individuality. . . . We must grow into and become one with the Person dwelling in every breast, and thus come to apprehend the saying "I and my Father are one"—that is, perceive that all souls have a Personal identity with God and abide in Him.

This is essentially the same idea with which Alcott had di
tressed Dr. Channing over thirty years before. It is the ide
for which he had contended with Emerson from the early da

of the "Transcendental Club," but always in vain. Just here, in fact, lay the widest intellectual gulf between the two friends, and that gulf was never bridged. Alcott insisted more and more upon a personal rulership of the world so powerful that it would finally blot out all human differences as the separate planets must one day be drawn back into the sun. Emerson could not accept this, whether because of some lingering Calvinism in him or because of his reluctance toward all intimate association. He wrote in 1863:—

> Alcott defended his thesis of personality last night, but it is not quite a satisfactory use of words. . . . I see profound need of distinguishing the First Cause as superpersonal. It deluges us with power; we are filled with it; but there are skies of immensity between it and us.

We may suspect that Personalism meant so much to Alcott partly because it gave a metaphysical and even a theological sanction to his social proclivities, and also that it meant comparatively little to Emerson because it emphasized a phase of experience in which he was seldom at his best. However that may be, Alcott, in his talks with Emerson as in every other human relationship, never ceased to speak the word "together" with a special intonation; but Emerson continued all his life to find a peculiar charm in the word "alone."

And yet one might easily make too much of these differences, for the two men did somehow maintain a noble friendship. Emerson was not oblivious to the truth that Alcott saw, for he wrote "The Over-Soul" as well as "Self-Reliance," and Alcott often tried, against the grain, to speak and think well of solitude. Perhaps all that we have here is a difference of emphasis upon a truth that has two aspects. We may say that every human soul lives alone, and cannot break out of its loneliness; but then we must also say, more seriously and deeply, that it lives united

[495]

with every other soul of the present or past or future. In t
cactus-forests of the American Southwest the individual pla
are seen standing far apart, each of them as it were a separ
fortress armed and bristling and hostile. One foot below the s
face of the ground the roots of those same plants are inextrica
intertwisted so as to form one continuous fabric.

Emerson's preference for solitude and Alcott's dependence up
association represent two aspects of one truth, but there can
no doubt which of these was more in keeping with the loft
temper and intelligence of the country after the Civil W
"Alone" had been a sufficient motto for the Puritan and the p
neer, but now that the States had been reunited by a huge cc
mon effort Whitman was beginning to "utter the word *en mass*
and Alcott, with a Yankee's dislike for mere promiscuity, was p
posing the cooler word "together." Such proposals are never
stantly accepted, and one cannot say that the "Rugged Indiv
ualism" of which Emerson is by far the noblest exponent I
even yet died out of the land. One can say, however, that it
dying, and that Alcott's strong emphasis upon association as
only sure means of individual freedom and happiness places I
in the vanguard of to-day and the ranks of to-morrow.

The sources of Alcott's Personalism are as deeply hidden
those from which he drew his transcendental thought or
theories of teaching. At first glance one would say that the
Louis group of philosophers, with their Hegelian reverence
the State, must have taught him much of this; and the suspic
is strengthened when one considers that George Howison, a me
ber of that group, later taught a set of ideas strongly tinged w
Personalism both at Harvard and at the University of Californ
where it may have had some influence upon Josiah Royce. 1
fact is, however, that the main elements of personalistic thou
are easily traceable to the beginnings of Alcott's intellect
career. He had always been a "personal theist." From the ti
of his first stay in Boston he had upheld the doctrine, which

[496]

was later to find in the Vedanta philosophy, that the human spirit is identical in essence with the Spirit of the Universe. From the period of the Temple School, if not before, he had always felt a conviction that an association or social group of any kind is somehow greater than the sum of its parts. He was still a young man when he made the arresting remark that whenever even two minds meet they pay deference to an invisible and silent third, vaguely felt as present. Throughout his life he was increasingly aware of an idea which is only to-day becoming clear to any large number of Western minds: that Deity is not so much above as it is about and within us, as the binding element which makes association possible, as the ether through which we communicate each with each. If any of these elements in the body of thought later known as Personalism were discussed during Alcott's visits at St. Louis, it was not he who learned them for the first time. So far as he was concerned, the source of them was probably Spindle Hill. There he had gained his lifelong awareness of an indwelling and all-sustaining Divine Person. There too, in that close-knit society, he had found his conviction that we act most wisely and well when we act together.

The ideas implicit in Personalism are discoverable in nearly everything that Alcott thought and said and did. Here is the clue to the labyrinth of his life and the integration of its apparent miscellaneity. Always a teacher, recognizing always that good instruction is a sympathetic sharing of a common good, he carried forward what he had learned in teaching children into his theory and practice of the Conversation. Why were his eyes uplifted while he talked with little companies in Massachusetts, New York, Ohio, Kansas, and Wisconsin? Because he was listening upward and hearkening inward for the voice of that Divine Person who presided, he thought, over every human assembly. Ordinary men, world-hardened and dusty-minded, assume that such allegations as this are mere empty figures of speech. Alcott was not an ordinary man, for the reason that he believed such things in com-

[497]

plete simplicity of mind. Consider that incident at the Temple School in which Miss Peabody had urged a private dealing with the private conscience but Alcott had held that the conscience of the entire group would be higher and more sensitive than that of any individual it contained. Whether right or wrong, he was advocating then precisely the same doctrine that filled the thought and the talk of his later years. Only the name of that doctrine was then lacking.

One important exception must be made, however, to the statement that the ideas involved in Personalism ruled Alcott's entire life. In our discussion of the Fruitlands episode we have seen a man who was not naturally a reformer temporarily pushed and pulled out of his course by tendencies too strong for him to withstand. During his later years Alcott habitually referred to the Fruitlands adventure as an example of "Individualism." In his recovery from that adventure he felt that he was returning from his separate self to the Divine Person—that is, from eccentricity to normality, from all that holds men apart to all that unites them, from strife to peace. Thus it was that he became "the serenest man in Concord." Thus it was, and not by the timid conservatism so frequently incident to old age, that he reached the prevailing orthodoxy of his later years. One may say that he kept his sympathy with the motives and purposes of reform but lost confidence in its more violent measures. At the meetings of the Free Religious Association and of the First and the Second Radical Club he was a frequent attendant and speaker, but was more and more distressed by the "extreme Individualism" of those organizations. When seventy-five years of age he attended a meeting of the New England Labor League and listened with keen interest to such "declared radical men" and "communists" as Colonel Green, Stephen Foster, E. H. Heywood, and John Orvis. He himself spoke at that convention, expressing approval of its general purposes and suggesting some of the quieter and less destructive ways by which reformers might do their work. One interested to learn that he dined that evening at the Parker House with the President of the League.

It should now be clear in what sense one says that Alcott, in his later years, made no intellectual advance but even turned back upon his course. Personalism was not a new idea to him but a coalescence of thoughts and attitudes with which he had been all his life familiar. Worked out by his habitual integration of his own native materials, it was more valuable to him, and far more creditable to his powers as a thinker, than any advance into new philosophic territory could have been. It rounded his thought and character, binding religion to philosophy and both of these to conduct. All things considered, one must call it his main intellectual triumph.

Alcott's contemporaries believed, rightly or wrongly, that he was the first clear formulator of the Personalistic position—in which case his influence upon American thought must have been far more extensive than has been supposed. Samuel Johnson of Salem believed and asserted Alcott's priority, and so did Dr. Joseph Cook of Boston—both of them, it would seem, with the implication that in this important respect Alcott had shown himself a more acute and a profounder thinker than Emerson. In the sixties and seventies it was felt by many persons that the early transcendentalists, with Emerson at their head, had fallen away into pantheism, and that Alcott had gone onward almost alone. The implied comparison between the two friends is fairly clear in certain remarks made in 1877 by so well-informed a man as Dr. C. A. Bartol:—

> To one transcendental philosopher, Mr. Alcott, we are in debt for his vital conception of Personality. A pure mystic, subsisting on the thin sweet grass of the Mount of Vision, in the full sweep of the pervading theory that blew like a trade wind against the conception of a conscious and willing Deity, he has kept his footing

and saw God keeping his. In all his Conversations, East and West, expounding matters so singular and hard to penetrate, he has held by selfhood as the strict anchor of Creation, and rendered a service for which his memory will be honored and dear. He is the true transcendentalist, teaching that the soul is no ephemeral thing, but lives beyond the momentary impression, in the past, the future, and in that eternity where time disappears, or all times are alike.

Against this passage one may set an entry in Alcott's Journal for the twenty-second of March, 1878:—

Return Thomas Taylor's translation of Jamblichus' book on the Mysteries to Emerson, and dine with him. The old topic of personal immortality comes into our discussion, and I find my friend as persistent as formerly in his Individualism. His faith is purely ethical, and demands the certainty of facts experienced individually. His idealism hesitates and pauses, appalled at the dread facts of the Personality. True to his convictions, he modestly rests in his Individualism, and is silent concerning what lies beyond. Perhaps he may be classed as an ideal theist, with that film of pantheistic haze that hovers always about that school of thinkers. This latent Pantheism has from the first characterized the New England school of Transcendentalists, and has not yet cleared itself from the clouds—most of its disciples being still touched with its indefiniteness, unable to find the certainty they seek. While it has modified favorably the materialistic tendencies of New England thinking, it has failed of planting itself upon the intuitions of the Personal and Immortal.

The comparison between Alcott and his far more famous frien was often made in the chorus of praise by which America tri to atone to the elder man for a long period of neglect. Thus,

[500]

take only one example, the *Chicago Tribune* remarked in a review of Alcott's *Tablets* that "Mr. Emerson has been to Mr. Alcott as Plato to Socrates. He has elaborated where the elder thinker did little but meditate and converse. He has written for the world what his senior contemporary has wrought out in his closet. Alcott was an Emersonian transcendentalist before Emerson, and if the latter has been the greater master of literary exposition, the former was the earlier student and teacher of this new philosophy. . . . He is a teacher to whom Mr. Emerson always refers with reverence."

Nothing could exceed the complete and beautiful modesty with which Alcott took the praise of his contemporaries. In May of 1872 he found that a New York newspaper had attributed his poem "The Goblet" to Emerson, as a London magazine thirty years before had attributed Emerson's first book, *Nature,* to him. He said in his Journal:—

> I should be proud to write verses that any poet might take to be his. But how these, first printed in the *Commonwealth* several years ago and again in my *Tablets,* came to be taken as his I cannot conjecture —unless it be that my book has found but few readers and, the verses sounding perhaps Emersonian, like his "Bacchus", are attributed to him. . . . I ought perhaps to distrust the having poetic gifts after Emerson's telling me I had neither ears nor eye for melody or metre. At any rate, I have written too little verse to claim the poet's inspiration.

There are certain men to whom the Fates owe a serene old age, and Bronson Alcott was one of them. He loved to be old, and he gathered the best fruit of longevity. He was amazingly hale and hearty, so that at an age when most men hug the fire he still took pleasure in working in his garden. At almost eighty years of age he enjoyed a long ride in an open sleigh over the plains of

Wisconsin with the thermometer at thirty-five degrees below zero. "The great expecter," as Thoreau had called him, looked forward until the very end, just as the young pedlar he had once been had looked eagerly on toward the next house, the next turn in the road. At seventy-five and at eighty he was still making plans that would have required decades for their execution. In his glad welcome to every advance of science and invention, to every important new idea or new book, he seemed not an old man at all but a youth who was to live the bulk of his days in the coming century.

A main reason, no doubt, for the almost complete success of Alcott's old age is to be seen in the way he filled it with youth. In the month of December following his eightieth birthday he lectured on the sixth at Amherst College, on the ninth at Divinity Hall, Cambridge, and on the nineteenth at the Young Men' Christian Association in Boston. "Without youth," he said, "wha were any world conceivable? Heaven must be populous with dam sels and beautiful boys, babes, and children. I see no room fo old people." Throughout his eighth decade one of his deares friends was Miss Ellen Chandler, a young schoolteacher of Fram ingham who eventually married William Goodwin, Professor of Greek at Harvard. His ability to attract and hold the affectionai admiration of younger men was shown in his relations with Ma ston Watson, the famous horticulturist of Plymouth, with Dani Ricketson, who had first been a friend of Thoreau's, with H. G. C Blake, Thoreau's disciple and editor, with F. B. Sanborn, f many years Alcott's close friend and finally his biographer, ai with W. T. Harris, who was both the child and the ablest i terpreter of Alcott's thought. Not the least remarkable sign his enduring vitality is the fact that his admiration for W: Whitman as man and as poet grew steadily with the years. O of the last entries in his Journal records the gift of a barrel apples sent to him from Esopus-on-the-Hudson by Whitma friend John Burroughs.

Alcott's delight in youth and his devotion to the ideal of Family came together in his feeling for his own daughters:—

> Ah, that my old eyes are honored and blessed by such generous recognition of my children! [he wrote in 1879]. It glorifies her with whom my human lot was graced, the spot of my birth, the vicissitudes of our mutual fortunes, our family endearments. Call it accident? Call it rather a blessed Providence that from such humble beginnings such ample benefits flowed. I should be ungrateful were I not susceptible to the praises bestowed upon my children. . . . I derive a deeper self-respect in every honor paid to them. What is theirs becomes hers, becomes mine in a truer and livelier sense than mere selfishness can own.

It had always been Alcott's way to attribute whatever gifts his daughters might reveal rather to their mother than to himself, and in this he only anticipated the belief and feeling of most other observers. The conviction grows upon the student of Alcott's life, however, that his characteristics, whatever may have been the contribution of his wife, were distributed with remarkable impartiality to Anna and Louisa, Elizabeth, and May. Elizabeth, we have seen, was most like him and was most fondly beloved. The serene and dignified Anna, a good wife and mother and a woman of decided histrionic talent, was also entirely after his own heart. Abby May, the youngest, was perhaps a little more worldly than her sisters, but she too resembled her father in her gift for the plastic arts. Louisa, the greatest of Alcott's successes, was precisely that one of his four children from whom he had hoped the least. There were traits in this second daughter which he did not fully understand, just as there were qualities of his own mind which she never quite comprehended. The rhythms of her emotional life were to him strangely abrupt and uneven, like her speech, like her handwriting, like the prose she wrote. Her moods, her language, sometimes her conduct, showed a violence both of affection and of dislike that was foreign to his nature. Yet there were certain traits in this daughter that he had in himself: strong fidelity, enduring enthusiasm, and a power of prolonged concentration upon one thought, one task, amounting to a temporary mania. She was capable, too, of a fierce devotion to those whom she loved—and she loved chiefly her own father and mother and three sisters. All the passion that other women spend upon their lovers, their husbands, their children, Louisa brought to a burning focus upon the little family group. When she wrote well she wrote about the family, and it is highly significant that when she wrote best of all she was producing precisely those books for children for which her father had begun to sigh before she was born. (Shall I ever be able to write them myself, he had exclaimed at the age of thirty, or will they be written by one whom I have taught?) When Louisa wrote for money—and she seldom was able to write for any other thing—it was in order that her father's debts might be paid and that the family might have a few of the simpler comforts of life. Her fame, when she could be made to understand it or to think of it at all, seemed to be an impertinence, a wholly unwarranted intrusion. What mattered to her far more than fame or the art of letters was that Henry Ward Beecher should offer her three thousand dollars for one story and that her publishers could send her thirty-three thousand dollars as the royalties of one quadrennium. One sets down these facts not to her discredit but to the honor of a brave and gallant woman. She was a mercenary soldier, but she fought with body and mind and soul in the holy cause of Family.

Bronson Alcott's own books had at least all the success they deserved. For thirty years after Emerson told him that the manuscript of "Psyche" was hardly fit for publication Alcott had written for himself alone, toiling through the annual volume of Journals and making it a larger volume with almost every succeeding year. As with Margaret Fuller and Wendell Phillips, he ever, his natural mode of expression was that of speech, in which he was one of the more gifted persons of his time. In the writing of his Journals, which gradually came to be an easy and simple conversation with himself, he did a large amount of good though seldom distinguished writing. Compared with these Journals, his books are flat, dull, and lifeless. Yet the *Tablets,* published in 1868, the *Concord Days* of 1872, and the *Table Talk,* appearing in 1877, had for the most part a "good press" and went, each of them, into two or more editions. *Sonnets and Canzonets* and *New Connecticut,* published in 1882 and 1887, are not discreditable work for an octogenarian who had never quite learned the simpler rules of versification, but both of them show the smoothing and capable hand of F. B. Sanborn. The best extended piece of prose that Alcott published in his lifetime was undoubtedly his long essay *Ralph Waldo Emerson,* privately printed in 1865 and published in 1882. The best of his poems is *Ion,* a threnody for Emerson which owes much to Sanborn but more to Milton's *Lycidas* and Shelley's *Adonais.*

It is a fact which the friends of Alcott will never cease to regret, but which they should never try to conceal, that he did not learn to write consistently well. In his "Orphic Sayings" there are better things by far, to be sure, than those who prefer to take their literary opinions at second hand suspect. In his numerous brief characterizations of contemporaries, as of Thoreau and Whitman, he fell far below the graphic power of Carlyle in the same kind of writing, of course, but he often went far beyond the same master in sympathetic comprehension. What his prose style chiefly stands in need of is a great many more little shining nailheads of fact, driven home. What he needed most of all to learn as a writer was the truth of Thoreau's superb sentence: "A true account of the actual is the purest poetry." Was there ever a more compact transcendental utterance than that? And yet Alcott, in some ways the most comprehensive and consistent transcendentalist that America has ever had, could live with Emerson and Thoreau for many years without ever fully discovering the open secret of their style. Burgh's *Dignity of Human Nature* was never quite outgrown in his writing, nor was Bunyan's *Pilgrim's Progress* quite lived up to. One feels sure that he would have thought it beneath his own dignity to tell the world that Thoreau's trousers usually looked too long, and we learn not from any of his writing but from a reporter's notes upon his casual talk that Thoreau's arms were covered with a thick dark hair, "like a pelt." In all his hundreds of admiring pages about Emerson he never speaks of his friend's habit of concealing a half-smoked cigar under the railing of the front fence when he went into the house. The world, to be sure, can do without such information but there is some question whether a prose style can permanently do well if it habitually avoids all such hard and factual detail.

It is one of the beneficent effects of longevity that a man who has been regarded as ridiculous for a sufficient length of time may eventually come to be accepted as a fixture, almost an exhibit, which newcomers, at any rate, are expected to admire. Something of that sort was Alcott's experience in Concord. It was not that the townsfolk ceased to laugh at him as the years rolled by or that they found it any less absurd than formerly to see him, with uplifted finger, lecturing a schoolgirl on the Mill Dam to the general effect that "Love globes; affection cubes." Still it was known that people had paid to hear this man talk, even as far West as St. Louis, and it was also known that Mr. Emerson had somehow been able to put up with him for a long time. Such things were important, and had their effect. Furthermore, the town was gathering more and more persons of fine intelligence with whom Alcott found himself immediately at home. Two weeks before his seventy-eighth birthday he moved with his family from Orchard House to the house on Main Street in which Thoreau had lived and died and which Louisa had purchased for four five hundred dollars as a home for the widowed Anna.

But Orchard House was not to be entirely forsaken. The outstanding success of Alcott's old age, and in some respects the crown of his life, was the Concord School of Philosophy, which ran through nine successive summers, from 1879 until the year of his death. Alcott had been planning for this school, dreaming about it, talking of it, and vaguely working toward it for exactly forty years, when finally, to the astonishment of the villagers, all the lodging-houses began to fill with strangers, many of them from the West, and on every morning and afternoon there was a stream of people flowing down the Lexington Road toward Orchard House. The Boston newspapers were most respectful. Boston people came daily and in droves, by the cars. Concord, which had recently come to regard Mr. Alcott with the amused tolerance which an oyster may be imagined as feeling toward its pearl, rubbed its eyes.

No attempt can be made in this place toward an adequate consideration of the Concord School of Philosophy. It was a dignified, wholly beneficent, and somewhat "Victorian" institution, entirely successful in what it undertook and highly creditable to the many persons concerned in its nine sessions. Although the meetings of the first summer were held in Alcott's old study and thereafter in the "Chapel" erected in his orchard, quite as much of the credit for the final organization is due to Sanborn, the permanent secretary and Treasurer, as to "the Dean." The success of the undertaking was assured, furthermore, less by Alcott's own contributions than by the frequently brilliant lectures of William T. Harris, Ednah Dow Cheney, Professor Benjamin Pierce, Thomas Davidson, Denton J. Snider, Frederic Hedge, E. P. Peabody, Noah Porter, Emerson, and Dr. Hiram K. Jones, the Platonist of Jacksonville, Illinois.

And yet the School was called "Mr. Alcott's" by the newspapers of the day and in the talk of the town. To no small degree it was built round Alcott, as one may infer from the remark made by George W. Curtis in the "Editor's Easy Chair" of *Har-*

per's Magazine: "It was not thought best to admit teachers of the so-called positive, or cosmic, or evolutional philosophy. This way of thinking was thought to find its refutation and solution in the more spiritual philosophy taught by Mr. Alcott." Even the great Benjamin Pierce was admitted to the "Faculty," one suspects, chiefly because he was believed to hold sound views on the priority of Souls and Ideas. His presence there reminds one, however, that the lectures of the School were by no means confined to philosophy, even in the broad sense that Alcott habitually gave that word. He lectured with surprising power on "Cosmogony." Mrs. Cheney, who had been before her marriage one of the closest and most admiring of Alcott's friends, talked like a master upon æsthetics and the history of art. Denton J. Snider, having apparently overcome the grave doubts of Alcott which he had entertained in the days of the St. Louis School, discussed Shakespeare Emerson, with the help of his daughter Ellen, read lectures on "Memory" and "Aristocracy." Alcott himself discussed his old themes of "The Scale of Being," "The Lapse," and "Genesis." Probably the most impressive lecturer in the group was William T. Harris, although the speed and precision of his "dialectic still went far beyond Alcott's understanding. Dr. Jones amazed the company as much by the uncompromising idealism of his thought as by his powers of vocal endurance. At each annual session H. G. O. Blake read passages from the manuscripts of Thoreau.

More to the present purpose is a recognition of the several ways in which the Concord School of Philosophy rounded out and fulfilled Alcott's interests and aspirations. With such men as Jones and Harris and Snider to represent the West, it was a proof what he had long been saying about the intellectual predominance of that region. It brought the West into the East so that Concord and Boston, even Emerson himself, could not fail to see and as Alcott hoped, to admire. Also, it was an application on a great scale of his theories of Conversation as a means of culture;

in his mind, at least, the discussions were more important than the lectures. We may regard it as a lineal descendent of the Symposium or "Transcendental Club", which had also given rise to the Free Religious Association, and possibly even to the Radical Club of the seventies. One sees, too, that it was valued by Alcott as a group of "Minds" coöperating toward results beyond the reach of any individual the group contained. Women played a large part in it, both as auditors and as speakers. It raised the social temperature of Concord, at least for the time being, by several degrees. And finally, it gave Alcott a confident assurance that he at last "belonged." From the opening day of the School until the day of his death he remained the Dean of the Concord School of Philosophy. After his death it was disbanded.

Death! Since Elizabeth's going Alcott had thought much about that great summons and translation. For the most part he had thought cheerfully, and always without fear. His faith in personal immortality was so simple and childlike that he was often asked to speak at the funerals of children. He was to need that faith, for to him as to every man of large social experience who attains old age life became a series of farewells. In 1862 died Henry Thoreau, whom Alcott had loved almost as a son. In the following year Alcott's mother died, at ninety. John Pratt, Alcott's son-law, died in 1870, leaving two sons. In the same year Alcott learned of the death of Charles Lane. Samuel J. May entered into his well-earned rest in 1871, and William Russell in 1873. Alcott's dearest companion, his wife for almost half a century, went from him in 1877. Two years later his youngest daughter died in Europe, leaving an infant child. On the twenty-seventh of April, 1882, at ten minutes to nine in the evening, Ralph Waldo Emerson breathed his last long weary breath. Louisa wrote that night in her Journal: "Illustrious and beloved friend, Good-bye!" This event, though so long foreseen and so many a time rehearsed, may almost be said to have taken more out of the world than it left behind for Alcott. Never to hear again that silver voice which had interlaced with loveliness those fifty years? To see only in memory henceforth that eagerly listening look, the light of those eyes which had been by itself an intellectual beauty? In Emerson's death Alcott too began to die. His hold on life began to loosen because life seemed less worth holding.

Emerson, most strangely, had not been a firm believer in the persistence of the individual after death. He had thought that we go down like drops of water into the vast sea. Oh, cold, cold! Always here in time Emerson had held his friends at a distance and now he thought to escape them for eternity! True, they would both belong to the "Over-Soul," but this passionate pilgrim from the Many to the One could not still the dull ache at his heart however his head agreed, by that dusty answer. He remembered how one day, when he and Emerson had been walking together he had finally brought forth a shy and tremulous request that his grave might be near that of his friend. And so that was what now lay ahead.

There must have been many times in the late summer of 188 after the School had closed, when Bronson Alcott felt lonely. He made no complaint, even in his Journal, and he went about his many small tasks with the vigor and regular dispatch he had always shown; yet his daughters must have wondered, as they watched him, upon what fund of inward happiness he could drawing.

He would have told them that it was enough to have them with him, and also his stalwart grandsons and little Louisa May Niereker, May's daughter. He was living with Anna now in house on Main Street where Henry Thoreau had died. Louisa bought her that house. Bronson Alcott liked it well enough, he liked particularly well the large, almost square room that had built for his own study and library on the ground floor. had built that room with money earned in his Conversation the West. There he had all his books—two or three hundred books that had once belonged to J. P. Greaves and that had been in the library at Fruitlands, with others bought in recent years and some few that had come from Thoreau. He would take down Thoreau's *Week* from the shelf and hold it and turn a page or two, remembering the day in Boston when his friend had brought t to him from Munroe's shop—remembering also those winter nights when he had heard it read in the hut at Walden, oh, long gone by. And there, too, were the fifty volumes of his own Journals, all neatly bound—not, as people said, with Louisa's money, but at his own expense. Fifty volumes! No other man in Concord had written so much. They amounted to a life work. And yet, who would ever read them? To what end, all that enormous labor, extending back to the dim years in Cheshire?

On fine days, when the autumnal glory was burning in the maples along the street, he would go down to look at Orchard House—for he could still easily walk the mile and a little over. Harris was living there now—was thinking of buying the place. it had to go to anyone, Harris was the best man one knew to enjoy it. But that house had once been home. It had been like one's child, one's wife. Standing by the gateway and looking up the old brown gables, he saw the window where his wife had used to sit when the sward was paved with afternoon, when the robins called in the April trees, or when the snow was falling. And there was that farther window where his youngest girl used to sit with her clay and canvas. Her dear and beautiful body was molding now in a land he had never seen. And Elizabeth? Ah, Elizabeth! . . . Leaf after leaf of tarnished gold sank through the still air from the huge elms. They covered the roof, the gables, and all the grass with their brief glory. Soon the trees would be bare.

And then on the homeward way he would stop beneath the those chestnuts and look for a long time at the square white house by the road-forks. The blinds would be drawn in that room

[511]

to the right on the ground floor, but yet as clearly as though he stood within the room his memory brought before him the round table with its three curved legs and the writing-pad and inkwell upon it, the rocking chair with its cushions, the sofa, the chest of drawers for manuscripts, the bust of Dante, and the picture of the Three Fates. He could see the Plato, the Coleridge, the Montaigne in the long bookcase against the wall. There were a hundred things in that room that he could have found with his eyes closed. But there would be no fire on that hearth. . . From the chestnut trees at the gate the large gold leaves were falling. Heavy and thick and undisturbed they lay on the white marble walk.

With his last surviving sister Alcott visited Spindle Hill. It was tangled and overgrown, forsaken. The fields where he had plowed with the yellow oxen, meadows where he had so often swung the scythe beside his father, were smothered in hardhack and sweet fern now. Stone walls he had helped to build round his father's pastures ran now through the dense, dark woods. Houses where his own folk had lived had fallen to the ground, were deserted, or were given over to strangers. The mill was gone at the falls. The swimming-pool had been broken. The house of his birth had disappeared. . . . . All over Spindle Hill the leaves were twirling and falling.

Bronson Alcott wrote cheerfully to himself in his Journal. He gave the last touches to his essay on Emerson and to the threnody Ion. He played with his granddaughter. He wrote two sonnets on Immortality. Was there anything left to be done?

On the twenty-fourth of October, 1882, he had an apoplectic stroke. He never wrote again.

THE CHAMBER LOOKING
EAST

{ 1882-1888 }

Sudden pause—"The chamber looking East"—Louisa's last charge—Fifty volumes of Journals—The backward vista—"Up"

WHAT does an old man do when his life lies all behind him, when the silver cord is loosed and the golden bowl has been broken? Say that he has been an active man, a worker with his hands, a wanderer, and that now he can scarcely walk from his bed to his chair. Say that he has always been a lonely man yet one with many friends, many dear companions, and that now for week after week—yes, and for weary months and years—he sees hardly anyone but the doctor, the nurse, his two daughters, his grandsons, and one little prattling child. Say that he has touched the heights of his life in conversation, and that now he can hardly speak. And let him be a man who for twenty years has written down at evening the thoughts of every day; but now his hand is palsied. What does such a man do?

Little is known, and little will ever be discovered, about the

[513]

last years of Bronson Alcott. After the crushing blow of his apoplectic stroke he made a slow but never complete recovery, learning as a child does to speak and to walk a little, but always with difficulty. He was given every possible comfort and domestic attention. Apparently he had little pain. There is abundant evidence in the Journal and letters of his daughter Louisa, in the records left by his friend Sanborn, and in the tradition of his own family, that his mind was, for the most part, clear, although his memory of recent events was shattered. His bed was in the newly built study at Anna's house on Main Street, and before the first winter of his decrepitude was out he was able to rise and to spend a few hours daily among his books. He was even able to attend as a silent listener, three more sessions of the Concord School of Philosophy. In September, 1885, Louisa took him to stay with her in her Boston house at 10 Louisburg Square—that comfortable and dignified isle of quiet on Beacon Hill, with something of an eighteenth-century charm still lingering about it, where an English scholar had built his thatched cottage and had grown his English roses beside a little fountain two hundred and sixty years before. The old man was fond of his upper room looking out on the trees and grass of the garden. If he could not be at Orchard House, this would do. Louisa, who had known her *Pilgrim's Progress* from childhood, called it his "Chamber Looking East." Although he returned to Anna's home in Concord for the summer of 1886 and spent the final summer of his life at Melrose, that chamber was the next to the last of Alcott's earthly lodgings. The pedlar had only one journey yet to make.

There had been a time when Alcott hoped, and even expected to round out a full century of life, but now he wanted more than any other thing to "go up." Louisa records that the first word he spoke when he was struggling back toward speech was the symbolic word "Up"—a word that might have been the motto for his life's endeavor. She tells us that one day in March, 1887, her father laid down his newspaper and said to her: "Beecher is go

[514]

now. All go but me!" When she took him to ride in Boston he loved to drive down Tremont Street so that he could see once more the mighty transcendental fountain—"the Mystic," as he called it—tossing its rainbowed spray high into the air among the trees and mightily striving to return to the level of its source, crowned with splendor. Oh, beautiful, never-defeated hope, forever pushing and rushing upward and forever up!

Louisa was tired too—oh, very tired! Since her return, twenty years ago, from the army hospital at Georgetown, she, once so powerful and buoyant, had known scarcely a day of health. She was one of the most famous and "successful" women in America, and her life was one long increasing misery. When this final task was done, this last loving duty, how gladly she would lie down to rest! She brought home one day a little poem that had been found under the pillow of one of her friends, a crippled soldier of the Civil War who had been dying for two decades. She read a stanza to her father:—

> I am no longer eager, bold, and strong,—
>   All that is past;
> I am ready not to do,
>   At last—at last.
> My half-day's work is done,
>   And this is all my part.
> I give a patient God
>   My patient heart.

For her father on his eighty-sixth birthday Louisa wrote a poem which stands next in beauty, among all her accomplishments in writing, to her lines called "Thoreau's Flute." Affection and skill work together in this close application of *Pilgrim's Progress* to the details of the old man's life:—

> Dear Pilgrim, waiting patiently,
>   The long, long journey nearly done,
> Beside the sacred stream that flows
>   Clear-shining in the western sun;
> Look backward on the varied road

[515]

Your steadfast feet have trod,
From youth to age, through weal and woe,
    Climbing forever nearer God.

Mountain and valley lie behind;
    The slough is crossed, the wicket passed;
Doubt and despair, sorrow and sin,
    Giant and fiend, conquered at last.
Neglect is changed to honor now;
    The heavy cross may be laid down;
The white head wins and wears, at length,
    The prophet's, not the martyr's crown.

Greatheart and Faithful gone before,
    Brave Christiana, Mercy sweet,
Are Shining Ones who stand and wait
    The weary wanderer to greet.
Patience and Love his handmaids are,
    And till time brings release,
Christian may rest in that bright room
    Whose windows open to the east.

The staff set by, the sandals off,
    Still pondering the precious scroll,
Serene and strong, he waits the call
    That frees and wings a happy soul.
Then, beautiful as when it lured
    The boy's aspiring eyes,
Before the pilgrim's longing sight
    Shall the Celestial City rise.

There is this one thing that we can be sure about concerni̶
Alcott's last few years: he did "look backward on the vari̶
road." It is remembered in his family that he would sit all d̶
long and every day, at his table in the study at Anna's hou̶
reading and reading over again his own Journals. Fifty volu̶
there were of them, containing about five million words, all ̶
long slow scripture of a steady, persistent, slow-pulsed hand. ̶
could not lift those volumes now, and he could not have writ̶

[516]

the shortest word they contained, but he could turn the pages; and as he turned and turned he found out for what good though unconscious purpose their thousands of pages had been written: they were his memory. He discovered to what reader they had been addressed: himself.

The days and the nights were long and still in the study at Anna's house. Now and then the old man could hear the voices of children going by on their way to school, the distant knoll of a church bell, or the leisurely *clock-a-clock* of some farmer's heavy horse jogging down to the Mill Dam. Children, church, farm! These had been his teachers, but now they were fading far away. Best of all living sounds was the light quick step of his little granddaughter at the door, and wisest of all that he heard now was her merry and innocent laughter. But he was listening for many a voice that was still. He was waiting for a final mysterious footstep that would not come.

To few minds has it ever been given, one would say, to review so vividly as Bronson Alcott did, and in so beneficent a quiet, the associations and events of such a long and varied life. As one is made to feel in other periods and aspects of his career that what happened to him must have been deliberately planned for the shaping of a human mind and spirit—and planned, too, with an artist's delight in fitness and proportions—so here. From his final defeat Alcott may have gained more than from any other. He gained the boon, so rare in American life, of recollection. He was given the time, the place, and the means for drawing himself finally together, so that he who was going back from the Many to the nameless and ineffable One might be entirely one himself. He was granted a long interval of that pure contemplation which has always been regarded by the wisest minds, whether of the brooding East or of the active West, as the supreme good that life can offer.

[517]

We can only guess what things in the dying man's career stood forth as of first importance while he turned the pages of his Journals day after day; but after following the total curve of his life and after having learned the very habit of his mind and mood we can guess with some assurance. Not his endless writing, not his adventurous and inveterate reading, not even the oceanic volume of his talk, would impress this man who had never asked "How much?" The central thing was that he had "set forth from the ground of Spirit," and had never left that ground. His life, he saw, had been essentially and continuously religious, although in no orthodox or pious way. He had never forgotten, nor had he once denied, the Presence on New Connecticut Hill. If he had been a reformer at all, it was chiefly because he had tried to follow Jesus simply and at once. He had tried to teach like Jesus; and when they would no longer suffer the little children to come unto him, that had been his cross. Once or twice, like Plotinus and Saint Paul, he had been lifted up out of the senses and had seen things unlawful to utter; and although that vision had faded he had found Spirit everywhere—in children's faces, in the garden at Orchard House, in the mystical fountain, in the death of Thoreau, in the mind of Emerson and the heart of Elizabeth and wherever two or three had been gathered together. Most clearly of all he had found it in the Family. For what was Spirit? Jesus had said that "God is Love," and to that he could now answer that "Love is God."

How wonderful that the total gains of eighty years, with their journeyings into the dim past and over the wide land, the numberless books and faces, their many sorrows and few triumphs, could be named at last in three short simple words! How right it was that after living for half a century among the most intricate of the world's philosophical systems he should be able to sum up the real good of them in a phrase which any child could understand! Simplicity was one final test of truth, and another was that it should be not a hidden thing but one set clear in all men's sight, if they would but look and see. It must be a knowledge familiar to childhood. And this deep truth that Love is God was no new thing to him. He had known it always. He had learned it from his mother's smile.

When he came to think of his career in its more worldly aspects Alcott must have been impressed by its beautiful symmetry, as of a rising and falling fountain. Spindle Hill—had he not always been striving to rise once more to that high source? All that he had ever known was what Spindle Hill had taught him. All his life he had been a true son of the stubborn and rocky Connecticut hills, raising dreams and thoughts and ideals where nothing else would grow. Yes, his entire life had been like that wonderful dream that came to Jacob when, having laid his head for the night "upon the stones of the place," he saw ladders of glory climbing the heaven's height with angels upon them ascending and descending. The stones of his father's fields had been the seed of a wide, rich harvest. He had looked so long and lovingly at the poor bare facts of his life as they had been given him that they had come to shine with an inward luster. Whether a self-made or a God-made man, his life had been fashioned of home-grown materials. It was like that beloved violin he had carved long ago out of a maple stump brought down from his father's pasture. A crude and clumsy thing it had certainly been, yet altogether his own; and he had made it sing forth what music there was in him.

Bronson Alcott may well have felt, while looking back along the vista of his years, that in almost any other age, in almost any land other than America, he would have been less lonely. If only he could have lived in the school of Pythagoras, or as one of those companions who had walked by Galilee, or even in some hermitage among the Himalayan snows! Better still, because his thoughts were always forward-bent, he would have liked to live in some as yet unguessed America of the future—an America quieted, thoughtful, using her wealth and power for the highest and holiest ends, in which the spiritual element of her inheritance shall no

[519]

longer be a hidden and shamefast thing. Yet he must have known that there was nothing peculiar in his loneliness and that most of the world's finer spirits have felt more or less astray among the centuries and the meridians. At any rate he had come to a time and a country that needed such men as he.

The Journals led the old man's thoughts far back, even to his infancy and to the little house at Petucker's Ring which had long been a heap of ruins, to the housewarming and the Negro fiddler and the custards. They brought before him the vanished house of Captain John where he had been born, and also the little house of his childhood with his mother knitting beside the huge blazing hearth while his father smoked in silence. The little gray school-house, Cousin William, Uncle Obed, Uncle John, the eclipse of 1808, the wind and wet on New Connecticut when he was search-ing for lost sheep, the heat and ache and happiness of mowing be-side his father, many faces of boys and girls who were all dead now, brothers and sisters he had not seen for fifty years, the stone walls he had laid, the yellow oxen, the maplewood violin, the Hessian tailor—all came glimmering back. Then the first step into the world: New Haven, New York, Norfolk, the roads of Virginia, the dogs that barked and then gave over barking, the slave quarters, the planters' houses, libraries, gentle manners and kindly hearts. Then there was the interminable sandy road through Carolina with William beside him, swimming rivers, wading bogs, drinking from stagnant pools, and the long fever in the stifling upper room, and William still there. (That ever-faith-ful William had been dead for thirty years.) He remembered the Great Dismal Swamp, how he had been lost there at nightfall with a tempest coming on, and had found his way by lightning flashes among the crashing trees. (Was not that, too, an emblem of his whole life?) He recalled the drowning pedlar he had tried to save and how he himself had been dragged down and had nearly died. At home once more with his costly coat, there was his sadly burdened and aging father, and there were the astonished maidens of the countryside. Then came William's kindly reproof, another journey Southward, the stay with the Quakers and the total change of mind, home, Fall Mountain School, the school at Cheshire, Brooklyn, Abigail May, and Boston. He had known that city for sixty years, and Concord for more that fifty. His Journals led him through the thickets of the reform period. They brought back Channing, Russell, Garrison, Brownson, Sewall, Miss Peabody, Margaret Fuller, Parker, Thoreau, Emerson—all but one of them now dead and gone. What a huge company of noble men and women his lonely heart had known! The Journals took him to England, to Fruitlands and Hillside and Orchard House. They carried him to the Mississippi and beyond. They brought back heartbreak and joy, defeat, and victory born of despair. He could see, as he read, his mother's smile; he could hear Elizabeth's voice; he could feel the loving presence of his wife. Turning page after page, he caught the ghostly flapping of flames on that hearth in Emerson's study which now was cold.

And what did it all amount to when the last page had been turned? With what pure and never-to-be-forgotten gift had he enriched his country? Emerson had called him "the most refined and the most advanced soul we have had in New England"; and yet, as compared with his foremost contemporaries, what learning had been his, what force of argument, what skill in action, what power, even, of memorable utterance? Why, none. Yet even in the humility of his old age Alcott cannot have forgotten that he had maintained a noble friendship for almost half a hundred years with the loftiest mind he had ever known. He must have seen that he had done something toward the liberation of childhood. Out of pure love and longing, moreover, he had created a home which was known and beloved now, through the words of his own daughter, by all the world. His light had been only that of a little candle, but he had let it shine among men. No deed of his, no institution, no book that the world could not let die, would keep his little fame alive in the coming time; but this old, old teacher knew that the influence of a nameless and forgotten life which has been wholly given away works on forever among mankind in harmony with all spiritual power.

And as the end approached would not his thoughts grow simpler, reaching back to the old familiar image of the road? The pedlar had called at many houses. From a few doors he had been thrust forth with scorn and reviling, but also he had been taken in as a welcome guest at many a slave's hovel and master's mansion. He had given away all that the world would take, and so had made but little money. He had walked a weary way. Now he was going home, with his amulets and garnets and pearls unsullied and unsold.

On the fourth of March in 1888, two days before the death of Louisa, Bronson Alcott died.

BIBLIOGRAPHICAL NOTE

IN writing this book I have depended chiefly upon the huge mass of manuscripts left by Bronson Alcott and now owned by his great-grandson. These manuscripts are of five sorts, of which the first may be called autobiographical. Here belong the fifty annual volumes of private Journals written between 1826 and 1882. Six volumes of the series, including four lost by Alcott himself, are now missing, but the gap thus left for the years 1840–1845 has been partially filled by including several volumes of Mrs. Alcott's Journals. Selections from Bronson Alcott's Journal for 1841 were published in the second volume of the *Dial,* and portions of the Journal he kept in England have been preserved in letters written to his wife. In his old age Alcott came to feel that this extremely ample record of a long life would be somewhat too extensive for the uses of a possible future biographer, and accordingly he drew up a compact "Autobiographical Index" in which every major event of his career from his birth to the year 1850 is succinctly recorded. He also prepared, with great care, several large volumes called "Autobiographical Collections," into which he gathered thousands of sketches, photographs, newspaper clippings, railroad time tables, admission tickets, advertisements, printed announcements, pamphlets, and broadsides, to which he added a considerable amount of comment and factual statement in his own hand. To these records of his own life he added, for

[523]

the most part in 1852, several more volumes, also very carefully prepared, concerning his ancestry.

Alcott never ceased to deplore the loss of the Journals dealing with his visit to England and his stay at Fruitlands, and one finds evidence among his papers that he often tried to write them out anew. Probably a more serious loss was that of his earlier Journals, begun when he was twelve and extending to 1825, which were "destroyed" at Philadelphia in 1833. Again and again in later life he tried to set down the substance of these volumes, using old family letters and the Journal kept by his brother Chatfield to assist his memory. Some part of what he was able to recall is preserved in the verse and prose of his book *New Connecticut*.

The second category of the Alcott manuscripts includes three slender volumes entitled "Observations on Childhood," in which the first years of Anna and Louisa are recorded in minute detail. Here too belongs the manuscript called "Psyche" which Emerson decided should not be published. These volumes show Alcott at his best, as teacher and parent.

Somewhat more distant from the center of Alcott's thought but still highly revealing are the extensive records, many of them stenographic, of his public Conversations. His own careful accounts of his ten "Tours at the West" belong in a related but somewhat different category. And finally, making up a fifth group there are among these papers several hundreds of letters written by and to Bronson Alcott and the members of his family over a period of rather more than sixty years.

Here, then, is a large body of original and authentic "source material" which not only has never been published but, for the most part, has never before been studiously read. Having such wealth at my disposal and wishing to see Alcott's life and time as much as possible through his own eyes, I have drawn upon the material constantly in every chapter of my book, not only by direct quotation but by paraphrase and restatement, and not for facts alone but even more for interpretations. Where I have attempted to suggest motives for Alcott's conduct, to give some hint of his emotional life, or to trace the inward movement of his thought, it is to be understood that his Journals are almost always my authority. The external events of his career might have been made out from other sources, but the thirty thousand pages of his Journals, illustrated and supported as they are by numerous other manuscripts, have suggested the possibility of following the man's changes of mood, of constructing something like the history of his mind, and even of indicating certain traits in his thought and character of which he himself was unaware.

Although they have seemed to me less important for my purpose than the Journals, I have not entirely neglected other sources of information and suggestion. Among the books that have been oftenest in my hands while this book was growing I should mention, first of all, *A. Bronson Alcott, His Life and Philosophy,* by F. B. Sanborn and William T. Harris (Boston 1893). Following this, and arranged approximately in the order of their importance for the present task, come the Journals of Emerson and of Thoreau, Bronson Alcott's *New Connecticut*—valuable chiefly for its notes —his *Tablets* and *Table Talk* and *Concord Days,* Sanborn's *Recollections of Seventy Years,* Mrs. Cheney's Life of Louisa May Alcott, the Rowfant Club's admirable reprint of the *Dial* with its two-volume Introduction by George Willis Cooke, and *Emerson in Concord* by the late Dr. Edward Emerson.

The materials of my first chapter were gathered partly on Spindle Hill itself and partly from Samuel Orcutt's *History of the Town of Wolcott from 1731 to 1874.* For my discussion of peddling in general I am indebted to this same work, to Timothy Dwight's four-volume *Travels in America,* to Alcott's *New Connecticut,* and to Mr. Richardson Wright's vivacious *Hawkers and Walkers in Early America.* William Andrus Alcott's account of the journey taken by the two cousins through the Carolinas and Virginia is in his *Rambles at the South,* published in New York in 1854. Upon Cousin William himself there is an article in tł fourth volume of Barnard's *American Journal of Education* ar another by Herbert Thoms, M.D., in the *Bulletin of the Socie of Medical History of Chicago* for April, 1928.

In my discussion of Alcott's career as a teacher I have hε much valuable assistance from an unpublished dissertation ϲ "Bronson Alcott, Progressive Educator" presented at Yale Ur versity in 1936 by my friend Dr. Dorothy McCuskey. The not in *New Connecticut* give a vivid picture of the schoolhouse Spindle Hill, which may be supplemented by William A. Alcott prize essay *On the Construction of School Houses* (Boston, 1832 by his *Confessions of a Schoolmaster* (Andover, N.Y., 1839 and by six articles appearing in the *Connecticut Observer* b tween January 25 and April 12, 1825. Further knowledge of tł schools in which Bronson Alcott first taught may be gained fro Samuel J. May's "Errors in Common Education" (*Americc Journal of Education* for May–June, 1829) and from the repo of the Connecticut School Committee for 1833. Thomas J. Mur ford's *Memoir of Samuel J. May*, published in Boston in 187 has been the main source, always excepting Alcott's Journals, ϵ my acquaintance with Alcott's brother-in-law—who is, howeve a famous figure in the annals of Connecticut Unitarianism.

Alcott's Journals, begun at Cheshire in 1826, are at first litt more than a record of daily happenings in the schoolroom. Fϵ the Boston of Alcott's earlier years I have depended chiefly upϲ *The Memorial History of Boston,* in four volumes, edited in 188 by Justin Winsor, although a more entertaining description ϵ the city is to be found in Edward Everett Hale's *A New Englar Boyhood.* Lilian Whiting's *Boston Days,* though sentimental ar unpleasantly "feministic," gives at least the "atmosphere" ϵ the city in later years. The best treatment of Alcott's teachiɪ in Boston to be found outside of his own Journals is that ϵ E. P. Peabody's *Record of a School* (Boston 1835, 1836, 187⁴ and in the *Conversations with Children on the Gospels* (Bosto

[526]

1836, 1837). My discussion of Alcott's earlier Conversations is based upon a study of stenographic reports and upon contemporary newspaper accounts.

Probably the most trustworthy and certainly the most interesting treatment of the American reform movement in which Alcott was involved is *The Stammering Century*, by Mr. Gilbert Seldes, published in New York in 1928. Richard J. Purcell's *Connecticut in Transition* shows that Alcott had at least the beginnings of reform about him even in his boyhood. In the chapter on "Alcott House" my main authority has been a long manuscript, lent to me by Miss Clara Endicott Sears, called "Bronson Alcott's English Friends." Written about 1895 by William Henry Harland, this manuscript is based upon some five hundred letters and numerous other documents concerning the English transcendentalists. It was used to some extent by F. B. Sanborn in the preparation of his unsatisfactory monograph on *Bronson Alcott at Alcott House, England, and Fruitlands, New England* (Torch Press, Cedar Rapids, Iowa, 1908). Further information about the group is to be had from Emerson's article "The English Reformers," published in the third volume of the *Dial*, and from Charles Lane's "James Pierrepont Greaves," which appeared in the same volume. For the relations between Alcott and Carlyle I have used, besides Alcott's letters to his wife and the Carlyle-Emerson Correspondence, a brief entry for July 28, 1864, from Mr. M. A. De Wolfe Howe's *Memories of a Hostess*. The same delightful book is my authority for the tale of Hawthorne's dissatisfaction with Mrs. Alcott as a neighbor.

In my eighth chapter I have been chiefly indebted to *Bronson Alcott's Fruitlands*, by Miss Clara Endicott Sears, in which there is a reprint of Louisa Alcott's "Transcendental Wild Oats." Repeated visits to the Fruitlands farmhouse, now owned and kept as a museum by Miss Sears, have had some effect upon my account of the enterprise—in which, however, I have been obliged to piece together many faint indications gathered from family letters and from the Journals kept by Mrs. Alcott and her two elder daughters.

Toward the end of my book I have been able to depend more and more upon Alcott's Journals. The manuscript of Ellery Channing's satire upon Alcott and Thoreau is owned by the Concord Free Public Library and is quoted here by the permission of the Trustees. Alcott's Western journeys are fully recorded in his own manuscripts and in the newspapers of the time. For the St. Louis School of Philosophy I have consulted chiefly William T. Harris's *Journal of Speculative Philosophy*—to which Alcott was a minor contributor—and Denton J. Snider's *A Writer of Books in His Generation* (St. Louis, 1910).

The materials for an exhaustive study of Alcott's work as Superintendent of the Concord Public Schools lie ready to hand in his own voluminous annual reports, published by the Town; but I have not been able to make room, in a book already overcrowded, for a consideration of that valuable work. In the little that I have been able to say about The Concord School of Philosophy I have used the several accounts by F. B. Sanborn, *The Genius and Character of Emerson* (Boston, 1885), and an article by Professor Austin Warren published in the *New England Quarterly* for 1929. I have also read many contemporary accounts of the school which appeared in the newspapers of Concord Boston, and Springfield.

My last chapter is based upon family traditions and upon such hints as one can glean from Mrs. Cheney's *Louisa May Alcott Her Life, Letters, and Journals*.

INDEX

INDEX

[531]

litical leanings of, 265; follows Jesus, 267–268; attracted by Garrison, 274–276; his lack of the historic sense, 276; visits Emerson, 279; at Groton Convention, 281–282; at Chardon Street Convention, 284–285; an occupation for, 295–298; increasing social contacts of, 298; and his daughters, 299; sails for England, 303; his ignorance of history, 312; calls upon Carlyle, 313–319; at Alcott House, 320–328; discovers the doctrine of "Birth," 325; his theory of reform, 326–327; travels in England, 337–338; buys books, 339–341; returns to America, 342; arrested, 354; moves to Fruitlands, 356; effect of English journey upon, 358–359; at Fruitlands, 361–380; leaves Fruitlands, 380; wishes to die, 381–384; a change in, 384–385; a tragic character, 385–386; cured by Nature and labor, 389–392; a typical year of, 392–393; as a gardener, 393–401; his love for Concord, 404–405; disappointed by Concord, 406–412; builds a summerhouse for Emerson, 413–415; as a father, 416–419; returns to Boston, 421–422, his Conversations, 423; described by Lowell, 425; poverty of, 426–434; satirized by Ellery Channing, 435–437; diet of, 437; his "apotheosis," 437–439; his vegetarianism, 439–441; his life in Boston, 441–445; studies his ancestry, 445–453; the mind of, 447–448; his theory of "Genesis," 453–462; at Walpole, New Hampshire, 463–464; in New York, 464, 466; at Orchard House, 469–472; his tours of the West, 472–488; Superintendent of Concord Schools, 476–477; discovers America, 479–480; appearance of, in old age, 485–486; his success, 489–490; his intellectual pause, 490–491; his mental habit, 492–493; his "Personalism," 494–500; his *Tablets*, 501; verse of, 501; old age of, 501–502; the books of 505; prose style of, 505–506; at Concord School of Philosophy, 507–509; loneliness of, 510; his farewells, 511–512; his apoplectic stroke, 512; last years of, 514–518; reviews his life, 517–521; his death, 521.

Alcott, Mrs. Bronson, her first meeting with Bronson Alcott, 106–107; writes to Alcott, 108; meets Alcott a second time, 112; arrives in Boston, 122–123; visits Alcott's school, 124; growing acquaintance with Alcott, 129–130; courted by Alcott, 130–132; marriage of, 134, 223–224; a friend of Garrison, 275; dislikes peddling, 296, 342, 343; Journal of, 344; her contest with Charles Lane, 346–347; quoted, 347–348; a reformer, 348–349; her feeling for her husband, 349; a letter to, 353; quoted, 355; at Fruitlands, 371–373; quoted, 372, 373; and Charles Lane, 378; letters of, 381; and Hawthorne, 407; in Boston, 421–422; quoted, 433; referred to, 436, 437; in Boston, 441; death of, 509, 511.

Alcott, Elizabeth, 218; seventh birthday of, 364; quoted, 419–420; death of, 467–468, 469, 470, 471, 503, 509, 511.

Alcott, Junius, 17; birth of, 55; a letter to, 279; a letter to, 351; a letter to, 388; death of, 444–445.

Alcott, Louisa May; birth of, 151; used as an example, 183–184; in childhood, 218; and Thoreau, 298, 342, 343; her "Transcendental Wild Oats," 344, 350, 355; and Fruitlands, 357; quoted, 379, 382–383, 402; at Orchard House, 412; "demonic," 416, 418, 427, 463, 471, 487; character of, 503–504, 506; quoted, 509, 514, 515–516; her death, 521.

Alcott, William Andrus, his serious disposition, 6; as educational reformer, 12; confirmed as an Episcopalian, 30; corresponds with his cousin, 30–33; goes South with Bronson, 57; nurses his cousin,

[534]

Channing, Dr. W. E. (*continued*)
trusts Alcott's methods, 173–174;
disagrees with Alcott, 174–176;
Alcott's changed opinion of, 176;
and the Symposium, 247; Alcott's
disagreement with, 249–250; influence of, 250–253; quoted, 253;
timorous, 266; at Chardon Street
Convention, 283–284; quoted, 293–
294, 295; death of, 492; Alcott's
disagreement with, 494.

Channing, W. H., in the Symposium,
248.

Chardon Street Convention, 283–
288.

Charleston, South Carolina, 57, 58;
Emerson at, 73.

Chaucer, Geoffrey, quoted, 187, 244.

Cheney, Mrs. Ednah Dow, quoted,
424; a friend of Alcott's, 442; at
Concord School of Philosophy, 508.

Cheshire, Connecticut, the Academy
at, 9, 266; Alcott teaches in, 75–
76; Alcott's reforms in the school
at, 77–78; opposition to Alcott
in, 96–99, 172.

Children, attitude toward in Connecticut, 7, 10, 81–83; Alcott's
love of, 80–83; few books for, 123;
a problem, 139; need discipline,
167.

Christianity, Alcott's attitude toward,
92; in Boston, 118–119; "a system of education," 126.

Christian Register, defends Alcott,
194, 204.

Church, the, and slavery, 271.

Civil War, the American, 491, 496.

Clarke, James Freeman, defends
Alcott, 194; in the Symposium,
247, 299.

Clergy, the New England, Alcott's
attitude toward, 79–80, 116–119;
the power of, 117; Alcott disappointed by, 119–120; condemned
by Alcott, 126.

Cleveland, Ohio, 485, 486.

Cobbett, William, 311.

Coleridge, Samuel Taylor, the idealistic teachings of, 36; his *Aids to
Reflection,* 151, 155, 159–160, 161;
the poetry of, 157, 158, 171;

quoted, 177–178, 209; his teaching and Nature's, 217; talk of,
228, 239; Dr. Channing's association with, 252; his *Biographia
Literaria,* 258, 322, 392, 476.

Columbia, South Carolina, a "canal
project" at, 57, 59.

Combe, George, his *Phrenology* and
Constitution of Man, 142.

Comenius, Johann Amos, his *The
Great Didactic,* 95.

Come-Outers, 271; convention of,
at Groton, 281–283.

Companionship, Alcott's need of, 22;
63.

Comstock, Anthony, 264.

Concord, Massachusetts, the meadows
of, 25; Alcott's first visit to, 199;
days and nights in, 201; Alcott
moves to, 291, 391, 399; Alcott's
love for, 404–405; disappoints Alcott, 405; coldness of, 406–412;
487; Alcott's old age in, 506.

Concord River, 398–399.

Concord School of Philosophy, referred to, 94, 129, 413; discussed,
507–509, 514.

Condorcet, Marie Jean, 335.

Congregational Church, theocracy of,
82.

Connecticut, population of, 19; Alcott's debt to and love of, 111;
Boston's opinion of, 222; reform
in, 265.

Connecticut Courant, 19, 32, 111, 266
292.

Conversations, Alcott's, on the Ol
Testament, 174; on the Life o
Christ, 174; value of, 178–179
increasing attention to, 209, 213
214; religious aspect of, 226, 236
237, 243–245; in Boston, 423; fee
paid for, 432–433; in the Wes
434, 485, 497, 508–509.

Conversations on the Gospels, th
180–196; recorded in a book, 19
public reception of, 192–196, 32
329, 337.

Conway, Moncure D., 272.

Cook, Reverend Joseph, 169, 49
499.

Cooper, James Fenimore, 311.

Cornwall, Reverend Mr., starts "opposition school" in Cheshire, Connecticut, 99.

"Correspondences," Alcott's search for, 156.

Cousin, Victor, Alcott's reading of, 160.

Cowley, Abraham, 394.

Cowper, William, his *Life and Letters,* 50; quoted, 400.

Cranch, Christopher, 281, 299.

Crandall, Prudence, 210, 272.

Crosland, Newton, 321.

Cudworth, Ralph, his *Intellectual System,* 294.

Curtis, George W., quoted, 507–508.

Daily Advertiser, Boston, 136, 192.

Dana, Richard Henry, 177.

Daniel, Samuel, quoted, 202.

Darwin, Charles, his study of a child, 141; his *Origin of Species,* 457.

Darwin, Erasmus, his *Temple of Nature,* 157.

Davidson, Thomas, at Concord School of Philosophy, 507.

Davis, Thomas, 298, 392, 427.

Defoe, Daniel, his *Robinson Crusoe,* 33.

Deism, 157, 445.

Dial, 195; named by Alcott, 279; first number of, 292; ridiculed, 293; quoted, 323, 326, 337.

Dickens, Charles, 158, 428.

Dix, Dorothea Lynde, Alcott's meeting with, 121; a reformer, 269.

Doddington, Bubb, and the Hell-Fire Club, 320.

"Dove Cottage," 291; regimen at, 351–352.

Dubuque, Iowa, 483, 485, 486.

Dwight, J. S., in the Symposium, 248.

Dwight, Nathaniel, his *Geography,* 9.

Dwight, the Reverend Timothy, quoted, 62–63; referred to, 101; the dead hand of, 111.

Dyer, Benjamin, 356.

EDDY, JAMES, 427.

Edgeworth, Maria, her stories for children, 123; her *Frank,* 168.

Education, public, in Connecticut during Alcott's youth, 9; moral aspects of, 11; reform in, 11–12; not the only means of intellectual advancement, 13–14; in New York and Philadelphia, 120; English ideas of, 121; Alcott's theory of, 183.

Edwards, Jonathan, 36; his remark about children, 81; Alcott's departure from, 82.

"Elegance," Alcott's brief period of, 63–66.

Emerson, Ralph Waldo, and Nature, 25; at Roxbury, 27; his summer-house, 46; quoted, 53; graduates from Harvard College, 68; effect of the South upon, 73–74; his love of fine manners, 74; his *Self-Reliance,* 86; a Boston clergyman, 117; first heard by Alcott, 126; quoted, 142, 144, 150, 155, 158; his *Nature,* 159; quoted, 161; his etymologies, 170; Alcott's acquaintance with, 177; reads "Psyche," 181; visits Temple School, 184–185; quoted, 185, 191; a letter from, 197; his growing friendship for Alcott, 197; Alcott's association with, 198–201; his lectures, 198; as a listener, 199; a "rhetorician," 199–200; not an American, 200; his use of Alcott's Journals, 200; an invitation from, 206; his address on "The American Scholar," 206–207; quoted, 207; his solitude, 224–225; quoted, 225; compared with Alcott, 225–226; advises Alcott, 227; a hesitant talker, 229; quoted, 229–230, 233; face of, 236; his lectures, 198, 238; quoted, 241, 243; topics of, 244; quoted, 245; a master of rhetoric, 245; quoted, 247; his address on "The American Scholar," 248; at home in the seventeenth century, 255–256; quoted, 256; his *Nature,* 259; theology of, 260; his self-culture, 263; and reform, 263; his recognition of evil, 264; not a reformer, 269; quoted, 270, 272; at Chardon Street Convention, 284, 286–287; quoted, 288; his

[537]

Emerson, Ralph Waldo (*continued*) *Nature* attributed to Alcott, 292; Alcott's closest friend, 298; quoted, 299; a letter from, 300; his feeling for Alcott, 301; describes Alcott to Carlyle, 301–302; his liking for England, 309; quoted, 319; and reform, 326–327, 339; quoted, 354; and Fruitlands, 357; quoted, 359, 360; visits Fruitlands, 366; quoted, 390, 391, 393, 394; his feelings for Nature, 398–399, 401, 402, 404; Alcott's relations with, in Concord, 408–410, 415; lectures of, in Boston, 423–424; quoted, 428, 438, 441, 443; describes Alcott's thought, 447–448; quoted, 452, 453, 459; his disagreement with Alcott, 459–461, 462, 468, 475, 476, 484–485, 487; decline of, 490, 492; quoted, 493; his controversy with Alcott, 494–496, 499; compared with Alcott, 499–501, 506; at Concord School of Philosophy, 508; death of, 509–510; his house, 512.

Emerson, Waldo, death of, 300.

Emerson, William, a student in Germany, 259.

England, letters from, 291; belongs to the past, 292; Alcott's dislike of, 306–313.

Episcopal Church, the, a form of "dissent" in Connecticut, 15; Alcott confirmed in, 30.

Equality, human, 334–335.

Evanston, Illinois, 485, 487.

Evelyn, Sir John, 394–395.

Everett, Abraham, 298, 363.

Everett, Edward, a rhetorician, 200; a student in Germany, 259.

FAMILY, THE, as the best of schools, 14; the source of society, 18; a golden mean, 327; Charles Lane's view of, 346; reform begins with, 360; basis of right living, 388–389, 471, 503, 504, 518.

Farmington, Connecticut, 14, 449.

Flavel, John, his *Treatise on Keeping the Heart* peddled by Alcott, 41.

Follen, Charles, 259.

Fountain, the, in Boston Common, Alcott's delight in, 462–463, 515.

Fourier, François Charles, 289, 327, 359, 389.

Fox, George, his *Journal* read by Alcott, 69.

Fox, W. J., 312.

Francis, Dr. Convers, in the Symposium, 247; a reader of German, 259, 260.

Francis, George, 321.

Franklin, Benjamin, 36, 44, 163, 170, 288–289; quoted, 289, 291.

Free Enquirers, the, of Boston, offer Alcott a teaching position, 133.

Free Religious Association, the, 498.

French Revolution, the, 163, 268, 270, 322.

Froebel, Friedrich Wilhelm, 173, 211, 422.

Frothingham, O. B., quoted, 241–242.

Fruitlands, and the convention at Groton, 281; a forecast of, 326 338–339; Charles Lane's part in 344; purchased, 356; Alcott's part in, 357; made in England, 357–358; unique, 360; reasons for fail ure of, 360–362; outward event at, 361–380; result of failure at 381–388; Alcott's debt to, 387–388; Journals of, lost, 388; an ex ample of "individualism," 499.

Fugitive Slave Law, the, 272, 27.

Fuller, Hiram, an imitator of Alcot 204.

Fuller, Margaret, a remark of En erson's to, 73; records Alcott Conversations, 181; goes to Prov dence, 204; answers Harriet Ma tineau, 209; education of, 218; student of German, 259; describe 277–278, 293, 339; death of, 44

Fuller, Thomas, quoted, 470.

Furness, Dr. William, a friend Alcott's, 121, 138.

Fuseli, Henry, his "Lectures Painting," 158.

GALLAUDET, DR. THOMAS HOPKIN 269.

Gannett, Reverend Ezra, called upon by Alcott, 112; at Federal Street Church, 117.

Gardening, Alcott's, 391–392, 393–401.

Garrison, William Lloyd, Alcott first meets, 136; as reformer, 165, 205, 239, 263; and Boston clergy, 267, 269; described, 274–275, 288; describes Alcott, 303–304.

"Genesis," Alcott's theory of, 453–462.

Germantown, Pennsylvania, Alcott invited to, 135; teaching in, 140, 161–162.

Godwin, William, his *Political Justice* read by Alcott, 125; Alcott's enthusiasm for, 158, 265.

Goethe, Johann Wolfgang, his Theory of Colors, 294; readings in, 392, 393, 480–481.

Goldsmith, Oliver, his *Deserted Village*, 23, 33.

Gospels, the, read at Temple School, 168.

Graeter, Francis, at Temple School, 167.

Graham, Sylvester, 186, 205; a vegetarian, 440.

Gray, Thomas, 335.

Greaves, James Pierrepont, his exposition of Pestalozzian methods, 85; his reading habits, 157; reads *Record of a School*, 208; letters from, 291, 292; influence of, 328; life of, 329; his thought, 330; quoted, 332; the mind of, 332–333; Carlyle's opinion of, 333; his teachings, 334; influence of, upon Alcott, 324–325, 340; his opinion of Alcott, 358; his doctrine of "Birth," 445, 452.

Greeley, Horace, quoted, 165; meets Alcott, 466.

Greene, Christopher, 299.

Greene, Reverend William Batchelder, at a Conversation, 240.

Greenwood, Reverend Francis, at King's Chapel, Boston, 117; performs Alcott's wedding ceremony, 134.

Grimké, the, sisters, 269–270.

Groton, Massachusetts, convention at, 281–283.

Gunsaulus, Frank, 402, 486, 487, 492.

HAINES, REUBEN, invites Alcott to Pennsylvania, 135, 137; death of, 161.

Hale, Edward Everett, 192; quoted, 287–288.

Hale, Nathan, declines to print letter from Alcott, 136; attacks Alcott in Press, 192, 197, 287.

Halleck, Fitz-Greene, his poem "Connecticut," 51.

Harris, William T., 402; meets Alcott, 467, 472, 473, 481, 482, 484, 492; referred to, 502; at Concord School of Philosophy, 507, 508, 511.

Hartford, Connecticut, 111, 272.

Harvard College, Emerson at, 74.

Hawthorne, Nathaniel, 232, 350, 391; shyness of, 407, 410, 487.

Hecker, Isaac T., 337; at Fruitlands, 366; his comment upon Fruitlands, 369.

Hedge, Dr. Frederic H., in the Symposium, 246; a student in Germany, 259; at Concord School of Philosophy 507, 508.

Hegel, Georg Wilhelm Friedrich, 475, 476, 480, 484.

Heine, Heinrich, 309.

Helvetius, Claude Adrien, 335.

Heraud, John A., letters from, 291; at Alcott House, 321.

Herder, Johann Gottfried, read by Alcott, 160.

Hervey, James, his *Meditations among the Tombs*, 33, 71.

Hesiod, his *Works and Days*, 294, 395.

Higginson, T. W., 242; a lecture by, 397.

"Hillside," Concord, *see* "Wayside."

Hoar, George Frisbie, 241.

Holmes, Dr. Oliver Wendell, and Bostonian conversation, 121.

Holbrook, Josiah, founds the American Lyceum, 121, 236.

Horne, Richard Henry, 321.

Hosmer, Edmund, 295–296, 391.

Howison, George Holmes, erudition of, 482; his "Personalism," 494, 496.
Hume, David, the skepticism of, 254.

IDEALISM, Alcott's natural and original, 94.
Imagination, Alcott's emphasis upon, 170–171.
"Infant, Observations on an," begun, 141; growth of, 144.
Irving, Washington, 252.

JACKSONVILLE, ILLINOIS, 483, 485, 486.
Jamblichus, his "Life of Pythagoras," 440; on the mysteries, 500.
James, Henry, the Elder, a contentious talker, 231, 239; quoted, 407.
Jefferson, Thomas, 178.
Jesus of Nazareth, his love for children, 81; Alcott's model and master, 91; not divine, 92; Alcott's imitation of, 95; a supreme teacher, 95–96; in Boston, 119; a radical thinker, 120; an instructor, 126; a great man, 127; the mind of, 148–149; Alcott's heresy concerning, 174; Alcott's remarks about, 179–180; his talk, 228, 265; quoted, 291, 428, 518.
Johnson, Samuel, of Salem, 499.
Johnson, Dr. Samuel, as a model of prose style, 32; his Lives of the Poets, 158; popular in Boston, 271, 335.
Jones, Dr. Hiram K., 486; at Concord School of Philosophy, 507, 508.
Jones, Jenkin Lloyd, 487.
Journals, Bronson Alcott's, begun, 78, 83; early concentration upon teaching in, 79; self-dedication in, 92; a change in, 147; quoted, 148; influence of Coleridge upon, 159; source of, 171; Emerson's use of, 200; quoted, 223, 227; loss of, for Fruitlands period, 368–369, 388; 392; quoted, 392–393, 445, 459, 464, 490, 504–505, 511; reviewed in his old age, 516–517, 520–521.

"Juvenile Library," a, formed by the Alcott cousins, 33–34.

KANT, IMMANUEL, Alcott's reading of, 160, 481.
Keagy, Dr. J. M., corresponds with Alcott about Pestalozzi, 84; in Philadelphia, 138.
Keats, John, read by Alcott, 157, 158; quoted, 245, 394.
Keys, the Reverend John, 13; teaches the Alcott cousins, 31.
Knapp, Isaac, in Anti-Slavery Society, 136.
Krusi, Hermann, his exposition of Pestalozzi's methods, 84.

LABOR, ALCOTT'S, in boyhood, 10; and Parker's, 276; at Concord, 292–294, 389–392, 399, 400–401, 434.
Ladd, William, a prophet of pacifism, 121–122.
Lakes, the English, compared with Wolcott, Connecticut, 19–20.
Lamb, Charles, his Essays of Elia, 158.
Landor, Walter Savage, as master of conversation, 231, 393.
Lane, Charles, a letter from, 291, 320; a speech by, 324, 336, 338, 341; character of, 343–346; Emerson's estimate of, 344; his conflict with Mrs. Alcott, 346–347; attacks Government, 353; buys Fruitlands, 356, 365; among the Shakers, 373; his controversy with Alcott, 377; leaves Fruitlands, 380, 384; a letter from 387, 389; visits Alcott, 392; leaves America, 393, 439; death of, 50●
Lane, William, 341.
Lao Tsze, 289.
Larned, Samuel, at Fruitlands, 36●
Lavater, Johann Kaspar, his Physiognomy, 50.
Law, William, his Serious Call read by Alcott, 69; his Way to Divine Knowledge, 294.
Lecture, the, Alcott's estimate of 198; and the Conversation, 23● 244–245.

[540]

Lee, Mother Ann, founds Shaker colony, 373; her "revelation," 374, 375–376.
Leland, Charles Godfrey, as Alcott's pupil, 162–163, 211.
Liberator, The, 275.
Lieber, Francis, 259.
Lincoln, Abraham, 477, 478–480.
Littlehale, Ednah Dow, *see* Cheney, Mrs. Ednah Dow.
Locke, John, his *Essay on the Human Understanding* first read by Alcott, 50; Alcott's early acceptance of, 133, 139; Alcott's departure from, 152, 163, 253, 257, 291, 335.
London, Alcott's remarks upon, 307–309, 313.
Longfellow, Henry Wadsworth, an address by, 248, 252.
Longfellow, Samuel, 464.
Lowell, James Russell, 252; his essay on Thoreau, 280; quoted, 321; his description of Alcott, 424–425; referred to, 445, 478.
Lyell, Sir Charles, his *Principles of Geology,* 457.

Maclure, William, corresponds with Alcott about Pestalozzi, 84.
Mann, Horace, his opinion of Alcott, 211.
Mansell, Dr. Henry, 321.
Marsh, James T., his edition of Coleridge's *Aids to Reflection,* 159, 258.
Marston, John Westland, 321.
Martineau, Harriet, quoted, 116, 165, 177, 208; answered by Margaret Fuller, 208, 329; quoted, 450.
Mather, Cotton, 466.
Mather, Richard, 36.
May, Abigail, *see* Alcott, Mrs. Bronson.
May, Colonel Joseph, adored by his daughter, 107; called upon by Alcott, 122; death of, 295, 427.
May, Reverend Samuel Joseph, as an educational reformer, 104; his first meeting with Alcott, 105; his description of Alcott, 106; visited a second time by Alcott, 112; describes Alcott's school, 124;

advises his sister, 129–130; in Anti-Slavery Society, 136; a visit to, 206; friend of Garrison, 275; "God's chore-boy," 276; a letter to, 281; referred to, 389, 429; death of, 509.
Meriden, Connecticut, an outfitting place for pedlars, 66.
"Micawber, Mr.," Alcott's likeness to, 108, 428.
Milton, John, 33, 397.
Miller, Hugh, his *The Old Red Sandstone,* 457.
Millerites, the, at Groton, 281–282, 313.
Money, Alcott's attitude toward, 64–65.
Moore, Abel, 393.
Morality, Alcott's emphasis upon in teaching, 169–170.
More, Henry, 256; poems of, 294.
More, Sir Thomas, his *Utopia,* 158.
Morse, Jedediah, quoted, 98–99.
Morgan, J. M., 312.
Murat, Achille, a friend of Emerson's, 74.

Nature, Alcott's feeling for, 22, 24–25, 393–401; Emerson and Alcott concerning, 256; the "Ministries" of, 389–390; to be subdued, 399–400.
Neef, Joseph, his exposition of Pestalozzi's methods, 84.
New Connecticut Hill, the Presence on, 27, 37, 70, 80, 184, 217, 386, 518.
New England, and the South, 52–54.
Newgate Prison, Alcott's visit to, 41.
New Haven Register, the, 19.
New Testament, the, Alcott reduces the Bible to, 110; Alcott's study of 125.
Newton, Sir Isaac, and Alcott, 140; influence of, 255.
New York City, Alcott in, 464, 465.
Nierecker, Louisa May, 510.
Non-Resistants, the, 279.
Norfolk, Virginia, 47, 60.
Northcote, James, his *Fables,* 162–163.

[541]

Porphyry, his treatise "On Abstinence," 311, 440.
Poverty, Alcott's, 225–226, 295, 426–434.
Pratt, John 509.
Preaching, Alcott's interest in, 116–119; compared with teaching, 119; Alcott's disappointment in, 120, 126; in Boston, 175; and reform, 266–267, 484.
Prose Style, in New England during Alcott's youth, 32; Alcott's, becomes more "elegant," 65; Alcott's simplified, 386; 505–506.
"Psyche," Alcott's manuscript, 143, 145, 181; Emerson's opinion of, 200, 227, 262, 504.
Psychology, a pioneer in, 141, 148–150, 181.
Puritanism, and *Pilgrim's Progress*, 37; escaped by Alcott, 54, 169, 226, 270.
Putman, Israel, 104.
Pythagoras, 155, 289, 440, 487.

Quakers, influence of, upon Alcott, 69–70, 80.
Quarles, Francis, his *Emblems*, 162.
Quarterly Reviewer, The Boston, 195–196.
Quincy, Edmund, 278, 283; visited by Alcott, 297.
Quincy, Josiah, at Temple School, 180, 184, 189, 211.

Record of a School, the, published, 166; referred to, 168, 173, 187; in England, 208, 307, 320, 329.
Reed, Sampson, his *Growth of the Mind*, 258.
Reform, in education, 12–13; Emerson and Alcott disagree upon, 263, 327; in New England, 263–280; in Old England, 311–312; at Alcott House, 336–337; as due to "individualism," 494, 498.
Religion, of Alcott's parents, 27–30; of the Quakers, 70; Bronson Alcott's, 92, 110.
Richards, Colonel Streat, 5.
Ricketson, Daniel, his comment on Alcott's Conversations, 241, 502.

Ripley, George, his view of Alcott as an "atheist," 37; a Boston clergyman, 117, 204; helps in founding the Symposium, 247; a student of German literature, 259; as reformer, 263, 268, 281, 293; visits Fruitlands, 366.
Ripley, Mrs. Sarah, 412.
Robbins, Reverend S. D., 231.
Robinson, Edwin Arlington, quoted, 427.
Rockford, Illinois, 483, 485, 487.
Rousseau, Jean Jacques, not a source of Alcott's theories about childhood, 82; his "conversion," 83, 335.
Russell, William, his *American Journal of Education*, 83, 99; publishes Alcott's first printed writing, 108; first meets Alcott, 112; described, 122; quoted, 124; assists Alcott as a teacher, 135; in Germantown, 140; influence of, upon Alcott, 145–148, 159; lives with Alcott, 209; a letter from, 212; visits Fruitlands, 366; death of, 492, 509.

St. Louis, Missouri, Alcott in, 474; The Philosophical Society of, 474–476, 477, 480–484, 496.
Salem Street School, the, Alcott's teaching in, 123–124.
Sanborn, Franklin Benjamin, **492**, 502, 505; at Concord School of Philosophy, 507, 514.
Saturday Club, the, Alcott an "after-dinner member" of, 441; a meeting of, 457–458.
Schelling, Friedrich Wilhelm, a foe of Lockian "Sensationalism," 254; his idealism, 258.
Schleiermacher, Friedrich, a German transcendentalist, 245.
Schoolhouse, the, at Spindle Hill, description of, 6–7; discomforts of, 12.
Schoolhouses, of Connecticut, 97–98.
Schoolmasters, remuneration and social standing of, in Connecticut, 8.

[543]

[544]

lery Channing, 435, 441; his *Week* published, 442–443, 446, 454; in New York, 464; referred to, 468, 475, 477, 487; death of, 492, 502; quoted, 505, 506, 508, 510, 511.

Ticknor, George, a student in Germany, 259.

Tolstoy, Count Leo, 268.

Town and Country Club, founded by Alcott, 443

Towns, little, Alcott's mistake concerning, 23–24.

"Transcendental Club," see Symposium.

Transcendentalism, Alcott's, and Noah Webster's Speller, 11; induced by Spindle Hill, 26; strengthened by *Pilgrim's Progress*, 37; intensified by Quaker influence, 70; a natural tendency of his mind, 94; confirmed by William Russell, 145–146, 172; in Conversations, 244.

Transcendental Movement, The, a motto for, 156; a foe of, 195; service of, 253; beliefs of, 254–255; personnel of, 255; central idea of, 257–258; and reform, 268–269; an index of, 340; individualism of, 412–413.

Trollope, Mrs. Francis Milton, her *Domestic Manners of the Americans*, 310.

Trowbridge, J. T., quoted, 242; 337.

UNITARIANISM, Alcott's, 95; Alcott's movement toward, 116; the clergy of, Harvard men, 117; prospers in Boston, 126; Alcott's divergence from, 127; too restricting, 249; triumphant, 253; conservative, 265.

VAUGHAN, HENRY, 256; quoted, 451.

Vegetarianism, 310–311, 351, 439–441.

Virgil, 395.

Virginia, as a school of manners, 52–54; Alcott's first itinerary in, 55; great houses of, 69.

WALKER, JAMES, invited to join the Symposium, 248, 303.

Walpole, New Hampshire, Alcott's residence at, 463–464.

Waterbury, Connecticut, 14.

Watson, Marston, 502.

Wattles, John, 299.

"Wayside," Concord, 390; purchased by Alcott, 391–392; gardening at, 393.

Webster, Noah, his Spelling Book, 5, 11–12, 58, 61; continued influence of, 123; his emphasis upon morality, 170; quoted, 170, 213, 248–249, 289, 313.

Wendell, Barrett, 252.

West, Alcott's Tours of the, begin, 432–433; discussed, 472–488.

West, the New, Alcott's preparation for understanding, 72–73.

Western Messenger, the, 195.

Wethersfield, Connecticut, 449.

Whitman, Marcus, 221.

Whitman, Walt, his knowledge of the South, 72; and Nature, 401; Alcott first reads, 463; Alcott's association with, 464–465, 466, 478, 480, 496, 502.

Whittier, John Greenleaf, quoted, 264.

Wilderspin, Samuel, as a reformer of education, 121.

Wilkes, John, and the Hell-Fire Club, 320.

Willard, Simon, quoted, 405.

Wister, Dr. Owen, a pupil of Alcott's, 211.

Wolcott, Connecticut, books in, 14, 33–34; description of, 17–20; population of, 17, 19; prosperity in, 18; customs and morality of, 19–20; Alcott's pride and pleasure in, 21; a self-contained state and society, 23; Alcott's illusion concerning, 23.

Women, discussed by Alcott with Miss Abigail May, 107; Alcott's theory of, 127; excell in conversation, 231.

Woodbridge, the Reverend William C., an interpreter of Pestalozzi in Connecticut, 84.

Woodward, the Reverend Israel, as a Calvinistic preacher, 28, 29.

Woolman, John, his *Journal* read by Alcott, 69.

[545]